OLD BOYS

OLD BOYS

THE POWERFUL LEGACY OF
UPPER CANADA COLLEGE

James FitzGerald

Macfarlane Walter & Ross
Toronto

MACFARLANE WALTER & ROSS
37 A Hazelton Avenue
Toronto, Canada M5R 2E3

Canadian Cataloguing in Publication Data

FitzGerald, James, 1950–
Old boys : the powerful legacy of Upper Canada College

ISBN 0-921912-74-9

1. Upper Canada College – History.   2. Upper Canada
College – Alumni and alumnae – Interviews
I. Title.

LE3.U72F4 1994   373.2'22   C94-932279-2

The publisher gratefully acknowledges the support
of the Ontario Arts Council

Printed and bound in Canada

This book is dedicated to my brother
Michael Ewart FitzGerald
with love and respect

Men must be taught as if you taught them not,
And things unknown proposed as things forgot

Alexander Pope

CONTENTS

PART TWO

PART THREE

ACKNOWLEDGEMENTS

I WOULD LIKE TO THANK the many people whose support, guidance, and advice substantially influenced me in the course of the creation of this book over the past four years.

Jan Walter and Gary Ross, from the very beginning, have brought to this project a rare combination of intelligence, professionalism, and humanity for which I am most grateful. Gary Ross's acute editorial instincts were instrumental in shaping the massive amount of interview material. Without his creative guidance, this book simply would not have been possible. Additional thanks go to Sara Borins and Bernice Eisenstein for their invaluable editorial assistance.

I am indebted to John Fraser, the former editor of *Saturday Night*, whose book *Telling Tales* was an early model and inspiration for my own book. I am also indebted to a host of friends and colleagues who patiently indulged and encouraged me in my worst and best moments. They include: Patrick Allossery, Rob and Nancy Boyter, Catherine Bridgman, David B. Chilton, Linda Conlon, Paula Costello, Peter Dales, Lee Daugharty, Suzanne DePoe, Craig Doyle, Fred Di Gasparro, Michael FitzGerald, Shelagh FitzGerald, Karen Fountain, Bill and Kate Greenfield, Kathryn Hanford, Linda Jones, Jackie Kaiser, Ken and Susan Ludlow, Jay D. MacDonald, Margaret McCaffery, Tim Morawetz, Peter Murdoch, Trina Preece, Terry and Jan Priddy, Steve Roney, Joa Roth, Jack Schaffter, Mark and Allison Smyka, Derek Suchard, Susan Tolusso.

Heartfelt thanks go as well to Carol Daugharty, Sarah Duncan, and Marietta Lash who laboured countless hours in helping me transcribe the taped interviews. I am also grateful to Paul Winnell, director of the Upper Canada College Foundation, who helped me track down some of the old boys whose names were not listed in the Upper Canada College directory.

INTRODUCTION

THE OFFICIAL HISTORY of Upper Canada College is to be found in the pages of *Colborne's Legacy: Upper Canada College 1829-1979*, published on the occasion of the school's sesquicentennial. Richard Howard, a former UCC student and headmaster of the preparatory school, offers a detailed account of the origins, growth, and evolution of UCC from a small government-funded, non-denominational grammar school in 1829 to one of Canada's most prestigious private educational institutions.

Sir John Colborne, later Lord Seaton, a British career soldier who fought in the Battle of Waterloo and became a lieutenant-governor of the province of Upper Canada, founded UCC in the small British colonial town of Muddy York, now Toronto, during the days of the oligarchic "Family Compact." Based on the English public school model, Upper Canada College was conceived in part to produce an educated, governing elite to counteract the subversive democratic and republican influences from the United States.

For patricians and parvenus alike, the school serves as a powerful beacon of the Canadian Establishment. Its four-faced clock tower today casts a panoptical gaze, like Father Time, over the school's sprawling, leafy, thirty-eight-acre island of tax-free land located in the single most affluent neighbourhood in Canada. Eight generations of Upper Canadians have passed through the portals of UCC since January 4, 1830, when fifty-seven boys first enrolled in the school at its original location in Russell Square. The initial tuition fees were £8 for day boys and £25 for boarders. In 1994, roughly one thousand boys aged seven to nineteen pay annual day-boy fees of $12,500 or boarder fees of $22,500. Much has changed in 165 years; much has also remained the same.

Both as a journalist and as a UCC old boy with family ties to the school, I have long been intrigued by the powerful mythology of UCC and its often indelible influence on so many influential people. My own maternal ancestors were among the first generation of UCC boys. John Ewart, my grandmother's great-grandfather, an architect who built the original UCC administration buildings and boarding houses in 1829, sent his two sons to the school, where they became head boys in 1836 and 1838 respectively. Beginning at the age of nine, my father, Dr. John FitzGerald, boarded at UCC from 1926 to 1934. My brother and I followed in his footsteps as day boys at UCC, where I spent ten years (1958-1968) under the influence of many of the same masters who had taught him a generation earlier.

Because of its unique history, location, and constituency, UCC offers a clear window onto the attitudes, mores, and values of an exclusive, privileged community which historically has produced a disproportionately high number of leaders in all fields of Canadian life. Because of the high concentration of wealth and power within "the UCC family," and because of the profound impact the school has had on so many of its old boys, I realized that to interview selected old boys would be to mine a unique deposit of Canadian social history.

Over the past 165 years, Upper Canada College, like Canada itself, has survived a succession of internal crises and external threats to its existence. For many people, UCC remains an inspiring symbol of the tenacity and longevity of traditional, classical, monarchical, patriarchal values in the face of encroaching, subversive, postmodern egalitarianism. For others, UCC is an anachronistic, still predominantly WASP old boys' haven which embodies and perpetuates many of the social, economic, and political ills of the late twentieth century – sexism, racism, homophobia, self-serving elitism, and endemic social Darwinism. For still others, UCC simply provides an academically and athletically challenging learning environment which will assure its graduates entry into the best universities.

In 1990, Upper Canada College published a directory of many, but not all, of its roughly eight thousand living alumni. Using the directory as a major source, I set about to interview a cross-section of old boys and UCC masters drawn from all generations from World War I to the present. I tape-recorded the memories, feelings, and opinions of three hundred old boys aged seventeen to ninety-five. I systematically chose several prospective interview candidates from each graduating year stretching back to 1915. From this pool of interviews, I transcribed, edited, and juxtaposed a series of selected oral histories of the eminent and the anonymous, the rebels and the conformists, the athletes and the scholars, the revered and the reviled. Together, the many diverse, subjective voices form a dynamic and often ironic roll call stretching over seventy-five years, linking the microcosm to the macrocosm, the private to the public, the past to the present.

One of the enduring myths of UCC is that it has produced a disproportionately high number of lawyers, stockbrokers, financiers, and businessmen who toil in the towers of Bay Street. The school itself has published no objective breakdown of the chosen professions of its alumni, partly because of incomplete records. But certainly there is truth to the public perception of UCC as a greenhouse for budding executives.

When UCC solicited career information from its alumni in 1990, approximately half of its eight thousand old boys responded. Of this group, by far the single greatest concentration – nearly 30 per cent – were working as stockbrokers, bankers, realtors, accountants, management consultants, and insurance and investment brokers. Another 28 per cent were loosely identified as "businessmen," working either independently or within corporations. The next highest concentration – over 12 per cent – consisted of lawyers and judges, followed by health professionals (dentists, doctors, etc.) at 7 per cent, teachers and educators at 6 per cent, and media professionals at 5 per cent.

Of course, these figures are based on a skewed and incomplete sample, but they do give a strong indication that UCC has effectively prepared the majority of its graduates for mainstream professional careers. What is less certain is how many old boys' lives do not easily fall into any conventional categories of success.

In my own graduating year, for example, I was struck by the radically contrasting trajectories of some of my classmates. The leaving class of 1968 alone produced a Progressive Conservative cabinet minister and an old boy who served time in prison for killing a man while under the influence of drugs. UCC has had its share of tragedy and scandal, which also fuel the enduring mythology of the institution.

Of the three hundred oral histories completed to date – coincidentally, the same number of UCC old boys who were killed in both world wars – seventy-one have been chosen to comprise the substance of this volume. Divided into four sections, the book begins with members of the class of 1922 and ends with members of the class of 1993. The four sections are organized roughly to coincide with four of the last eight principalships of Upper Canada College. Each section also falls loosely into a distinct historical period – the 1920s and the Depression, World War II and the Cold War period, the 1960s, and the post-sixties era.

Part I picks up the story of UCC in the post-World War I era, when W. L. "Choppy" Grant had recently assumed the principalship of the upper school and J. L. "Duke" Somerville was headmaster of the lower, or preparatory, school. Part I also includes oral histories under the relatively brief principalships of Terry MacDermot (1935-1942) and Lorne "Butch" McKenzie (1942-1948).

Part II spans the principalship of Reverend Cedric Sowby during the postwar years 1948-1965.

With the retirement of Cedric Sowby in 1965 – and of Alan Stephen, the headmaster of the prep for thirty-two years, in 1966 – Upper Canada reached a critical point in its history. Part III portrays the turbulent ten-year period of 1965-1974 when Patrick Johnson and Richard Howard ran the upper school and preparatory school respectively. Many of the traditional "character-building" components of the UCC curriculum which had endured for generations – the compulsory cadet corps, compulsory boxing tournaments, and corporal punishment – were disbanded during this period of rapid social change. The house system, in which senior boys assume positions of leadership as prefects and stewards over the younger boys, remains intact to this day, although the English public school "fagging system" within the two boarding houses has long since disappeared.

In Part IV, the most recent generation of old boys talk about their experiences during the post-sixties era under the principalships of Richard Sadleir (1975-1988), Eric Barton (1988-1990), and the current principal, Douglas Blakey. While many other boys' private schools opted for coeducation during this period, UCC has chosen to remain as one of the few all boys' private schools in Canada.

In the words of the American poet Rita Dove, "Memory has a reputation for compassionate inaccuracy." The highly subjective nature of this book is based on the belief that human memory is fallible yet indispensable to understanding ourselves. My modus operandi rests on the premise that because an interview subject has chosen to remember an event in a certain way, the recollection is the truth for him. The fact that, ten years later, he may choose to remember it differently, or fail to remember it at all, is an unalterable fact of human psychology. While it was obviously impossible to verify the objective truth of every vignette or anecdote related in this book, every effort has been made to verify the authenticity of the salient historical events.

James FitzGerald
Summer 1994

PART
I

HARRY WILSON

1919–22

Financier

U PPER CANADA was in the country in those days. You'd take the streetcar to Avenue Road and St. Clair Avenue and then walk up to the school from there. I lived below the hill on Avenue Road, so sometimes I'd roller-skate to school. I'd fall periodically. In those days, we wore long stockings and my mother would be very annoyed at the great big holes in my knees. Occasionally Dad, who was a wholesale grocer, lent me the car and I would drive to school in our old air-cooled Franklin.

The west side of the school, Forest Hill Village, wasn't built up at all. We used to have the annual steeplechase all around the countryside. We had to struggle through a stream, which has since vanished underground.

I only weighed 117 pounds, so I used to take quite a battering in boxing. I was a skinny little rat. In football, I was too light for the first team. I played flying wing for the second team. I used to get quite a lot of clobbering. I still have a bad knee from it. I don't know how many times I had my nose broken at UCC.

I never liked the cadet battalion, but I always thought it was a good thing because it instilled a sense of discipline in the boys. Sergeant Major Carpenter, an old army man, was a very knowledgeable fellow who ran the Rifle Company. He turned out a darned good unit. They dressed smartly and marched smartly and drilled smartly. However, times change, and you've got to change with them, so the batallion was disbanded. It's still a pretty darned good school.

I remember we used to call Allan Lamport "Mr. Upper Canada" because he strutted around as if he owned the place. Foster Hewitt was also at the school at that time. He was a nice fellow and a good friend of mine.

William "Choppy" Grant was the principal of the upper school and J. L. "Duke" Somerville the headmaster of the prep.

I didn't like Choppy Grant, but I admired him. His father was the principal of Queen's University. Choppy was very effective as principal at a time when UCC was changing. In fact, he initiated a lot of the changes. I gather that the school had been deteriorating under Henry Auden, his predecessor. When Grant took over as principal in 1917, he did a very effective job pulling it back up again. The health of UCC is very important for the health of the country.

After Upper Canada, I started in as an office boy running messages at the National Trust. I stayed there all my business life, ending up as president. I'm not a very exciting person. I'm a stick-in-the-mud. I think it was the people I met at school that helped me later on, rather than what I learned at school.

The boys who went to UCC usually ended up in pretty senior positions. One of the great advantages was that if you wanted to find out some particular thing, you would call up Joe Smith and say, "Joe, can you help me out on this?" That's the big advantage of going to a school like Upper Canada.

When you come to think of it, UCC is probably the most important educational institution in the country. It's the biggest of the Little Big Four private schools. It attracts people from all over the place. Of the boys who go there, a large number turn out to be leaders in various fields.

My son Michael has achieved the highest position in politics of any Upper Canada old boy. He had a great time at UCC, I think. He became the number-two man in the country as minister of finance under Brian Mulroney. I wish he got out sooner than he did. He said he was going into politics for only ten years, so he overstayed his time. He was formerly second in command at Dominion Securities. It cost him about thirteen million dollars in income to go into politics.

When I was chairman of the board of governors at UCC from 1962 to 1967, the school gave me a coffee table made from a tree that stood on the grounds. I think it was made from one of the old elm trees that started to go bad from Dutch elm disease. I appointed Pat Johnson as principal in 1965. I had to fire Reverend Cedric Sowby, an Anglican clergyman, who was really out of touch with things. He was a nice man, but rather a weak fellow. I felt he had to be replaced, so we gave him a good pension and kissed him goodbye and Pat Johnson took over. It was a good move because the times had really gone ahead of Cedric. The school is probably a pretty happy combination of Canadian and English now.

I had an awful portrait of myself painted by Alan Collier. I intended to give it to Upper Canada, but the family liked it so much, they said, "Nothing doing. It's staying here." It wouldn't have mattered. Nobody at UCC today would have known who that old bird was.

ALLAN LAMPORT

1919 – 23

Former mayor of Toronto

THE PEOPLE who run things in this world have got to be very disciplined, with the ability not only to discipline others but to discipline themselves. You had to be disciplined to carry out orders in football, hockey, the Rifle Company, boxing, and all the other things I participated in at UCC.

I was heavyweight boxing champion, shotput champion, and captain of hockey. I set a record as a football player, and of course I was a steward and a prefect. When I was at UCC, I also rowed with the Toronto Argonauts. I went down to the waterfront at 5:00 A.M. and was back at school by 8:00 A.M. Then I got the rowing team started at the school.

I also became adjutant of the Rifle Company, or second in command. It was a great thing. They should still keep those things up because they are great teachers of respect, discipline, law and order. They are the principles of a high-class, well-governed country which has regard for the Crown and all that it stands for. If you don't have traditions, you don't have discipline.

I always thought disbanding the cadet corps in the 1970s was a very foolish thing for UCC to do. That kind of training is the greatest thing in the world – to march together, to be on time together, to know what commands are, to know what the services put up with, to know what is expected of the individual soldier, to know that he can lead men.

My father, who was a lawyer, thought I should go into boarding in my last year at UCC so I wouldn't let my studies down. To be a boarder was a great experience. I was a floor prefect. We had a lot of tough guys there, like Cam Seagram. I met people who I stuck with as friends all my life until they passed away. Harry Wilson was at UCC in my time, whose son became finance minister.

We had a great bunch on my floor in boarding. Once I remember I was studying and I heard a noise in the hall. I didn't pay attention and then I heard some water splash. In those days, we had washbasins and pitchers. I went to my door and looked down the hall. Suddenly I got some water in the face. It was meant for the guy in the next room to me.

I said, "What the hell are you guys doing? You guys get out here." Then I got my pitcher of water and let it go. Dickey Potter, the floor master, was a great guy who had a high regard for me and my sports capacities. He came up the hall and caught me in the act of throwing the water. Of course, he had to discipline me. He said, "Is this what goes on in my absence?"

Everybody else was in their room. I wasn't going to say who else was involved. It looked as if I was in on an initiation. So I said, "Well, there was a bit of water thrown around. You just came in too early, sir." He said, "You come in here, Lamport." He closed his door and got out the cane. He said, "Lean over that chair." I leaned over the chaise longue beside me. He hit the chaise longue three times, then he hit me three times, so the other boys could hear six blows.

Isn't that cute? He really didn't hit me that hard, but he really hit the couch hard. All the students felt sorry for me because they got me in the bloody thing. I never did tell them. Nobody else got caned. The victim becomes the hero!

When I later became a comptroller and then mayor of Toronto, I ran across UCC old boys in every walk of life. It was always a delight. They would seek me out for things. I kept close to UCC in everything I did. All the things I was asked to do, I would do, like referee a hockey game. I played the old boys hockey.

My last UCC hockey game was in the new Maple Leaf Gardens. Conn Smythe, who was a UCC old boy, as well as his two sons Stafford and Hugh, gave us the Gardens to have a game. Then, of course, a lot of the old boys got together and built the Patrick Johnson Arena on the school grounds. But the old boys always had the use of Maple Leaf Gardens.

Then along comes Harold Ballard, who was also a UCC old boy, although just a couple of years. We were great friends in Parkdale when I first went to Queen Victoria Public School. He was a very aggressive young man. He and I thought a lot alike because we were both aggressive and risk-takers. He became head of Maple Leaf Gardens. He was always anxious to see that I went to the games. He would send me tickets here and there and even made me an honorary member of the Hot Stove Lounge.

Ballard was a champion speed skater. His tube skates were about sixteen inches long. He would beat the United States and Canadian champions. He was a great athlete and boat racer. He was a member of the Sea Flea Group. He managed the hockey team that won the Allan Cup and he took a great pride in it. He left UCC and went into his father's tube-skate business, as well as claw-cutting machines.

He and I were the closest of friends at UCC. He didn't make friends easily. I brought him along. You didn't have to teach Harold Ballard anything because he was a very, very wise guy, a great head on his shoulders. But he didn't have any patience for training. He wanted to climb to the top quickly. He was the same till the end. He kept reaching for the stars and he was right. He was a great money-maker but a poor administrator. The detail of administration he just hated, as a lot of us do.

When I was mayor, there was a drive to put Avenue Road right across the UCC grounds, which would have cut off the football field and the area where the hockey rink is now. All that corner would have become housing. But because of my fight, I saved it. In fact, some of them wanted to go right clean through the school property up Avenue Road. Toronto was expanding rapidly back then. St. Clair Avenue was all mud. It was a pretty hard thing to hold back, but I got a lot of us together, in particular those in city council.

I did a lot to bring along the TTC into the new world. No city ever became large or important without a subway system. The British had it in London with horse-drawn cars. So you see how far ahead they thought. New York was next. Paris had had them before the turn of the century. Toronto built the first subway in Canada. The biggest move I made was when I forced through the east-west subway line. It cost us $200 million and it's worth $3 to $4 billion today. I opened the Yonge Street subway line in 1954, my last year as mayor. It was quite a fight to get it through. The construction upset Yonge Street badly. The merchants were just livid.

I don't have any sons. Both my daughters went to Havergal College, as did my wife. If anything, I am prejudiced about girls' ability. There is no question about their capacity. It's much better than men's when they are younger, on the average. But they have to get the proper home discipline. Again, it starts with discipline.

In my last speech at a UCC rowing dinner, I said, "Let's not get UCC into coeducation. It's very disruptive. The forces of the future are damning and dangerous. Girls don't think they are doing the damage they are doing by meeting boys after school and having a little kiss. But it's there. It never gets better, it gets worse. It digs down to the depths of degradation, to the point of starting too early, before they sow their wild oats." Boy, I am very much against it.

I've got great-grandsons on the list to go to UCC. You've got to put them in early. They will give priority to old boys' families. Any fellow who has a chance to go to UCC will be well rewarded if he has enough sense to take it all in and realize he is there for training and not to be an independent rowdy.

Anybody can be a resister. There is no sense or class in behaving like that. We never, ever had any rebellion at ucc in my time. We never even thought of it. Everything was smooth. They gave in where they should, which is the smart thing to do. I would say to people who resent the school, "You people were rebels because you couldn't get your own way." That's usually the type that won't be told what to do. My God, what's the use of going to the school if you don't believe in it?

Anybody who is resentful of ucc, I wouldn't think it would be worthwhile putting their name in this book. I think it would be an insult to the college. These people have no judgement.

GUY PURSER

1919 – 27

Gas station manager

I WAS ONE of the many boys who were sent to Upper Canada College to be got rid of by their parents. I saw many of them, when the parents saw fit to visit, standing at the foot of the driveway by the prep. As the parents would drive away, the boys walked away, mopping the tears out of their eyes.

I had an extremely unfortunate youth. I was an only child. My mother left me and my father when I was two years old. She ran off with another man. I came out from England with my father when I was four years old. The boat we came out on, the *Tunisian*, was torpedoed on its way back.

When I was six, my father literally abandoned me at the corner of Brunswick Avenue and Bloor Street to go to the war in 1914. He got on the streetcar and left me there. I lived at a boardinghouse. I was the "war baby" of the woman who ran the boardinghouse. I stayed there for five years until my father came back from the war. It was bloody awful. What I particularly regret is that I never had any milk, so it accounts somewhat for my slighter build. I never had any milk until I went to board at Upper Canada College when I was eleven. In those growing years, I had no milk, just tea.

When my father came back from the war, he said, "I'll never leave you again, laddie." Then he sent me to board at the Upper Canada College prep school. It was a bitter experience. I was in no way fit for what I had to face at UCC. I was not of a particularly high IQ. I was not studiously inclined and, what was worse, I wasn't athletically inclined. I was looked down upon with contempt by everybody, including the faculty. I can well remember the geometry teacher, Mr. Parlee, in the upper school, having a new boy named Bradshaw move from another class to his. Mr. Parlee said, "Bradshaw isn't much good at geometry, but he's great on the rugby field." I think that tells oceans of truth.

My father wasn't paternally inclined. He didn't want any children. He used to say, "How your mother could have left a beautiful child like you, we could never understand." But he did understand it. He was a prize phoney. He lived to a great age. He lived long enough, I think, to regret how full of self-deception he was. He was thrown out of the retirement home, Belmont House, for making passes at the nurses.

I tried to be attentive to my father even though he disgusted me. I visited him regularly. My mother was a nut and my father was a nut. You're looking at the son of a nut. It's a wonder I knew enough to come out of the rain. Honest to God, it really is.

I was under the benign influence and protection of my grandfather on my mother's side who lived in England. He was a wonderful man who paid for all my tuition at Upper Canada. My father worked as a salesman for his father, who was a manufacturing jeweller. My father was no good as a salesman at all. He went to the war, he told me afterwards, so he would be shot and my grandfather would have to look after me. That was considered an intelligent reply to my question about why he went to the war.

I was just a damn nuisance. My father, however, did do one wonderful thing. He married again, a wonderful woman, the greatest woman who ever lived. How she ever put up with him and his nonsense, I don't know, but she did. She was the editor of the homemaker's page in the *Globe and Mail* for twenty years under the pen name of Polly Peel. She was also the superintendent of the Women's Building at the Canadian National Exhibition. She was a very talented woman.

But my father had absolutely no interest in me whatsoever. I was made to feel everything was my fault. My father worked that into me thoroughly. I was defective. "You're a mess," he said to me once. I was in my early teens at that point. Now, my stepmother didn't approve of that at all. She was a dear woman. My greatest regret in my life is that I never showed enough appreciation to her for all her love and devotion.

My father told everybody that he had put me through Upper Canada College. He even told his brother. I was complaining about my father to my uncle, who said, "Well, he put you through Upper Canada College." I said, "He did? Let me show you some literature. I've got letters showing my grandfather complaining about the expense." I was an extremely ungrateful grandson, too. As a grandfather, I now find my grandchildren are extremely ungrateful, but I've learned to swallow it when I think about how I was.

I wasn't adaptable at sports at Upper Canada. I was thin and unmuscular and I was led to believe somehow that everything was all my fault. That gave me a complex which has stuck with me all my life. I can't resist saying this – most of the chaps of my generation who were mighty on the rugby field and mighty with the scholarships are now all dead. And here am I.

At this moment, I could beat any of them at anything. I'm in pretty good health. I just had a cancer operation, but I've come through it pretty well. I've lived twelve years beyond the life of the average man, so what am I bellyaching about? It's funny how life turns out.

In the prep with Duke Somerville, the principal, I was on a daily report. If my report wasn't up to scratch, I was caned. My grandfather always wanted to see me. Twice during school periods, two weeks at a time, he ordered my father to come to England to visit him. This was a bad thing because it took me out of circulation for two weeks.

The Duke's attitude to me was shameful. He used to completely ridicule me in front of the class. We started to learn algebra in the top form of the prep. I had missed two weeks at the start of it. It didn't mean anything to him. I was supposed to have caught up. I wasn't too bright anyway, but it was hard to start off with these guys further along in the book than I was. He should have arranged for somebody to help me get caught up.

One day the Duke said, "There's a boy in this class who says he gets caned every day." You could hear the class titter. He said, "Class can dismiss and Purser will remain for his daily caning." I said, "I can't remember telling anybody I get caned every day. I don't get caned every day." It really worried me, but I wasn't one to argue.

At that time, I was a day boy. I said to my stepmother, "Did I ever tell you that I get caned every day?" She said, "No, and I know what you're going to say. We told a friend of ours that you were occasionally caned and she spread the news that you were caned every day." She got Duke Somerville on the phone and told him this. Somerville never apologized to me or explained to the class that he had been misinformed. That was bad. I'll never forget that.

I might have been caned once every two weeks. I tried to arrange it otherwise. Of course, you don't get caning any more. It's illegal, both in the college and the prep. Lots of guys were caned dozens of times. I can give you names of all kinds of fellows. One guy got thirty whacks in succession. He boasted about it.

The canings in the prep made me shy. In the upper school, I was never caned, although they did some brutal caning. They used a stick as thick as your thumb and they would hit you in front of the class. I avoided that. It had that effect on me. I wasn't going to submit to that. I arranged that I wasn't.

There were two masters, one in the prep and one in the college, who were very dear to me. They were excellent teachers and wonderful people. In the prep, Mr. Spooner was one of those masters who could keep rigid discipline, but there was a laugh all the time. The masters all used to cane, but I never resented it from Mr. Spooner. He was great with the sports, but he never made a nasty thing about it for those who weren't sports-inclined. I knew more Latin in the prep in his class than I knew when I wrote my matric. It's a fact! He was a wonderful person.

In the college, Mr. Darnell was a dear man and an excellent teacher, very much the same as Mr. Spooner. I'll never forget after injuring myself boxing, I turned up the next morning with my arm in a sling. He asked if anybody knew the answer to a question he was asking. I answered it. He said, "That's right. By the way, Purser, I'm awfully glad to see you here today." I'll never forget that.

The chap that I chummed with had problems. Joe was a manic-depressive. He had a hell of a time in school, worse than I did. He got caned, I don't know how often, for obstinacy. The funny thing is that he just never caught on to the principle of studying. He had to write his matriculation twice.

But the strange thing is that I introduced him to his wife and he introduced me to mine. When he got married, they spent their wedding night in our living room. He had four marvellous children by her. She died very suddenly.

Joe had parental problems similar to mine. His father was a lawyer and an alcoholic. His mother was where the manic-depressiveness started. Both he and his brothers had it. He would get to a state where he just wouldn't talk to you at all. You can imagine what that would be like for his wife.

He stopped talking to me. I didn't see him for two years. I can only tolerate him so much. I feel very sorry for him. He's so sour grapes about everything under the sun. He's fashionably interested in music. That's our big tie.

Joe has an absolute mania for taking the opposite position. For instance, Horowitz is almost undoubtedly the greatest piano player on earth. Joe can't stand Horowitz for that very reason. His mother didn't have his natural sense of culture. I remember going into their house one afternoon. We used to do our homework together. His mother was playing a record of some jazz of the time. He took the needle off the record, picked up the record, and smashed it.

The cultural level in the school was dreadful in those days. The principal in the upper school, Choppy Grant, thought there were things we should be subjected to. He brought the Hart House String Quartet to the school. He never should have done it. Sir Ernest MacMillan, who wasn't knighted then, gave a talk. I can remember in the corridors afterwards Wiley Grier saying to somebody, "If he thinks he's going to keep the boys awake with that stuff, he's out of his mind."

I can remember a Jew in my class in the college. I hadn't paid much attention to him. It was in the winter in Wiley Grier's class. We used to tilt our chairs back a little bit. This guy kicked my chair from under me. The master wasn't in the room at the time. I went down flat. Before I could get up, the other guys grabbed the Jew, took his pants off, opened the window, and threw him out. He landed on a whole bunch of burr bushes underneath the window. He had to come back in without his pants. That gives you an idea of the brutality of youth.

I think being in an all boys' school probably affected my attitude towards girls and women later. I'm quite sure some guys got utterly carried away. There are two wrong ways – indifference and overenthusiasm. I think that worked both ways with some of them. Joe was definitely against girls. He didn't know what to do with them. If I hadn't introduced him to a girl who seduced him, I don't know what he would have done.

An incident took place at UCC which changed my whole life. I've got a steel brace in my thumb on my right hand. In those days, in first year in the upper school, all the new boys had to go into a boxing tournament. By a strange irony of fate, the only athletic activity I was good at was boxing. In an elimination tournament you fight with somebody your own weight until you lose.

There was a Mexican chap who was a very good boxer. Latin-American youth are much further advanced physically than Anglo-Saxons. This chap had the physical maturity of a boy of twenty. I was fourteen. I had won about four bouts and I finally came to him. He knocked me out cold. He knocked everybody else out cold, too.

A. L. Cochrane, the phys ed master, came to me afterwards and said, "You musn't be too ashamed that you lost to him." Before the Mexican knocked me out, I hit him and I broke my thumb. I went to the school doctor who said, "That's all right. It will straighten out. Put a little iodine on it and keep it in a sling for about three days." Who was I to doubt him?

Naturally, it didn't set properly. My right thumb is now half an inch shorter than my left thumb. This means nothing to an ordinary person, but do you see all this music? See the piano over there? Music is my life! I was studying with Ernest Sykes. I wrote my matriculation in ancient history in the morning and played my piano exam in the afternoon. My thumb was sticking out.

I was trying to master piano technique with this bad thumb. Down the years, it got worse and worse. When I left Upper Canada, I finally had to give up the idea of becoming a professional musician. No one gave a damn about it.

Thirty years later, running my Esso gas station, I used to play classical music in my office, which often aroused the curiosity of the customers. When the elite of Forest Hill came in to sign their credit cards, I used to say to them, "If you can tell me what's playing, I'll tear up your bill." Very few of them could. Once I asked the ladies of the committee for the Toronto Symphony Orchestra, who were very prominent socially, if they could tell me the difference between Ravel and Debussy. They couldn't. I used to say, "They think Ravel is a detergent."

Once I was invited to a party in Forest Hill for Garrick Ohlsson, the great American pianist, after his concert in Toronto. When I arrived, they said, "Come on in. What would you like to drink?" I said, "Where is Garrick Ohlsson?" They said, "Who? Oh, yes, he's in the other room." That's how much the elite knew or cared about the arts.

For forty years, I ran the gas station in Forest Hill Village, which I call "The Golden Ghetto." The company is called Esso now, but it was Imperial Oil back then. I met lots of Upper Canada old boys at the gas station. The ones from my generation are just about all dead now. Those who aren't dead might as well be.

I would encounter snobbery from old boys who would say, "Get this, get that, do this. I'm Mr. So and So." You know the kind? A classic case was Mr. Bunting, whose son was the chairman of the stock exchange. Mr. Bunting was at one time, too. He came into my station once and said, "Purser!" I said, "Now look, don't call me Purser. Call me Guy or Mr. Purser. I'm not at school!" He said, "I'll be glad to give you all my business, but when I come into the station, I want all my windows cleaned every time."

I said, "Now, Mr. Bunting, I just can't do that. If you ask to have your windows cleaned, we'll clean them. We'll clean your windshield and your rear window and we'll give you the other free services. But I cannot instruct my help to cater to you and you alone. I can't tie them up to that extent." He said, "If you feel that way about it, okay."

He went over to Shell. He went over to Gulf. Finally, he came back to me. It was a hot afternoon. There was quite a run on for gas. Mr. Bunting was waiting to get in and Mrs. Patterson was also waiting to get in. Bunting pulls out of the middle and, before she can come in, he gets in ahead of her. She comes over to me and says, "Mr. Purser, I'm outraged. I've been waiting all this time and this man barges in."

The next remark I made cost Imperial Oil a lot of money. I said, "That just goes to show that the age of chivalry is dead." Bunting gets out and says, "I could have done without that remark." He goes downtown and presses every button on the desk: "Call the president, call the vice-president, call the general manager. Do you realize what this man said to me?"

It just happened that this woman was the wife of the legal adviser to Imperial Oil. He came in and said, "Guy, if you have any trouble, let me know, will you?" So that's how we fixed Bunting. Every time I see him in the Village, I say, "Oh, hello, Mr. Bunting, how are you today?"

I still walk into the Village almost every day. I got to know an enormous amount of people over forty years. Most of them are pretty doddery now. It's interesting to see how life treats them. Some of the alcoholics have managed to hang on for I don't know how long. Women alcoholics used to come in to sign their bill. I was on one side of the desk, but they didn't want to get that close to me because I could smell their breath. They would take the bill and go over by the window and sign it.

I remember a UCC old boy, a prominent lawyer, a wonderful person. I won't mention the name. He lived in a mansion on Dunvegan Road. Very nice people too. A taxi comes into the station. All I can see is the driver. He motions to me to look, so I look in the back seat. This guy is on the floor and he is handing me a signed cheque. He wants me to cash his cheque, which of course I do. They were going down to the liquor store.

Bruce Matthews was a real snob. His chauffeur used to come into my station. Right through the prep, he had a sickly smile on his face that really got my dander up. His father was the lieutenant-governor of Ontario.

I used to know John David Eaton quite well. He was a hell of a nice boy at the prep. He used to say, "If they knight me, they are going to have to call me Lord Dunvegan." He was a great athlete as a boy. I saw him swim the length of the tank twice without coming up.

There was nothing snobbish about John David Eaton. He had trouble with his kids. One son was fed up with his father because he wouldn't buy him a new car. He had one already. Out of rage, he drives his car onto the beautiful lawn, climbs underneath, undoes the crankcase, and lets the oil out onto the lawn. It's partly due to the parents, though, just being soft and perhaps lazy about discipline. I've also seen the reverse, sons who were highly disciplined and lived disciplined lives.

I couldn't have afforded to send my son to Upper Canada. I wouldn't have sent him anyway. A hothouse arrangement, where you have a concentration of males, cuts you off from the common herd. My children went to public schools. I think the public school system is a much better preparation for life than Upper Canada.

MAVOR MOORE

1927

Actor, writer, director

I WENT TO Upper Canada by a kind of fluke. My father was an Anglican minister and my mother, the daughter of a university professor, was an actress. By that time, my mother had had a great deal of experience on the professional stage in the United States and Britain. My parents were splitting up. We were poverty stricken, but I had a wealthy godmother. My father, in trying to smooth over the situation, decided that he would send my older brother and me to a really good boarding school. He persuaded my godmother, who was a member of the Laidlaw clan, to pay for us to go to UCC. She paid for the outfitting, the clothes, and the whole bit. Otherwise, there was simply no way it could have been done.

I rebelled against the whole system at Upper Canada, which I thought sadistic and totally unimaginative. It had no room in it at all for creative work or unconventional thought. There was just one incident of real suppression after another, including canings. I thought the headmaster, Duke Somerville, was just like the sadistic Charles Dickens character, Wackford Squeers. I was caned two or three times. I thought each time it was very unjust. There was no doubt in my mind that Somerville enjoyed it. There was a real sadistic strain in the man. He was a specialist in intimidation. It was his whole stock and trade.

Nearly all the teachers at UCC were English. The matron, Mrs. Cadenhead, or "Mrs. Cabbage Head" as we called her, was in Somerville's pocket. He and Mrs. Cadenhead had a sort of vaudeville act going. She would be nice to everybody while he would intimidate everybody, so it was the old good cop/bad cop psychology.

I got really very ill towards the end of that first fall term of 1927 at the prep. There was no home, by this time, for me to go to. I spent about ten days in an alcove off the dining room of the Duke's house. I was a terrible embarrassment to them because they really didn't know what to do with me. I had mumps and measles at the same time.

I had a very, very high fever when my mother finally came and rescued me and took me out of the school. When she saw me in this condition, she was not well herself. She broke all the health rules. She didn't even wait to call a doctor. She just bundled me in my clothes and put me in a cab. She smuggled me onto the train up to Ottawa, where I spent the rest of the winter with my grandmother. I was very close to death.

I have since read a good deal about the private schools in Britain and in America, as well as in Canada. I think they have been really warped institutions to a considerable extent. I recently read my old friend Noel Annan's book on Britain called *Our Age*. He went through the public school system in Britain at exactly the same time I was at UCC. Though he himself is very balanced and healthy, he describes in some detail how the English public school system has warped the young men of several generations.

I'm sure my sickness was partly a response to my unhappiness at the school. I had terrible nightmares. I was under some emotional stress to begin with, which Somerville should have realized. It should have been his first order of business. I later learned that one particular teacher, who became my champion and stood up to Somerville for me, got fired for it. The whole thing really was something right out of *Nicholas Nickleby*.

STANLEY RYERSON

1919 – 29

Historian

E GERTON RYERSON, the founder of the public school system in English Canada, was my great-grandfather. There was a touch of scandal in the fact that the children and grandchildren of the founder of the public school system went to a private school. I remember in the hall one day at Upper Canada, a boy named Birks, of the Henry Birks jewellery family, said to me, "Egerton Ryerson! Egerton Ryerson! He was a socialist!"

Whatever else he was, and he was quite a few things, a socialist wasn't one of them. Many years later, when I was doing some work on the background of Confederation for a book, I came across a document where Egerton Ryerson was being accused of being a Communist because he was in favour of letting the children of workers get schooling, which might radicalize them. It made me think of UCC, and Birks's indignant blast.

I have often asked myself how Upper Canada College could have produced a rebel in the form of a notorious Communist intellectual. How could such a thing happen? I began to trace it back. The main element was my friendships at UCC with Andrew Bell, Ross Parmenter, Frank Park, Bill Fleury, and Howard Lindsay. Howard Lindsay was the editor of the *College Times* in 1927, the year before I was editor. His family was Orange Crush.

Howard Lindsay was an atheist and I was very religious. When I was seven, I used to preach to the urchins on the steps of our house on Delisle Avenue, reading passages from the Bible. Howard and I would get into endless arguments.

Another main influence on me was the French master at UCC, Owen Classey, who had been the tutor to the children of H. G. Wells. When I got my first scholarship, he had marked it. We had pseudonyms and mine was "Barnacle." Classey said I had "stick-to-it-iveness." Because he had worked with H. G. Wells, Classey conveyed an element of the Fabian socialist approach which questioned the old established fiats.

Every so often very distinguished vistors would come to the college to speak. Admiral Earl Beatty, who was one of the great naval commanders in the Great War, came to speak in the prayer hall one day. All the masters sat on the dais in their gowns. When we went back to French class, one of the boys said to Classey, "Sir, you weren't on the dais this morning." Classey said vehemently, "I hate flags and all people who wave them." So we learned that education is internationalism. There was an element to our education that all you really needed was a large question mark. Owen Classey is the person I owe most to in terms of thinking and rethinking, situating an interest in science and history, a history of the world and not just the British world.

In the school library I came across a book called *New Worlds For Old* by H. G. Wells. It was about the idea of rationality in relation to society. On the street, you have the milk wagons of one company and the milk wagons of another company, wagons with yellow wheels and wagons with red wheels. I can remember the clip-clop of horses' hooves going along Delisle Avenue and seeing the various competing companies' wagons, like Eaton's and Simpsons. Wells's book was about the relative irrationality of a free-for-all in a socioeconomic jungle.

So I first got the idea of an alternative society to that of corporate business in the Upper Canada library, and in my arguments with Howard

Lindsay over religion. I had also my reaction to the instruction in the confirmation class in the Church of England at Christ Church, which I realized was a total whited sepulchre. I knew there was a big chunk of hypocrisy somewhere in there. Howard Lindsay had put his finger on it.

The only rebellion that I was really aware of was the religious one. I wouldn't stand up in the prayer hall, for instance. Howard Lindsay and I were outcasts in terms of religious respectability. In a sense, these were the seeds of a future social sedition, which didn't bloom until later.

I've always had a certain fascination with history. On the one hand, my family is steeped in history, and on the other hand, my experiences at UCC deepened and amplified my appreciation of it. Sir John Colborne, Lord Seaton, the lieutenant-governor of the province of Upper Canada, founded Upper Canada College in 1829. We sat under his portrait each morning in the prayer hall.

It was frequently told that Lord Seaton fought in the Peninsular War and that he was a hero at the Battle of Waterloo, but the story always ended there. We were never told about his role in smashing the 1837 Rebellion in Lower Canada. I thought it slightly odd the way in which the progression of classes developed in the school. We had Canadian history up to the War of 1812, but never beyond. After that, we went back to British history and ancient history.

The first small book I wrote was about the 1837 Rebellion, *The Birth of Canadian Democracy*. It was then I discovered the role of my school's founding father. The French also called Lord Seaton "Le Vieux Bruixeau," or "Old Incendiary," because he burned their houses. Not many old boys know that the hero of Waterloo was also the hero of putting down rebellions and instituting the era of the Act of Union when Lower Canada vanished.

I boarded in Seaton's House at Upper Canada, even though our home was only a few blocks away. A combination of a multiplicity of cultural threads, quirks of my own particular development, and the tensions in my family resulted in my being happy to be a boarder. Being out of the family orbit also played a part in my development. I later realized that Upper Canada was my prehistory which gave me things from the existing world, as it was, that were enriching. It was easier to appreciate it after the fact than it was just after I left Upper Canada.

This convergence of threads laid the groundwork for what happened to me after two years at the University of Toronto, when I went to Paris and moved to the political left. As a result of some radicalizing experiences in Paris in the early 1930s, I joined the Communist party. I remember going to a meeting of protest about what was then going on in Indo-China.

There was a terrific regime of repression of which the French army and gendarmerie were the dominant operating force. In that meeting, one of the speakers from Vietnam spoke about how a cage would be put on their chests with a rat in it, which would eat its way out, all under the supervision of the French military police.

Coming out of the meeting, we could hear the whistles of the military police charging a crowd of several thousand people. Nobody had done anything. We were leaving a meeting which had been a protest against French imperial repression in Indo-China. People were being bashed in the head. I was knocked over in front of a café.

I had just been reading in Lenin's *State and Revolution* that the state was essentially a collection of armed men in prisons. There is a dimension of violence in the very nature of the state. That night, I experienced it both on a scale of world empires and on an internal, personal scale.

When I came back to Canada in 1934, I taught at Sir George Williams College in Montreal for three years. At the same time, I was lecturing under a pseudonym at what was called the Workers' University, which involved radical workers' education in the east end of the city. Across the road, the Jesuit fathers had opened an office in what was their educational drop-in wing. One day they went to the administration at Sir George Williams and said, "Did you know that you have a notorious Communist on your faculty?"

So that ended my academic career in 1937. For thirty-three years thereafter, I was out of academe. I did freelance work and translations. I wrote three or four books. I worked in various organizations like the Workers' Defence League and the Communist party. Following the Soviet invasion of Czechoslovakia in 1968, I left the political left and we moved to Montreal. I had written a book in 1942 called *French Canada*. Mackenzie King had sent me a note of appreciation for my book on his grandfather and the 1837 Mackenzie Rebellion. He also wrote a letter to me about my book on French Canada. So even though I was more or less submerged underground, I wasn't totally cut off. After a year on unemployment insurance in Montreal, I was approached by the University of Quebec, where I taught for twenty years. I retired on New Year's Eve, 1991, at age eighty.

At Upper Canada, I wasn't all that struck by the omnipresent weight of the world of business. Only in retrospect was I struck by the galaxy of business elite that attended the school in my time: Wood and Gundy of Wood Gundy, Ed Gurney of the Gurney Plough Company, Heintzman, Seagram, Birks, Crean. I remember the room next to me on the third floor outside the prayer hall was occupied by Crawford Brown, whose family had a large chunk of Massey Harris.

A critique of Upper Canada College as an old-boy network is totally logical in relation to a critique of Canadian society as a whole. If you look at the school as a particular manifestation of the development of society, then an integral element of male chauvinism is inescapable. The dimension of imperial power that had been a part of Choppy Grant's work at Oxford University on colonial history, and of Sir John Colborne's presence in Canada, was part of this reality.

Meanwhile, all along, women were in the position of wives-as-servants who cooked, cleaned, and served as sex objects in relation to the sex that runs the world. It's all an inescapable part of the tissue of corporate business society, as well as the societies that try to replace it. I remember in the Soviet Union having supper with somebody from the Soviet News Agency, TASS. My wife and I were there, and I started to help with the dishes. They were horrified: "That's women's work!" And this was the motherland of socialism!

Of course these patriarchal attitudes go back to Genesis and the rib. I have migraines so I can't drink alcohol. The prevailing attitude is that if you can't drink, you are not a man. An institution like Upper Canada is in some ways the pinnacle of this pattern of attitudes. So a critique of the old-boy ethos is solidly founded.

I often think of something my dad had said around 1922 at the medical school at U of T. Walking down the halls, he said to me, "See those doors? The first one is a professor of hematology, the next one is a professor of endocrinology, and so on. Each one teaches as though his subject is the only thing there is in the world. He gives his students reading without really consulting his neighbours about what they are giving their students to read."

He was talking about the shut-in-ness of the institutionalized disciplines that are a part of the division of labour. The separation becomes an end in itself. My father used to say, "We have a vast curriculum, but no course on health." He wanted to start a school of health education. He was an associate dean, which carried a certain amount of weight, but the faculty said to him, "Okay, if you want to do it, go ahead. But on one condition: it must be outside the faculty of medicine." Here was a beautiful description of the built-in contradictions in the professions and the elite and their relation to society.

The fact that I moved to the left was really rough on my father and mother. When we became legal again in 1942, the leadership of the Communist party was incarcerated in the Don Jail in Toronto for ten days for violating the War Measures Act. There were a dozen of us, all men. We had been writing pamphlets and opposing conscription in the first stage of the war.

The Ontario premier, Mitchell Hepburn, who hated Louis St. Laurent's guts, used to blast the anti-Communist orientation of St. Laurent. So Hepburn came to the Don Jail and brought us chocolate bars, which we appreciated after ten days on a prison diet. My mother also came to see me and talked through the bars, which for her was quite something because she was horrified by everything that I had been involved in. But my father didn't come to see me. It was hard for him to talk to me. He was very shut in on himself, and so was I.

I didn't go back to Upper Canada for a long time after I left because of the sociopolitical gap. I remember when I went to an old boys' dinner in the 1960s, I met a guy who never used to mince his words. He said, "Are you still a fucking Commie?" I said, "That's one way to describe it." About five minutes later, somebody introduced me to another old boy. It turned out he was an RCMP inspector who had been probing and surveilling my activities.

JOHN MACDONALD

1921–30

Civil servant

OUR FAMILY PIONEERED a substantial amount of land in Toronto, stretching back from Bathurst Street into what is now Forest Hill. There were only three houses in that area in the days before World War I – the Ritchies', the Fosters', and ours. Living in that undeveloped area of Toronto had certain real disadvantages for me because I essentially grew up as a country boy. Until I got to Upper Canada, I didn't have any contact with other boys at all.

During World War I, infantry troops did a lot of their training in the St. Clair and Spadina area, charging across the fields with fixed bayonets. We had high wire fences around our place. As a small child, I could see whole waves of soldiers climbing over the fences and rushing across our lawn, which was quite substantial. They'd run across country to the ridge where a big Jewish synagogue is presently located. The trenches they built there lasted for years and years after the war.

I started at Upper Canada in 1921 when I was nine years old. It was a murderous establishment, just absolutely brutal. I was in terror of being put down all the time. I didn't fit into the group and I couldn't talk to them in their language. They had grown up together going to Brown School, south of St. Clair on Avenue Road. I'd grown up raising rabbits in a more rural setting, which made me a bit of a loner. I was neither intellectual nor athletic. I was physically small. I did stand in the first three or four in the class, but I'd never stand first. I was too lazy and I don't think I was bright enough.

In the prep, the bullying was extreme. Very quietly going on all the time was a homosexual undercurrent which mostly came from the headmaster, Duke Somerville, and another master, Mr. Spooner. Spooner used to work on my friend Roger Mitchell, which is why I know a fair amount about it. He'd bend boys over and operate on them with a cane. The Duke did pretty much the same thing. It was a very bad show. It should never have been tolerated.

There was nothing the Duke liked better than to get boys to sit on his knee up on a platform and make fun of them in the class or at the school meetings. Spooner did it after lunch. He'd tell the boys to go up the "Golden Stairs." Other guys told me that after he caned you, he'd pick you up and put you on his lap. He'd then rub your behind and start to cry. I was lucky. I got caned but not in this homosexual way. I was never attractive enough.

This stuff is never talked about. Somerville has gone down in history as a great man, but he was a big shit. I don't know how he became headmaster. I got a number of views of him because Dad had been a boarder at the school and Dad had no use for him at all. Somerville had some uses for Dad because he wanted Dad to donate a bell for the tower of the college.

I don't think Dad knew what was going on sexually. I don't think any parents did, or if they did, they didn't do anything about it. It was just too far removed from their imaginations. I don't know how extensive it was. I do know that Somerville had a stable of boys and that Spooner had another one. I think these guys enjoyed caning in a sadomasochistic way.

I never directly experienced Somerville's homosexual ritual, but someone very close to me was ruined by him. Somerville clearly enjoyed tormenting my friend, who didn't have the kind of fortitude required and was scared of his own shadow. When my friend couldn't stand it any longer, he started to drink. He had a bad time at Upper Canada, although God equalized things for him by giving him five wonderful sons and a daughter. He leads a happy life now.

There was also an awful lot of homosexual play and fooling around among the boys. I witnessed it and I participated in it. I think it probably did us harm. When I was sixteen, I turned my attention to girls and I don't know whether that was any better or not. The only thing I know is that the girls and I had a hell of a fine time.

Even though Upper Canada was an all-boy environment, I met lots of girls. The girls' parents organized coming-out dances. They had to scurry around to find enough boys to make sure that there were always boys waiting to dance. You couldn't have a girl at a dance standing by herself. We knew our job, which was to make sure that the girls didn't get stranded. We boys all had a hell of a fine time. We got to know all kinds of girls. I wouldn't say it was a puritan sexual atmosphere, but it was much more cautious. Since birth control didn't exist, you had to get out fast if you got in.

If a girl got pregnant, you could tell the guys who were fairly well off. One would get caught once in a while and everything stopped. If his family wasn't very wealthy, he ended up running a gasoline station. There were a lot of guys running gasoline stations or some kind of a dead-end job. You couldn't have a scandal. The boy had to marry the girl. They both knew their duty. The results could be very unhappy.

I started a fairly involved sexual relationship with a Havergal girl when I was seventeen and in the sixth form in the college. We had a great life together. I thought the sun rose and set with her. Before her, I had had another girl who was at BSS [Bishop Strachan School]. We got involved with sex a little bit but not very much. I knew the dangers but I also knew there were quite a large number of girls available. The thing was to get somebody you really wanted to be with. I don't know how many beds I've fallen into. We were not chaste.

I treated the UCC masters in an awful fashion. Alan Stephen had just arrived at the school from a rich, fairly gentle lifestyle. I don't know what the hell happened but Roger Mitchell and I decided to see if we could make him mad. We started to do things in class and Stephen lost control of the situation. Everybody in the classroom was yelling. It was awful.

Somerville got called. He looked like the ruler of the King's navy. Very severely, he said, "Who is responsible for this?" Dead silence. The silence could not go on forever, so Roger and I turned up. He grabbed each of us by the collar and dragged us up and down each aisle of the classroom, whacking us with the cane as hard as he could. I've never forgotten it. It was a scene of carnage. Alan Stephen and I subsequently became best friends. The villains and the good guys were all mixed up together at UCC.

I can also remember being caned by a guy by the name of Mowbray. I can't remember what it was for. He'd say, "Come to my office," and you'd go. He'd go to his rack of canes and select one. He could really hit you hard. You'd usually get "six of the best." I had great respect for Mowbray. He was a man of integrity but dull as dishwater. I guess he deserved to eventually have one of the day-boy houses named after him.

Caning was just part of the business of being at UCC. Once I got into a fight in the locker room with a guy who subsequently became a doctor. I don't know why we were fighting but we were bashing each other about. Somebody reported it and we were yanked up to see Somerville, who caned both of us quite strenuously.

I don't think I got a very good education in my nine years at UCC. Any education I got, I gave myself. The school wasn't much good at sorting out who was a good teacher. I don't know how anybody could have let guys like Spooner and Somerville loose in that place for so many years. Somerville was a sadistic bastard who should never have been in charge of a school.

My impression of Choppy Grant, the principal of the upper school, was also not very high. I preferred his son, George Grant, who came under my charge when I was a counsellor at camp. He was an unobtrusive little thing who probably had a hard time with his father being principal of UCC. My impression of Choppy was that he didn't feel for other people.

But there were also good things at UCC. Some of the masters were worthwhile people. Billy McHugh was my idea of the perfect teacher. He made mathematics easy for me and anybody who could do that was okay. He would lay it all out on the board calmly and lucidly. Then an awful morning came in 1929 when it was announced that he was dead. Everybody knew that it was a suicide. I think it was the stock market. An awful lot of people committed suicide in those days.

ROBERTSON DAVIES

1928–32

Writer

I WAS STARTLED the last time I went into Upper Canada. I was talking to some of the boys and they didn't recognize the portrait of Lord Seaton, the school's founder. That portrait was an icon in my day because it hung in the prayer hall right behind the dais, where everything went on. Every morning we prayed for Lord Seaton and all other UCC benefactors.

I don't think they do that any more. In fact, they don't have prayers in the mornings. By golly, we had a Bible education. The sixth-form Bible class was taken by the headmaster, who was remarkably good. We had a brilliant, free discussion. You weren't chained down to the party line at all, so it was very good stuff. I'm wholeheartedly in favour of it.

At least once a week, Dr. Grant used to lecture us at prayers in the morning. His words were, "Much has been given to you and much will be expected from you." He rubbed it in and he made it stick. It was true. We were told flatly that we were a privileged group and that we would be expected to measure up. My father was also explicit about expectations. He quoted from the Bible: "Him to whom much has been given, much shall be required."

We carried with us a set of expectations, which I think is a good way to educate people. I used to tell my students when I was teaching at the University of Toronto that the people of Ontario were paying a lot of money to put them in those chairs and that they had better measure up. They never thought that anybody was paying for it. They thought their miserable fees covered their presence at the university. How they thought a nice place like the university was kept up, I don't know.

I am a wholehearted supporter of the UCC system, but I recognize that it isn't possible to apply it to everybody. I'm a believer of elitism in the good sense of the word. Our instruction was to rise as high as we could. It was a sort of nineteenth-century thing, but thank God I came along in time to get some of it.

I know one or two old boys who have ended up as panhandlers and they are embarrassing, but you must expect that. In any group, you are going to get some people who are going to go astray. They can't stand the pressure. That's too bad and one is sorry. But it is not a thing that is going to apply with 100 per cent effectiveness.

In those days, Upper Canada had a fagging system which was very tough on new boys. You were awarded to somebody as his fag, and then you were virtually a slave. Fagging entailed polishing shoes, making out the laundry lists, sending the laundry, getting the laundry back, putting it away, looking after the fagmaster's luggage, fetching him glasses of water during study – menial tasks of one sort or another. I had a fag when I was in Grade 13. I did what we were told you were supposed to do with a fag. He did things for me and I did a few things for him. I helped him with his homework.

I was in Wedd's House. William Mowbray was the housemaster, a very just, formal sort of man. He dressed formally and was very formal in his way of speaking to the boys and dealing with them, as all the masters were in those days. Most of the masters wore gowns when they were on duty. You always had to stand up in the presence of masters. A master was not supposed to see a boy sitting down. The etiquette was quite strict, which I think was a very good thing. There was a very formal way of doing things, but within the formality there was a great deal of freedom.

I wasn't any good at sports, so nobody wanted me on their team. There were a great many clubs, which were a very effective thing in the college. There was a travel club, a stamp club, a photography club, a music club, and an art club. The Curfew Club, the top club in the college, was for sixth-formers and senior boys, who would talk about current events. The clubs were very good indeed, giving the boys a great deal of occupation and education.

I was very interested in the Little Theatre at UCC. The director was Freddie Mallett, who was also the chemistry master. Freddie Mallett was a prominent amateur actor in the Hart House Players' Guild, along with his wife, Jane Mallett. Various people like the actress Dora Mavor Moore and Frank Rostadts, who was an amateur actor of considerable reputation, used to come and talk to us, which was interesting.

I acted in a lot of the Shakespeare, Gilbert and Sullivan, and Bernard Shaw plays for the Little Theatre. Also under Dr. Grant's urging, we had a curious sort of drama festival for the junior boys who got up and performed a one-act play. There was an adjudicator who decided who had done it best. Each one-act play was under the guidance of a boy from the upper school who was a member of the drama club. He didn't direct the play, just kept an eye on it. He saw that people would get to rehearsals and that they took it seriously.

Alan Stephen, the headmaster of the prep school for many years, had been one of the history masters in the upper school in my day. He asked me if I would write a play specifically for the prep, so I wrote *The Masque of Aesop*. Then they asked for another one, so I wrote *The Masque of Mr. Punch*. The plays deliberately included a large number of boys, giving them the kind of thing I thought they could do well. For years, they have played in the school. Insofar as there are any royalties, they get them.

Choppy Grant's son, George, was in the Gilbert and Sullivan productions. He was a charming schoolboy, much younger than I. In *Iolanthe*, I was the Lord Chancellor and George was my train-bearer. He was a very pretty little boy. It was astonishing when he grew up and became a big, fat, queer-looking man. But he was a delightful person. All three of his sisters were awfully nice. Alison Grant, who later married George Ignatieff, was the first girl I ever took to a dance, the Rifle Company Ball.

The Grants were a fascinating family because they were extremely lively minded. Mrs. Grant was a delightful, intellectual woman who could talk splendidly to boys. She and her husband were a first-class pair to be at the head of a school. They really knew how to deal with young people, not in a patronizing way. They always treated you as if you were grown up. He took you seriously if you were serious. I remember the mathematics master, Butch McKenzie, once called me a liar because I hadn't done something he said I should have done. I went to Dr. Grant and said that I would not be called a liar. Grant took me very seriously and took me out of McKenzie's class.

McKenzie later on became headmaster, but I don't think he was a successful one. He was a very difficult man. He had an uncontrollable Scottish temper. His face would become the colour of brick and he would fly into rages. He was a good teacher for people who were very good at math, but he had no patience with anybody who wasn't. He was a rotten disciplinarian. I understand when he became principal, in the 1940s, he had trouble with the staff and eventually was removed. I talked to some of them subsequently who said he was impossible as the head of the staff. He used to lose his cool when he was caning boys.

There was something about Grant's regime which subsequently has led me to have very great respect for him. He had a staff which contained an extraordinary number of men who had returned from the First World War. They were very decorated. On Prize Day, they appeared with all their medals. It was astonishing what they had. But they had found nothing in civilian life except being schoolmasters. Some of them were very resentful and difficult. I think they must have been a hard group to deal with, but Grant did deal with them very skilfully. The result was that the teaching was on a high level. You did feel sometimes that these men were so far above the work they were doing that it wasn't funny at all. But it was the only job they could get. One or two of them were a little bit strange, but Grant was very patient with them.

One poor master, Dickey Potter, who had been shell-shocked in the war, had a silver plate on top of his head. Every now and again, Dickey used to climb the water pipes in his classroom and teach from up there with his gown hanging down. Nobody raised an eyebrow. I memorialized him and some other UCC masters in my novel *Fifth Business*. I remember one day Dr. Grant came in to say something to him. Dickey was up on the pipes and Grant never winked an eye. He just said what he had to say and went away. He was very tactful and gentle with those people.

Doggie Mills, the Greek and Latin master, had undergone a terrific crisis in his early life because he had been brought up a Protestant. Then he had very much wanted to convert to Catholicism and become a priest.

After agonies that made Cardinal Newman look like a patsy, he decided not to do so. We were always aware that Doggie was a man who had undergone very great spiritual stress, so we respected him. We used to tease him a lot in class, but we all respected him.

One of the things the boys used to do was rather dreadful. Doggie had catarrh, so he used to spit every now and again. He was a very gentle fellow. He would walk down to the back of the class where you weren't supposed to know that he was spitting out of the window. He did it very quickly. Wicked boys used to cover the window. He would then have to follow the spit, dab it with his hanky, and clean it up.

There was another man who had terrible injuries called Parlee, who walked with a dreadfully inhibited gait. His legs had been crushed in some kind of air accident. He was a man who suffered from deep resentments. And there was Daddy Darnell, a frightful drunk. He was the one who threw a wet boxing glove at inattentive boys and then retrieved it on a string, as I described in *Fifth Business*. Subsequently, the headmaster got rid of him because he was really rather a problem. He sank down to being the superintendent of an apartment building.

These types of eccentric teachers were infinitely more educational than the teachers I'd had at Kingston Collegiate, who were all products of the Ontario training system. The UCC masters had been in the navy and the army and had seen service all over the place. They had travelled in the East or had been in the intelligence corps. They brought a world with them from beyond that narrow world of the Ontario College of Education.

The character of Boy Staunton in *Fifth Business* wasn't based on any particular UCC old boy, but he was a type which was very well represented in that school – the rich, privileged person who had it made, who was clever and not a bad person, but unaware of much about life. But there were also a lot of boys who didn't come from rich homes. Some of them were the very brightest of the lot. Sam Hughes and Stanley Ryerson were absolutely stars. When I became editor of the *College Times*, I was aware that I had better mind my hide because I was following in the footsteps of some pretty remarkable editors, like Stanley Ryerson, B. K. Sandwell, and John Ross Robertson.

When I recently went to the seventy-fifth anniversary dinner for the Little Theatre, a master told me that he found all sorts of boys who had read *Fifth Business* and yet hadn't recognized the college. They didn't know that "Colborne College" in the book was based on Upper Canada. The bleak stupidity of Toronto Tories is a miracle, you know.

PETER GOODERHAM

1923–33

Businessman

C HOPPY GRANT was one of the people at UCC I could have squashed. I hated his guts. He used to come into the prayer hall first thing in the morning. He never glanced at his masters. He ignored them. He would come in with his flowing gowns billowing. I used to say, "There is Choppy, milord." It was good that I did not have him as a master because he was an overly nasty little man. He was very self-important in his own right, and his son George used to feel it. Choppy was mean to him.

Choppy Grant commanded the cadet battalion, the silly old fart. Boys could not go any higher than the rank of captain in those days because Choppy Grant was a major. I had a portable typewriter and I was able to type, so I was made an adjutant. I had my own office, my name on the door, and a sign which said No Admittance. I put up the notices and orders on the wall. I signed them and then took them to Choppy to initial to make them official.

I remember the governor general, Lord Beaverbrook, came to inspect the Rifle Company one year. The big inspection day creeped up and Choppy had to be out there first with his beret on. Because of my position, I was in the main party. I swear that Beaverbrook knew that Choppy was an ass. Beaverbrook turned to me and said, "Would you tell me who is that gentleman over there with all the braid?" I said, "Yes, Your Excellency, that is Major Grant." He said, "Major what?" Choppy was so afraid that I was going to do something awful, he congratulated me afterwards.

But I liked Choppy Grant's wife, who was a peach, and his daughters. I used to get in on some of the Sunday evening get-togethers in Grant House. Mrs. Grant was pretty funny. She would say, "Now, Peter, you can look anywhere you like in this house because your grandfather paid for it." She was so nice about it, whereas Choppy would not mention it. He tried to let on that he had paid for it.

As a boy, I was never allowed to forget our family connection to the school. My grandfather had graduated from UCC in 1871. He was a grand man and a great patron of UCC. He was chairman of the board from 1912 to

1934 and chairman of the Old Boys' Association at the same time. He was a real philanthropist, but he never allowed anything to be named after him, on purpose. He was a very modest man who did not want anyone to know where the money came from in case they kept chasing him again. He would say to all his pet charities, "Do not mention where this money came from or that is the last nickel you will get."

He liked giving away money so much he gave away all his own off-springs' money. He gave away what would have been my inheritance. His father had left too much money. When my great-grandfather died at age seventy-five in 1905, he left behind $25 million, the equivalent of $500 million today, which came from the Gooderham and Worts distillery. Family sources of funds were all over the place.

My father, who graduated in 1911, happened to hold the hundred-yard dash record for years. While I was at the school, he still had it. I was aware of his track records and history at the school, but I was never allowed to mention it. I used to win the Gooderham Writing Prize every year, but I was never allowed to keep it. Grandfather would give me one hundred dollars instead. It was crazy. I mean, a writing prize is hardly a scholarship.

In those days we had grand, expensive debutante parties. The girls would ask the boys. UCC boys were always on the top of the list. Parents would prepare a list and UCC boys were at a premium. It helped if you had a name that meant something in Toronto. They were good parties, but no drinking. It just was not done. We used to carry a Mickey occasionally if it was a party at the Royal York Hotel. If it was a wide-open party, we would have booze with us. The better the band, the better the party. It was good music, jazz, the whole works. Your dance programs were the important thing. The sooner the girls had it filled with names, the more they could relax. There was always a supper dance, which you had your best girl for. Those were fun days.

I was always interested in anything to do with the family from an early age. Grandfather used to talk to me about the family more than any of his nine sons. It got to the point that it was almost embarrassing when Grandfather asked for me. Even Uncle Ed, who was my godfather and the chief take-over of the family businesses, used to wonder why I was always cited.

Grandfather started selling off the family businesses in the 1920s and 1930s. He was head of the family by then, although he used to quote his father. The family was involved with about eighteen different businesses they had started – the distillery, the bank, hotels, railways. They had a hotel in Temagami called the Ronnoco, which is O'Connor spelt backwards, the King Edward Hotel, the Lake Hotel at Niagara-on-the-Lake, the Clifton.

Long before the days of telephones, my great-grandfather George would send down for Grandfather from his house, which he built at the corner of Bloor Street and St. George. It was called Wavoney, after the river my family came from in England. Grandfather would have to get his horse and buggy out and drive up to his father's. Grandfather lived down on Trinity Street, so going up to Bloor and St. George was a hell of a distance.

One day, he was let in and shown into the library. Great-grandfather put his shoes on the floor and said, "Will, see how you fit those." When my grandfather put them on, his father said, "Okay, you are taking over." Of course, it was not the size of the shoes that mattered. He just had to have an excuse to make a choice.

When Grandfather ran the family, everyone listened to what he said. They were afraid of what he would say. Even though they worked for the company, they each had a $500 allowance per month, which was a hell of a lot of money in those days. But it was crazy because he never gave them any independence at all. My wife's father was exactly the same, brought up by a domineering grandfather. And I mean really domineering: "Sit at that desk, not that one."

Even Grandfather's two daughters were on an allowance. The eldest one, my beloved aunt Eileen, came every day and had tea with him. The tea was brought and she poured it. When she dared to spend one month in Muskoka, her allowance was cut off. He was a nasty man. She was not there for tea, so to hell with her.

Dad should have stayed with the distillery, but I think his father's influence really affected him. He moved out of it – mind you, very close at hand. He was in the stables of Gooderham and Worts. His biggest job was shooting flies. He was a crack shot to start with. He would sit at his desk in the office, which was built of teakwood, and shoot flies. I remember horses' hooves ruined the whole teakwood base.

My father got into the business of cartage, which had to do with loading gravel for building projects. The first contract he got was building the St. Clair Avenue bridge across Mount Pleasant. He had very high-class English Leyland trucks. He was able to take one load of booze from the distillery out the back door, land it in Windsor, and make fifteen hundred dollars. So it became part and parcel of his scope. They even got so far as to put a pipe under the St. Clair River from one end to the other.

But my father said, "Father always had his spies out." I do not know how he did it, but my grandfather knew what every son was up to, all nine of them, and the girls, too. He knew everything that they were doing, and if they were found out, they were called to the office.

Arthur Ball, who was Grandfather's private secretary, would call the sons in at a special time to see their father. They would come in and Grandfather would say, "You sit over there." He would talk to Dad about the stock market. One morning he said, "You have got too much nickel. Sell your nickel." Dad said, "But, Father, I think it is going to go to one hundred." It was then at seventy. Grandfather would say, "Let the other fellow have the thirty." If he had held on, Father would have been a millionaire when he died. But no.

He was called into the office again and Grandfather said, "You are not the only damned fool in the family. Alex is a damned fool. He lost two million dollars." So, as Dad is walking out of the Flatiron Building, he runs into his brother Alex. He smiled and said, "Alex, you are a damned fool. Father says you lost two million dollars." Alex said, "Father is the damned fool. It was nine million dollars." Easy come, easy go.

One Saturday, I remember my father coming home for lunch from the stock market. Mother was serving scrambled eggs, and he said, "Well, Olive, today was the day." She said, "What do you mean?" He said, "Well, it has come. And it came very quickly. I was two hours down there, and I lost three million dollars." Mother said, "What do you mean? Why did you not tell me about it?" She was trying to say, "Look, I would have spent it before it got lost."

When the Mitch Hepburn government took over in Ontario, they started picking on wealthy families for inheritance. All my grandfather's sons and daughters had been given houses as wedding presents, so they had to be added into their estates. Dreadful. One of the uncles decided to fight it by taking it to the Privy Council in England, which could overrule the Ontario government in taxation matters. The Privy Council ripped the Hepburn government up the arse, and how. A lord gave a terrific speech in the House of Lords which made Hepburn look like such a bloody fool.

Choppy Grant and my grandfather both died the same month in 1935. I was the only grandson invited to Grandfather's bedside as he was dying, which was very embarrassing to Dad. Here was his twenty-year-old son being asked to sit beside his own father. I remember the faces of the nine sons all around me, staring at me, wondering if Grandfather was going to change his will.

A few years ago, at an old boys' dinner, I was able to say to the principal, Eric Barton, "That is my grandfather's portrait hanging over there, and I am proud of one thing. He educated over six hundred boys at this school through his scholarships."

[This interview took place on August 15, 1992. Peter Gooderham died on January 12, 1994.]

JOHN McCORDICK

1927–33

Diplomat

I ENJOYED the cadet battalion at Upper Canada. I joined the colour guard. The sergeants all wore a bright red sash, which made for a very colourful group of uniforms. One year, we were taken down to the Canadian National Exhibition as part of the entertainment. We marched around and drilled in our uniforms, which was very well received. We had to train like mad in preparation for the event. Day after day, we went through various drills, maneuvers, and rituals. We trained ourselves so that no one ever clinked their bayonet against someone else's, dropped a rifle, or moved in the wrong direction. We were almost like a Prussian unit. We were damn good.

My lifelong curiosity about languages was largely stimulated by a UCC master named Jacques de Marbois. I was very much under his influence. He wasn't a very good teacher, especially for the duller boys, but he was a very good teacher about life because he had seen a lot of it. On a hot spring day when he thought it was too hot to teach, he would open the windows of the classroom. He'd sit cross-legged, Buddha style, on his desk and tell us stories about life in Shanghai. I'd come home brimming with all this stuff and unload it on my parents. I'd say, "I learned the most fantastic things from this fantastic master."

I spoke French quite well by the time I was fifteen. I started taking German fairly early in the upper school and had an affinity for it, so I got marks in the nineties in the matric. I had difficulty in choosing a career, so I went to Dr. Grant, the upper school principal, during the summer for advice. I said, "What should I do? I'm pulled two different ways." He said, "The best advice I can give you is, don't make a choice based on the prospects of making a lot of money. Try to analyze yourself to see where your own bent is. Follow that."

After UCC, I ended up taking physics at the University of Toronto. In 1937, when I was twenty-one, I went away for one year to Germany, where I also studied physics. I also went to the University of Paris for a year, where I took Russian. I was able to dovetail the work I was doing at the Science Politique with another institute where they taught Arabic,

Turkish, all the Slavic languages, and dialects of Indian, Chinese, and Japanese.

They had fabulous professors. I was able to take their lectures as well as my political science ones. So that formed the grammatical base of my Russian. I liked the old-fashioned way of teaching, the one that says: There is no shortcut. This is a difficult language. You face the difficulties. You don't learn like a baby, parroting it. If the grammar is complicated, you have to learn it.

In the summer of 1939, I went up to Estonia, which was still a free country, because it was known for having teachers of Russian used by the British armed forces. I lived with a Russian family and took Russian lessons from them. I lived an intensive nineteenth-century Russian social life for the four months I was in Estonia. Then the war started in early September 1939.

The Russians had signed a non-aggression pact with Hitler. The Russians were already putting pressure on the Baltic states and some of their troops moved in. I didn't get out of Estonia until the middle of October. The only place to go was to Finland or to Sweden. If you went south, you got into Nazi-occupied Poland. I managed to get on a ship going to Stockholm. I never took Russian instruction again, but I already had a good working knowledge of the language.

External Affairs was a very small government department in the prewar years in Canada. They were going to have a competition and exam for admission in January 1940, so I informed them that I would write the exam. But I never did because I joined the Canadian army instead.

I was in the army in England in June 1941 when the Russians came into the war, having been attacked by the Germans. The British were looking for Russian-speaking officers at that time. They put together a special course in Cambridge under the future Duke of Wellington to train them in conference technique, military vocabulary, and so on. The British had my name because I had been at the previous German course. They asked to have me sent. The Canadian army at first demurred, but someone said to General McNaughton, "Oh, why don't you let him go." So I went.

I was in Iran in 1942 when I was told to take part in the transportation of former Polish POWs to England. When the Russians joined the Germans in 1939 in attacking Poland, the Russians had taken prisoner hundreds of thousands of Poles, who they then shipped to Central Asia. Now that the Russians were our allies, the hundreds of thousands of Polish prisoners could be released to the British. They were to be brought from Central Asia to the Caspian Sea, put on oil tankers, and dumped ashore in an Iranian port on the Caspian, en route to England.

The British commandeered a lot of private trucks with open backs. The Poles just stood in these trucks. Staging posts were established right down to Egypt. I was in charge of one post at a provincial city about 120 kilometres northwest of Tehran. We had as many as 5000 Poles a day coming through. They were in such poor health that we had several deaths per day.

I was a young captain, and I did the negotiations with the Soviet authorities over the transportation of the Poles. I went by train to Palestine. I was not very well at the time, as I had dysentery rather badly. I was so ill that the British brigadier who saw me said, "You can't go any farther. You're too sick. Drink orange juice until you get better." After two weeks in Palestine, they let me go on to Cairo. It was arranged for us to meet a ship leaving from a port on the Red Sea. We went down to Capetown, where we spent two or three days between changing ships.

We were put on the *Laconia*, which was about 22,000 tons. It was built right after World War I and used on the Southampton-New York route. The layout of the decks was quite unlike anything I'd seen. I'm not superstitious, but for the first and only time in my life, as I went up the gangway, I had a foreboding that this ship was doomed.

One of the peculiarities of the *Laconia* was that what would have been the first-class area was almost below the water level. It was a very low deck, not up above the way they usually are. The British officers had their meals down there, so I did too. Out of boredom we tended to linger at the table and have extra cups of coffee.

On the third evening out of Capetown, I said to the others, "I'm not sitting around this evening. I know what will happen when I get back to the Canadian military headquarters in London. I will march in and say, 'I'd like to go on a few days leave.' The answer I get will be, 'First of all, we need a report from you.' I can say, 'It just so happens that I have it here.'"

I wanted to finish the report, so I went up to the cabin that I shared with three other officers and spread out on my bunk the papers I'd been working on. It was then that two torpedoes struck. It was about five minutes since I'd left the dining room, just after nightfall. No one in the dining room had a hope. The torpedoes went straight into that part of the ship. So if it hadn't been for that report, I would have been finished.

It was an unforgettable experience, of course. I remember the particular smell of the torpedoes. I had never smelled those kinds of explosives before. In the course of the night, the ship sank. I was one of the last people off it because I was part of the small group of officers in charge of a large number of Italian prisoners we had on board.

The reason they put me in charge was that the guard for the Italians were young Poles, coming from the Middle East to become airmen in

England. They were made the guard of the Italians, but they only spoke Polish and Russian. None of the British officers on the ship could communicate with them, until someone discovered that I could speak Russian. So I was put in charge. One of my duties was to stay on the ship, if a disaster struck, until the last possible moment.

During the ordeal in the water, watching people die, part of my salvation was figuring out that I had to somehow get through to dawn. Not that dawn was a guaranteed salvation, but I had a better chance in the light. I knew I had to conserve my energy. I saw a lot of people, some of whom I had known on board, thrashing about in a panic. These men were far stronger than I was. They were wasting their energy and I was conserving mine. That strategy helped me survive.

I clung to the wreckage. I saw people drowning and bleeding all around me in the sea. I was able to swim to a lifeboat in the morning as soon as the sun was bright enough. We floated around for five days in the South Atlantic in the lifeboat with absolutely nothing around us. We were well off the coast of Africa, three days' sailing from Capetown. We didn't know if we'd be picked up. The drinking water was running out. We found that the crew was getting at it. The water, which should have lasted for several more days, had actually run out at the very moment we were picked up by a French battleship.

The things that sustained me, I can say quite unashamedly, were not religious beliefs. They were habits of self-discipline, of mind, of thinking, logic and deduction. These I attribute to a combination of my education at UCC and the fact that at university I studied physics and mathematics. But universities do not give you the things that Upper Canada gives you. It's the type of logical thinking that UCC endows you with. It is not very easy to describe, but I owe a debt, perhaps even my life, to those influences.

After we were picked up in our lifeboat by the Vichy French, they put us behind barbed wire just outside Casablanca. Two months later, in November 1942, the British and the Americans landed on the coast of North Africa. The British were on the Mediterranean coast and the Americans were on the Atlantic. We were released by the Allies and taken in the hulls of liberty ships to Norfolk, Virginia. I was brought up to Ottawa. The rest were all British people who had to cross the Atlantic once again. What an ordeal!

When I got to Ottawa, the adjutant general saw me himself. He said, "McCordick, I'm delighted you're alive. You were posted missing and possibly dead. But I have bad news for you. Because we didn't know where you were or whether you were even alive, we couldn't wait any longer. So we appointed another officer to the diplomatic job in the Soviet Union. We've just brought him out from England. He's in Ottawa. You can meet him if you like."

He was a Russian Canadian who eventually became a very good friend of mine. Then the adjutant general said, "Run up the street to External Affairs. They urgently want to see you." In a way, I was lucky, because the work that I would have done as an assistant military attaché in the Soviet Union was not nearly as interesting as what I ended up doing as a diplomat. After the war, External Affairs asked me to stay on. I almost have to thank a German submarine commander for my wartime entry as a diplomat into External Affairs.

I started my diplomatic career when they sent me to Moscow in 1943. I served mostly in Eastern Europe, largely because the Russian business started it all off. I was ambassador in Austria and Czechoslovakia. I was ambassador in Poland just before I retired.

I have never considered myself a militarist, but I consider that the kind of training I got at UCC played a useful role in forming my character. I remember how public opinion was shifting in the 1960s against militarism. I regretted it very much. A country like Canada no longer knows quite what to do with its young people. It's a pity that the old traditions have drifted into the past.

My son Brian went to UCC for a few years in the early 1970s when I was ambassador in Vienna. We thought we were doing the best thing, but it didn't work out too well. He didn't enjoy being a boarder. He got ragged and bullied rather a lot. He's now six feet three. He's good at looking after himself, but he wasn't when he was fourteen or fifteen. He had only been to French schools and had a slight accent, and never fit in as well as he might have.

That's the one grudge I've held against Upper Canada. I don't think they handled him the way they should have. My wife went to see Patrick Johnson, the principal, when we were still living in Austria. He put her off very much. While I can't absolve my son from all responsibility, I think the school let him down. Boarding schools are supposed to serve the function of *in loco parentis*. UCC didn't exercise that responsibility. After four years at UCC, my son went to Ashbury College in Ottawa for Grade 13.

I regret the erosion of British values in Canada and in Canadian institutions like Upper Canada College. I also regret the charge that some people in Canada today will make against a person like myself, even though all I do is express a mild word of regret. They will tell me that I'm colonial-minded, that I belong to the old British boot-licking brigade.

I say, "You're completely wrong, but I'll never be able to explain to you why I feel the way I do." After all, I was in a department of government which was designed for Canada to paddle its own canoe. You can't say that I worked to retain or prolong Canada's colonial status. But it was a world unto itself. I was closely associated with the British forces during the war and I can't forget that experience.

When people, as they often do these days, go around shouting about Canadian national identity, I seldom have any opportunity to add my two bits' worth. When the subject does come up, I say, "Look, I was born in 1915, but I've never been in any doubt about my identity. I don't have an inferiority complex about it. Nor do I have a superiority complex about it. I'm quite comfortable in my own skin."

[This interview took place on November 17, 1991. His Excellency John McCordick committed suicide in his Ottawa home on May 23, 1992.]

MICHAEL SHALOM GELBER

1931–35

Psychotherapist

A T UCC, I WAS very much interested in religion. Jack Davidson, a master, organized a religious discussion group in his home on Sundays. He arranged meetings of boys from four or five of the snob schools. George Grant, Hart and Lionel Massey, Bill Goulding, and Jim George would come. I was the only Jew in the group, but they thought that was kind of quaint. I later went to theological school and was ordained as a rabbi.

George Grant was interested in ethical values rather than in explicit concepts. I could see the conflict that he had, as a man of grace, who was suffering under the nineteenth-century oppression of some of the UCC masters. Caning boys is ridiculous. It's just unacceptable. We had to take PDS, or punishment drills, which involved going around the damn quadrangle as punishment for some ridiculous thing that happened in class. It was a disgrace. It reduced the whole thing to stupidity.

Despite that element at UCC, the principal, Choppy Grant, George's father, was a good guy. Unfortunately, he had to accept UCC as it was. The school was dominated by a group of fellows who thought that they were

Englishmen when they were actually farm boys from the backwoods of Ontario. They appropriated all the techniques and the language of Englishmen. UCC hired an awful lot of Englishmen who were incompetent teachers.

My suspicion is that Choppy basically would have been a liberal. I didn't know him when I was mature, but I knew him well because his son George was so close to me. If I was a big boy then, I could have said to him, "Dr. Grant, why do you have us walking around in that damn quadrangle when boys do something wrong? It isn't going to do them any good. It makes them look like silly asses when they have done some minor thing." He would have said, "Well, perhaps you're right." But he couldn't change what he had inherited.

I am eternally grateful for what he did for me personally. An Englishman wrote a book about the danger of war, when I was thirteen, called *Cry Havoc*. I was a pacifist because we were all influenced by the post-World War I period. At Huron Street School, where I went before I went to Upper Canada, boys and girls would come out on Armistice Day. I remember our wonderful teacher, Miss Walker, a lovely woman whom we all loved. She had lost a brother in the war. We'd stand there, little kids of six or seven, and see her sobbing on Armistice Day, remembering her brother. It tore my heart strings. Poor Miss Walker! It was incredible how she influenced me just by crying.

When I went to Upper Canada, I was involved in everything. The school did Gilbert and Sullivan operas beautifully. They interested us in music. They had a wonderful art room. They had great sports. I loved to do all of these things. But I decided I would not take military training. My mother said, "All the Gelbers have gone to Upper Canada College." I said, "Well, I just don't want military training. I love Upper Canada. I love the people. I love my friends. But I won't take military training."

My mother, who was a dear girl, wrote a letter to Choppy Grant. She said that she didn't want to contravene the rules of the school, but she also had an obligation to her son. At the age of thirteen, her son was a pacifist who refused to be in the Rifle Company. I was to take the letter and give it to Grant's assistant. I was called down and I came in. Grant was sitting on the edge of a long table, wearing his gown. He scared the hell out of me.

He said, "Gelber, I've received a letter from your mother. You know that it is compulsory for all boys to go into the Rifle Company at Upper Canada." I said, "Yes, sir." He said, "What do you think about that?" I said, "Well, sir, if I have to go to another school, I'll simply have to go to another school, because I don't believe in war and I don't want to participate."

He said, "If you feel that strongly about it, I think I'm obliged to agree with your mother. You will not have to take military training, but you might have to do other things, like washing windows or something like that."

On my Lord, what I lived through! The officers in the Rifle Company gave me a hard time, although the really important guys didn't object. The master who ran the battalion, Sergeant Major Carpenter, didn't give me a hard time. He was very nice to me because I was athletic. Sergeant Major Carpenter was of a world long gone.

There was a British hangover in Toronto in those days. Everything that was British was worthwhile. You caned the boys to make men out of them. Butch McKenzie was my math teacher at UCC. He eventually became headmaster, which was ridiculous. He said, "There is a rumour around here that I cane boys. I don't cane boys. I flog them." This was my math teacher!

One day Jim Biggar told me to deliver something to Choppy Grant's office. His secretary said, "Gelber, I know the head wants to see that very badly. You better go in." I went in and Choppy had three guys in my class who were being punished. He caned them in front of me. That particular episode bothered me. I'm a big guy and everything else, but I'm hypersensitive. A lot of those kinds of things bothered me. I was just so embarrassed to see my own classmates caned.

I'm sure a lot of George Grant's difficulties came from Upper Canada. UCC was very macho and George was anything but macho. I'm a clinical psychologist, so I can see an awful lot of these things that I could never have seen before. George was a very close friend and I can understand clearly how difficult it was for him.

George had a terrible relationship with a UCC master, Mr. Parlee. I never had Parlee as a master, but I would imagine that Parlee would have been nice to George because he was the boss's son. Parlee appears to have gone just the opposite to prove his independence. He shoved George around. If I were a teacher, I would have found George an interesting fellow. He was bright, well disposed, not nasty. But Parlee gave him such a hard time.

Hart Massey was a wonderful friend, too. His father, Vincent Massey, commanded a tremendous amount of respect and deference because of his wealth. He identified himself with the intellectual community, but he was not really an insightful man. He was the governor general of Canada, but he had nothing really to say about the future of Canada.

At Batterwood, the Massey estate in Port Hope, Vincent would often speak to the locals in the same way as an English lord speaks to the peasants. There were always more maids and butlers in the goddamn place than there were guests. But the Masseys were very nice to me. I had a great love for them. I used to go with Hart to Batterwood, where there were always a lot of artists, musicians, and politicians. Hart always sat with me in school at prayers. I was so tall and he was so short. I would always sing the hymns louder than he would. He still visits me in New York.

Terry MacDermot, who succeeded Choppy as principal after Choppy's death in 1935, was a colourless guy who had no personality at all. He was a dullard. His pretensions as part of his Montreal intellectual liberal group didn't mean a goddamn thing. I knew him before he was principal at Upper Canada because he used to visit the Masseys' place.

But the Upper Canada Board of Governors before the war had a sense of aristocracy that didn't exist. They had delusions of grandeur. They brought in crazy guys like Terry MacDermot and Butch McKenzie to be principal when Toronto was replete with good, competent, talented people. They could have hired some guy from Humber Collegiate or UTS [University of Toronto Schools] who was a charming, delightful man as the head of the school. But they had to choose these screwy guys.

Even though I liked my UCC friends, I left because I thought it was too militaristic. I said to my mother that I would like to go to a regular high school. She said, "Do what you like. You're a big boy now." So after Grade 12, I went to North Toronto Collegiate, where I didn't know anybody. It wasn't the least bit like Upper Canada, but it had a nice quality about it. There were nice, friendly people there.

My father wanted all four of his sons to go into the family business. He was disgusted with me because I didn't. He nagged me because he wanted me to. I couldn't be in that business. My brothers Marvin and Arthur have hated my guts since childhood. I was different. I was taller. I was head of my group at camp. I was a prefect at North Toronto. I was in the theatre. It's not my nature to be interested in any snobbery – I was just doing things.

I simply had to move away. I love Toronto. I would have stayed if I didn't have family. My brothers Arthur and Marvin went into the family business. Lionel and I didn't. Lionel did some writing and he was in the air force. During the founding of the state of Israel, he was very active at the U.N. for some years. He wrote about five books on international affairs.

I wanted to go to Columbia University in New York. But then when the war broke out, I wanted to go to war. The Canadian military told me, "We'll call you when you are needed." So I took my B.A. at Columbia. Then I joined the air force as an aircraftsman second class. I begged to go overseas because I wanted to participate. Eventually I got commissioned and went overseas.

I was a pacifist, but George Grant was much more courageous than I was. I joined the Royal Canadian Air Force, but he went over and looked

after the people in the east end of London who were being bombed merci-
lessly. He endured the Blitz and brought those who were hurt into hospi-
tals. He was a remarkable fellow. When he got pneumonia, they sent him
home. I was still in Canada in the Canadian Air Force at the time. I would
go over to visit him quite regularly. He would tell me stories about the
things that happened. Then he got TB, but he transcended the adversity
and went back to England. Goddamn it! That's a courageous fellow for
you! Frankly, I was scared pea green when I went overseas.

Sergeant Major Carpenter's son, who was a big shot in the military, met
me in Trafalgar Square. He said a very moving thing to me, which I have
never forgotten. He said, "Gelber, I'm not surprised to see you. My father
always used to tell us, 'Leave Gelber alone. When the war comes, he'll be in
it.'" He understood.

During the war, I had no idea about the Holocaust. When the news of
the death camps came out in 1945, our commander in London said, "We
ought to send Line Officer Gelber down to Germany." So I went down
with a guy called Smith from Ottawa, who was a marvellous fellow. When
we got to Bergen-Belsen, we were taking in refugees from all parts of
Europe who were homeless, who had no money, who had nothing to eat.
We brought in thousands of refugees who had been in other concentration
camps. We also buried the dead in Bergen-Belsen, which was horrific. We
were there, so who else was going to do it?

I worked at Bergen-Belsen for nearly a year. I came back a wreck. I was
just played out. I ruined my stomach. The doctor sent me home. I was as
thin as a rail. I stood aghast at what we accomplished within no time,
though I don't take any of the credit for it. I just participated in the whole
thing. They brought in musicians, including the famous Jewish violinist
Yehudi Menuhin. We set up the *falsch Schule*, where people could learn to
build things. We got equipment from the Nazis.

UCC asked me to speak to the boys when I came back from overseas. I
talked about my experiences at the concentration camp. The kids were all
very disturbed by it. I told stories about people that we had saved and what
had happened. I was glad that I was invited because I wanted them to
know. It made a profound impression.

When I came back from the war, I took my M.A. and Ph.D. in New
York. I took a second Ph.D. at Union Graduate School. While I was going
to that school as a clinical psychologist, I became even more interested in
religion. I had always been interested in religion as a boy. So I went to theological school. I was ordained and then I was made head of the school,
which I ran for a while.

I've just finished three books on religion. As a guy who treats patients with emotional and psychological problems, I've got to try to deal with the superego. In dealing with the superego effectively, I have organized a group called the Family Synagogue. We have been meeting in each other's homes for many years.

I drive some rabbis out of their minds because I'm so liberal in my position. But my liberal position is more effective in my opinion in advancing the cause of Judaism than the traditional prayer book or even the Reform prayer book. The Reform Jewish prayer book is a piece of junk, which is why I've written my own prayer book. I'm hoping that what I'm doing will be even more relevant to our needs.

It seems to me that one has to have a context in order to be able to perceive an intelligent approach to day-to-day living. If you feel that the only thing in your life is money, it forms a context. The guy who writes a book has got a context. The guy who is a musician has a context. Much of my theological training came from UCC. I could never have written my own prayer book without having an Upper Canada background and context. I can still sing the songs I sang with Jack Davidson and the religious discussion group. I've still got in my apartment the prayer book we used. They were wonderful songs. To this day I often sing them in the shower.

KENNETH McNAUGHT

1929–36

Historian

I N MY THIRD YEAR in the upper school, George Grant, Michael Shalom Gelber, and I all read some books like Beverley Nichols's *Cry Havoc*, and biographies of ammunitions makers. We became pacifists. George, Shalom, and I went to Choppy Grant and said we didn't any longer wish to go out to the cadet battalion. In the 1930s, the battalion was the heart and soul of the college, apart from cricket. We were really challenging the Holy Grail.

Choppy didn't like it very much, but what I found most impressive was there wasn't any big struggle. The school allowed us conscientious objector status and we did alternative service. Sometimes that would take the form of helping build new tennis courts, but more often in my case it took the form of learning how to do drypoint etching with Mr. Kettle up in the art room.

So I benefitted in two ways. I learned what real liberalism means and I also became an artist of sorts. I learned that tolerance could coexist with the complacent idea that we were destined to become rulers of an ordered society, that our route was predesigned to Bay Street. I learned that the toleration of dissent was a fundamental aspect of the establishment position. This is one of the things that makes me happy that I went to Upper Canada, and rather proud of the school. Conformity is a big problem, but I firmly believe that there was genuine tolerance at UCC, based upon a very conservative view of life. I don't think at any of the public schools that we would have been allowed to be a conscientious objector against the rough-and-scruffy little cadet corps.

On one wonderful occasion, when we were trying to make our point about pacifism, we encountered Sergeant Major Carpenter, an ex-Indian army sergeant major who was the supervisor of the cadet battalion. He cornered us in the locker room. It was a very strange sight because he was on his way out from the shower and getting dressed. He wore a laced-up corset because he was so corpulent. It made his position somewhat ludicrous from our point of view.

He gave us the tired old line: "What would you guys do if you saw a Hun coming to rape your mother?" It was just classic. But he was standing for one side of the tradition and continuity of the college. But an even more important side was also there being safeguarded all the time. It was a terribly important experience. A lot of my friends, of course, gave me a rough time, but by that time I was gaining quite a bit of confidence as a dissenter.

The same year, I took my first course in Canadian history from Count Nicholas Ignatieff. He organized the League of Nations Club which met in the principal's room. Terry MacDermot had by this time succeeded Choppy Grant as principal. Ignatieff gave me the essay prize in the class for an essay on the CCF. The prize was MacDermot's book *Recovery by Control*, which I thought was delightful because it was a much more politically moderate line of interpretation than the CCF was taking. Another of my masters, Johnny Davidson, was a CCFer. So was Geoff Andrews.

I came to love UCC. We had such tremendous opportunities that none of the high schools of the day could provide. There was a wonderful art room. Godfrey Rideout was in my class when we first took music from Ettore Mazzoleni. Godfrey Rideout became a very prominent musician who composed a great deal of fine music and directed conservatory orchestras. At UCC, he was one of the principal organizers of the Gilbert and Sullivan operettas.

On Tuesday mornings we'd go down and watch the Toronto Symphony practise for that week's concert. We would, as a privileged little group, go trailing in and sit in Massey Hall and listen to the whole damn concert. Then we would go back to the college, and Mazzoleni would go to the board and describe the makeup of the orchestra: "The first violins are here, the double bass are over here, there are always eight double bass." He would give us a breakdown of the whole structure of a symphony. This was totally outside of the ordinary curriculum. You had offbeat experiences like that. Masters like Jacques de Marbois, Herbie Little, and Hugh Bremner were terrific characters. It was very unlikely you'd find the same kind of person in a high school at that time. It was a very enriching experience.

The genesis of my CCF ideas happened while I was at the school. My parents were strong supporters of the CCF and the League for Social Reconstruction. My father was an advertising account executive who also spent a lot of time moonlighting in journalism. He wrote for the *Canadian Forum* a lot. Whenever he wrote anything particularly radical, he'd use a pseudonym like Forrest Glen or R. B. Tollbridge. When I got my driving licence, I was several times delegated to go down to the station and pick up J. S. Woodsworth, the founder of the CCF. He stayed at our house while he was doing speaking engagements.

So it was right inside me, but I found no difficulty with that, as one might have expected one would at an establishment, conservative school. We ran mock elections in 1935 or 1936. I formed a little CCF club, two years after the party was born. I brought in the local CCF candidate and presented him to the school in the prayer hall. I was a little bit nervous because I was very young, passionate, and idealistic. I looked down my nose at the guys who just trotted along in daddy's footsteps, though I, of course, was doing exactly the same thing – they just had different daddies.

The unhappy fact is that you can get a better education and better advantages at such schools. About three-quarters of every Labour cabinet in Britain has been educated at English public schools. A socialist is not necessarily a conformist, nor indeed is a conservative necessarily. I've always been CCF/NDP, but inside I know I'm a small *c* conservative.

I guess we were pretty snobbish. It's amazing to look back on it. Of course, it never occurred to me that going to a Granite Club dance or a formal Forest Hill house party was the kind of society so far out of the ordinary person's ken as to be a different world. I managed to swallow my CCF principles and enjoy those parties pretty much. The Battalion Ball was a very big whoop-de-doo. I can remember feeling rather embarrassed because the thing to wear was kid gloves and I wore white gloves.

Sir George Parkin, after whom the prep building was named, would have been very happy with the argument that old boys should hire other old boys to work in their businesses. The same argument was used to run the British Empire. That's how a class interest is developed, held together, and remains dominant. But the old-boy network doesn't have to be spelled out in conspiratorial groups. It's simply self-recognition and self-perpetuation which is spontaneous. The old boys' network is thriving.

I'm not in it myself. I've never enjoyed the UCC Old Boys' Association, principally because I went to two meetings and spent most of the time fending off people who wanted to sell me insurance policies. But the other, far more pragmatic, reason was that if I hadn't been able to afford my sons to go there, should I be endowing other people to go? Which perhaps is small-minded of me.

I am not convinced that it is necessary to open all institutions on the grounds that they might be considered discriminatory. There are so many obvious necessary exceptions to that, starting with particular religious institutions like synagogues. If you're running a Thai restaurant, you don't hire Frenchmen to cook. It eventually becomes very anti-liberal. It ends up being politically correct. It gets to the point where you can't read anything written by a dead European white male. It's ridiculous.

Upper Canada College is not going to remain an exclusively male WASP bastion forever. That's probably a good thing, just as it's a good thing that Toronto has changed. It was a pretty narrow-minded, parochial, bigoted, racist city in the 1930s. But there are probably fewer basic issues gnawing at UCC than are gnawing at the country. At the moment, I'd say Upper Canada College has a better chance of surviving as it is than the country does.

JOHN WEIR

1932–38

Stockbroker

W HEN I SENT my son John to Upper Canada, I remember going in to see Al Harris. He was my mentor at UCC. He had caned me when I was in the prep. In the 1960s, you weren't allowed to touch anybody, which I thought was damn stupid. I told Harris, "If my son needs a caning, he gets a caning and I don't want to hear anything more about it." Harris said, "What does your wife think?" I said, "She agrees with corporal punishment and discipline." Harris told me, "We aren't allowed to touch the boys." Then, when the cadet corps collapsed in the 1970s, that was the end of discipline at UCC as far as I was concerned.

I enjoyed the cadet battalion at UCC. We used to shoot on the rifle range. I thought the discipline was good. If we didn't measure up, we had pack drill. You'd carry a pack and walk around the quadrangle. It was run by Sergeant Major Carpenter, who was great. He was a disciplinarian and that's what kids need. They really do. This mollycoddling is dumb.

In 1938 I went with the Queen's Own Rifles as a lieutenant to Niagara-on-the-Lake for a course. UCC is affiliated with the Queen's Own. I felt the discipline helped me later in my life. Kids don't even like the word "no," for Christ's sake. They are certainly going to get it when they enter business. They get it soon enough in the cadet corps. I think it should be reinstituted at UCC, but there are so many pacifists around that they won't go for it.

It was a competitive environment at Upper Canada. All the paper marking was competitive as hell. You either got your 50 per cent or 56 per cent. The marks were made public, so you knew what you got in relation to everybody else. That's good too. All this A, B, C stuff is crap.

I did okay in boxing until I got into the intermediate class and then I got the shit knocked out of me. I got in the finals once, maybe twice, but most times I got clobbered. It was good fun. I was an oversized louse who didn't get hurt. During the war I took a commando course. The boxing was a tone up for me because it gave you good reflexes.

When the war started in 1939, I went into the air force because I just damn well didn't want to go into the trenches. That's where my father was in the first war. He got gassed and ended up with asthma. My uncle was killed in the trenches and the other uncle was in the trenches too. I said, "Balls to that! If I'm in the air force, I will come home to clean sheets every night or I won't come home at all."

I got into combat eventually. We effectively started in January 1941, when we were doing some sweeps and intercepts over France. We used to fly over France and try and create the impression that we had more planes than we did. At first I was flying Hurricanes, then Spitfires. We were outnumbered. It was interesting. There were dogfights with Messerschmitts.

The average survival time in combat was six hours. That's how many people were killed. We didn't know that statistic until after the war. I flew about five hundred hours in combat. Hughie Godefroy, my friend at UCC, joined the same squadron as me and he went right through the whole war. He was great. He shot down about eight German aircraft. He was a wing commander at the end, DSO with bar, DFC with two bars. He was very quiet about it.

I didn't shoot down any planes that I could claim. I was close. I saw some but I couldn't claim them. We had cameras and sometimes you'd be firing and the guy would disappear in the clouds. You might see something come off the plane, but that doesn't mean you shot him down. Lots of our guys came back with parts of their tail missing.

Going up into combat, I don't think it really sunk into us that it might be our last day on earth. It did as we lasted longer and longer. You'd say, "Well, I've got to keep my eye on things." Sometimes you would get over-confident. That's what happened to me. We flew in pairs. My partner got shot down, so I had nobody on my tail. The guy who shot him down over-shot me and I shot him. His number two got me.

My plane blew up. I ejected as it was on fire. I was burned on my face and hands. I had to pull the parachute right away. I jumped at 26,000 feet. Luckily, I have a low metabolic rate, or I did then. Most people couldn't survive above 15,000 feet.

When I landed, I was trying to get to a little French village where I once went to school. I thought I would find my teacher. I was blind because of my burns. I was numb by then. I wasn't in any pain until I got to the hospital later on. Then there was a lot of pain.

I made contact with the French underground. I had the password for the day because I could speak French. I changed from my uniform into civilian clothes. They were going to get me back to England if they could. But I went blind, so they had to leave me in the woods until the Krauts caught me. They took me to a hospital in France, and then I went to Germany as a prisoner. So the war was over for me.

At first, I was in Stalag Luft 1 and then I was in Stalag Luft 3, the famous "Great Escape" POW camp. It was a great experience. Nick Laidlaw, a psychiatrist and a UCC old boy, was in the same prison camp. It was amazing having somebody from the school in the same prison camp.

The movie *The Great Escape* was pretty historically accurate, but the motorcycle scenes with Steve McQueen were a Hollywood touch. Some of the events in the movie did actually happen, but not in the correct order. There were four or five of us who managed to escape a few times. I got away on a marching route one time. In my third escape, when we were being removed from Bremerhaven to Lübeck, I got away until the end of the war. It was great.

Of the four of us who tunnelled, three of us had worked in mines. Every tunnel up until then had been a failure, so we decided that we would build it like a mine. We dug a shaft and lined the tunnels. We built a railway and a pump system for fresh air. We thought the Germans had some type of sound detection boxes, so we had to go down sixty feet.

The greatest problem was getting rid of the sand. The sand was quite yellow down below and it was quite brown up above. As we were dispersing the sand, they could tell in a second if we were tunnelling or not. So we contrived all kinds of methods to get it hidden under other huts. It got so the goons couldn't crawl underneath the huts because the sand level kept rising. They twigged to that. We couldn't get rid of the sand, so we had to stop the operation completely.

The goons were sniffing around getting awfully close, so we thought we would give them one tunnel. We let them find it. They put dynamite along the tunnel. I said to my buddy, "I bet you anything they didn't cover it." When you put dynamite on top of the ground, all it does is blow a little hole and it steams up. He said, "We should move back." I said, "I bet it blows the roof off the hut." It did. We all laughed.

They got around it by dumping manure in the tunnel. You know what an outdoor privy is like? That's what we had. Every so often they had a cart that came. We called it the "Honey Wagon." They would pump it out and use it as manure on non-root vegetables. They pumped it into the tunnel. There was no way we were going to use it. Because they thought that they had found what they wanted, we managed to get the other tunnel going again. That was fun.

By coincidence, there was an Allied air raid the night of the Great Escape. If it hadn't been for that air raid, we probably would have got about two hundred people out. The lights went out, so we had to use candles and start it over again. We were afraid the goons were going to come in and search the place, as they often did, so we stopped. But we did get nearly one hundred guys out. It was a howling success, except that fifty of the guys were shot by the Germans. Some of them were shot in a field. My tunnelling colleague, Bertram, was shot. About four or five Canadians were shot just outside of the prison.

I didn't go on the escape myself because I was in Frankfurt in the hospital getting some plastic surgery done, lucky for me. The Swiss had come in and said that I should get my eyes operated on if I could. I had both eyelids turning inside out.

A doctor had performed the first of several operations on my face after I got out of the French hospital. He used no anesthetic. We studied self-hypnosis. We practised for two weeks before each operation and really worked hard at the concentration. You think of the most wonderful thing that's happened to you and the most wonderful sensation you've ever had – and it can't be sex!

It worked, it really did. I can still do it sometimes. I felt very little pain. If your mental block breaks down when the pain gets pretty excruciating, he would just quit the operation. He would start over again in a couple of weeks. I was there three months and probably had four operations. He was a fabulous guy. Since the war, I've had operations regularly, about every other year.

I took three Canadians with me on my final escape in 1945. We were being moved from Bremerhaven to Lübeck. I don't know how long we were away, but it was until the end of the war. I collected three guys and a "tame goon," as we called them. We promised him amnesty providing he worked with us. We used to travel through villages in a cart. The cart would be sent back and we would take another cart and continue on. He expropriated them. He would just say, "I've got prisoners to move."

If any cars came along, we got off the carts and he trained his rifle on us. We pretended we were his prisoners. It worked well. We always had at least one guy awake, twenty-four hours a day. We gave the goon half the ticket, and one of us kept the other half. When we got to a place near Lübeck called Trenthorst, we gave him the other half. He was okay, but not too bright.

I had learned to live off the land during a summer when I was at UCC. A UCC master, Count Nicholas Ignatieff, and a few of us went out to Peace River in 1933 or 1934 for six weeks. We had learned to live off the land pretty well from an Indian guide in Algonquin Park who taught us an awful lot. Then I took a commando course as well and I had camping experience.

There is no way anybody should starve in the woods as long as it isn't frozen up. There are beetles and worms that you can eat. It's easy to get them. You can fry worms and they taste quite a bit like bacon. It's difficult to face swallowing them unless you are really starving.

During my last escape, we lived off the fat of the land. If we saw anything we liked, we lifted it. One day, I saw some grey snails on a wall as we were walking. I said, "The time will come when we'll be starving. We'll collect these." I had a box. I collected 120 of them.

The Indian guide had told me about eating snails. He said, "You can't eat them for about forty-eight hours because there is a green sac inside them which would kill you if you ate too many. That green sac is their storage system which they can live on for about forty-eight hours. After that you can cook them and eat them."

I was about ready to cook them when we ran across some Belgian guys. I don't know where they came from but they were going in the opposite direction. They said, "What have you to trade?" and I said, "What have you got to trade?" They said, "A side of bacon." I said, "I've got some snails. They've been starved, so you can eat them today." They knew all about that, of course. So we got a side of bacon for the snails.

The only time we almost got caught was by a group of ss. We were fishing on one side of a pond. We heard a rustle in the bush and along came these guys. They had grenades. I said, "Henry, you run right and I'll run left. One of us will get away and tell the story at least." They lobbed the grenades into the pond and killed fish for us. They dove in, we dove in, they grabbed their fish, we grabbed ours, and they took off, with lots of laughing. They knew we were thinking we were going to get it.

We had seen the peace mission two or three days before, going down the autobahn. I said, "We should get ourselves found pretty soon." I knew that they were going to sign the peace to end the war. We knew we were getting close to Lübeck because we could hear the guns. I thought maybe we should go and see if we could find our guys. So when we got near Trenthorst, there were our guys. All the prisoners had been collected. We walked in and got shit for being away for so long. They said, "Where the fuck have you been all this time? We thought you were dead."

After the war, I joined Wood Gundy, where I'm still working. I like the brokerage business, but I don't know how much longer I'll stay. My father worked until he was eighty-two. He was the founding director of the brokerage firm McLeod Young Weir in the 1920s. I like booze quite well and I think if I retired, I'd be very busy around the bottle, so it's just as well I don't.

Stockbroking is not a business for females. The private school boys have got old-boy connections, so it's a case of who you know, not what you know. The feminists can go to hell as far as I'm concerned. In this business, women usually end up by being stressed out and not female and they don't last. We had one woman who lasted a long time but she was a real hornet. She lost her sex. That's what happens.

The feminists have done a lot of harm for themselves. They are trying to get legislation for equality. It's like legislating love or hate. You can't do it. They are equal, all right, but a lot of things they can't do. A lot of things we can't do.

I don't think Upper Canada should become coed. I'd like ucc to do nothing for at least another ten years and see what happens. Then you will see by the graduates how it has worked. I think it's better to have a boys' school and a girls' school. I know the guys would love to get in with the girls, but it's just as ridiculous as having women in the elite corps of the army. It just seems to me an awful waste.

When a woman insists on being called Ms., I just say, "Ms. Carriage."

Who's kidding who? Are you proud of being a female or not? Are you embarrassed if you're not married or not? You can be Miss or Mrs. and what's wrong with that? What are men supposed to be instead of Mister or Master? I'm not hiring any more, thank God. You get the civil rights people coming in telling you who to hire.

I'd rather hire somebody from UCC, TCS [Trinity College School], SAC [St. Andrew's College], or Ridley than any place else because I know basically what they are like and what their response will be. You wouldn't say UCC old boys are predictable, but you have a better idea of their responses because of the male bonding. I don't mean in the fruity way. You know the cooperation you probably will get. You know that they do respond to discipline. I don't know whether they do as much now.

That's why I think the cadet corps was a really good idea. I'd like to see it back. The battalion made it easy to take orders. Once you've taken orders, you can take them again. Once you've given them, you can give them again. There's no question that UCC prepared me for the war.

GEORGE MARA

1930 – 41

Businessman

MY GRANDFATHER was in the retail wine and spirit business. My father was a manufacturer's agent who inherited the business. I started at Upper Canada in 1930 at age nine. For my tenth birthday present, my father built a full-fledged hockey rink in our backyard with a row of boards, lights, and a couple of nets. During bad weather, he would hire a guy to come and flood the rink all night. So we had ice when Upper Canada did not. The school team would come and practise at our rink.

I remember my father pointing out the window at the rink and saying, "Now that is either going to make a man out of you or a horse's ass." That was his way of doing things. He'd been a football player for the Toronto Argonauts. From a very early age, he really wanted me to be a football player. He pushed me hard. Maybe that was part of it. I didn't dislike it, I just went the other way. I didn't want any interference.

When I was invited to try out for the first-prep hockey team at UCC, I could hardly sleep all night. I remember going to Varsity Arena at 6:00 or 7:00 A.M. I made the team, which was beyond belief. Earl Elliott was the coach. For me, it was better than the National Hockey League.

That year, 1933, we won the minor bantam championship. I was hooked on hockey, although I did play a few other sports. The prep team practised every day at the Maple Leaf Gardens and played all our games there too. In those days, it was really sensational. The Gardens was brand new, having been built in 1931 by a UCC old boy, Conn Smythe. We were big shots. We had our own dressing room. From the time the Gardens opened, I think I spent half my time in it. I went to all the Maple Leaf games. It was great fun.

Years later, when I became president of Maple Leaf Gardens, I offered the Gardens to Upper Canada College, but they would not accept because they had their own rink. Some of the boys who represented the school were pretty cranky when they found out.

Conacher, Primeau, and Jackson played for the Maple Leafs in the 1930s. Joe Primeau became a coach for Upper Canada College the year we won the championship in the big team. He was a wonderful fellow. We became very good friends. He subsequently became coach of the Leafs.

I made the first team in the upper school when I was fourteen. So I played for the first team for four years. When I left the school, I played for the Toronto Marlboroughs. I played junior for five years. I remember playing for the first team one day at Varsity Arena against UTS. My wingmate, Simpson, had just recovered from a semi-concussion. He had been out for quite a few days. There was a fellow by the name of Pogue playing for UTS, who wasn't a bad guy. I wanted to score goals, so I didn't spend much time putting people through the end of the rink.

In those days, I was a pretty fair size for a hockey player, particularly in that league. I weighed about 175 pounds. Simpson had been banged into the boards by Pogue. I didn't take great exception to it. As it happened, I was coming around the back of the net. I just kept on going and put Pogue into the boards.

There was a crazy old guy by the name of Mike Rodden, who was famous for years as an athlete and a *Globe and Mail* correspondent. He was then in his eighties, so he really wasn't totally with it. He'd ring the bell and chew tobacco all the time. When I was sixteen, he was about eighty-three.

He rang the bell and gave me a forty-minute misconduct. I said to him, "Mike, there is no such thing as a forty-minute misconduct." He said, "There is now." So I sat in the penalty box. A UCC master, Mike Bremner, who was a wild-eyed guy, came waltzing down, shook his fist at me, and said, "You will never play another game of anything for Upper Canada College. This is disgraceful." But his edict didn't stand.

At Upper Canada, I was on what was called a negotiation list for the Detroit Red Wings of the NHL. The Maple Leafs had made a deal with Detroit, so I went up to the Leaf training camp in Owen Sound in the fall of 1946.

Connie Smythe was like the sergeant major at UCC. He used to referee the UCC old boys' games. He saw me around the Gardens for years. He knew who I was, but just didn't figure this kid was going to amount to much. I used to have a convertible car and all the stuff that he abhorred. He thought I was an undisciplined rich kid.

At Maple Leaf Gardens, he came up to me. I said, "Hello, sir. How are you?" He had been injured and was limping. He was very gruff. He said, "I hear you are going up to the training camp." I said, "Yes, sir." He said, "What did you do during the war?" I said, "I was in the navy." He said, "I guess you were an officer, were you?" I said, "Yes, sir." He said, "Well, you never did anything. You were born with a silver spoon in your mouth. You won't get on a Maple Leaf team unless you make it on your own goddamn ability. You never did anything that I know of on your own."

He asked, "Are you going up to the training camp on the bus with the rest of the players?" I said, "No, I'm not. See that convertible car? That's mine and my golf clubs are in the trunk. The car parked in front of it is owned by Billy Taylor, who as you know has been arrested for gambling and black market activities. The car behind it is owned by Sweeny Shriner, who is also under indictment for black marketeering. Neither of them participated in the war." It was not a very satisfactory exchange with my new boss to be, confirming his worst suspicions.

At training camp, all the good players were back from the war. There were about sixty players at the camp. In those days, they kept statistics of goals scored at camp. Until Conn Smythe arrived, I had a sensational camp on the scoring side. In fact, when I left, I was the leading scorer.

We practised twice a day. One afternoon, I was playing centre against Billy Taylor, who was kind of a dope, but a brilliant hockey player. When Smythe arrived, Taylor suddenly got much more aggressive and chippy. The speed of the whole damn practice seemed to pick up. I couldn't understand what the hell was going on. What I hadn't seen, but they had, was a light grey fedora going around the top of the rink. That meant the boss had arrived at the camp.

I remember Taylor took a big swing at me with his stick. There was a place between your pad and the shinguard before the boots improved. If you were really a shit, you could whack somebody in there and get him good. I thought, What the hell is with him? This attack was unprovoked. He didn't seem to be that kind of a player really. I later realized he was just gung ho because Smythe had arrived. Smythe of course coined the famous phrase "If you can't beat 'em in the alley, you can't beat 'em in the rink."

Smythe stayed for three or four days, then I got called into Happy Day's office, the coach. He said, "Do you want to go to Pittsburgh?" Pittsburgh was the Leafs' farm team. I said, "No, you know I'm not going to Pittsburgh. I'm not going to go to Detroit, so I'm not going to Pittsburgh. We discussed all this, Hap. Is this your idea?" He said, "You're not hungry enough to play for the Leafs." I said, "Is this your idea?" He said, "No." I said, "Is it Mr. Smythe's idea?" He said, "Yes." I said, "Well, see you around."

So I went and packed up my bags and put them in the car. When I walked into my mother's house, sitting in the living room was the famous Lester Patrick, who was a contemporary of Smythe's. He had been a great hockey player. Connie Smythe put the New York Ranger team together and then they fired him. Lester Patrick took it over.

I had never met Lester Patrick, but I knew him on sight. I said, "What brings you here?" He said, "When they took you off the negotiation list, they had to go through headquarters of the National Hockey League." The day Smythe arrived at the camp, he took my name off the list. Before I got the boot, they had three days' notice. He took my name off, so they could put somebody else's on. He didn't even bother trying to make a deal.

Patrick said, "Come and play for New York. You'll get even with that little bugger." Of course, it is so appealing when you are still young. I said, "Well, I'll come to New York and see." I did and it was really depressing. I was living in a crappy hotel next to Madison Square Garden. Nobody in New York knew anything about the hockey team.

By now, I was twenty-four. I had been in the navy. The wartime accelerates your thinking a bit. It wasn't nearly as exciting. There was so much off time, particularly in a city like New York. I spent my time in pool halls or the movies. It just didn't have the right feel. So I came back. I played Senior OHA hockey for a little while. Then the Olympics came along. I won a gold medal at the 1948 Olympics in St. Moritz as a member of the RCAF Flyer hockey team.

I played centre very briefly for the Montreal Canadiens in the playoffs one year. My winger was Cliff Malone. I had four or five points that night until a huge son of a bitch damn near put me through the glass and separated my shoulder. It was very painful. You can't get over that kind of injury very quickly. My hockey career was over.

Many years afterwards, in the late 1950s or early sixties, Connie really got going with me. One day he called. He never said, "Hello, George," just went off in a tirade. I didn't know what the hell he was talking about. Although it seemed like he was telling me that I had been appointed to the Board of Directors of Maple Leaf Gardens, nobody had mentioned this to me. When he finished, he didn't wait for an answer. He hung up.

My office was at the Harbour Commission building downtown. I drove up Bay Street. I still hadn't figured it out. I was going to call somebody to see what Smythe was talking about. On the front window of the *Telegram* building, there was a big section of pictures and headlines of the group called the "Silver Seven," who were taking over the running of the Maple Leaf hockey team. My picture was among them, even though I had not accepted. It was a foregone conclusion.

John Bassett was one of the Silver Seven and so was Stafford Smythe. I was the only hockey player among them. I was tempted to cut my nose off to spite my face, but it was too intriguing not to see what this was all about. So I became a director of Maple Leaf Gardens.

I still thought that Connie and I were not going to get along. Having regard for his peculiarities, we couldn't have gotten along better. He was terrific most of the time, but unpredictable as hell. Anytime that anything went wrong, he'd try and bait me in meetings, but I wouldn't get cranky with him.

When I became president of Maple Leaf Gardens in the mid-sixties, the first call I got was from guess who? No congratulations, no anything. Conn said, "I've been talking to the treasurer. Get me a Buick." I said, "Could you start back a sentence or two?" He said, "You know what I'm talking about. I've always had a Cadillac. My deal at the Gardens, as former owner, is that I get a car of my choice. What are you going to do about it?" I said, "Mr. Smythe, I suggest you do whatever you want. If you want a Rolls-Royce, go get one and send us the bill." He said, "Well, that's better." Bang! He was unbelievable.

Once, the subject of my unfulfilled NHL hockey career came up. Smythe said, "I did you a favour." I said, "Yeah, but you really didn't think you were doing me a favour at the time. What was your real reason?" He said, "Well, you weren't going to do anything you were told. You were going to be a bad influence on the team. You were a good hockey player, but it wasn't worth having you around."

I was disappointed that I never really tested myself in the NHL, but I played against top-flight players in the armed services league. The best players were playing in that league because the NHL deteriorated during the war. When I went to Ste. Hyacinthe for a signals course, I played for the Montreal Royals, a farm team of the Canadiens. I played against all the best players of the era, like Maurice "Rocket" Richard, Elmer Lach, and Billy Reay. So from a self-satisfaction standpoint of measuring myself, I was able to compete. But if I had had my druthers, I would have liked to play for the Maple Leafs for two or three years, just to have done it.

JOHN GARTSHORE

1935–43

Musician

I LEARNED to be a sexual masochist at Upper Canada. I'm not kidding. On more than one occasion, when Geoff Andrew caught me masturbating, his way of dealing with it was to cane me. The poor man probably did not know how else to deal with it, but caning is a rotten method of teaching anything. What it taught me, of course, was the erotic connections of caning. They are still with me.

I also got caned by Skull Bassett, an upper school history teacher. He looked like a human skull, so we nicknamed him accordingly. He caught me chalking on the wall along the door of his classroom the word *Golgotha*, which is from the crucifixion story in the Bible. Golgotha is the place of the skull. Wooo! He caned me for that, probably quite rightly. It was terribly disrespectful. I was caned a lot. I worked it out. In three years in the upper school, I was caned 1.14 times a week. I got not to care, because why should you? I can remember a number of masters saying, "I do not know what I am going to do with you. Bend over." When they had finished, I would dutifully say, "Thank you, sir." I became inured to it.

Early in the prep, there was an awful lot of "mini-caning" right in the classroom. It was very common to be pulled up to the front for a couple of swats. Putting up with that and going and sitting down again was just one of the honours. I was quite a crybaby as a kid. You learned pretty quickly not to be. It was a very tough environment.

Corporal punishment is a rotten teaching method. It does not work. That's the test. I think it made me into a bit of a rebel. I have a great deal of "fuck you" in my makeup. I came by that early because by the time I came to the upper school, the housemaster, Geoff Andrew, recognized it in me. He tried to harness it but it didn't work. It was what the army used to call "dumb insolence." I adopted the attitude, Don't talk back, but do not cooperate. Do as little as possible.

You learn those behaviours from somebody. In my case, it started in the prep. When you are required to go out for hockey or cricket, you go because you are going to be beaten if you do not. But I did not join in very much, mainly because I was never any good at it. I was one of those kids who was always chosen last for things, which leaves a mark.

I also learned to hate hockey at UCC. The idea of making hockey into a religion at places like Maple Leaf Gardens is awful. When you take children to see professional hockey, they learn that the rules of the game are that you break the rules. Look at the number of penalties and the amount of fighting. Professional hockey players who fight should be banned for life. I don't care how good they are. Bill Hewitt, the son of "Hockey Night in Canada," was at UCC in my time. He was a spoiled little brat who was universally disliked.

I remember one night I had parked my car at the back of Maple Leaf Gardens. Six very macho men who had been at a Maple Leaf hockey game were getting into their car. They saw me getting out of my car. All six of them started yelling at me, "Hi, faggot! Hi, faggot!" It is my mischievous nature that I said, "Hi," and started walking towards them. They all frantically got into the car and locked the doors. It was one against six. You never saw six guys get into a car so fast. They were very brave across the parking lot.

Upper Canada for a gay person in those days was just awful. There's nobody to blame for it. It was just the times. Coming out would have been suicidal. I'm not even sure you would physically survive. The word *homosexual* did not really exist. Nor did words like *queer* or *fag*. You might hear somebody saying, "Is he all right?" Maybe you were the one person who did not have a date this weekend. You were either "all right" or you were not. If you are faced with that choice, what are you going to be? It is the choice between desirable and undesirable, which is no choice at all.

I had a very close friend in the prep and we drifted apart in the upper school because I was a boarder and he was not. I have not seen him for forty years. We were very close friends, probably because we had a lot in common. We were scared of the same things and had the same dislike for games. In a very good sense of the term, you might even consider our relationship to have been a love affair. It was absolutely non-sexual, but I can remember being called in by the principal, Terry MacDermot, and being told that I should give up this friendship because he did not think it was healthy. Now I realize what that was double-talk for.

One of the troubles was that none of us had any language to talk about things. I can remember talking to my priest, years after UCC, trying to get some of this stuff out. I am sure the poor man had no notion what I was talking about. When I now work as a counsellor for the Community Homophile Association of Toronto, I encourage people to use dirty words, if they feel like it. If people want to say, "I love being fucked in the ass," let them use those words. If you ever said anything like that at Upper Canada, of course, you would be beaten right away.

This was a problem in my family as well. No complaint or problem was ever heard without first evaluating the grammar that it was spoken in. If I had a family complaint, I can remember that my voice would rise, as it does when you are emotional and your throat tightens. The first reaction was, "Do not whine, dear." To hell with what's wrong! I have heard people say, "Oh, my goodness, the vulgar language." Never mind the language. Mind the pain! How can you hear the pain of what they are saying if you cannot get past the language? We simply did not have words.

I do not know how many of the UCC masters were gay in my time. I knew of at least one, but there was not a breath of any improper behaviour towards me. This master was known as "Homo." He was a Scotsman with a strange sense of humour. He'd say, "Your head is like heaven, for there is no parting there." You see, I learned something from him.

I remember there were also a lot of sexual rumours about Willy Orr, the classics master. He was at UCC for nearly fifty years. He spent a lot of time putting together all the handwritten timetables on a humongous sheet of paper. He scratched his balls every place he went. I do not think that he ever came on to me, although he caned me enough times. He'd say, "Well, dear, I hope you liked it." It's too late to be mad at him.

There was a little sexual hanky-panky. There was a cleaner who would always goose you as you walked by. I just took that as natural behaviour and goosed him back. But we were all goosing each other all the time. There were a fair number of circle jerks, and that sort of thing. Actually, circle-jerking was considered the way to get to somebody, whether you liked them or not. You got a lot of guys to hold him down and then jacked him off. Amongst us, this was acceptable behaviour, though certainly not amongst the staff. You got caned for it. But for peers, it was part of the fun. You would play the victim one day and somebody else would be the victim the next day. Nowadays it is a variety of sex I love.

In the course of the school year, there were a number of dances at the college. They would tart up the gym. One was required to produce a date, female of course, or one would be provided. There was an awful lot of very macho talk about what was going to happen. It was not just a matter of dancing with the girl and taking her through the supper line. There was a great inventory of all the dark corners in the school where one could take her, but what was going to happen was not really made very specific. I don't think they really knew what was supposed to happen. Of course, afterwards there was much boasting.

I can remember somebody producing a condom. Whoa, this was serious. We did not use the word "condom" then. There were other words for it. I was terrified because I thought, Here is something that I have no knowledge of. I did not even know whether I had a desire for it. Whatever it was, I could not imagine why it would be interesting to anybody.

Officially, of course, all of that sort of talk would be considered dirty. If anybody overheard it, you would be punished. But among peers, it was normal. You were either normal or you were not. I did not know I was gay. It was terrifying to even try and face the fact that I might not be normal. So I would do a certain amount of boasting. I got fairly good at listening to all this macho talk, putting together some of the phrases. Then I'd say, "The rest of it is none of your business." I played a role. It was all bullshit.

At the actual dance, you would report to where the bus arrived and be introduced to some poor creature. You would take the girl to the gym. I hated dancing. It was not until years later when I started dancing with men that I found out that it was fun. Now, if I had the stamina, it would probably be fun with women, too, because I have finally stopped being afraid of women.

Sooner or later, I would park the girl amongst the female wallflowers and cross the room and join the male wallflowers until a master would roust us out and say, "Go and dance with her." At the earliest possible opportunity, of course, I'd deliver her back to the bus and get rid of her. I was in mortal terror the whole time, wondering, What is she hoping that I will do in the dark corners?

After Grade 12, I went to UTS. By this point, I had become very aware of male beauty. I could not put any of the right words to it. But I can still look at the *College Times* and breathe fire at the real pleasure of looking at some of those beautiful boys. At UTS, I fell into some very deep clothes fetishes. In Grade 13, the UTS school sweater became a very important garment to me. When I eventually managed to get mine, it was an important day. When I put it on, my mother was disappointed because it was crew neck, not a V-neck or turtleneck. Mother's comment was, "That's really not suitable to wear to school, dear. It is all right for the playing field."

That was a childhood trauma, as well. All my clothes were bought by my mother. To wear that sweater to school, which was very important, was a peer thing. I had to smuggle it to school because I was inspected before I left the house every morning. It was called "Give your mother a kiss," but it was really an inspection. I remember she caught me taking the sweater out of the house one time. I said, "I need it for games, Mother," which was an outright lie. I would proudly wear that damned thing. It is full of moth holes, but I still have it.

It would have killed my father if I had told him that I was gay. I never did come out to my father, who died in 1970. I now remember him as a very caring and sensitive person. I am still trying to get out of the bloody closet. There is no such thing as ever being completely out of the closet. As long as there is one person in this world who does not know that you are gay, you are still in the closet.

I told my mother when she was about eighty. Her initial reaction was very honest. She said, "Thank God my friends do not know." It's what we now call "parental closet." Parents of gays go through the same closet experiences we do. I gave up being ashamed of being gay long ago. I am apt to get quite violent with people who insist that I should be ashamed about it.

There is a lovely line in a Robertson Davies novel of a conversation between a number of drunken men in the middle of the night. One of them gets himself into a frightful temper. A man says to him, "I perceive that you are angry about this. You may strike me one moderate blow if it would help." I think it's a wonderful line, and I have used it as a counsellor in sessions. Nobody has taken me up on it yet. They laugh at me, which is fine. They say, "You think I can get over this by just hitting you?" I say, "Well, you might. Try it."

My parents thought I was going to grow up to be a captain of industry in the ucc mould. It always upset my mother that I never had more than two or three people under me in any job. The measure of success was to have hundreds of people "under you." I would say, "No, no, no. I am into the sort of business in which the measure of success is how few people you can make do with." She could not understand that, because ambition, size of office, carpet, and furnture were everything. She had all the traditional values.

The traditional Upper Canada values are ones that I gave up very early. After uts, I started buying some other ties. Years later, when I thought it would be fun to wear my Upper Canada ties again, I discovered my mother had given them all away. They were so grungy that they really were not very wonderful keepsakes. My contact with the old-boy network has been limited to people canvassing me for life insurance. I was so put off by the experience, I thought, I am not going to use the old boys' network for anything.

When people say, "Look at all the winners ucc produces," I say, "Look at all the losers it produces." I was made into a nobody by that place. Part of that was my own perception. I was invisible. It always amazed me to find out that somebody actually noticed me. I just did not think that anybody knew me. Today, if I run into somebody and they say, "Oh, Gartshore. I used to know a Gartshore at Upper Canada," I say, "Indeed. Indeed."

GALT MacDERMOT

1937 – 42

Musician, composer

I WAS SIX YEARS OLD in 1935 when my father, Terry MacDermot, moved from Montreal to Toronto to become principal at Upper Canada. When I was eight, it was time for me to go the prep school. I don't think it was ever considered that I'd go anywhere else.

Our family lived in Grant House, the large principal's residence on the school grounds. I remember it was always cold. My two sisters didn't like it much. They felt a little embarrassed and outnumbered by all the UCC boys. But Grant House was a great place to live for a kid my age. It was close to the rinks, so I could skate. There were apple and pear trees. The football games took place right outside our window. I used to train on the track in front of the house. I used to love listening to the cadet battalion band. I used to march around behind it as a little kid.

There was a tremendous emphasis on sports in the prep. I liked all the sports – hockey, football, soccer, and cricket. I don't remember learning much in class. I remember Mr. Harris scaring the shit out of me and everybody else. I guess he taught us something, but I don't know what. I can't even remember what the subject was.

I think Dad tried to make UCC more academic when he was principal. He really believed in education. I didn't and I still don't. I can't remember anything I learned in school now. When I have to do my bills in restaurants, I can hardly add.

I know that my father had some major fights with the Upper Canada Board of Governors. He was a good friend of Bobby Laidlaw who was on the board, but he didn't approve of a lot of the other guys. He let them know that he thought UCC should be the best school in Canada academically. They didn't think so. They just wanted UCC to be a good old-boy type of school. But I think Dad got most of what he wanted done in the seven years he was principal.

Dad was considered a radical and an intellectual. He could talk about anything. He was a big collector of D. H. Lawrence books. He was interested in the sexual theories of Kinsey, Havelock Ellis, and Sigmund Freud. Once I rememeber Dad asking me, "Is there any homosexuality in the school?" At the time, I didn't even know what homosexuality was. He explained it to me, and I said no. In the prep, there was nothing because there were so few boarders. Whatever boarders there were, they were despised. We just felt sorry for them because they had to live in the school. They couldn't go home to get a decent meal.

A lot of conservative Toronto people didn't think my father should have been the principal of Upper Canada College. Apparently some joker wrote a nasty pamphlet about him when he first arrived. I remember my mother was very upset. There was opposition to him because he was a left-wing radical. I think he voted CCF a couple of times. He was a Bernard Shaw fan and believed in socialism. He didn't think the government should be changed through violence. In fact, he wrote a book called *Recovery by Control* in the Depression. Like Franklin Roosevelt in the U.S., he advocated fixing the economy through government action. I think that he became much more neutral as he grew older. When economic prosperity returned after the Depression, there was no need for that approach.

Dad believed much more in the English tradition than I do. I happen to actually dislike the English, but Dad for some reason didn't. He had certain reservations – he said, "You've got to watch them or they will walk all over you" – but he admired certain British traditions, including their educational system. I don't know if he liked the elite English public schools like Eton or Harrow, but I think he wanted to turn UCC into that kind of school. When he first took the job as principal, he took a trip over to England looking for teachers at the elite schools.

Personally, I have a big problem with English people when I work with them. I think it's partly from having Englishmen as teachers at UCC. Alan Stephen was all right, although I never really dealt with him. But there was always some Englishman at UCC who was a pain in the butt. They give out orders in a way that's very offensive. I don't know whether that's just my Irish blood coming up.

My father was also a great piano player. He used to play every day and I would play the violin with him in Grant House. I had started playing the violin at the prep. There was quite a lot of good music in the prep. We did the Gilbert and Sullivan operas. We used to sing every day. Dad would buy all the popular songs and sing them. I remember him buying a song called "I'll Never Smile Again." He used to play Beethoven, Mozart, and Haydn symphonies with my older sister, who was quite good. My mother, who had been a dancer, also used to sing. Music was not something that any of us considered as a profession at that time. We just did it for fun.

In 1941, my father and I took a bicycle ride down to Montreal while he tried to decide whether to go into the army. He had been asked to teach officers at RMC [Royal Military College]. He wanted to take a week where nobody could reach him by phone so he could think about it. So we rode our bicycles from Toronto down to Montreal. I was twelve years old. There was very little traffic in those days, so we had the road to ourselves, just the two of us. I got to know Dad for the first time. A father, when you are young, is a distant person who you are slightly frightened of.

World War I had had a terrible effect on my father. He was in communications, putting up wires. He saw all the carnage in the trenches. It was appalling. He really thought after the First World War that there shouldn't be any more wars. He loved the League of Nations and he believed in it. After the bicycle trip, he decided to go into the army.

As a young man, I didn't experience the typical UCC pressures to be respectable and make money. I remember a UCC friend, David Greey, saying, "I'm going to be a chartered accountant. I'm going to be a millionaire." Even then, I thought, What a dull life. I ran into him many years later and he was obviously very successful. But anything other than making money was a suspect pursuit. That's just foolish. Upper Canada was full of assholes, but I liked them.

I left UCC when I was about twelve or thirteen, which is a very impressionable age. I was lucky. I went to UTS, which had some great teachers. I was only there for a year or two, then we moved to Montreal. I finished school at Montreal High, which had a big effect on me. Oscar Peterson, the jazz pianist, was a couple of years ahead of me at that school. He used to play the piano at recess.

After living in Montreal for two years, we moved to Ottawa. When the war ended in 1945, Dad went into External Affairs. Over the years, he was Canadian ambassador to South Africa, Greece, Israel, and Australia. I listened to a lot of boogie-woogie, Oscar Peterson, and Duke Ellington's orchestra on the radio. I thought it was fabulous stuff. That era of music was just incredibly creative. Now music is another word for money. When they make a movie, they look for a composer not to make music, but just to enhance their income.

When Dad was posted to South Africa after the war, I went to Capetown with him to study music. I took a bachelor of music at Capetown University from 1951 to 1954. I learned to play the organ in Capetown well enough to carry a job as an organist. When I came back to Montreal, I had a job in the Westmount Baptist Church. I had married a

Dutch girl who I met in South Africa. I was just barely managing to make a living.

Then I had a hit song in London called "African Waltz," a jazzy boogie tune. John Dankworth recorded it and made a hit out of it. It freed me from the church. I left Montreal and went to London for a year and a half. Then I moved to New York City in 1965. Two years later, in 1967, I met two actors, James Rado and Gerome Ragni, who had written a book of lyrics which had no music. They said, "Do you want to write the music?" I said, "Sure." So I wrote the Broadway musical *Hair*, which became a worldwide success.

Initially, I wrote a tune for the song "Age of Aquarius" which the authors and I weren't crazy about, so I rewrote it. It was the only tune in *Hair* that I rewrote. The lyrics are kind of pretentious: "When the moon is in the Seventh House and Jupiter aligns with Mars, then peace will guide the planet and love will steer the stars."

Hair opened on Broadway on April 29, 1968, exactly two years to the day after my father died. It was a fabulous time, the year of the Chicago riots, the peak of the 1960s. I liked working on *Hair*. At the time, it was considered radical, although it didn't seem radical to me. The powers that be certainly didn't like it. I know that J. Edgar Hoover, the head of the FBI, hated it. The Senate had to pass a law to allow *Hair* to play someplace. It got that kind of attention. I don't know what my father would have thought of it.

It was the first show to show nudity and the first to take a really honest look at race relationships and sex. Basically, it was an honest look at everything. There was no pretence in it. It celebrated everything. It was full of energy. The idea was that some hippies were trying to evolve a new lifestyle that they believed in. They didn't like the Vietnam War, the Establishment, or the dominant cultural values of the 1950s and 1960s. They were trying to figure out another way of living.

Hair ran on Broadway for five years. It takes a lot of energy to play, so we were all really quite glad to close it. We were tired. I didn't play the show all the way through, but I played it for quite a while. I'd play piano for eight performances a week.

I'm still writing music. People come to me or I write something and take it around. But it's hard to get a show on now because the money is very tight. Also, New York reverted quickly back to a very conservative type of theatre. As soon as Richard Nixon and the Republicans came into power in 1968, things really dried up. The theatrical establishment likes theatre to be more genteel and low energy, the kind of thing Andrew Lloyd Webber does. It's pretty contrived, controlled and predictable.

Luckily, I don't have to compromise my own musical integrity because the money keeps coming in from *Hair*. I made a lot of money at the time and it continues to pay well in residuals. It's been running solidly in Europe for fifteen years. There is a touring company that just never stops. Currently there's a production of *Hair* in Sarajevo. Right in the centre of the civil war, they are performing a musical about peace and love. Soldiers come in and see *Hair* and then they go back to fight.

I still remember some of my friends in the prep, including Dave Gossage, Fred Hadden, Mike Meredith, and Jim Bacque. Jim Bacque later wrote a controversial book, *Other Losses*, about the maltreatment of German POWs during the Second World War. He was kind of a controversial guy even in the prep. He was in trouble most of the time, as most of us were.

I haven't really kept in touch with anybody. When you leave at thirteen years old, you take a different route. None of the others went into music as far as I know. There was a guy in the prep named Bill Glassco who later became prominent in the theatre. He was the only guy I knew of my generation who went into the arts.

I don't really even consider myself an Upper Canada old boy. I just went to the prep because my father was there. Academically, I wasn't very brilliant at all. I paid no attention. School was an imposition on my time, as far as I was concerned. But I liked it. I had fun. They had some great skating rinks. Other than that, it was just a typical school, something you wanted to get out of as soon as you could.

JAMES BACQUE
1936–47
Writer

I VIVIDLY REMEMBER V-E Day. God, the end of the war! We were sitting in Freddy Mallett's 3A chemistry class at about 10:30 A.M. on May 8, 1945. It was a beautiful spring morning, the leaves blossoming outside. We had sung our hymns in prayers. The windows were open in the old college building, so the warm spring air was drifting through the class. Walking up the elm-lined avenue, if you happened to be late for prayers, hearing the boys singing through the open windows of the old prayer hall really was quite beautiful.

On this morning, Freddie Mallett left the class. We were all in a very strange mood. We were restless and calm, hopeful and apprehensive. We were taken out of ourselves. We knew the end of the war was about to be announced. Through the open windows we could hear the sound of church bells, fog horns, and ships' sirens all over Toronto. It was a magic moment. There were boys who had graduated from Upper Canada, barely able to shave, who had been obliterated. Now, people who were hopefully still alive would be coming home. I think we were taken to the prayer hall and I'm certain we went home early.

Our family had been devastated by the war. We had been a close-knit family of seven, five children and two parents, with servants, living in Moore Park. We had a dog and lots of fun. When the war came, everybody rushed off in uniform. My father, my big sister whom I adored, my big brother, and then my other big brother, all went off to war. My big brother Graeme was in the navy and all his friends, whom I looked up to, were in the forces. Graeme landed at D-Day in Normandy, Hugh was in the air force training to be a parachutist, and my sister was with the RCAF Women's Division. During many of these years, my father was away in Ottawa working in the war.

Just the three of us were left. All the servants were gone too. I'm not saying that I pitied myself because we didn't have servants. On the contrary, we had fun and we learned things. It was a fine time. I was very glad of it. But it was a huge adjustment to make. I resented it, not because the luxuries were gone but because I desperately missed my brothers, sister, and father. It was really awful to think that they were always at risk of being killed! It was terrible … awful!

I was sixteen when the war ended. Up to that point, we all talked about going overseas to fight. One guy would say, "I'm going into the navy because my brother's in the navy." Another would say, "I'm going into the air force because I want to fly a Spitfire." But things were suddenly quite different. There was a sense of a future that Upper Canada was preparing us for that was radically different from before. Up to that point, there was no question we would go straight into the armed forces and go to war. Now, we would have to go to university or into the work force and earn our living as citizens.

I knew I wanted to be a writer early in life, but I wouldn't admit it to myself. It was a dangerous thing to be a writer in this country in the 1940s and 1950s. It was as if you had said that you wanted to paint your face green. I remember my father saying, "There's no money in it."

It may well have been the case that if I had gone to a small provincial school outside Toronto, I would not have become a writer. UCC gave me a grounding in math, history, and English. But who knows? Certainly Upper Canada has produced a number of writers and artists out of all proportion to the general population. On the other hand, there are fewer than one might expect, given the advantages. You can make a judgement on the quality of the institution from that perspective.

The academic education in my time was adequate, perhaps even better than Canadian standards. But in my eleven years at the school, the only time I felt that my mind was coming alive was in the upper school with a few individual masters. One of them was McCubbin, who taught physics very well indeed. Another was Ettore Mazzoleni, who was a tired and cynical guy but nevertheless a good teacher.

My memory of Mazzoleni is that he was quite an unpleasant person. He felt frustrated in having to teach at UCC and yet he did it extremely well. Perhaps he was a failed artist. He taught English and was a musician. He was a very good teacher who taught me the rudiments of English which have put me in good stead all my life. Some time after graduation, I began to see that the grounding we had learned was far superior to that of kids from other schools. Certainly many American and English people that I met later did not know the language or the vocabulary nearly as well as I did. They didn't know what the subjunctive was. They didn't have a lot of knowledge you can use to improve your writing and speech. So I felt that aspect of the school was absolutely first-rate.

A few other teachers at UCC had an influence on me. I thought Jim "Piff" Biggar taught history well. Mike Bremner taught mathematics. He was not a very bright guy, but he did know his subject. With his limited mind, he was able to handle a limited subject. I did feel in his class an incredible excitement in discovering that Euclidean geometry was absolutely logical and perfect.

On the debit side, there were masters like I. K. Shearer, who was a notorious homosexual, little-boy watcher, and molester. He beat up on the kids. Nevertheless, he was shamefully treated when he was summarily fired in the 1970s after teaching at UCC for over thirty years. If he was going to be fired, why the hell had he been kept on the faculty so long?

Then there was the tragedy of Lorne "Butch" McKenzie. McKenzie became principal of the school in 1943 after filling in as acting principal after Terry MacDermot resigned. As far as I could tell, he never should have been a teacher. He was violent, bad-tempered, and stupid. He taught calculus and binomial theorem to our 5A class, but we just weren't getting taught.

When Butch was teaching, he scared the bejesus out of the boys. I'm not a coward, but I was terrified of this guy. The terror was not only of his sardonic and sarcastic attitude, but of the potential violence and the possibility of being expelled. I actually developed an ulcer. It wasn't just from him being a bully and talking to you, which in itself was a worrying thing. We simply weren't learning anything.

In those days, Grade 13 exams were a source of terror. Your life depended upon whether you passed the exams. I know boys to this day who are hopeless in life because they didn't apply themselves to get through those exams. We were expected to perform. A great deal of pressure was put upon us by parents, by ourselves, and by the teachers. Contained within this 5A class, but separate from it, was sixth form, made up of five or six of the brightest boys in the school. They were kept back a little bit in order to get good marks, as far as I could see, and be intellectual leaders. Tommy Crerar, Walter Massey, and Bob Johnston were among them.

Some time around Easter, there was a rebellion in Butch's class. Walter Massey and Bob Johnston went to the administration to complain. Thereafter we had to come to school after hours and on Saturday morning. I think Butch was removed from the class and we were given an emergency supply teacher. I don't know what the percentage was that got through the exams, but a tragedy had been averted by the courage of these boys. They confronted a very violent and powerful man, who shortly thereafter left the college.

Another master, Owen "Buzz" Classey, who had been H. G. Wells's secretary, would hit boys in class. It was awful. His classroom, which was at the top of a wooden staircase, had two doors. As the boys would be working, he would leave by the big door at the top of the stairs and leave it open.

It was a trick. He would wait until he heard too much noise in the class. He would burst suddenly in through the other door with a loud crash. If he didn't like you, he would come up behind you, talking to you, waving a book at the back of your head, then smashing you with it. He literally beat boys about the head. One boy had his head slammed on the desk so hard that blood came out of his ears. This was the atmosphere.

I think Upper Canada in those days inculcated violence in the boys. Boxing was not a necessary thing for a boy to do. I did well at it, so I'm not speaking with the resentment of a loser. I won all my bouts until I ran into a kid called Murphy in the upper school when I was about fifteen. Murphy's arms were about a foot longer than mine, so I didn't have a prayer. He bloodied me up pretty good. I ended my boxing career not liking the idea of losing, which I had never experienced before.

But I began to see what I had been doing to a kid called McLeod, who was the next-best boxer below me. All the way up the ladder, McLeod was always up against me but he could never beat me. There was nothing he could do to beat me in the ring. I just had him in the mind. We were thrown in like two bears into a pit. It was really awful, worse than my own experience against Murphy.

I remember seeing a vicious fight between two guys who went at it tooth and nail. The one guy just didn't have a chance, but he didn't quit. He got mad. His face was streaming blood. It may even have been coming out of his ears. He could barely stand up. The other guy just hammered him. It was what they were put in there to do. I don't know why the referee didn't stop the fight. It was a scandalous bout that was the talk of the school. I remember thinking at the time how stupid and wasteful it was. Here was a boy's young mind being given a concussion.

For our final year at UCC, my brother Gord and I were sent into boarding. Graeme had been in a terrible accident, so he required a great deal of care. He had come home from the war unscathed by D-Day and then bang, he was nearly killed in a car crash. He was learning to walk again. My mother said, "Well, I just can't take care of all of you boys here. I'll have to send you to the school to board."

Boarding was like prison. We were treated like common criminals, regimented, kept down, kept in. The food was very bad. Everything was institutionalized. We were scarcely allowed to make a phone call. We were allowed to have dates with girls twice a month. One had the feeling that girls were less likely to want to see you because your access would be limited.

I remember feeling quite lonely. I couldn't see any reason for it. I hadn't had these kinds of restrictions as a day boy, so why was I being restricted like this? A lot of it was because it was simply convenient for the administration. It was very easy to lose a privilege and be kept in. I can't remember the number of times that happened. We were allowed to go home on Sunday night for dinner. I remember thinking, Why the hell do I have to go back to school after dinner? Why can't I stay the night at home? I haven't done anything wrong.

The boarders always wanted a girlfriend. It was a damn shame that we weren't allowed to get out more often. Normal, healthy young men wanted to have girlfriends and impress girls. The denial of their presence tended to put them in a separate category. To a certain degree, boys were victimized. They approached women as if they were goddesses. I can remember falling in love with Nanno Fair when I was in boarding. I remember saying prayers out the window, "First star I see tonight, make that girl love me." I remember sneaking into the principal's office to make phone calls to her. We weren't allowed to have very many minutes on the phone in the boarding house.

I remember beginning my journey into literature, beyond the Hardy Boys, comic books, and the books we had taken in school, when I was in Seaton's House that final year at UCC. Graeme had a copy of *War and Peace*, which I took. I was living in the same room with Alfie Moyer from Sudbury. I remember sitting at my desk doing my homework that year. I was so worried, I was literally pulling my hair out. My desk was just covered in hair. I don't know why I didn't go bald.

After lights out, I would snap my light around and read *War and Peace*. When the patrols in the hall had quieted down and my light had run out of fuel, I would tiptoe into the can to go on reading. Jim Biggar, the housemaster, caught me there one night, sitting on the floor at 2:00 A.M. The masters were always patrolling the dorms, probably because they were terrified the boys were doing unsavoury things with each other. Anyway, there I was. He was quite nice. He asked me what I was reading, so I showed him. My memory is that it was a rather comic little scene, very underplayed. That was the beginning of my acquaintance with the joys of literature. I thought it was a great thing to be able to open up a person's mind the way Tolstoy did.

I didn't really know what I wanted to do when I left Upper Canada. Underneath it all, there was this sense that I wanted to write. It was like coming out of the closet. Finally, I did. Some time in third-year university, while my parents were in Florida, I spent a whole weekend in our house with an awful headache. I was so angry. What would I do? Law? Medicine? Go into my father's business?

When I thought about it, I felt as if I was part way up a mountain on an expedition against my family. My family had brought me as far as the 20,000-foot level by giving me a private education. Was I simply going to go back to the bottom and repeat everything they had done – wear a suit, work in a business, and make money? There didn't seem to be any point. Why shouldn't I climb to the peak? The climb is terrible. But then it is terrifying to go back down to the bottom and lug all that stuff back up again.

There was an additional feeling that the conventional route would have been very boring. It had already been done. When you talk to other artists and writers, you find that they are interested in the new and the creative. They just don't want to repeat patterns they have been witnessing since they were kids. Why do it all over again? Even though the prospect of making a living as a writer terrified me, I finally decided that I would become a writer. That night, the headache disappeared.

I knew a young man from UCC, a former head boy, who had a different experience. He wanted to write and be a history professor, but his parents were not for it and told him not to do it. He was a great success at what he did, but at the age of forty-nine he killed himself. After his death, I discovered a manuscript he had written.

One of the most difficult things I've ever done was writing *Other Losses*, which is about the unreported high death rate of German prisoners in World War II. In that book, there are a great number of statistics. I couldn't have written the book if I hadn't had rigorous mathematical training at UCC. I would have given up. I was able to analyse the statistics only because Upper Canada College had properly taught me Euclidean geometry. While it was algebra that I was using, Euclidean geometry had shown me that there is perfection in the symbolic world of mathematics. No part is missing or redundant. When I looked at the army statistics, I knew that they must be falsified. They could not be perfect on their own terms.

I sat late at night at the same rosewood desk my mother had given me, making myself get the statistics right. I knew there must be an answer. My experience when I was fourteen at UCC became my experience when I was fifty-six, sitting in a hotel room in Washington, D.C., alone and dead scared. It was exactly the same fear I felt going into Mike Bremner's Euclidean geometry class at UCC and not having my homework done. It was not a fear of being caned or beaten, but a feeling of humiliation at not living up to my standards – standards which were to some degree planted in me by UCC.

When we graduated from UCC, I remember, we thought, God, what a stupid place. It trains kids to be stockbrokers. What an awful way to enter life. Hugh Stephenson was my best friend. He was head boy in 1947, and his brother Ted later taught at the prep. Hugh and I both went to Trinity College at U of T. We later talked a lot about our experience at UCC, agreeing that it wasn't a very good school.

Part of my rejection of Upper Canada was because I felt it was too snobbish. There was a certain amount of anti-English war-guest feeling, a certain amount of anti-Semitic, anti-black, anti-French-Canadian feeling, although it wasn't terribly severe. The only widespread hatred I encountered at that point was against Germans. It was by far the most prevalent, inculcated prejudice and hatred in the country and in the school, even after the war was over.

I remember seeing a system of control at work in the steward and prefect system. The guys wearing white stewards' blazers, the guys catching the great pass to win dramatically over Ridley in the football game – they were the favoured sons. But those guys generally did nothing spectacular in later life. They are like ivy. They climb high up the wall and spread their leaves in the sun very early. But they have no strength of their own. They will cling to the wall for the rest of their lives. Those who have different qualities will grow up a strong tree.

I think you can see that in a guy like Peter Newman. He didn't do much at UCC, but he's certainly made up for it since. Galt MacDermot didn't do much at the school, but look at the creative energy behind *Hair.* I would bet he hasn't stayed in touch with any of the old boys. You tend to find that the loyal old boys who shone at the school are the ones still trying to relive their glory days.

When I graduated, my friends and I felt contemptuous of UCC. We felt that the school promoted mediocrity, not excellence. It was highly competitive, yet mediocre in a lot of ways, which is a very bad combination. There was no excellence that we could see, except on an individual basis. My feeling was that UCC was very snobbish, overly tied to monarchism, and academically inferior. Peter Newman and I vowed that we would never send our sons to Upper Canada. I kept that vow.

MICHAEL SNOW

1942 – 48

Artist

U CC WASN'T the happiest of times for me, but I don't blame the school. I don't blame myself, either. That was just the way it was. Mostly, I was afraid of everything, which came out by my refusing to do almost everything. Somehow or other, I managed to get through school and to pass, so I did do something. But I had an incredible lack of confidence. Because I passively resisted, I didn't learn how to learn. I suppose there's a little more psychology involved in teaching now.

I first started to play the piano at Upper Canada. My friend Dave Lancashire, who later worked for the *Globe and Mail* as a foreign correspondent, wrote a piece called "Blues in the Clock Tower." He played trombone in some of the bands I played in in the 1940s. By 1947, when I was at UCC, I was playing in bands.

The old clock tower used to have piano practice rooms. Neither of us were studying piano. He played trumpet and I'd play piano. They didn't like it that we played in the clock tower because we weren't supposed to be there. It was only for piano students. Sometimes we were chased out.

Another old boy, Ken Dean, also played in the band. He was one of the

first people I had met at UCC who was interested in jazz. The most important thing that happened to me at UCC was discovering jazz. It really gave
me a raison d'être. Meeting Ken, who was already a pretty accomplished
musician, was fantastic. So I taught myself how to play piano. That's how it
all started. I continue to play.

This was totally extracurricular, because I didn't study. My mother was
a very, very fine pianist, and still is. She wanted me to take lessons, but I
wouldn't do it. Then I heard this music which really moved me, and which
I wanted to imitate, so I started trying to teach myself. It wasn't done in a
total vacuum. I asked questions of other people. I do have a pretty good
understanding of theory, despite the fact that I'm self-taught.

There used to be compulsory sports at 3:30, which I used to try to
dodge, partly because I was afraid I couldn't play properly and I was a
skinny wretch. I avoided sports at all costs. I must have played sometimes.
In fact, I remember enjoying it once. I made a touchdown playing football.
It was probably the second time I played football, but for some reason it
didn't encourage me. I don't know how I got away with cutting sports, but
I really don't remember doing it very much.

I got forced into boxing. I won my first bout. My opponent was even
more afraid than I was, which is hard to believe. In the second one, I fought
Foster Hewitt's son Bill, who really cleaned me up. It was awful. I was just
really very alarmed when I advanced after the first fight, because I didn't
want to be there at all. There was no escape. Hewitt beat the shit out of me.

But when I discovered jazz, I met some other ne'er-do-wells, some of
them high school dropouts, who were just as converted to jazz as Ken Dean
and I were. I used to hide my bike in the bushes. I'd sneak out when it was
sports time and ride down to Promenade Music Centre, a record store.
One friend used to bring a little metal thermos of gin and Tom Collins mix
and little silver glasses. We'd sit in there and drink and listen to this wonderful music, and then I'd somehow get home on my bike.

Art class had more to do with the school itself. I remember very, very
well some compliments that a prep art master, John Hall, gave me about
some drawing. I was really, really hungry for encouragement. He was
extremely complimentary, and it stayed in my mind. He said that when I
drew the faces out of imagination, I had the capacity to make all the parts
fit in a way that it seemed as if it was a unified, realistic face. All the charac-
teristics of form that a face might have were there. He said it was a certain
kind of talent that I had.

The next memory I have is getting the art prize in my graduating year.
Yulia Biriukova was the art teacher in the upper school. I remember the
prize as being a surprise because, over the years, I don't remember doing

anything much different in art classes than anybody else. So, when I got it, I thought maybe they were trying to tell me something.

I didn't know what to do, as a lot of people don't know what to do at that stage, so I went to the Ontario College of Art. I didn't think about being an artist until two days before I graduated. I went to OCA really because of the UCC art prize, which is pretty fantastic. I don't remember Yulia Biriukova being specifically complimentary or helpful. She was a knowledgeable artist herself, but somehow or other, I can't remember her classes very well. But the final result is that I got the art prize, which turned out to be pretty important.

The war was on. I still have a lot of drawings from then, which all have to do with Nazi planes being shot down. I drew a lot of comic strips, a lot of which involved the war. Comic strips were very influential. They were sort of the TV of the time. It was really a strong period for Superman and Batman. I read them all and was very influenced by them.

I think that I was dumber than kids today would be. My little boy is a lot older than I was at nine. It is amazing that my wife and I are considering sending him to UCC. Twenty or thirty years ago, I would have laughed or screamed or cried at the thought of sending him. He's my only child – as far as I know. His closest friend went to UCC in fifth grade, so he's interested in UCC because of his friend. But a lot of what he hears, he really doesn't like. He's very against uniforms. The high fees and the lack of girls are an issue for my wife and I.

I remember quite clearly my father talking about the benefits in going to UCC. I recently found a letter from him which was about my report card at that time. He said, "You have to remember that these people you are going to meet are people that you are going to know the rest of your life." It has turned out that that was not true. The old boys' network hasn't happened very much with me.

One would have thought that my father might have opposed me becoming an artist, but it was a case of "Do whatever you want to do." They may have been disappointed, but they still said go ahead. Probably my father was a bit disappointed. He was disappointed about many things, especially going blind and losing all his friends in the war. He had a lot of very depressing things to cope with. Tragically he lost one eye, when I was about five years old, in an explosion in Montreal. During the time I was at OCA, the other eye started to go.

Eventually, I had some shows. I remember he came to one of them at the Issacs Gallery. He could see colours, but everything else became indistinct. He got very, very close to a canvas and said, "That's a nice colour, Brother." My nickname in those days was "Brother." Apparently it started when I became a brother to my sister.

I think one of the contributing factors with people who become artists is the tendency to solitary play during a certain period of your life. You build up some kind of inner life that wants to keep on continuing. I was like that. I have talked to other people over the years to try and find out if there is any resemblance. In a lot of visual artists, it's been like that.

I was brought up before TV. A lot of the time, I used to doodle, which was all in my own mind and under my own control. Much of our time is now taken up by passive entertainment, where that kind of imagination isn't being indulged because TV is all input. I wonder what kind of long-term effect that will have. I think one of the important things about preschool time is the freedom to play and discover things on your own, which seems to be less and less possible. I was very much of a solitary player, playing my own games and indulging my own imagination. It can make for an asocial kind of thing because you're trained to be alone.

I had a retrospective of all the *Walking Woman* works which toured. I remember at a museum in Cornell, I was talking about the work and a very solemn-looking woman said, "What did you think about feminism back then?" I said, "It didn't exist. I know this is hard for you to believe, but no one thought about it. I might have known that there were suffragettes, but no one thought of women's issues in the ways that you think of them now."

She really wouldn't believe that because she was interpreting *Walking Woman* in the context of the oppression of women. Many bad, oppressive things must have been happening to women back then, but we weren't as conscious of them because there was not a lot of information about them in the media. Obviously it must have been going on. The WCTU [Women's Christian Temperance Union] was the spearhead for prohibition because there were so many drunken husbands beating their wives.

It's very interesting to think about the kind of effect UCC, as an all boys' school, had on people. Historically, even in tribal societies, the men worked together and the women worked together, so you could make up some kind of argument for male bonding. For some reason, for some kind of mutual understanding, it's easier for men to work together and women to work together, than necessarily for them to mix. But they have to mix. So, there should be training for that.

Because of UCC being all boys, it was hard to meet girls. But somehow or other, I did meet some. I remember trying to take somebody to the Battalion Ball, but I couldn't dance. It was just horrible. I suppose that I felt socially awkward on leaving UCC. If there had been girls in the classroom, I might have got laid earlier. I became very interested in that, but it was difficult to achieve.

If I was in any way rebellious at UCC, in a way it might have been the music. It wasn't popular music that I was interested in, in fact there was really a big difference. I wasn't interested in Frank Sinatra and all that kind of crap. I don't think the UCC environment was hostile. I think that they meant well. I wanted to conform, but I was too afraid to. But it wasn't a reasoned opposition in any sense. It had more to do with my own weaknesses than anything. Maybe it was good for me to be at UCC.

Of my UCC contemporaries, I see Ken Dean occasionally at the market. I saw Jim Bacque a few years ago when he was working on his book *Other Losses*. Bill Kilbourn, who I see occasionally, has written some marvellous things. Peter Newman and I got honorary degrees at Brock University, and we talked about UCC a little bit.

I still have some books from school. We used to have these little books where you'd write down what the homework was. Mine is full of jazz stuff. It's all kinds of things like playing with designing labels, writing out tunes and chord type progressions. I was doing a lot of that when I was there.

I remember one particular occasion, we got together at somebody's house and listened to records and drank beer. I walked back to Rosedale, where I lived, from this guy's place at Broadview and Danforth. We walked back talking about the various clarinet styles of Johnny Dodds and Pee Wee Russell and all these particular issues about how the clarinet should be played. Louis Armstrong's Hot Five, and all that kind of stuff, was very underground then. It wasn't popular, although there was a following all over the world. I heard a few things on the radio that were revelatory.

We walked all the way back and sat on the front porch. My father came out to get the paper at eight or nine in the morning. We were still sitting out there talking. It was wonderful. I'll never forget it. A lot of my energy went into the music.

I still have a lot of tapes from our band, Ken Dean's Hot Seven. There were no tape recorders then, but we met a guy who used to cut discs, so I have quite a few things from 1948. Some piano solos actually were quite good. It's really quite surprising. I'd only been playing about a year. When we got organized, we played regularly, just for fun. Gigs came up, sometimes at Centre Island. It was fantastic. It was like New Orleans.

In the summer, we'd play in the Balmy Beach Canoe Club or sometimes at university frat dances. We were paid very little, but it was really amazing. We were just totally into the music. We'd spend hours listening to records and discussing what so and so played, who played this and who played that.

Being a musician also helped attract girls. I first got laid on Centre Island after one of the concerts. Sorry, Thelma.

PART
II

PETER NEWMAN

1945 – 49

Author, editor

I EMIGRATED to Canada with my family late in 1940 from Czechoslovakia, where my father had been an industrialist. He owned a big sugar refinery. We could only come to Canada as farmers because of the immigration laws. After leaving the farm, my father moved to Toronto and started an import-export business. My mother was a concert pianist.

I went to many different schools in Canada because the family moved around. My parents wanted me to be in a boarding school. They very wisely realized if I stayed home and spoke Czech and German, I would never get rid of my accent. In 1945 Upper Canada had an informal wartime scholarship program. The principal, Butch McKenzie, made it possible for me to go. The school paid about half the fees and I paid the rest.

I became the president of the radio club, the first time in my life that I was actually elected to something. We had a little cubbyhole up in the clock tower where we made crystal radio sets. For about fifteen dollars, you could make a radio out of the crystals. I could listen to it on earphones, which was fun. At first, I couldn't figure out why so many wanted to join the radio club. Then I realized they wanted to join because the tower was a good place to smoke cigarettes. Michael Snow played piano up in the tower and I played drums with him occasionally. He was very good.

I volunteered for the drum corps and eventually became the drum sergeant, who stands in the front row on the right side and leads the band. If there was only one drummer playing for the whole band, that was me. We would march around the school fields and went to St. Paul's Church on Bloor Street for Sunday church parades. Whenever we marched, wherever the band was, I was the chief drummer, which was a great honour for me. I remember one battalion inspection where I got into big trouble because I switched to a jazz beat. The kids loved it, but the masters didn't.

I was very conscious of the war because my home country was being invaded. In fact, I got a very strong military feeling out of UCC. The military legacy stayed with me, because I later joined the Royal Canadian Navy and eventually became a captain.

It was the kids, not the teachers, who made me feel like an outsider at UCC. Some of the teachers became a bit protective of me because they could see what the other kids were doing. Even Butch McKenzie, who I didn't think liked me, would call me in a couple of times a year and say, "How's it going?" Now it would appear patronizing, but at the time it was appreciated. The kids would tease me about my accent. They were all rich WASPs. I was Jewish and poor.

I've never known whether it's an advantage or disadvantage to have gone to Upper Canada College. For me, the big drawback was that it wasn't coeducational. It was okay if you were a day boy and you had a family and a street life on weekends. But for a boarder to come out of that environment into university, where suddenly there was no structure and there were women all over the place, you felt like an alien from another world.

I was terribly shy. I didn't know how to approach women. I don't think I was alone in that. It was a real problem. We had two dances a year at UCC. Of course, we didn't know any girls, so they would truck them in from BSS. It was just a totally unreal atmosphere. They would be there by 7:00 P.M., be gone by 10:00 P.M., and we'd say, "Where did they all go?" Girls became objects of mystery because you had never touched one. I don't mean in a sexual way, just having conversations with them.

I didn't get to go home too often, maybe only two or three long weekends a term. In the summers, my last two years at UCC, I worked in a gold mine in Northern Quebec. I made enough money to pay the rest of my tuition. I was in a mineshaft which had no safety rules, which meant that they paid us a lot of money. I may be one of the few people who actually worked his way through Upper Canada College.

Because I was lonely at times, I did a lot of reading in the boarding-house, which proved very valuable to me. I read mostly non-fiction, nothing to do with the curriculum. You don't think of that as part of your education, but in a way it's the most valuable part. Once you get a job or even go to university, you don't have that much time to read.

I wrote in the old boys' directory, "Like war, I'm proud of having been at UCC – and prouder still of having survived it." I got beaten up two or three times. I wish I could remember what it was for. The overall experience wasn't that happy, but the other side of the quote is relevant too. I'm glad that I went to UCC because it meant that I learned English and picked up the idioms of everyday speech.

If you learn English in a Berlitz school, you don't learn the way the language is really used. There are immigrants who came to Canada at my age of similar background and intelligence who still have strong accents in their fifties and sixties. They didn't have the kind of immersion I had. At UCC, you were by yourself and you had to learn. Every time you made a mistake, ten kids would laugh at you. That's a real incentive. At UCC I learned how to survive in Canadian society.

While I was at Upper Canada, I wanted to build radios as a career. My ultimate career path as a journalist had nothing to do with the school. The school simply made me less awed by the establishment. When I came to write about it, I could write very objectively. I'd seen them in showers, I'd seen them cry when their team lost. There was nothing extraordinary about them.

I've been back to the school a couple of times to give speeches. I found it very strange because I remembered being in the prayer hall as a boy listening to the speeches. I thought I was a poor immigrant boy who would never amount to anything. Here I was back at Upper Canada College, and I was now the one giving the speech.

TED ROGERS

1941–51

President and CEO, Rogers Communications

M Y FATHER DIED when I was five years old. It's very hard to compete with your father. It has always driven me. My father started the radio station CFRB and Rogers Majestic Radio. He invented the AC tube, which meant that radios could plug into the wall current for the first time. In 1925, his invention was introduced at the CNE. The radios would run on great big feed batteries, which would leak acid on the carpet. It was the first radio in the world that worked on an electric household current. He died suddenly at thirty-eight of an aneurysm, without having much life insurance.

Two years later, my mother married a wonderful man named John Graham, who had graduated from UCC in 1930. I went to board in the prep at age seven in 1941 because John was overseas during the war and my mother wasn't well. I remember the prep boarding house had bars on the windows in those days. In the dorms, you'd line up at night and they'd ask you, "How are your bowels?" I tried to be polite. Then one night I said to the nurse, "Mine are fine. How are yours?" I got caned for that. I used to get caned quite a bit.

Maybe Upper Canada was a surrogate father for a while. After my father died when I was five, my pediatrician advised my mother that I should go to a boys' environment because if I stayed home with my mother and a nanny, I'd grow up to be a sissy. So at age seven, in the course of a week, I went from having somebody brushing my teeth for me to being caned if my teeth weren't clean enough. There's nothing wrong with that, but it was a bit of a shock.

Alan Stephen was the prep headmaster at that time. I used to sneak in crystal sets and radios when I was in boarding in the prep. I put an antenna like a clothesline across Alan Stephen's garden. I didn't think he'd notice, but he did. So they moved me away from a window cubicle to the other side of the dorm. Then when everybody was away, I put the wires underneath the linoleum. The linoleum ripped, so again I got caned. "Three of the best" would be quite normal.

In the prep, to make us feel that we weren't the privileged few, they gave us the same small amount of food as the people in the war in Europe. Sometimes boys would cheat because their parents would bring over a sandwich. But by and large, we all honoured it. Occasionally, they would gather us around to tell us that somebody's father had been killed in the war. I remember a boy named Logie just standing there in the dining room. He was pretty upset. So were we all. You grew up pretty quick.

I boarded all the way through the school except my last year. It was particularly hard at the end of the war when the dads came home and many of the boarders went home. That was hard for me. Everybody has their share of unhappiness and I certainly had mine.

In the upper school in Seaton's House, we weren't allowed TV sets, but I designed a TV antenna on the roof. The pole lay down flat so no one could see it. Mr. Biggar, the housemaster, was so pissed off at me for getting into trouble all the time that he put me right next to his own office at the end of the hall. Right by Biggar's window, I rigged a wire down the wall through a lot of plants. At night, I would start to pull on it. It would start to come up very slowly. I had an arrangement with the prefects that I would turn the lights off. They would then turn the switch back on that controlled the electric outlets as well as the lights. They would come and watch the TV, which was in the cupboard, with me. We could watch a Buffalo TV station from 1948 on. I would lower this thing back down, lock the cupboard, and nobody would know the difference.

One winter night it was very icy. I started to pull and it wouldn't come. I had to put all my weight on it, and the thing came crashing down through the nurse's window. It then bounced down to the junior house-master's window and smashed through that, too, onto the concrete in the basement. The prefects went running out and denied they were any part of it. I had to take the rap. I got six of the best for that too. But I still like to say it was the first Rogers TV cable system in Canada.

Of the boys in my time at UCC, Hal Jackman and I have stayed friends through the years. We've been very active in politics together. We each put up ten thousand dollars for a half interest in the *Sutton Reporter* and I'm happy to say that we went bankrupt. So Jackman is not a perfect busi-nessman and neither is Rogers. Maybe you've got to do things like that when you're young. I know Hal would say, "Yes, do those things when you're young. Do them when a small amount of money is involved and do them in partnership with someone who is as much a bloody fool as you are."

Peter Newman and I have also stayed in touch. I'm fond of him. Con-rad Black is another old boy who has done phenomenally well. He is an unbelievably clever individual with a mind unequaled by anyone I've ever met. I also knew Bill Hewitt, but he went right into his dad's radio station, so he had it fairly easy. I love the Foster and Bill Hewitt Athletic Centre at UCC. It was very good of Bill Hewitt to donate one million dollars to the school. Foster must still be turning in his grave because he never gave a nickel to anybody when he was alive. I also knew Butts Campbell, who was the head of the battalion one year. Arthur Whealy, now a criminal court justice, was also head of the battalion one year. He was a good person.

In any school you go to or place where you work, there's an old pals' network. But there's nothing like the Family Compact as there was in the last century. I don't think I've ever hired anybody from Upper Canada. I've hired people I knew in politics. Phil Lind, a senior vice-president at Rogers, is an old boy, but I knew him through politics. I've got a friend from Upper Canada, Toby Hull, who runs the Hull Group of insurance companies. He's on the board and he handles our insurance. But we've done that sort of thing all our lives together. My stepfather, John Graham, has been part-time non-executive chairman of Rogers Communications right from its beginning thirty years ago.

I think I came away from UCC bitter. Maybe bitter is too strong a word, but I thought it was unfair. I'm not complaining because I've had a lot of good luck in my life. Having had some adversity helped me. My experience in life is that people who have had some adversity tend to work harder, particularly if they are new Canadians from Europe or Asia who have been dispossessed. They are more driven. If everything is handed to you on a plate, you're less likely to struggle.

I don't know if I had any kind of vision of the future when I was at the school, although I had a long time to think. It was like being in jail. I do think UCC gave me something in terms of my future business success – an entrepreneurial sense and also a sense of individuality. Of course I think UCC did turn out some people who conformed to what they perceived to be a mould of the old English aristocracy. But Peter Newman and I weren't that way, and neither were many others. Like a lot of other places, UCC turned out very different people.

BILL "BUTTS" CAMPBELL

1944–50

Soldier

I USED TO PROTECT Ted Rogers at UCC because the guys would want to beat up on him. He was as skinny as a rake. They used to call him "Bones" because he was so thin. I was the middleweight boxing champion at the time. I would get the guys aside and say, "If you pick on him, you have to go through me first." They never did.

There was a fagging system at Upper Canada in those days. New boys had to do all kinds of stupid things for the senior boys, like shine their shoes and do whatever the hell they wanted you to do. You couldn't buck it, because it was either do it or you never knew what the consequences would be. You did it. Fagging was not pleasant. Some of the guys could think of the weirdest bloody things just for the hell of it, just because you were a new boy.

The prefects caned boys in those days. I got caned. I still have scars on my ass from the masters' canings. The principal, Butch McKenzie, used to have his cane soaking in alcohol right beside his desk. I. K. Shearer, the French master, caned me once. He used to roll dice on his desk to see how many strokes we'd get. For me, he rolled a two. He said, "Don't worry. There will be a six in every stroke!" I had to lean over his desk. I thought he was going to drive me through the wall. All the other guys were waiting at the bottom of the stairs for their turn.

One time I hit Shearer. I was not a good French student. There was nobody else in the classroom, just the two of us. He was leaning on me really heavy. He used to put his foot on your seat and kick you. He would just about drive you off the seat. He'd say, "Put your head down. Study! Study!" Then he would hit you. Finally, I whacked him in the face. I was seventeen. Shearer was a tall guy, but he wasn't chunky. He didn't do a damn thing in retaliation because he knew there was more where that came from if he wanted to make a fuss about it.

I was light middleweight champion, light heavyweight champion, and then heavyweight champion. I was a bleeder. One whack on my nose and I'd bleed, but that never bothered me. I was also a numero-uno swimmer. I was captain of the swimming team. I was also a sprinter. I didn't do long distance because I smoked. That's why I'm called "Butts." I did the one hundred yards, fifty yards, the quickies. They were wonderful times.

We played twenty-two football games and never lost one. Bill Hewitt was quarterback, Bob Bazos was the running back, and I was the wide receiver. At about 180 pounds, I was the second-lightest guy on the team. Those were the days when you played both offensively and defensively. The nurse, Miss Barrow, patched me up many times. Today, at sixty-two years of age, I'm still goddamn sore. The old injuries come back.

Miss B. was like a surrogate mother for the whole college, particularly the athletes and battalion officers. You never got your picture on Miss B.'s wall unless you were somebody. I think she was in love with the school doctor, Dr. MacTavish, but she never did get married. She was married to Upper Canada College for over forty years.

When Dr. Sowby succeeded Butch McKenzie as the new principal in 1948, the only one he could really count on was me. I was the lieutenant-colonel of the battalion. He had me into his office. He didn't say, "I need your help," but it was obvious he did. He said, "You're not going to have a revolt." McKenzie, the previous principal, had had to deal with a student revolt. The boys had walked out on him. I think Ted Rogers was the leader of it.

I guess Sowby didn't want the same thing to happen to him. He knew that if I just took everybody and said, "Don't show up," nobody would. He called me into his office because I was a steward and numero uno and therefore I could control the student body. I had authority. It didn't take him long to figure out that I was his key. He was a hell of a nice guy.

UCC is affiliated with the oldest regiment in Canada, the Queen's Own Rifles, which was the twenty-seventh brigade mobilized to go to Europe.

When I was lieutenant-colonel of the UCC cadets, I said, "I'd like to go with the Queen's Own." They said, "Like hell! You're going to Officer Candidate School."

On May 18, 1951, I went into Office Candidate School. We started with eighty-two guys, just kids of eighteen or nineteen. They wanted to find our breaking point, physically and mentally. They put us through murder. My stepfather had died when I was seventeen and I didn't know my real father. I said to myself: "You're not going to break me because I have no place to go. I have no family." Only twenty-one of the eighty-two candidates graduated.

I lied to join the army. I said, "I've got Grade 13 senior matriculation." They never asked much. They were really scraping the bottom of the barrel to get volunteers to go to Germany and Korea. I ended up in Korea with the Vandoos, which was a wonderful regiment. Don't you play around with the Vandoos. They take care of their own. No matter how bad you are, they protect you.

I commanded a medium machine-gun platoon in the Korean War in 1952. Don't ask me how many Chinese we killed. We fought at night. During the day, we slept. You could always count on it if there was a full moon. At midnight, you knew darn well the Chinese were coming. You could set your clock by them. They attacked in waves.

I had eight machine guns. All my firing was between 11:00 P.M. and 4:00 A.M. We were firing through blankets in a dugout to suppress the flash. One night, we fired 170,000 rounds with my eight guns. When you have constant rapid firing, it burns out the gun barrel. The next day, a three-quarter-ton truck was coming up the main supply route. I said, "What's going on?" They said, "New barrels for your guns." Our guns were all burnt out.

We lost only twelve men in the course of fourteen months. I don't know how many Chinese were killed because they never left any bodies behind. We'd have a hell of a shootout. The next day, we'd send a patrol out, but we could never find any bodies.

After Korea, I stayed in the army. When I retired, I went to work as a management consultant for the Department of National Defence. I was a lieutenant-colonel when I retired. If I had stayed in a little longer, I would have made full colonel or maybe brigadier-general. But thirty years is plenty. I don't regret one minute of it, good times and bad times. As long as you did your job, you were okay. I never had any problems because I had superb officers. It's the old story: If you fuck with the bull, you are going to get the horns up the ass. I'm the bull. The army was like my family. It was home.

The cadet training at UCC really helped my career. It was very structured. You play the game or you are going to be a loser. Yes sir, salute smartly, what can I do for you? Those days were discipline, discipline, discipline. If you followed the rules and you did what the college required of you, you would have no problems. But if you tried to buck it, you were in big trouble.

I have damn good memories from Upper Canada. It was a wonderful experience. You learned whether you wanted to or not. There was no way you couldn't because they wouldn't leave you alone. They just kept beating on you. UCC made me because it was challenging.

When I visited Toronto in 1991, I thought I'd look up old Bones, Ted Rogers. I hadn't seen him since UCC. You can easily confuse Upper Canada College and Ted Rogers' house on Frybrook Road because they are about the same size. A maid came to the door. I said, "Is Mr. Rogers home?" She said, "Yes. Who are you?" I said, "Just tell him Butts Campbell is here." I waited a minute at the door. Then she came back and said, "Well, I'm sorry, Mr. Rogers is terribly busy." So I didn't get to see him. Of course, he's a billionaire now.

HAL JACKMAN

1945–48

Lieutenant-Governor of Ontario

WHEN I WAS A NEW BOY, we were the first class that didn't have to fag for the older boys. Everybody above Grade 9 had been a fag when they were new boys, so there was a huge resentment by the upperclassmen that they had been cheated out of their fags. There was still caning in those days. The masters could cane, but the prefects couldn't cane any longer at that point.

The principal, Butch McKenzie, usually made announcements each morning just after prayers, then he would leave and the prefects would take over. The discipline was collapsing. There was howling and shrieking in the assembly when the prefects were in charge. People would boo. Often, prayers would take up almost more than half the first period as a result. Butch McKenzie didn't do anything about it, probably because he was a little reluctant to break with tradition.

The cadet corps was most unpopular in my time, right after the war. The Upper Canada College cadets were run by the students themselves. The students didn't know anything about the army, so all they did was the same old drill. I don't think the drill had changed since prior to the First World War. About 25 to 30 per cent of the boys would simply not show up to the early-morning drills.

At morning prayers, the adjutant would read out the names of the people who had missed the drill: "The following will report to the orderly room." With every name, there were huge cheers. One morning, there were about 130 guys lined up outside the orderly room. Guys would say with a straight face, "Well, I got up early, but the Yonge Street streetcar broke down." Twenty guys behind him in line would put up their hand and say, "I was on the same streetcar."

My younger brother Ed, who is now a Catholic priest, followed me into UCC and boarded for a full ten years. I decided to leave UCC after Grade 11 for UTS, where my father had gone to school. I thought the difference between UCC and UTS was like night and day. The spirit was very bad at Upper Canada. I don't know why. We had a good hockey team and a good football team, but there was a general cynicism. I think it had something to do with getting rid of all the structure, like the fagging system, and not finding anything to replace it with. I don't know if the school imparted any leadership qualities. I think I was in a very bad year. I think it is a good school, don't misunderstand me. I just think those years were bad years.

UTS had better school spirit and was also a much more demanding academic environment. Upper Canada seemed to be struggling for its role. Academics were hard to justify. They didn't have the material, they didn't have the money to pay the teachers, and they didn't have good students. They had what they called a sixth form, like a Grade 14. Boys would hang around the school for an extra year. Some of them would get scholarships and perhaps be made a prefect or steward. I think you should spend that extra year at university.

I believe you are privileged if you go to Upper Canada, but I think it was much less obvious in my day. I remember the school did not have a waiting list. Anybody could go if they could pay. I think as the city gets bigger and wealthier, and there are more people from all over the world coming in, then a school like Upper Canada is pushed up into more of an elite position. I don't think when Lord Seaton founded the place in 1829, it was really an elite school. It was just all there was. Upper Canada College was the first school historically in the province of Upper Canada, but it was not so clear that it had that same significance then as it does now. Anybody who says, "I joined the elite when I joined Upper Canada College" is saying that from the perspective of looking back from the 1990s.

In my day, it was a very cynical age. At university, when the war veterans came back, they would tear down the goal posts. People were supposed to wear coats and ties in the great hall of Hart House, but they just ignored it. The warden of Hart House had to resign. It was that kind of age. The war shakes you up. A lot of people are killed. The old values from the old generation failed because of the war.

I think UCC would help my son's generation more because they are brighter people. My son Henry, who graduated in 1984, enjoyed UCC. I think his class will provide a generation of leaders in all fields. I think that's more clear for his class than mine. I'd have to look at the old issues of the *College Times* because I can't remember who was all there.

Unfortunately, when you go to the old boys' dinners, there are too many guys who say, "The best years of my life were at Upper Canada." That should never be. Because of their memories, their hearts come back to it. But they should think about what they can do in the future. Many of these guys think UCC is just the cat's meow, but it's nothing but a training ground. If they are good, then it's a case of going on to the next stage. You're just still a kid. You've got to get to university and then go out in the real world. There are too many guys whose high point in their lives came when they were eighteen years old at Upper Canada College. I still see those type of guys around. I really don't know what the hell UCC was preparing you for in those days.

JOHN CRISPO

1946–52

Professor of political economy,
University of Toronto

I HAVE ONLY ONE really clear memory of Upper Canada. That is when I realized that the way to succeed was to fail. To be head of house or head of battalion, spending an extra year in Grade 13 really made a difference. I was just livid about this. Don Elliot, an undertaker's son, and I went to the principal, Dr. Sowby, because we wanted the school to bar anybody from any student office who failed academically. We did not get much satisfaction. But I thought that you should not get further ahead politically by failing.

When I went to UCC, they accepted anybody with connections and money and did not care whether you were good academically. Now they can get people with connections, money, and a reasonable academic ability. If you are no good, unless your father is E. P. Taylor or the equivalent, they will throw you out because they have such a lineup of candidates who will pay them big bucks. In my time, they were willing to take the bucks and compromise the standards, which I thought was wrong. It penalized those of us who were working hard and trying to complete high school in the normal five years.

I cannot even remember whether on balance UCC was a happy or unhappy experience. I really have a problem with recollection, which probably indicates that I have some deep, inner-psychological problem that I do not want to come to grips with. I have blanked out so much of my life, it is frightening.

I made a lot of friends at UCC that I still have. I was in the prep for a couple of years. I never held any office. I do not even remember if I was a prefect or steward in McHugh's House. I did not get a good education. They were appalling in maths, physics, and chemistry, in what I would call the hard subjects. In a lot of the courses, the way they taught you Grade 13 was to tell you, "Go buy Coles cribs." We would memorize all the answers to the previous years' examinations. That is how I passed Latin and God knows how many other subjects.

I think that they did give you a well-rounded life, in the sense that they compelled you to play sports and participate in the battalion. I am not sure that I enjoyed either one, but I think that it was a good experience to have. I think that I boxed one year and hated it. I never was very athletic. I was an abject failure in the battalion. I got to be corporal. Barry Rogers, myself, and another guy were all corporals leading the three ranks of a platoon. Just to be different, we said, "No matter which way the lieutenant orders us to turn next time, the centre rank goes straight and the other two ranks go in opposite directions. Pass it back." Of course when we did that, there went my corporalship.

Looking back on it, I wish I had gone to a coeducational institution. I did not get to know what women were all about until I got to university, which is a terrible gap. In non-business areas, that probably is the biggest single regret of my life. Upper Canada did not give you much exposure to women. My parents frightened me to death about sex, which was probably just as inhibiting. I would not blame the school entirely, but I would rather have gone to a coeducational school.

I got caned once by I. K. Shearer, who was a diabolical creature. He happened to pop by one day when I was throwing a spitball. He came into the room, and I died. He pointed at me and told me that I had to come into his office after school and get caned. I will never forget his cupboard full of canes. I did not dislike him, but I think that he was a bit sick. When I came after school, he said, "Now, Mr. Crispo, there is a choice of canes here. Let me explain. This is the whippy one. It gives you a little more snap, but it does not have quite the weight of one of my stiff ones. Now this one really gives you a crack, but I cannot swing it as hard because it does not have any whip to it."

I remember Shearer saying, "You pick your cane." I do not remember which one I picked. I just remember this crazy guy saying, "Take down your pants." I have forgotten how many whacks I got, but I knew that I had been whacked. But I never really resented it and I have not ended up being against corporal punishment.

Years later, I was invited back twice to address the boys in the prayer hall. I gave an address called "Upper Canada College Students in a Sick Society." I told them that their parents, by and large, were ripping off society. I said UCC boys were not constructive members of society because they were spoiled brats. They owed something to society but they would probably never repay it because they were going to follow in their parents' footsteps onto Bay Street, ripping off people with inside information and conflict of interest. If you were a failure, you would not have to worry. The insurance industry picked you up because presumably you had some social skills and you could use those to con the friends you had at Upper Canada into buying insurance and keeping you alive.

I got a standing ovation. The students had never heard heresy like this before. I will never forget the principal's reaction. He was just appalled. He said, "My Grade 11s and 12s can take it, but what about my 9s and 10s?" He just took off from the platform. Unfortunately, I had left my coat in his office, so I had to go back in. There is a tradition of serving tea for the speaker. When the poor secretary started bringing in the tea, the principal said, "No tea! This man is not staying!"

I am a disgrace as a graduate. I have never been to an old boys' reunion, which probably says something about how I felt about the place. There has to be something in me, deep down, that is fairly bitter and negative about UCC. I have never contributed a nickel to the school, which I guess indicates some lack of gratitude.

Somebody at OISE, who is writing a book on success, asked people, "Who are the two people who contributed most to your success?" I said my father, because I fought him, and that gave me the urge to go and learn about things so that I could fight him better. There was also a left-wing professor of industrial relations at the U of T who was terribly discriminated against his whole life. Once I took his course, I got all the ammunition I needed to fight my father about unions. He hated unions. Then I was down at MIT and did industrial relations. But none of that was in me when I was at Upper Canada.

My father was pretty harsh. Once I got to the point where I realized that I did not agree with him on a lot of things and I had the guts to stand up to him, the friction, oh Jesus. In fact, I feel very guilty about the way I treated him. I treated him like shit and I now realize that he was a very good man. But if he said something was black, I said it was white, and off we went. He was a very strong-willed man and I ended up being very strong-willed. Clash, clash, clash. Oh God, it was just terrible.

My father never accepted my choice of profession. We argued until the day he died. He was a TCS old boy and a manufacturer's agent, and I think it's fair to say he hated much of his job. He eventually said, "Look, what you really want to be is a lawyer." I have never forgotten what he said: "Law will give you the most diversified licence to steal on the face of the earth."

ROBERT MORRIS

1948 – 53

Lawyer

WHEN I WAS in my final year boarding at UCC, I remember two fellows who were a year or two behind me. One of these boys was slightly older than the other, but they became great friends. My first gay experience was with the two of them in the senior boys' shower in the basement of Seaton's House. They'd say, "If you meet us at six in the morning, we'll have a little fun and games."

Why did they pick me out of everybody in the house? Did I look that way or something? I don't know. Now, I'm sure that it was only an experiment. Both of them went on to marry women. One of them is now a high-profile old boy. God, I was eighteen, one must have been sixteen and the other perhaps fourteen. This happened no more than a couple of times. We ended it, but not because somebody told us to end it. It just didn't go any further than that.

Those few episodes were my only sexual experiences until, God, I was practising law many years later. I was so naive. I didn't even masturbate until my final year at UCC. I remember a prefect in my boarding house giving a new boy hell for masturbating. He said, "You're disturbing other boys in the dorm. The house mother has asked me to tell you to cut back on it." After he left, I asked, "What's masturbating?" The boy went red and said, "Are you crazy or something?"

I didn't know my own sexual orientation at the time, but some of the masters gave me a sense of confirmation. In hindsight, I had the strongest feeling that the faculty members who made me feel most comfortable were themselves gay. I feel strongly that some of these men were very important in my own life and self-affirmation.

I thought the world of a gay master, John Linn, a musician and a teacher of music. I remember him pounding the old keyboard on some Gilbert and Sullivan production like *Iolanthe*. Willie Orr, the classics master who taught at UCC for over forty years, was a wonderful man. He knew we were using crib notes and he knew how to use a Coles crib against you, which was marvellous. Carrying on with his students in Greek and students in Latin, it was hilarious. But he devoted his life to the school.

Jay D. MacDonald was another remarkable master. I vividly remember him as a person whose love of theatre was such that it grabbed everybody. I still think of classmates of mine who were drawn to theatre. We had different backgrounds, but he seemed to inspire a feeling for what we could achieve and self-realize. Those years of theatre were tremendous for me.

I remember saying to Jay MacDonald, "What if instead of going on to university, I should go to New York to act?" I remember him looking at me sternly and saying, "Well, Bob, you know, for every actor working, there's ten thousand starving down there. You should know that it's rough." But honest to God, I still wish I had gone. I'd likely have been dead of AIDS many years ago. On the other hand, I think I would have realized a hell of a lot about myself.

When I look at my time at Upper Canada, I'm sure 80 per cent of the masters were memorable and positive in my life. They kept up the tradition, teacher to student, but you felt so comfortable as a student that it was very creative.

Looking back at pictures of myself at UCC, I should have known I was gay. But I had nothing to compare myself with. The faculty members who were gay would have known or sensed it, but they were totally prohibited from reaching out to adolescents. It must have been very difficult for them. I have a friend who taught for years in the Scarborough Board of Education and he said to me, "Bob, this student is gay. It's so frustrating. You can see it in a fifteen- or sixteen-year-old boy and yet you're not permitted to do anything. In fact, you could be fired for affirming the person."

In university, I did an unusual amount of drinking, and I'm sure if drugs had been available to me, I would have buried myself. I have a friend who is dying of AIDS. He's about six months older than I am – I'm sixty – and he sees so many different psychiatrists. He got married and his children are all grown up. It's just the last two and a half years that he's been out, but his whole life was affected.

I was about thirty-five when I consciously recognized I was gay. I tried to incorporate it into my law career in Kitchener. My private life was so detached from my professional life that it was ridiculous. You buy yourself in. My brother had a family, so I thought I would too. They were living in Kitchener and that was one reason I moved there in the mid-sixties. I thought, I can be useful by trying to help them out financially and in their lives. I had no sexual relationships.

In my forties, largely because I was repressing my sexual self, I had a nervous breakdown and I stopped administering my office. It was pathetic. My staff just couldn't get any direction and finally I just had to close down. There was just nothing I could do. I moved back to Toronto, and that was when I came out. I suddenly had to admit that I had been untrue to myself for twenty years.

I had buried myself in work and in religion. In 1988 I graduated with a degree in theology because I wanted to take on the advocacy of my genus in theological circles, particularly in the Presbyterian church, which may be the oddest group of people in Canada. It's amazing how they're always shooting themselves in the foot, clinging to traditionalist points of view.

My job with the Presbyterian Gay/Lesbian Alliance occupies my time now. I am mailing nationally all the time, sending material to clerks of session, moderators of church sessions, ministers. I attend Glenview Presbyterian Church, where so many of the people have connections to places like Upper Canada. They depend on tradition for their roots, which is understandable. But sometimes you've got to introduce them to new understandings. Times are a-changing.

We have a group at Glenview Presbyterian Church called Parents and Friends of Lesbians and Gays. It's amazing how young the parents' children are who are identifying themselves as being gay. For me, it's wonderful to see them do it at age nineteen or twenty. How fortunate they are in many respects. In my day, it would have been just unbelievable.

I learned that I am HIV positive in 1988. I feel a loss of energy, but I'm still able to work and carry on. My T-cell counts are down to around 250 or 200, so my time is limited. That's reality. I'll be lucky to live a few more years. There are things I'd like to see done, but I know that they're not going to be done, so I end up saying, "Who could I get to take this over?"

I have always remembered a guy at UCC named Richard. Dear old Richard. He was about five feet four inches and very athletic, but because of his size he could never make the school teams. But he was a hell of a fine guy. He has disappeared. Every year or two, I phone up the school and say, "Any news of Richard?" They can't find him. I think he went to Montreal. I'm sure he's gay. He probably came out in the 1960s when it was easier to come out. He may well have suicided. God help him.

I also remember a fellow in Greek class at UCC. His father was a retired British army colonel who insisted that he go into engineering. He wanted to get engaged to a woman he met at the university. His father forbade him marrying this woman, so he suicided. What a hell of a waste. You can't connect that to UCC, although these people seem to be drawn to that institution. There was a boy at UCC, nine or ten years younger than I was, named John Medland. He became sick of living and eventually killed himself. I'm sure he was gay. He made a couple of passes at me at the time. I didn't know what the hell was going on.

I really do feel that I've got to stand up with some gay UCC alumni. It's time we drew attention to this issue at UCC. David Medland, John's younger brother, is a UCC old boy who is very informed on gay issues. He's had four or five people die in his home, friends that he's lost to AIDS. I'd like to go to UCC and talk. They should think of developing a program to deal with the question of sexual orientation, especially in adolescence. Every board of education has to face this issue eventually.

STEPHEN CLARKSON

1945–55

Professor of political economy,
University of Toronto

THE OVERWHELMING MEMORY I have of Upper Canada was its Englishness. The headmaster at the prep, Alan Stephen, was very English, as was Tim Gibson, my first form master. There were certainly Canadian-born teachers, but you wouldn't have necessarily known it from the way they spoke.

I lived on an isolated farm north of Toronto as a child. My mother was

English and my father, while coming from a very established family of accountants in Toronto, had gone British by marriage, then by profession. He spent twenty years of his engineering career in England.

So this English influence meant that I was brought up reading Arthur Ransome, G. A. Henty, *Boys' Own Annual*, and my older brothers' old copies of *Chum*. I remember my mother, who taught me to read and write at an early age, reading to me from a book called *The Story of Britain*, which told of Queen Boadicea and "our country," which was England. We learned to pronounce words in particular ways, even if Canadians pronounced them differently. I said "out of doors," not "outdoors," or "forsigh-thia," not "forsythia." So there wasn't any culture shock going to the prep at age seven.

At UCC, I don't recall feeling any sense of connection with the city, province, or country. The school was, as it still is, geographically very much an island, isolated in its gorgeous grounds in the middle of Toronto and, although we didn't know they were on the verge of collapsing, its quite impressive buildings.

Beginning in 1948, the upper school was run by the Reverend C. W. Sowby, who had been recruited from an Anglo-Irish school, presumably because it was thought there wasn't anyone in the Dominion of Canada qualified to run a boys' private school. Dr. Sowby set a tone which certainly contributed to the isolated quality of the place. He had no real connection with the society, except through the old boys he had to deal with.

In the prep, I was in a choir and I played in the band. All I can remember is Gilbert and Sullivan, followed by Gilbert and Sullivan, after which we looked forward to another Gilbert and Sullivan production! There was no Canadian culture, literature, or history. I can't remember any Canadian art or music. I eventually became editor of the *College Times* and head boy. The prizes I would get on Prize Day would be books bound in leather with gilt lettering. I don't think I ever opened one. All the symbols were those of the imperial centre.

In those days, there was probably less corporal punishment in the prep than in the upper school, and less for day boys than for boarders. In the upper school, I was caned by I. K. Shearer, but it is not in my mind as a big thing. There wasn't homosexual abuse in my experience, but that's not to say it didn't exist.

The school's culture was its own world. The implicit and explicit message was powerfully elitist: You are the select. You are better than everyone else. Something is expected of you. The word *privileged* would have been implied, if not explicitly used. If you had been given a lot – intellectually, financially, or socially – a lot was expected of you.

I guess that's the good side of it. The other side of the coin was the enormous sense of superiority. Everybody else was considered inferior, including those at the other boys' private schools. As for people who went to public schools, it was quite amazing to find out that they could put two or three words together and punch away at a sentence. When it came time to emerge from the incubator of UCC into the real world, it was quite a shock.

The school could have been anywhere in the British Empire – India, Australia, South Africa, Canada. UCC was an implanted institution, with a culture and religion similar to other Commonwealth educational institutions based on the imperial format, particularly Trinity College at the University of Toronto, where I went after UCC. I then went to Oxford University, which was like going to the real thing for the first time. At Oxford I came up against English snobbery and the English class system, which made me aware of where I fitted in the Canadian social hierarchy.

I was a Rhodes Scholar. An interesting question is the extent to which the Rhodes Scholarship institution is both an imperial and a class-based phenomenon. A student of mine who got the Rhodes Scholarship in 1991 was asked in the interview, "How is it that you are so accomplished and yet you went to a high school?" She was amazed that the question would be asked. Clearly the Rhodes institution itself is based on the values that Canadian private schools adhere to and propagate. It's probably true that if I had done equally well academically, but had not gone to Upper Canada College, I would not have won the Rhodes Scholarship.

UCC clearly ill-prepared me for the real world. I make a distinction between formal education – learning to read, write, and do arithmetic – and cultural education. That I was taught cricket, so that when I was in the navy I didn't know how to play baseball, is a symbol of how the school consciously educated its clientele not to integrate into the society for which they were training to be the leaders.

At that time, Canada was still a pre-national colony, not yet a nation-state. I was at UCC from 1945 to 1955, which was the end of the one period when the Canadian university system had produced an indigenous social science. At UCC, I knew none of those names – Harold Innis, Donald Creighton, S. D. Clark, Brough McPherson, or, in literature, that of Northrop Frye. These men were teaching less than a mile away at the University of Toronto campus, but none of my UCC masters had any connection with that Canadian school of thought.

The inculcation of leadership was most powerful when people came regularly to talk to us in prayers. Every other day, there would be a speaker. My oldest brother, my only sibling who stayed in Canada, had been the aide-de-camp of Viscount Montgomery during the war. Because he had a bona fide British connection, he was eligible to come and talk to the boys at Upper Canada.

I finally got a sense of my own country by seeing what other countries were like. It was really a double experience. At Oxford I could see how I had been programmed to be a kind of mock Englishman. It didn't work, because the English certainly didn't think I was English, even though I had been born in England and had relatives there. I ran up against every prejudice that the English bestow on foreigners, expressed in the well-known phrase, "The wogs begin at Calais." You are not part of what they consider the best society in the world.

I went to Paris for a year because I felt I should know French as a Canadian. I had studied French at the University of Toronto but I hadn't learned to speak it. I ended up staying in Paris and doing my doctorate. I had a positive experience there, whereas Oxford had been negative. In France I saw a nation-state in operation. It was very conscious of the need to preserve and develop itself, spending enormous efforts on educating its own citizens and its own future leaders in an extremely rigorous way.

France was a country that knew what it was. Its elite was proud of what it was, and not without arrogance. The French think they have the greatest civilization in the world and they have some grounds for thinking it. France gave me a sense of what Canada wasn't. It gave me a sense of what the Canadian elite, which I had been educated to be part of, was doing – or not doing – in this country.

One can argue that UCC, as the pre-eminent private school in English Canada, has had a large impact on the country. In my judgement, it has been largely negative. As I see it, Canada's elite has been protected throughout its history by the Pax Britannica, which made it incapable even of conceiving a threat to its own integrity. There are thinkers who are exceptions, of course, such as the historian Stanley Ryerson, but Canada wasn't brought up with any consciousness of itself other than as an extension of some other society.

UCC was originally set up in 1829 to perpetuate the elite, at that time the oligarchy of the Family Compact, which needed to protect itself against the masses internally and against the American threat externally. The irony is that, as UCC has evolved, it has really defeated its own purposes. It prepared its elite to accept a continuation of imperial dependency that has undermined its own integrity. There are a number of paradoxes in this, since the new American imperial culture is less democratic, and more class ridden and polarized, than the present Canadian dependency.

The Canadian business community, but also largely the media and the academic establishments, are fundamentally incapable of seeing themselves, since they have always been an extension of other societies. I gather

Upper Canada currently prides itself on how large a proportion of its graduating class are accepted by American Ivy League universities. I take that to be quite in the tradition of the school, although it represents a wry switch from one imperial centre to the other.

The overall impact of UCC on the country is personified in Michael Wilson, an architect of the North American Free Trade Agreement and the GST and a contemporary of mine at UCC. Unless he is a liar – a word he used to describe John Turner – he epitomizes someone who is very comfortable with the values of the new empire. He can take the American prescription for what is good for Canada the way earlier generations – and the way his masters at Upper Canada – would have taken the British prescription for what was good for Canada.

In the pathology of Canada, namely its incapacity to perceive its own interests as different from and threatened by those of its dominant partner, there is something of a historic tragedy. Canada has come to the position where the only thing it can do is tag on to the economic and political system of a declining American hegemony. I see Upper Canada College as a microcosm of the problem.

What is the sense of community that powerful UCC old boys like Conrad Black, Ken Thomson, Ted Rogers, and John Eaton have? Is there any evidence that it is national? What would their actions have been had they gone to a school which gave them the sense of community they would have had as Frenchmen going to a French private school, or Brits going to Eton or Harrow?

Had influential UCC old boys absorbed a national culture, it is more likely that their role as leading capitalists in our capitalist economy would have enhanced our capacity to cope in the world. The tremendous advances that were made in the late nineteenth century – the development of Massey Harris, for instance, as the prime multinational, high-tech leader in an industry where Canada had some comparative advantage – were followed by our gradual sellout in the twentieth century. That happened presumably largely because our business class would rather manage an American multinational than compete toe-to-toe.

A comparison might be Sweden. At the end of the nineteenth century, Sweden was less developed than Canada in manufacturing capacity. Like Canada, it was a staple producer and exporter. But Sweden didn't allow foreign ownership. Its elites knew the difference between German ownership and Swedish ownership. They didn't have high tariffs and their banking system helped their entrepreneurs develop.

The Canadian banking system, staffed by a large number of graduates of Upper Canada College, seems to favour dealing in large sums with companies from New York than with companies from Quebec. In fact, Quebec goes to the American market for money because they can't get it in Toronto. If UCC had been able to affirm its own identity earlier, rather than keep the umbilical cord pulsing decade after decade, it might have helped develop an indigenous bourgeoisie that identified its fortunes with its own country. Many wealthy UCC old boys, with the possible exception of John Bassett, seem to identify with their fortunes, rather than with their society. It isn't just to say that this is an Upper Canada phenomenon: Campeau, Desmarais, and Bronfman, minor players in the global capitalist market, are other examples.

A few years ago, the school used John Porter's sociological data published in his book, *The Vertical Mosaic* – namely, that UCC had produced a disproportionately high number of leaders in all walks of Canadian life – as fundraising material. If UCC has indeed produced a disproportionate share, then the school has to accept some responsibility for where those leaders have led the country – to the brink of collapse.

MICHAEL WILSON

1949 – 55

Former Progressive Conservative minister of finance

I PLAYED SOME HOCKEY at UCC, but I wasn't a very good skater, which is a fair handicap in hockey. I played goal. I only had to go from one post to the other rather than one end of the rink to the other. I also started playing squash at UCC, and I've played ever since.

I was probably best in football, although I never made the first team. I used to enjoy scrimmages with the first-team players. They didn't take them very seriously, but I did. I said, "I'm going to show these SOBs that there is someone on the second team who can knock them around." They used to take me aside and say, "It's not done, Mike. These are practices. Don't scrap so hard."

Ted Buxton, the phys ed master, taught me how to box. I remember when I was living in Montreal and walked around the rough area of the city, I would get pushed around. So when I learned that there was boxing at UCC, I said, "I've got to take boxing. No one's going to push me around. No one's going to call me a ninety-eight-pound weakling and kick sand in my face." Buxton said, "If you get his glove between your shoulder and your head, hold his arm there and then hammer him." He knew all the tricks.

We were shit disturbers at that time. We were terrible with Rudolf Fluegge, the German teacher. I found out later that he had a fairly rough time during the war. One time, we hid behind the door and as soon as he walked in, we slammed it shut and turned the lights out. It was probably disarming for someone who had gone through some pretty rough times in the war, although that never crossed our minds.

We pulled a bunch of pranks. In the old building on the top floor, we would all start to shake our feet in unison and the old wooden floors would shake. The chalk would jump off the blackboard and inkwells would slide along the desks. It was silly, but fun at the time.

Corporal punishment was still in force. I. K. Shearer got after me. I had passed some answers on to one of my friends, who was not very good at certain subjects. Mr. Shearer caught us both and we were caned. It certainly wasn't something I'd go out of my way to repeat, but it wasn't terribly painful. I think what probably affected my future behaviour more was Shearer saying, "Don't forget your father is on the board of governors of the school. This is not appropriate for you to do. You should have a better sense of responsibility and the impact that can have on him." I think those words had more impact on me than my sore ass.

My father was a governor of Upper Canada College and ultimately chairman of the board of governors in the 1960s. After graduating from UCC in 1922, he spent his entire career at National Trust. My two sons went to UCC in the 1980s and one is now with National Trust and another with the Toronto Dominion Bank. My father was a community-minded individual, being the chairman of the United Appeal in Toronto and the founding president of what is now the Heart and Stroke Foundation. His sense of community service has been one of the key influences in my life.

The school made an effort to bring in leaders to talk to us. You had a sense that you were in an educational institution that was special. Implicitly, you were expected to use that. You were imbued with a sense of the importance of achievement. When people spoke to the assembly, the seeds were being sown. I can't remember the light going on and saying, "Gee, I want to be like that guy." It just evolved.

I was never an outgoing individual, not the rah-rah sort of guy, the actor, or the guy who would stand up in the class. Julian Porter, who was with us in the prep at UCC before he moved to UTS, was a great speaker. His father was a politician and Julian fit the mould. I remember saying to myself, I could never stand up in front of the class and do that.

I graduated from UCC in June of 1955 when I was seventeen. I wanted to go to university and I was good in numbers, algebra, geometry, and trigonometry. I knew I wanted something that made use of that talent, but at that point, I can't say I was thinking, When I grow up, I'm going to be the minister of finance.

TOM GODWIN

1947 – 55

Cardiologist

M ICHAEL WILSON AND I were each other's best friend for about eight years. I thought I related well with him. He used to come out to my dad's farm and I was over at his place quite a bit. We used to study a lot together. I really liked him.

In recent years I've been in contact with him just a few times. I remember he was asked about abortion at one meeting I was at. I knew what he thought about abortion – basically, if you want one, go get one. But he really didn't answer the question. I thought, Shit. Why don't you just say what you think? But of course, you can't do that if you're a politician.

Myself, I would never get elected because I would alienate every group. If I believed in capital punishment, I'd say so. Michael Wilson would have to temper his comments because that's how a politician works. It's funny: I was better in math than he was, and he became finance minister.

When I left Rosedale Public School and came to UCC, John Eaton and I were in the same class. By the time I graduated, I was two years ahead of him. I was reading the newspaper recently and the Eatons were visiting Vancouver, looking at a whole city block. Guess who's the head of the negotiating team? John Eaton. I thought, Holy shit! He was a nice guy, but he didn't have the brains. I think his brother Fred, who is now the Canadian high commissioner to the U.K., was smarter.

I liked the kids and masters in the prep, but when I got to the upper school, it was a different atmosphere. I guess a lot of my trouble at UCC was my own fault because I didn't like the discipline. Maybe I was a bit rowdy. I felt badly at UCC. I didn't achieve. I was never made a prefect, and I only got to the rank of lance corporal in the battalion, which I hated. I felt at Upper

Canada that I always got shit for having a poor attitude and not making the big effort. Yet I was always in the top third of the A form. I did well in my senior matric.

But I got shit for fooling around in the class and not paying attention. I thought it was so much better, especially if you had a good textbook, to go home and work like heck at home. I wasn't very bright. I had to work hard. I think I worked harder than most of my friends. I had a little bit of a problem. My older brother, Stuart, who was three years older, was definitely very bright.

When I came to the school, I think everybody, including my parents, expected me to achieve like my older brother had. In fact, my marks weren't that far off his, but he just walked through the school. He was excellent in math and science. I was better in English, and because I went to Quebec for a summer, I was good in French. I was better than the French teacher, I. K. Shearer, in French. That's how crappy his French was.

I had a terrible row with a Grade 12 German teacher, Fluegge, one of those guys who had no control of the class. Some guys in our class were real comedians. They just stretched the guy out of shape. I don't think I was the instigator, but I was right in there. One day I was talking when he came in. He walked up and punched me in the face. I got a fat lip. My father, who was an old boy, found out about it and hit the roof. The guy lost his job.

When I was in Grade 10, a teacher hit me across the ear with a cupped hand. I went out to football practice that night and then I went for a swim. When I got in the water, I had a terrific pain in my ear and I could hear a really funny sound. I went to the hospital and they found I had a perforated eardrum. Nothing was done about it because it was an "accident." The teacher's hand just happened to hit me on the side of the head.

I got into a lot of trouble at ucc. I just didn't fit in. I didn't enjoy going to school in the morning. I enjoy going to work every day at the Royal Columbian Hospital, where I've been almost twenty-five years now. I get on well with everybody. Everybody kids me, the patients and the nurses. As I get older, I'm becoming a father figure. I really like the place and I look forward to going in. I never felt that way about Upper Canada College.

I think ucc was bad in my time because Dr. Sowby was principal. To me, he was a despot. I remember I got caned for stupid things. In Grade 10, we had Sowby for Scripture classes. There was a Bible story about how a bunch of Philistines wanted to become Jewish. I didn't know what a Jew was because there was only one Jewish guy in our whole school at that time, Howard Marx. We called him "Harpo." Howard was a nice guy, but he was very quiet and didn't play any sports.

In the story, all the Philistines who were supposed to become Jewish had to be circumcised. I couldn't imagine why anybody would want to be a Jew in the first place, let alone go through circumcision. So I turned around to make a comment to the guy behind me and I heard a big bang on the desk. Sowby told me to get out. At the end of class, he called me back in and asked me what I was laughing at. I said, "Circumcision." He said, "I thought so. You should be caned for that." I got six strokes.

Then in my last year, I came into the prayer hall one morning and Stephen Clarkson was sitting in my usual seat. Stephen Clarkson was a very good boy and did what he was told. He was a model student, head boy, a steward, very smart. I said, "That's where I sit." He wouldn't move, so I just took him underneath the knee, pulled him out of the seat, and sat down.

He comes rushing at me, so I give him a little bit of a punch. He falls. Just then, the procession of masters comes into the prayer hall. The next thing I know, I get called into Sowby's office. I could have had a Saturday morning gating, but I had to go and help my father on his farm on Saturday. So I got caned instead. It makes quite a bruise. Nowadays, people would consider it assault.

Although I didn't like Upper Canada, you worked hard. In public school, if you were at the bottom of your class, you were a bit of a hero. At UCC, if you were at the top of your class, you weren't considered a sucker. I think I was motivated to work hard because I hated the system. I thought I could beat them at their own game. I could do it my way and still achieve.

If I had conformed to what they wanted, if I was malleable like my older brother, I would have been left alone. But I was outspoken in class. I think it is also because I was quite physical. I wasn't afraid to speak my mind even though they didn't like what I said. I got in a fair number of fights because I didn't like what happened to people.

Something else really annoyed me. After Grade 13, they had a sixth form which was designed to get you prepared for university. They wanted me to come back for it. They told me they would make me a prefect. I couldn't believe they wanted me to come back to that school! Didn't they realize how much I hated it?

My father had done quite well when he was at UCC. He could never understand why I didn't fit in. My father tried to sit down with me at home and discuss my problems at school. He wondered why I wasn't getting on and always getting crap for lack of effort, yet I would get good marks. I would say, "Who cares about the effort? Look at what the results are! I do well at school." I guess I was disrespectful. I didn't like the system. I didn't respect them and I thought I had reason not to.

I think my father was disappointed that his sons didn't take advantage of the old-boy contacts at UCC. I didn't need contacts, of course, being in medicine. When I finished medicine, I had lots of job offers in Toronto and I came out west by choice. One of the best decisions I ever made was to come out to Royal Columbian Hospital. I believe a sick heart patient has got a better chance at the Royal Columbian than anywhere else. It's nice to feel part of that team.

I get great satisfaction out of building things. When I was a kid, I liked manual labour, carpentry, and cutting trees. I worked on a fishing boat one summer. But at Upper Canada, to be a carpenter or plumber was just not on. You've got to let kids do what they want to do.

I think we have to revise our definition of success. I've got a neighbour who's a truck driver. He's got a really nice wife and four really nice kids. I often feel jealous of him. It would be great to come home in the afternoon after you've delivered your load, sit out on the porch, have a beer, and not worry that your place is a mess. He's laid back enough that he can do the things he wants to. A lot of people, including federal cabinet ministers, have achieved things in life by licking someone's ass.

I think I'm successful. I have a very beautiful family. My wife and I have four kids who really like us. We're good friends. I have a job that I enjoy. I feel that I'm doing some good. We have a 120-acre farm and a 100-cow-calf operation. We've planted 10,000 trees on the place. We salvaged a salmon stream which the previous owners had just about destroyed. I don't watch television. I got my pilot's licence and I like to fly my little homebuilt airplane with a souped-up engine in it. My life is quite rich.

ANDREW HUTCHISON

1950–56

Anglican bishop of Montreal

I FAILED PHYSICS at UCC in Grade 13, so I didn't officially matriculate. The family fortunes were in trouble and I felt ashamed of the burden of the expense of repeating a whole extra year. At the time, I didn't feel the system had failed me. It's only now, when I look back on it.

Failing was awkward because at the end of Grade 13 I had won the Herbert Mason Medal, along with Joe MacInnis, who later became an explorer. Joe won the gold and I won the silver medal. I had been CO of the battalion and a steward, and here I had missed a subject. Obviously, I couldn't go back to the school under those circumstances.

So I immediately went out to work for the Arrow Shirt Company, still a teenager. They shipped me off to Winnipeg, where I enjoyed running a territory. I then came back to head office and became their sales promotion manager at a very young age. From there, I started a wire and sheet metal production business of my own when I was in my twenties. John Eaton, a UCC contemporary, helped me out financially with it.

My company was probably the second largest of its kind in Toronto at that time. I designed and produced all the street corner news boxes, which in those days were either for the Toronto *Telegram* or the *Toronto Star*. I was not yet thirty. I had the kind of experience that a lot of people don't get until middle age. Then I looked around and thought, Is this all there is?

Under my leaving class picture in the *College Times*, my intended profession was listed as Anglican priest. I had been very serious about religion from an early age. I began to talk to my wife and she gave me a push. I went to York University just as they were inventing it. I nagged away at undergraduate studies at night. Eventually, I went full time. I went on to Trinity College to finish up. I was ordained in 1969. I came down to Montreal in 1984 as dean of the cathedral. In 1990 I became bishop.

At Upper Canada, I was a fish out of water in one sense. Despite all the family stock – my family's links with the school are ancient – there was no money around. My mother died of cancer when I was thirteen, so I came to UCC from Lakefield, where I'd boarded for six years. I found it difficult. I'd go off on a Saturday afternoon and watch the football game with John Eaton. I'd walk into his palace of a house on Dunvegan Road in Forest Hill and think, How can I return this kind of thing? The late John Bassett was also a friend. I'd pick him up on the way to school the odd time. How on earth do you balance that? Socially I felt on solid and equal ground, but financially I found it mind blowing and very difficult to cope with.

Upper Canada put a lot of responsibility on me. At sixteen, I was the youngest commanding officer that the cadet battalion had ever had. At that time, there were 480 boys in the battalion, so it was serious stuff. I remember discussing it with my father. The advice he gave me was, "Whenever responsibility is offered to you, take it. There are too many people in life who don't. If it has been offered to you, it is probably because you have something that you're not aware of that you have to give."

I learned how to cope with that responsibility effectively. I made a contribution. It reinforced my Burnsian belief that "A man's a man for all that." I found I was able to walk among the Eatons and the Bassetts and recognize that we are all fundamentally human beings and that one need not be impressed by the power of money, influence, or position. That was also part of the UCC legacy.

Another thing that really got reinforced at UCC was a sense of confidence and privilege. At the time, we were nauseated to hear yet another speaker in the prayer hall saying, "Boys, you've got the world in your hands. You can do anything you like." But it was, and remains, fundamentally true. You have opportunities and choices that most people would surrender their life to get. Upper Canada has produced men who are flexible, open, and adaptable to virtually any circumstance. Whether it be working at an old mission, on the streets in Thailand, or in the towers of Bay Street, there's a level of adaptability that's impressive. I'm certainly grateful to have had a piece of it.

At one point, I'd been away from both Lakefield and UCC for years. During the course of a few weeks, I went to an old-boy event at Upper Canada and then, later, an old-boy event at Lakefield. At the Upper Canada event, the typical response was, "Hutch, how are you doing? Let me give you my card." There was all that hustling, talking about what everybody was doing and how they were scoring in the business world. Certainly in my time at Upper Canada, there was a lot of hustle going on. Conrad Black made the ultimate statement of that kind of hustle by breaking into an office and selling exam papers to other boys.

When I went to the old-boy event at Lakefield, I met old Hugh Ketchum who had taught me a thousand years ago. He said, "Hello, it's good to see you. I just bought a lovely old house north of the school. I wish you could see the sunset at night over the lake." It is just a different sort of dimension in life altogether. Lakefield had depth, quality, and a deep awareness of privilege, but it was at a different level than UCC.

There was a qualitative difference as well between Lakefield and Upper Canada in religion. My experience at Lakefield was morning and evening prayers in the Anglican tradition, seven days a week. I loved it. It really was an anchor for me at a difficult point in life. Upper Canada, which was losing some of the Anglican trappings, was a terribly secularizing kind of experience. What was called prayers was never anything more than assembly. The principal said a couple of prayers, a boy read a lesson, and we sang a hymn. What's religious about that?

That's why I say that UCC had nothing much to do with my religious formation. I was supportive of Dr. Sowby and what he was trying to do as an Anglican cleric, but I can't honestly say that Upper Canada was a fundamental religious influence. The greater influence was Grace Church on-the-Hill, where I was deeply involved as a lay reader from an early age.

The spiritual roots just aren't present in society any more, which is a major problem for all of us. Everything that has been substituted has been found wanting. Of course, I understand that the church has let people down, particularly in Quebec. The abandonment of the religious institutions is thoroughly understood. The great sadness is that it comes just at a time when the spiritual needs worldwide are deeper than they have been for generations. I had a guy in my office just the other day who had millions in the bank. He had done so well materially, and yet he was in a mess. He said, "Please, will you pray for me and help me work through a few things about what it is like to be alive in the world."

Out on the street, there are more people in an obvious spiritual search than has been the case since the thirteenth century. I see it in people rushing into concerns about native spirituality, the environment, justice, peace, all kinds of things that never got talked about in the board rooms. These issues now occupy 60 per cent of the agenda. People are running in all directions in search of something. I'm not suggesting that we go back to nineteenth-century religion. Far from it. But we're going to be in major crisis if we don't awfully soon find a way of doing something serious and intentional about spirituality. The rest is going to let you down.

So a lot of what Upper Canada taught us was a lie. All the stuff that we thought would make life good and beautiful hasn't worked. What do you do about it? It's a problem for the school and it's a problem for society.

JOHN EATON

1945–57

Chairman, T. Eaton Company of Canada

WE LIVED right around the corner from UCC on Dunvegan Road, so as a young boy I was always aware of the school and, of course, the neighbouring sister school, Bishop Strachan. I remember seeing the UCC boys in blue and the BSS girls in crimson and grey going past our house.

I liked the school immediately. Going to the outdoor rinks was one of my favourite things to do. I'd put my skates on at home and try to skate across to Upper Canada. I don't think it did the skates any good. I'd skate for hours on the outdoor rink when I was eight or nine.

I remember in 1946 awaiting the arrival of a Vampire Jet, one of the first jet fighters, coming from England. We stood around and waited for a good half hour. The pilot was supposed to be over at 10:00 A.M., but he didn't come until about 10:30. It whooshed over. We kids were delighted.

The battalion always intrigued me. In the early days just after World War II, we hadn't really established that the Russians were our enemies. In the prep, we were always fascinated to watch the sham battles on the big oval at the upper school. There would be three or four upper school guys dressed in Nazi uniforms who were always triumphed over. Guys would fire blank ammunition and capture the Nazis. We were still toning down from the Nazi peril in Germany and the yellow peril in Japan. There was a very strong feeling for the cadet battalion.

The battalion was the only line of defence against the Fenian Raids in 1866. Not bad for a bunch of high school kids! I'm very proud that that's part of the history of the school, and I believe most old boys are. There was a period when some people at UCC said, "Shame! Shame!" I say, "Shame on them!" People with a uniform were spat on during the Vietnam War, but it changed around in 1992 when we were chasing Saddam Hussein across the desert.

I boarded for a year at the prep in the senior B dormitory. It was a lot of fun. The residence in the old Peacock Building was rather austere. You were allowed to put a couple of pictures up on your wall. It was very institutional, very barracks-like, but everyone was the same and you really didn't care. We got to go home once in a while. We also got to go to Norval, the school property in the country, which was more or less total playtime. We'd look for frogs, tadpoles, grasshoppers, and butterflies for biology or general science, as we called it in those days. That was a lot of fun.

Television didn't come around until I was in the upper school. Radio was the main entertainment. We tried to sneak the crystal radio sets into the dormitory so we could listen to them. Although we hid them, they were easily discovered by the masters. If you did your homework, your grades were good, and you were careful, they would let you have the crystal set. But if you were a bad or obstreperous kid, they took it away.

Corporal punishment existed in those days, but I don't think it hurt anybody. It hurt at the time, I can verify that. I remember being caned. It hurt, but you survived. They also hung the bad guys in those days. That wasn't all bad, either.

My brother Fred followed me to the school by a year, Thor some years after that, and then George. Thor and George were only there for a short period of time. George went to Forest Hill and Thor went to St. Andrew's because they weren't happy at Upper Canada.

I was never a rebel. My brother George was a rebel. Now he's probably more right wing than I am. What can I say? If the older brother, as I was, is Mr. Straight Conservative all the time, the other brother doesn't want to be in the same mould. He wants to cut out and do his own thing. It's better to do your own thing and be happy in what you're doing.

In the upper school, the team spirit was stronger in the boarding houses than in the day houses. I was a day boy in Martland's House and a boarder in Seaton's House. I thought it was an all around, very healthy atmosphere. In sports, you were taught to try and win and put your best foot forward. If the other guy can beat you, shake his hand at the end. It wasn't win at all costs.

I recall the Hall Dennis Report on Education coming out in the late 1960s. At the time, I was working with the Old Boys' Association. We were very concerned about the Hall Dennis Report, which wanted to do away with competitiveness in the classroom. Everyone was to be judged equally. It would bring everyone to mediocrity. I recall being very distressed because it was really going to ruin the raison d'être of Upper Canada.

UCC was training guys to be leaders. They were teaching them how to be competitive, how to exist in a world that is competitive. The Hall Dennis people did away with the Grade 13 exams, which started to make everyone an amorphous bag of mush. There were no distinct flavours any more. I felt that that was terribly wrong. As has since been proven, it sure as hell was wrong.

I would suggest that maybe the reason for some of the boys' schools like Ridley, TCS, and Lakefield going coed is purely economic. They couldn't fill the bunks, so they may as well let in the other guys. I think in Metro Toronto there probably will always be enough boys to fill the boys' schools. There will always be enough girls to fill the girls' private schools. There will be no need to have coed schools. I would not like to see Upper Canada go coed. I always believe: If it ain't broke, don't fix it. Upper Canada ain't broke in more ways than one.

Upper Canada is sailing along. Sure, you tighten a bolt here and there. She ain't young and beautiful any more. But she's got a couple of new buildings and she's looking pretty damn good. She can go a few more miles.

I've got fond memories of all of my masters – Wilf Gallimore, Frank Brennan, Mike Bremner, Piff Biggar, Ducky Mallett, Swifty Grant, Art Killip, Pop Law, Dick Sadleir. They are legendary, wonderful men – Walter Ruffell, Muzz Greatrex, Sam Foote, Al Harris, Tim Gibson, Dick Howard. These are people you always remember. You leave the school calling them "sir." Then, when you come back as an old boy to the first dinner and maybe have a few too many beers, you say, "Well, Joe ..." He says, "Yes, John," and suddenly it's over.

I loved UCC. The school offered me whatever I wanted. I had a lot of fun, probably too much fun. Some of my pals from there are still my pals, and I've been out for over thirty-five years now. But it's not for everybody. If you want a good, broad education and a lot of extra programs to help you and fill out your young life, it's the place for you. But you have to work for it. It isn't handed to you on a plate.

ROBERT MARTIN

1946–57

Professor of law
University of Western Ontario

L ONG BEFORE I ever read Thomas Hobbes, I understood what he was talking about: "The condition of man is a condition of war of each against all." There was constant fighting in the prep boarding house. When I went home on Sundays, my mother would tell me that I would have black eyes and cuts on my face. I remember kids would fight at the slightest provocation. They would be non-stop fighting everywhere, especially amongst the boarders.

It was a very bizarre, nasty, and brutish existence. I wouldn't want to go to the point of suggesting the masters were full-blown psychopaths, but there were some very unpleasant men who clearly derived enjoyment out of bullying and beating little boys. The relish with which the masters caned the boys was quite extraordinary.

I went to Upper Canada College at age seven because my father was killed in World War II. I lived in a very odd household of four women – my mother, my grandmother, my sister, and the maid. My mother had decided that I needed a male hand in my upbringing, so she sent me to board at Upper Canada.

At that time, there were sixty boarders in the prep, fifteen boys in four dormitories. There wasn't one kid who came from what you might call a normal home, normal in the sense that there was a mother and father. I was often very, very unhappy. I can remember lying in bed quietly crying to myself and thinking about my father. Many times I would have dreams that there had been a mistake, that my father hadn't really been killed and he was coming back home. I had a sense that my father coming back home meant that I wouldn't have to board at Upper Canada any more.

When I look back on it, the thing about UCC was the complete absence of any kind of compassion or tenderness. Charlotte Cruickshank, the nurse's assistant, was kind, but everybody regarded Charlotte as being kind of soft. You could get away with things with her. But I think everybody was very pleased and grateful that she was there because she was a very warm, tender, and compassionate person. In many respects, Charlotte was the only island of humanity that these wretched little boys had in that savage little world.

In contrast, Agnes McQuistan, the nurse, was a truly frightening, ugly Scottish woman who looked like Babe Ruth. She had tight little buns of hair behind each ear. Boys definitely trembled in her presence. We used to have to line up and be inspected every night after our bath before going to bed. There was a rule that you had a bath three or four nights a week and then you would wash your hands, face, and feet the other nights.

At the time, I didn't understand the peculiar coldness of Scotswomen. My in-laws are Scots and I've travelled in Scotland and I've found the Scots are peculiarly cold people. It was only years and years later that I realized Agnes McQuistan was a typical cold Scot. Before you went to bed, you went down to her office wearing only your pyjama bottoms and slippers and stood in line. We passed in front of the nurse and held out our hands. She would turn them over and look behind your ears. In a thick Scots burr, she would tell you that you were "filllthy daarty." Once I remember her sending a kid back to wash himself again and hitting him over the head.

There was an awful lot of beating going on at Upper Canada. Even Mrs. Milsom, the only female teacher, did it. You would go up to the front of the class and you would be told to hold out your hand. She would pull a wooden spoon out of her desk, whack you on the hand, and then she would give you a candy. It seemed like the only people who didn't have the authority to beat the kids were the waitresses in the dining room, but beyond that, boys were being beaten all the time. It was a very nasty atmosphere.

It was also very competitive. I remember being flabbergasted by my first encounter with John McMurtry at the track and field day in the prep. He was very athletic. He would have been seven or eight. McMurtry was running in the 75- or 100-yard dash. When he came second or third, he threw himself on the grass, crying and screaming and pounding on the ground. I had never seen anyone behave like that before.

When I think about it, the constant harassment of students in the prep was astonishing. If you weren't getting beaten, you were having to run around the oval in front of the building. Masters would do incredible things in the classroom, like throwing blackboard brushes at boys and hitting boys with yardsticks. If anybody was caught chewing gum in Walter Ruffell's class, you would have to go up to the front of the classroom and take the gum out of your mouth. Ruffell would take the casing off the pencil sharpener and you would hold out your hand. He would shake the pencil shavings into your hand, roll the gum in it, and tell you to put the gum back into your mouth and keep chewing it.

One of my masters was clearly sadistic. Some of the masters were hard, cold, and mean, but this one clearly enjoyed causing pain to little boys. I remember an experience when I was around nine. We went to Norval, the school's country property north of Toronto, which was actually always fun. They would load up this band of little savages into a bus, drive us to Norval, and then turn us loose. We'd range all over the property, dig clay, torment small animals, get burrs all over ourselves, run up and down and throw each other into the river. It was very exhilarating. I have quite positive memories of being at Norval.

One time, all this master talked about on the bus was how he was going to spend his time at Norval searching around the woods for the ideal cane. He broadcast this throughout the bus. When we arrived, he went off into the woods and found a long piece of stick. On the bus back, he was lovingly whittling the stick, talking about how he was looking forward to the first opportunity to use it. Who is going to be the lucky little boy who gets it first?

I cannot remember what I did, but I did something on the bus. You didn't have to do very much to get caned. So he told me to come to his room after I had my bath. I remember this incident vividly. He was caressing this cane, sitting in a chair. Because it was bath night, I was just wearing my bathrobe.

He said, "Take off your bathrobe." As I was standing there naked, he was just looking at me. I knew there was something unusual about this. This was just odd. Then he told me to bend over a chair and he whacked me six times. One of the ways that you maintained your dignity and your self-respect with these masters was not to cry. It was very, very important because, in a sense, no matter how much you were beaten, if you didn't cry, you felt somehow you had won. You had beaten them.

The master really laid into me. It really hurt, but I remember thinking, No fucking way am I going to cry! I really had a deep, persistent hatred for this man that stayed with me. I wouldn't have any difficulty calling him a sadist. Some of the others weren't very tender, but he clearly gained a lot of pleasure and enjoyment out of inflicting pain on little boys.

On the other hand, Alan Stephen, the headmaster, was just a magnificent man. Mostly what one felt towards masters was fear, but I really liked and respected Stephen. He was always intellectually stimulating and demanding, but not in an oppressive way. He gave one a very fatherly kind of feeling.

Dick Howard, who succeeded Stephen as headmaster of the prep years later, was an arrogant prick. I have a deep dislike for him. When I was about nine, I was in his class. He took me aside one day and just launched into a tirade, saying, "I don't know why you're here at this school. You're a waste of time and you're no good." I thought, Why are you saying this? What did I do? I didn't know what I did.

I guess I was just generally undisciplined. That's why I got caned every day. I challenged people. I still have a report in which Alan Stephen wrote the headmaster's comments. His main comment was something to the effect of "Robert always seems to be 'agin' the government." I'm not sure to what extent that was already in me or to what extent Upper Canada brought that out in me, but the generally oppressive atmosphere certainly encouraged it.

The main thing I got out of Upper Canada College is a lifelong hatred of authority, which in many respects is probably not a bad thing. Certainly, it was deepened by going to Upper Canada. When I look back, it was just a very odd way to grow up. But it wasn't remotely as awful as accounts I've read of British boarding school life. At least our dormitories were heated and the sheets were dry and clean.

But I've never in my life been subjected to such terrible, sickeningly awful food. The things that they used to feed us! It was years and years after I stopped boarding before I really began to like food. It was terrible. For breakfast, they would bring out kippers, little fish swimming in grease with their eyes looking up at you. I've never seen scrambled eggs that were so disgusting. Maybe they used powdered eggs, because I don't think you could make real eggs with such a revolting consistency and colour. Once a week for lunch or dinner, we'd have tongue. They would put a whole fucking tongue right in the middle of the plate. There was no attempt to disguise it. It was just this grotesque thing sitting in the middle of your plate. It smelled awful. We had to eat it.

There was a master sitting at either end of the table and you were supposed to clean your plate. If you watched the master at either end and if you were quick enough, you would get your paper table napkin, scoop whatever it was you couldn't face eating into your napkin, and put it into your pocket. Of course, then you would forget about it. Quite often I'd wake up in the middle of the night and run down to the toilet and throw up because the food was so horrible, unpalatable, and downright inedible.

I boarded for four years in the prep, then I became a day boy. My mother decided I'd had enough boarding. On Sundays, the boarders used to get paraded down to Christ Church, Deer Park, off Yonge Street. After church, we could go home. You had to be back in the dorms at 6:00 or 7:00 P.M. When I was at home one Sunday having a bath, my mother came in and looked at my rear end. It was in the condition that it usually was in – bruised and ridged.

She was really shocked and upset. She said, "What the hell is this?" I said, "What do you mean?" Being beaten was normal for me. She was very angry and went to see Mr. Stephen, which may have had something to do with my being pulled out of boarding. So I was a day boy for my remaining seven years at the school.

I can't look back on UCC and say I gained some inspiration, ideals, or purpose in life, but there is no doubt that I did get a very good and rigorous education. In my own life, clearly the most valuable thing that I gained from Upper Canada was that I learned to speak and write English very well. I know that that comes from the intellectual rigour of the education I received at Upper Canada, and I'm very grateful for it. I know that I had an incomparably better education than my two sons. The students I teach at Western are very poorly educated, but it's not their fault.

One of the things I find very difficult to accept about the culture in which we live today is the premium that appears to be placed on whining and complaining. At Upper Canada, it was clearly a challenge to be able to take abuse. You'd adopt the attitude "Beat me all you like, but you're not going to get any whimpering out of me." But it still amazes me that no one has ever tried to bring criminal charges against Vernon Mould.

When I look back on it, I assume that there must have been boys who were being, if not molested, at least sexually accosted by masters. This never happened to me, but it did to others. I remember a Latin teacher in the prep school, Tim Gibson, who would stand by one boy and fondle him. He didn't get down to fondling his genitals, but certainly would get his hand inside his shirt. This was done right in class!

Politically, I think I got a sense of Red Toryism at Upper Canada. I'm very conscious of the fact that the political left wing in this country has evaporated because of our obsession with what I call bourgeois feminism. We've abandoned any notion of class as a meaningful analytical or political concept. I used to be active in the NDP. I ran for them in the federal election twice in London. I now despise the NDP because I regard it as being far right today. All the parties are socially radical and economically reactionary – touchy feely, feel-good social policies and straightforward, unvarnished, let-'er-rip capitalism.

If the left were to revive itself in Canada today, it would be socially conservative and economically radical, which doesn't, in fact, seem at all paradoxical to me. That's what Red Toryism is all about. At UCC, I got a sense of Red Toryism from people like Alan Stephen and Jim Biggar. A lot of Biggar's social and historical notions were quite radical, although the mainstream ideas that we got out of the classroom about society and politics were very traditional, social democratic ideas about social responsibility and Keynesian views of economics. Certainly nobody at Upper Canada ever gave me a sermon about the glories of capitalism and how the free market solves everything. No one said, "If people are out of work, let them look after themselves." If anything, it was a very CCF-ish, welfare state-ish kind of ideology which I was taught. It never occurred to me that this was odd at the time.

Upper Canada clearly taught me there is a moral way to behave and an immoral way to behave. I don't recall anybody actually saying that, but I definitely came away from UCC with a sense of good and evil, right and wrong. But I tend to have a very Manichean worldview, which is a major emotional and intellectual flaw. I'm far too rigid. I suspect that may have a lot to do with the boys and masters of UCC.

There was a deep sense of loyalty and solidarity in the boys, us against the enemy, the masters. I really loathed anybody who would rat or inform, which was the lowest, most immoral, vicious form of betrayal. A sense of loyalty was one of the good things I learned from that environment. In my view, the world was very simple. There were boys and there were masters. If you were a boy, you were an ally and a comrade of every other boy in a fundamental, unequivocal war.

LIONEL CONACHER

1950–56

President, Canadian Tire Associate Store

I WAS IN GRADE 12 when I heard the news about my father. I was studying because I was having trouble at school. After football practice, I tried to get my academics straightened around. Miss Barrow, the nurse, came down from the infirmary and said to me, "I think you should go home." As I came up on the front steps at home, my sister told me. I can remember it very clearly. It was an unbelievable shock.

My father had been playing in a baseball game for charity that was run by the press against the members of parliament in Ottawa. He'd finished his professional sports career the year I was born, 1936, and gone on to be a Liberal member of parliament. Somebody threw a ball in from the outfield and caught him right on the temple as he was running the bases. It didn't do anything to him right then. He went back to the dugout and complained to a friend that he wasn't feeling well. My father went up to bat a few innings later, hit the ball, ran to third base, and collapsed. He had a cerebral hemorrhage from the blow. He died on the spot. He was only fifty-four.

The cause of death was announced as a heart attack because people didn't want the guy who threw the ball to be known as the guy who killed Lionel Conacher. He had an autopsy, and the family decided that the heart attack verdict was a reasonable decision. But at this late date, it doesn't matter any more. The funeral was massive.

At that point, I was finishing fourth form. I was born in January, so I was going to graduate at age nineteen, as opposed to eighteen. In fact, I wound up putting in another year and graduated at twenty. Miss Barrow pointed out to me that it didn't matter. It was important just to get it and get on to university. That next year I didn't do anything. The year after that I realized: Hey, I don't have a father. I don't have anybody in the world. I better get my act together.

The school put me through a very bad time. They were not very supportive. When I missed my senior matric the first year round, the year after father died, they didn't want me to write my second year. They almost as a courtesy let me stay at the school. Most of the guys were off to places like Meisterschaft. UCC wouldn't let them stay. Under the circumstances, they let me stay, but then they kicked me out of French and history class.

The only person who helped me was Miss Barrow. I was determined to get my senior matric. Barrow encouraged me to live one day at a time. She said, "You're bright enough, with all the sports you played. You have to be bright to handle all those." She encouraged me and I finally got my senior matric in spite of them. I went on to the University of Western Ontario and played four years of college football, then played professionally with the Montreal Alouettes for a couple of years. I went on to business school and graduated with second-class honours. My brother Brian, who followed me into UCC, later played hockey for the 1967 Toronto Maple Leaf Stanley Cup winning team.

I'm told by people who played against me in sports that I was a fierce competitor. I knew I had to be tough as nails. Just because my name is

Conacher, there were always a couple of guys who would try and get you. I grew up with that reality.

I won most of the sports I played at Upper Canada. I remember in Grade 11, they held the NCO tests for battalion and then listed the marks up on the board. The guys in the test with the top marks were the captains, then the lieutenants, the sergeants major, and so on down the list. My marks were up with the lieutenants and that is what I should have been named. But instead I was named a company sergeant major.

I went to see Ian Cartwright, the commanding officer. He told me, "You always win at everything, so we thought you should lose at something." I said, "Shit, you could have been a little less obvious. You could have at least put my name down with the sergeants major. Why did you leave it up there with the lieutenants? I got that mark!" He replied, "We know you did, but we are not going to let you win at everything."

In my years in the upper school, I remember some spectacular stunts pulled in morning prayers. A bunch of guys put flour into the organ pipes. It just screwed up the organ, but it was funny. I can remember in my first year, somebody hustled a collie dog into prayers. They had him in the elevated back platform they used in the old school. Somebody else smuggled in a pigeon. Somebody else, through the hole from the upper balcony before it was condemned, lowered and raised an alarm clock tied on a string.

Part way through prayers, the alarm went off. Sowby was just going nuts. He couldn't figure out where the alarm was coming from. As an alarm clock runs down, they have that one last final ding. When it finally stopped, Sowby was just about to turn to walk back and sit in his seat and it dinged one more time. He just about exploded. You couldn't have timed it better.

Once Joe MacInnis and I paid Don Martyn to read the Bible. We were going to pay him for every minute he went over the standard five-minute Bible reading. He went on for about twenty-five minutes. Nobody could figure out how to stop him. What are you going to do? Physically stop him from reading a Bible?

The stewards used to take over after formal prayers, making the stewards' announcements to the school. The head steward was doing the announcements for that day and he could be a bit pompous. All of a sudden, a whole row of guys stood up and they all made a throwing motion simultaneously. One orange came out of the crowd and belted him on the side of the face. The stewards had no idea who actually threw it. They knew the whole form had stood up and sat down, but they had no clue who actually threw it.

I'm glad I went to UCC and I'm comfortable, like most UCC people are, walking into any room anywhere in the world. At the same time, it's a weird set of standards. I guess what made me focus on it was going back and watching my three sons go through the same horseshit in the 1980s. But I think that my sons would probably tell you that they were pleased to have gone there and made great friends.

I've gone back to a few old-boy dinners, but less now than I did a while ago. When my kids were there, I got a second look at the place. I watched some shenanigans and knew some of the stories that were going on. As I watched some of the intricacies of society there, I guess I became more cynical about it than happy with it. I started to realize, looking back, that I almost didn't make it out of there. I was lucky to have Miss Barrow helping me live my life while I was there.

I had an immigrant friend who went to UCC, Jerry Diakiw, who is now a school superintendant. A few years ago, he wrote a critical article about UCC in the *Toronto Star*. I said to him, "Jerry, I didn't know that you felt that way. I have to tell you, I felt the same way!" He said, "How could you feel the same way? You were a Conacher!" I replied, "Yes, but we didn't have the money or prestige of the Eatons or all the other people. I was a jock and I suffered from the same things."

At the same time, I was accepted because I could do things that most of the guys there couldn't do. I was fortunate to have won all sorts of trophies in track, boxing, football, and hockey. I could beat a lot of them athletically, so I survived. UCC is certainly a place of survival of the fittest.

ALAN WALKER

1946–53

Journalist

I HAD A FASCINATION with reading and writing from a very early age, rather indiscriminately. I remember before I could even read and write, I spent hours with paper and pencils doing what I assumed to be writing. I was fascinated with linear sentences and I began to figure out what they were. When you're very young, you do not hear sentences, words, or punctuation. You just hear a sound. Gradually it dawned on me that something more was going on there, that there were divisions of sound, and that I loved to write.

Jack Schaffter realized that I was not a jock, not militaristic, not in the UCC format. I was a square peg in a round hole. I wanted to be left alone, do my time, get paroled and get the hell out of there. He detected an interest that he could directly influence, so he gave me all the help he could. I didn't have to go out and play soccer at night and freeze my ass off. I didn't get out of the compulsory games, but rather the semi-compulsory games. There were certain times of evening when you were sent out of the building. You weren't allowed to stay inside doing corrosive things like reading books. You had to get out. So, I was allowed off that.

I found my own way of evading compulsory games in the afternoons of most seasons. There were so many teams that the bastards couldn't keep track of them all. By second year, third year, I had found hidey holes all over the prep school in basement storage closets and janitors' holding areas. I would much rather sit in a small grubby room, reading a book for an hour and a half, than do all those horrible, disgusting games. The masters, by and large, were not aware of how devious we could be at getting away with things. It was part of the training, I suppose. At eight years old, I could pick a lock with reasonable confidence and raid the kitchen or the tuck shop.

In the prep, you had to write a letter home each week. Most of the kids wrote: "How are you? I am fine. I hate this place. I'm getting out." I liked writing letters home. I wrote fairly long ones. My mother gave me her old typewriter when I was nine or ten. I taught myself how to type. To this day, I can't type properly. I was soon typing letters, not only to my mother and stepfather, but to aunts and uncles.

Perhaps it was Jack Schaffter's suggestion that it might be fun to put out some sort of a little newspaper. I believe I was the editor. I still have copies of it. I wrote a poem, did little drawings, and wrote profiles on the different interesting people at the prep. The head groundskeeper, Tom Aikman, kept bees. Right in the middle of the city, he produced honey that won contests. I hung out with him for half a day, with Schaffter's encouragement. I asked him a bunch of questions, jotted down a bunch of answers, and wrote a profile. I did a number of profiles over the years. Two of them actually appeared in the *College Times*.

The masters all had their own canes, straps, yardsticks, or various weapons of choice. There was a selection of canes of various thickness and flexibility which masters could choose from. If you were told "no talking" and you were caught talking a second time, that was it. Kids got six of the best as a regular, daily fact of life. The infractions were so trivial.

One day I was having a fight with one of the kids and I called him a prick. A master grabbed me and said, "What did you call him?" I said, "A prick." I had no idea what it meant. To me, it was no stronger than twerp or idiot. He told me, "That's a very dirty word. You never say that." I was probably nine or ten. I couldn't convince him that I didn't know it was a taboo word. It was like I was speaking in a different language.

Maybe I'm reinventing history here, but I'd like to think that I was smart enough to have said, "Sir, if I'd known that it was a dirty word, why would I have yelled it in front of you and repeated it?" He wasn't going to understand a thing. I was punished for abusing a word that I didn't know the meaning of.

When I was in my last year in the prep, having developed a reputation for being a bookworm, one of the boys about my age walked into one of the toilets at some unexpected time. There were two kids in the same stall performing oral sex. One of the boys was about our age, twelve or thirteen, and the other was kid was maybe eight.

The prison code was "Never rat on anybody." But this spectacle really bothered the witness. Possibly the younger kid had been coerced, which made it even worse. So the witness went to two or three friends and they discussed whether he should report this incident. Then they ran into the problem of what words to use. They were terrified of stumbling into some black area where they were going to get into trouble themselves. We were trying to do the right thing, but our instinct was that the masters were going to punish us.

The only words these other kids knew were words like "prick," "cock," and "dork." They didn't know the proper language. I said, "Well, I believe I have heard adults call it a penis." None of them had heard the word. They had grown up with "dickie" or some such word. I said, "All you can do is go in and say, 'Sir, I caught X sucking the penis of Y.'"

That was where the story ends, oddly enough. But the impression it left was, again, that feeling of speaking a different language, and the terror that we had of even trying to talk to the masters. The lack of sensitivity on the part of many – although not all – of the masters was appalling. If we said or did something that they thought was a punishable offence, they had no sympathy and no interest in trying to understand. I suspect the witness never did report the incident in the toilet.

I was always aware of the school's elitist reputation and snobbery. They fed it to us all the time. As late as the 1950s, believe it or not, they still had a football cheer, in the official booklet of cheers, that went, "Nigger, nigger, hoe potater, half past alligator, ram, ram, bulligator, Chippewana duck. College! College! Rush 'er up!" There were maybe six blacks in the upper school. They sat there while everybody chanted "nigger, nigger."

The rich kids made it quite clear that they had a fairly low opinion of us. On Saturday or Sunday afternoon, chauffeur-driven limos would come to the boardinghouse to pick up the Bassetts, the Eatons, the Burtons, or the Dunkelmans of the Tip Top Tailors family. One of the McMurtrys and Joe MacInnis, the undersea diver, were also in boarding. There wasn't a great deal of snobbery, although one time I recall one of the Eatons being obnoxious. He had tailor-made uniforms and we had clothes off the rack. He said, "You can't afford clothes like this!"

I was an easy target for bullies. I was smaller and younger and I ate more than I should have. Of course, I was bone-idle lazy. Never stand when you can sit, never sit if you can lie down, never stay awake if you can sleep. I was fat. I didn't have many friends. At one point, I remember, I got into some sort of disagreement with a kid, who hit me. He was one of the very few kids who was less popular than I was. I suddenly found myself facing this kid, surrounded by other kids who were cheering for me! I was ashamed that I hit him back. I was guilty of the same sort of *Lord of the Flies* behaviour that many, many of the other kids had applied to me. This kid was weaker than I was and I hit him. Then, finally, I came to my senses.

In the boxing tournaments, boys were paired off, roughly by weight. I was thrown into the ring with some other kid whom I'm sure didn't want to be there any more than I did. I said, "I don't want to do this. Why should I hit anyone? He hasn't done anything to me." It was three one-minute rounds. For the first round, I just defended myself. He managed to land a couple of punches late in the second round or maybe in the third round. Because he wasn't expecting it, I did hit him. I was ashamed of what I had done, so I just withdrew and went back to my corner and that was the end of the fight.

What I remember most is not that something unfair happened to you now and then, but that from certain masters it happened on a regular basis. In Form 5 or 6, I would have been ten. There was a master who had an extremely vile temper and chain-smoked cigarettes. I hope they got to him eventually. He was capable of instant blind rages. He was cruel. He favoured kids who were in the jock mould or kids who were aggressive. He did not like boys like me who avoided physical activity.

At one point, somebody threw a spitball or a paper-clip. It landed on the floor fairly close to the master, who was writing on the blackboard. He turned around and said, "Who threw that?" Well, of course, we'd never confess. He then said, "Okay, everybody stand up." He said he was going to punish all of us if the culprit didn't confess, or if somebody else didn't tell.

After some minutes, the bell rang. He said, "All right, get off to your next class, except you, Walker, and you, Prestwick." Prestwick was a similar guy, a quiet bookworm. We just stood there while he worked at his desk. Finally I said, "May I say something, please?" He said, "What do you want?" I said, "May I ask why I've been kept behind? I did not throw anything. I didn't do it." He strode down the aisle, grabbed me by the arm, and said, "Come with me." We started towards the headmaster's office.

When we got to the headmaster's office, he said he was going to cane me. I would get six of the best – no evidence, no trial, nothing. He told me to lean over but I dug in, which for me was pretty odd. I was so enraged by the injustice of the situation that I simply refused to bend over. I said, "This is not fair. I'm not going to do it."

He took me back downstairs to his office. He wrote a note, sealed it in an envelope, and told me to take it to the nurse. When I got to the infirmary, the nurse opened it and read, with evident bewilderment, that a bookish ten-year-old boy was refusing punishment. He had instructed her to put me in the infirmary and give me an hour or so to think it over.

Finally, they got to me in the most evil, unfair way. They conferred among themselves. The nurse came in and said, "If you don't accept this punishment, we're going to have to phone your mother." At that time, my mother was sewing dresses for Simpsons and moonlighting as an RNA. The nurse said, "We're going to have to call in your mother. She'll have to leave work and lose pay. It's going to be difficult for her. It's going to cause her a lot of grief. Surely you don't want to hurt your mother?" Well, they had me. I said, "No, I don't want to hurt my mother, but it's not fair." The master arrived, took me back to the headmaster's office and caned me.

Fifteen years later, I was sitting with friends in the Pilot Tavern on Yonge Street. My former master comes in and sits at the bar, all alone. He was a little greyer, but he wore the same crew cut. I was maybe twenty-five or twenty-six. I had just graduated with a master's degree and been hired by *Time* magazine and was on my way to Montreal. I went over and said, "Hi. You once taught me, didn't you?" He said, "Yes." I said, "Many years ago, I was one of your students at UCC. My name is Walker." He said, "Yes, I do remember you." I said, "Then you will probably remember a particular incident." He said, "Yes, I remember that very well."

So I said, "Okay, here we are now, sitting here as adults. I'm telling you I didn't do it." He said, "Yes, you did." I said, "You didn't see me do it. You mean that after fifteen years, when I tell you I didn't do it, you can't accept that I didn't do it?" He said, "No, I can't." He was stubborn, he was wrong, and he wouldn't admit it fifteen years later. That sense of not being understood, of speaking a different language, was still intact. I said, "What are you doing these days?" He said, rather proudly, "I'm back at the University of Toronto doing my master's degree." I said, "Good luck. I got mine last year."

That caning incident has stuck with me for forty-three years. I'll never forget the madness, the unfairness, and the apparent ready cooperation of other members of the staff to support him. They never considered that I might be telling the truth. That was one of the characteristic patterns that I most disliked about the place. There was a complete lack of interest or ability in dealing with children. Luckily, when my mother remarried, I left the prep at age thirteen and spent my high school years at Etobicoke Collegiate, which was no picnic either. But I don't think I could have endured another five years of UCC.

I have never married. Having gone to the UCC prep school, I'm openly asked by some people, "Are you gay?" I say, "No." But I think the fact that I didn't get married is connected to the fact that I went through a private school. There is no place less private than a private school. Everything was communal, with wretched cubicles with walls that didn't reach the ceilings or the floors, built like public toilets, with a curtain across the front. After seven years of boarding, I developed a permanent, highly honed sense of privacy.

When I go home at night, I want to close the door. I don't want anybody else there. Some people say, "Well, the right woman didn't come along." I have to say that three or four times the right woman did come along. But I had an absolute need for privacy plus a lack of experience with women my own age until relatively late in life. I have had several relationships with women, but it has never come down to actually moving in with one for very long. I think it stems from school.

At UCC I used to daydream about the day when I was utterly my own boss in my own environment. I envisioned a pure kind of life in my little imaginary bunker. I would have everything in there that I wanted, like hot and cold running water, chocolate milk, Coke. Nobody could get in. I had daydreams about it.

That's still with me. I now live in a top-floor apartment with two locks on the front door. People visit me from time to time, but I'm not a social animal. I haven't been to a party in twenty years. I like living alone. I doubt very much whether I ever will get married. I believe that my seven-year stretch at boarding school, at an age where you're so influenced by your environment, had something to do with it. It retarded you, socially and sexually.

I remember when my mother and stepfather used to take me back to the boarding house after a brief visit home. They would drive me from

Etobicoke along Lakeshore Boulevard, up Avenue Road to the top of the hill. I remember as that damn clock tower, the "Four-Faced Liar," hove into view, I'd get that sick-to-your stomach feeling. Today, more than forty years later, whenever I pass the school, I get that same sick feeling.

CONRAD BLACK

1951–59

Chairman, Hollinger, Inc.

MY PARENTS, when we moved to Toronto from Montreal, lived on Warren Road in Forest Hill, which is only a few blocks away from UCC. My brother Montegu, who is four years older than I am, was happily enrolled at the school when we moved out to Bayview. I was seven years old and eligible to go into Grade 2, so my parents enrolled me. The conventional wisdom was that UCC was the best school in Toronto.

Not being terribly athletic, I didn't enjoy the compulsory games. Fortunately, I got some dental work when I was in about Grade 5, so I didn't have to box after the first couple of years. In all of the sports, I gave an honourable, mediocre account of myself. I wasn't so inept that I was embarrassed.

There were a couple of years that I was grateful to my eventual member of parliament, John Bosley, because John really was quite uncoordinated. People would pick on him and not notice that I was only marginally more coordinated than he was. He was one of those lads who was a bit overweight and messy looking. He had thick glasses always covered with fingerprints. He wasn't good at sports. He was bullied. My chief recollection of our relationship is of saying things to him like, "Oh, Bosley!" He's obviously been a successful man since, becoming a Tory MP and Speaker of the House of Commons. It wasn't easy for him and yet he came through it all right and made a success of himself. I tend to like people like him. I've always been a bit of a supporter of the underdog.

In Form 1 I had Mr. Archibald, a Canadian war veteran of that very English imitative type and very much a believer in the old hickory stick. Anyone who accumulated three demerits would get a big whack. I can still remember how frightened I was at the imminence of the first of many episodes of corporal punishment. But then I became a bit complacent about it. It wasn't anything serious. Then gradually, over the years, the whole process became more painful.

In Form 4 the master was George Galt, a jovial man who specialized in theatre and literature. But he too was a true believer in whacking his charges. I don't want to sound like a person who was completely horrified at the thought of a good kick in the derrière for misbehaving young boys. It is not necessarily the wrong thing to do in certain circumstances. But I started to feel uneasy. There was an unquestioned aspect to the discipline, and even a slightly fetishistic aspect to it.

I remember one day George Galt was about to take his stick to my posterior – I had assumed the position he commanded to facilitate the caning – when the door opened. It was Earl Elliott, who was the deputy headmaster, or whatever they used to call them. Elliott said to Galt, "Oh, I had wondered if I could see you for a moment." All he could see of me was the part of me that was proffered.

Galt said, "Oh, yes, but I'm just giving Black a well-deserved thrashing. May I just do that first?" Elliott said, "Oh, goodness, yes. I wouldn't want to get in the way of such a useful endeavour." So with this encouragement, old George Galt laid into me, with Earl Elliott nodding in approval. I found that experience quite degrading. It's odd how well and vividly one remembers certain incidents from one's youth.

I got by not badly in the prep. I had no desire to move to another school at that point. But I started to develop more and more reservations about the system as we proceeded. There were some emphases that I considered to be excessive. I was also beaten by Walter Ruffell, but I didn't really have an objection to that particular incident. I can see its point. A sign on his classroom door said "Examinations in Progress." A bunch of us in Grade 6 were making noise in the corridor. Ruffell came out and said, "Can't you read?" I shouldn't have said anything. I should have just shut up and gone away like the other kids. Instead, I said, "No, I'm receiving an inferior education."

Ruffell dragged me into the classroom by the scruff of the neck and beat me, spread over his desk, with a riding crop, in front of the other boys. In that culture, it was a reasonable thing to do. I had affronted him. After he finished, he said, "Please come back when you're feeling undereducated."

Oddly enough, what offended me more were the unnecessarily insulting comments by teachers. This was one of Vernon Mould's specialties. He was a talented man and often rather nice. But he would often hold a vote in the class about how a boy should be punished. He'd say, "Should Daks get a

Saturday morning detention or should Daks write out one hundred lines? Should Daks have two whacks with my stick? Four whacks? Six whacks?"

That was one of the things that outraged me the most. I felt that the students were corrupted by the system into a sort of Roman circus approbation. The masters broke our solidarity. UCC wasn't one great happy commonwealth, as Dick Howard reported in his book on UCC. The reality was that we could be co-opted at any moment to legitimize the excesses and outrages of our masters, which offended me.

Another thing that bothered me was there were a few teachers who were quite sadistic. One or more were rather active fondling homosexuals. I was caned by I. K. Shearer in the upper school, but I asked for it. He was a bit of a sadist and certainly a homosexual. But in this case, he caught me not doing my homework.

He said, "All right, you have a detention. I'll tell you what. We'll flip a coin. If you win, I'll let you off this time. If you don't, you've got a gating." I missed and I went for a double. He said, "All right. We'll flip one more coin. If you lose, I'll just give you two whacks." I thought, There's no way I'm going to lose three times in a row. But I did. But what he did was not excessive. He didn't hurt me. It was almost a good-natured thing. He was dangerous to some people, but he was not too severe with me.

Shearer was an amusing guy in a way and he certainly knew French well. Patrick Johnson told me he later threw Shearer out of the school after over thirty years' service. Then he apparently reformed as a man and went to Africa to teach Third World kids. He had his moments. He was an amusing man, but clearly a very neurotic character. I suspect he was more than a fondler.

I am not a gay basher at all. After the publication of my autobiography, *A Life in Progress*, I had an exchange of letters with Laurier LaPierre in the *Financial Post*. LaPierre wrote an extremely outraged letter about my reference to him when he was teaching at Upper Canada. I wrote back and apologized to him on one point only, which was a psychological presumption that implied a relationship between his subsequently declared homosexuality and his enthusiasm for corporal punishment in those days at UCC. I had no business saying that and I did apologize for it. But the rest of what I wrote about him was quite accurate.

Laurier did not personally cane me at UCC, but he did lots of other boys. He had a reputation as a caner. He was a very enthusiastic practitioner of that form of "education." A couple of times when my parents went on holiday during the winter, they put me in boarding for a couple of weeks. I really saw how that regime operated.

I remember one night when there was some kind of a pillow fight.

LaPierre and one other faculty member flicked on all the lights. The routine was you were all herded out and you had to bare your behinds and lean over your basin. LaPierre shared with another master the honour of battering us. I had the good fortune not to be on LaPierre's side of the row of basins. But I can attest, not as a recipient, but at least as a witness, that he completely overreacted. He hit the kids far too hard. What is so terrible about having a pillow fight? Most of the boys weren't even involved in it, but everyone was caned.

It was not unlike the Lidice solution, when the Nazis killed all the innocent occupants of a Czech town in reprisal for the assassination of the ss governor, J. R. Heydrich, in 1942. Actually, I don't want to be tendentious in bringing in that analogy. ucc was certainly not a Nazi institution and it's outrageous that I should say so. I am defaming it. I would wish either not to be quoted on that, or, if I'm quoted, at least quote my withdrawal of it.

I spent only one year in the upper school. A problem developed with Willy Orr, who was a very severe old guy. I had a double gating and I thought I was excused halfway through. You stayed for one hour if it was a single gating and two hours if it was a double. Some guy read my name so I left. When my absence came to light, Orr treated me as if I had skipped the gating altogether. He didn't say, "Well, fine. You've got a double gating next Saturday."

Orr used to cane kids in one of the portable classrooms on a Monday afternoon at a certain time. I was told to report there at the appointed time, so I knew what was going to happen. I had had enough experience with caning in the preparatory school, so I wasn't too concerned. But I thought this was odd because what I did was not terribly serious. I thought, Oh well, he'll give me one or two whacks and say, "Smarten up." Nothing to be too concerned about.

But he absolutely walloped me. It was a fierce and savage assault. He was very formidable in his way. He had a full-sized cane which he would hold in both hands like a baseball bat. It really hurt. This time, there was absolutely no justification for it. In the previous episodes with Ruffell and Galt, there is room for legitimate debate as to whether their remedy was appropriate. Certainly there had been considerable provocation on my part. But for Orr to lacerate me to a pulp for the most technical and trivial of infractions was just not on.

That particular caning was what started the final escalation. Orr identified me as someone who was disrespectful of the system. These guys are very experienced watching schoolboys go through the system. I guess they can tell the ones who naturally get on in the system, those who have a will to excel, those who are skeptical, and those who are potentially subversive. I guess he was making a pre-emptive strike. In that sense, he was an astute old schoolmaster. He saw that I wasn't really a true believer. I don't want to dramatize excessively, but it really was like so many episodes of oppression by undemocratic or colonial forces that lead to insurrections.

That's in a sense what happened. I became completely and perniciously insubordinate and undermined the entire school in various ways, culminating in stealing the examinations and selling them to boys in the school. It's not something that I'm proud of, but I'm not ashamed of it either.

My misfortune was to be at UCC during the Cedric Sowby era. I thought Sowby was an absolutely appalling principal. Patrick Johnson and Dick Sadleir, who followed Sowby as principals, were both very good English teachers at that time and fine, decent, sane men. I have no doubt at all that they really improved the school between them, but it was too late for me.

The aftermath of the exam-stealing episode was a clearer and harsher lesson than most fourteen-year-olds, in this society anyway, get in the fluctuations of their fortunes. Four of us were involved. I went very rapidly from being a person of some perceived power to being an absolute pariah. I had been friendly with people in the way one is in a school yard, where you know someone in school, even though he's not in your class. You were on some sports team with him or you share some interest in one of the clubs. Somehow or other, you just know him and you are friendly.

Then all of a sudden, it's as if you are a leper. Actually, it's not fair to say leper. It seems that people stay away from lepers because they are afraid of the illness, and it's sort of impersonal. But I was an evildoer who was the carrier of a kind of behavioral virus that could infect my friendly acquaintances if I even came close to them. It didn't last long, but the backlash was quite shocking. I think the denunciations of us came from boys to whom we had sold exam papers. When it was discovered, the four of us were called in singly to face Sowby, Orr, and old Dr. Bassett, who was a horrifying, scary guy. In fact, they all were. I must say they were all utterly hateful. Luckily, there were also good teachers in the school, like Johnson and Sadleir.

Anyway, they isolated us as the culprits. The school was convened the next day. The boys were told they had to rewrite the examinations they had written the day before. We were officially suspended. It was put in a way to maximize our unpopularity. They stirred up a kind of ritualistic, reflexive, angry reaction against the wrongdoers in their midst. If Sowby had said, "We will all now shake our fists in righteous indignation against these four fallen sinners," everyone would have done it. It was an altogether totalitarian process. When I was expelled, Mrs. Sowby, sitting there in her conical hat, with all her facial hair, said to me, "You realize your life is over." Can you imagine saying that to a fourteen-year-old? Dreadful!

I accept that I had brought great inconvenience to a lot of innocent people, students and faculty. I don't wish to sound too self-righteous. But with that said, I always felt it could have been handled within the context of a normal disciplinary framework. If they wanted to throw me out, they could, but it was not necessary, in my opinion, to stir up public approbrium against fourteen-year-old boys. It is alleged that in the aftermath, some boys planted a burning cross on my parents' front lawn. It's probably true, but I think my family and I were away at my parent's cottage at the time. If it didn't happen, it could have. It properly illustrates the spirit of things.

If I had been a few years older, what I did would have been a crime. It was undoubtedly an act of theft. Therefore, in one sense, the people who think I committed a criminal act in stealing the exams are right. But, in the first place, I think you temper things a bit in a case of provocation. In the second place, I think there is a well-settled point of both law and what we might call contemporary social moral philosophy that you soften the indictment for juveniles. In the third place, whatever the extent of my offence, I've paid for it, have I not? Therefore, having paid for it, I have been rehabilitated.

It is certainly a well-settled point of jurisprudence that when wrongdoers are apprehended, tried, sentenced, and serve their sentences, they are to be readmitted to society as if all had been put right. Somewhere in there, moving from not guilty by reason of provocation, through guilty as charged, convicted, sentenced, and expiated, I really don't think I deserve to be called a criminal today.

Again, I don't want to sound self-righteous. I did undoubtedly cause a great deal of inconvenience because the entire school had to retake the examinations. I can understand why great moral outrage was easily roused against me by the regime. But I was a bit surprised that the initial reaction was so overwhelmingly hostile to me. There was not a shading, as far as I knew, not a single individual instance of someone saying, "It was sort of amusing and enterprising what Black did. I don't approve of it, but if you're going to buck the system, this guy really did it with some panache or originality."

That came subsequently. Other people I met who had been at Upper Canada at that time said that to me subsequently when they could be more philosophical. My friend Brian Stewart, the CBC-TV journalist, is an example. I think we had seen each other, but not spoken, when we were at Upper Canada. When I went to Thornton Hall in the autumn of 1960, I think my very first meeting with him, he said, "Weren't you at Upper Canada two years ago?" I said, "Yes." He said, "Ah, yes, you were the central figure in that exam scandal, weren't you?" I said, "I was. People aren't still upset about that, are they?" He said, "Not that I know of. Certainly I'm not. I think it was the greatest thing that ever happened to that school. I hated the place."

That got our relations off to a very nice start and we've been very cordial ever since. He and his family moved to Toronto from England that summer. Their house in Forest Hill wasn't ready for them until the fall, so they were still staying in the Park Plaza Hotel. His father was ultimately the president of Simpsons. Brian would start off every school day having his breakfast in the Park Plaza. He told me that every single day for three months he literally vomited at the thought of going to Upper Canada.

When I was at UCC, I felt I was destined for something in life, but no thanks to the people at the school. I thought I was destined for something, but only because I sat at home reading Charles de Gaulle's memoirs at the age of ten. I was interested in poetry or Abe Lincoln, anybody who caught people's imagination. I was always interested in seeing how they did it and what they did to do it.

But that particular instinct was not fostered at all at UCC. In that school, if anything, I felt they were trying to level me and suppress that kind of instinct. They were not trying to pat me on the head and say, "You're right to think like that. If you play your cards right, work hard, and show some judgement in character, you can be an important person some day." I didn't encounter that approach at all.

I'm afraid I cannot credit UCC with imparting to me my love of language and literature. I hate to say this, but they did absolutely nothing. No, I take it back. Dick Sadleir, Pat Johnson, and, to a degree, Dick Howard, my English teacher in my last year in the prep, did. I want to be fair. But I was thirteen or fourteen by then. Prior to that, absolutely nothing.

Old Earl Elliott did certainly stimulate my knowledge of arithmetic. Elliott was a nice, dignified, fair, and, on balance, rather affectionate teacher, but from the old school and fairly severe. God, I've never forgotten how to multiply, divide, add, and subtract. It stood me in good stead. To this day, I never use a calculator. I always work things out in my head and I owe that to him. I probably owe more to him for such a career as I've had than any other teacher in that sense because my arithmetic is good.

David Beatty, the current chairman of the board at UCC and the president of Weston Foods, recently invited me to speak at UCC. I wouldn't really be too eager to go back. As I said in my book, I've let bygones be bygones. I think it's a good school, but I don't have any desire to make a symbolic return to it. I wouldn't say I'd never do it. I just don't have any motivation to do it. The people who do that, I think, are people who have some desire to be reconciled to the place in question or to be reaccepted by it. I suspect the guys who go back to old-boy reunions do so because their school years were their good years, or perhaps because they want to prove something or fight for some kind of recognition.

ucc has since asked me for money as an old boy, but I haven't given them any. My brother has given personally. Our company won't give them any money. To one place or another, we give a lot of money away. I give to some schools, but not to the ones where I was thrown out. After ucc, I was thrown out of tcs.

I have absolutely no grounds to complain about ucc. I set out to destroy the regime and they caught me at the end. They had a perfect right to throw me out and that's what they did. But the fact is, if they had been smart, which they weren't – Sowby, Orr, and Bassett were hopelessly stupid – they wouldn't have done what they did. They would have ascertained exactly if it were necessary for the entire school to rewrite the exams, and to be fair, it would have been necessary to rewrite some exams. But they wouldn't have named us at a public meeting. They would have been much more impersonal about it.

I think they probably would have had to do something fairly drastic. Orr's punitive method, corporal punishment, wouldn't have had any more relevance at that point. Making us repeat the year wouldn't have been fair because we hadn't failed academically. It may well be that they had to throw us out, but they shouldn't have done it publicly. They should have sent our parents letters saying, "We must ask you to withdraw your son." There was no need for anything else. You simply don't turn public hatred on fourteen-year-old kids, even if they do terrible things.

In the first edition of John Henry Cardinal Newman's *Apologia Pro Vita Sua*, he said: "I left Oxford University in 1845. Other than as one sees it from a passing train, I have not returned." In a subsequent edition, there's an asterisk. At the bottom of the page, next to the asterisk, it says: "Indeed, at the invitation of the Chancellor and governing body of the university, after my elevation to Cardinal, I did return to Oriel College and to the high table, after an absence of just thirty-three years."

I'm not comparing myself to Cardinal Newman. His case was a mighty intellectual and ecclesiastical controversy and my case was a very trivial incident. The manner of my leaving Upper Canada bears no comparison, but I cite it as a contrast. Newman didn't seek, obviously, the approval of Oxford, but he so loved Oxford and the bitterness of his religious change was so great, he clearly wanted an act of reconciliation.

The school threw me out. I have made my comments on the circum-stances that led up to it. I bear UCC no ill will. I think it's a good school and I wish it well. But I do not seek any acts, symbolic or otherwise, of reaccep-tance by them. Except for going surreptitiously one night on May 24 to put a Roman candle on the door of Grant House, the principal's residence, I don't believe I've set foot on the grounds of Upper Canada College since June 1959.

JOHN FRASER

1953–61

Journalist

I HAD SUMMER JOBS in journalism starting at age sixteen, through a UCC connection, John Bassett. I started as a copyboy at the old Toronto *Telegram*. In those days, Mr. Bassett owned the Sherbrooke *Record* in Quebec, so I did about three years working at the Bassett papers. Then I also worked on newspapers in Newfoundland.

When B. K. Sandwell, another UCC old boy, was editor of *Saturday Night*, the magazine spoke to the Anglo elite of Canada. Another old boy, Robertson Davies, had an association with the magazine as literary editor. I've heard it said that the reason I got the job as editor was because I went to UCC with Conrad Black, the present owner of *Saturday Night*. That's not true. I did get to know him, but we didn't know each other particularly well between UCC and his coming to England. It was simply the conjunction of his having bought *Saturday Night* and thinking of me. Once he moved Hollinger into a big press holding, it wasn't such a strange thing to hire me.

At UCC, I was certainly not oblivious to the challenge of trying to sur-vive. I remember one prep master, Tim Gibson, used to stroke young boys on the back of the neck. Once a boy told him, "I don't like it, sir." He said, "Don't you like it? It's nice." We didn't think anything of it much at the time. If you did like it, then you would be teacher's pet. No one would ever tell their parents. But Mr. Gibson liked stroking the backs of boys' necks and sometimes rubbing them over their shoulders and chests.

Once he was doing this when another master, George Galt, came to the entrance of the room to look for him. I remember his eyes, looking. Mr.

Gibson's hands pulled back. I can remember Galt saying, "Whenever you're ready." At the time, and even later, it was all sort of a joke. Now when we hear the stories of what happened, it's not thought to be such a joke any more. That sort of thing is now practically a criminal offence.

I didn't question the prep. In fact, I quite liked it. But I did question the upper school. I can remember questioning the values, partly because at home things were a little unsettled. I was dealing with instability in my private life, so I was looking more closely at things that were happening at the school. But I was headed for trouble anyway.

They had a double-streamed A- and B-form system. In the upper school, I went from 1A2 to 2B1 to 3B3, then out. After Grade 11, I went to Oakwood Collegiate. ThreeB3 was the way station in hell, but there was real camaraderie in that class. It was the class in which we held the math master, Walter Bailey, out the window of the new upper school. Mr. Bailey was a tragic figure to my mind. He obviously had personal problems. He made the mistake of trying to be friends with the boys. Of course, you just become a victim. The 3B3 guys were big sixteen-year-olds. We picked him up and hung him by his legs out the window of the third floor. He was screaming, animal screams. He was destroyed by that class. I think it was known that he was gay. I guess that incident was part of the whole sexual ambivalence of slightly younger boys. Later I heard he became an alcoholic. I could understand why.

I was not much of an athlete. In fact, I avoided sports at all costs. It wasn't until I was in the upper school and noticed some pictures in the corridors that I discovered that my dad had been the manager for the hockey team and the football team. I thought, That's a nifty way to get out of playing. So I got to be manager. It wasn't to follow in his footsteps. No one wanted to be manager and I thought it was quite wonderful. It got me off playing hockey and football.

I didn't manage to get out of all the sports. The big thing was to avoid hockey and football. I found out that if you enrolled for several sports, then you could tell the one sport that you dropped out because you were going to another sport. You would tell the same thing to the other departments and end up not playing any sports at all. It was sheer duplicity. If you signed up for two or three different things, you could eliminate all of them. That was a big breakthrough which I discovered on my own. It has been a great help in dealing with bureaucracy ever since.

I had to box in the prep, but I solved that problem very quickly. I discovered before I even got in the ring that they scratched the match at the first sight of blood. It was horrifying to have to get in the ring. So I simply did a fair amount of picking damage on my nose beforehand. As soon as the bell went, I'd go out and spar a bit, but then I'd be able to blow my nose and some blood would come out. They would scratch the match.

The battalion was more of a challenge. For the first two years in the upper school, I joined the band. In those days, the upper school was actually in portable classrooms because a new upper school was being built. I opted for the glockenspiel, having discovered that they split the band apart for rehearsals. The percussion instruments practised in the gym and the music-making instruments practised down at the prep school. But they could never figure out how to classify the glockenspiel. You hit it like a percussion instrument, but it did make music. They let me decide for myself which section I should be in, so I went home.

That worked fine until Field Marshal Bernard Montgomery came to the school for the annual battalion inspection. In the end, you still had to turn out for the marches in the spring season. The band wasn't very well prepared. Captain Keeling, the head of the band, wanted us to play "God Save the Queen." His last hissed instructions were, "If you don't know the piece, don't play." He brought his baton up with a great flourish and the only noise that was heard was the glockenspiel, just a mishmash of wrong notes.

I got bored with that after a while, so I joined the rebel platoon, which was full of a bunch of troublemakers. It was the sort of place where you obeyed every order to the nth degree. If a green lieutenant didn't know how to order a right wheel properly, he would right wheel us all into a fence and everyone would fall down like dominoes. It was a lot of laughs.

There was a natural dictatorial element at UCC. You slaved and then when you became a prefect or steward, you had the power. Certainly when you became a prefect or steward, you didn't have a sense of the injustices that you had experienced. On the whole, you just got even, taking it out on younger boys. It was a real slave mentality. But the bonhomie atmosphere, if you were rebellious at all, was quite wonderful.

I was a bit of a rebel. I was more duplicitous than the more open ones. I didn't particularly like getting caught because there were consequences, like corporal punishment. No one really questioned authority in those days. The only person I ever knew who did was Conrad Black. He stood up in a way that irritated masters. He was very cocky and would talk back. He got beaten a lot.

I was caned twice, once in the prep by Walter Ruffell and once in the upper school by I. K. Shearer, who was a sadist. I was caned for being rude to Mr. Ruffell, a bachelor, for saying he was having an alleged relationship, which I really didn't understand, with Miss Eckhart, one of the secretaries.

With Mr. Shearer, it was a caper in Grade 9. Someone had brought in a pair of real police handcuffs. We were in a portable classroom with a weak, ineffectual French master. We chained a kid we didn't like to the bottom of his desk and kept him out of view for most of the French class. But then he whimpered. The master came down. Instead of looking perplexed, he simply left the classroom and came back with Mr. Shearer, who was known as the "Beast of Belsen." He struck holy terror in us.

The key to the handcuffs had worked its way around the classroom. I was the last boy in the front desk of the farthest row. I ended up holding the key. Shearer went around the room demanding the key, boy by boy. When he came up the last row, he said, "If the key isn't in this row, I'm caning the whole class." We believed him. In the end, being a decent soul, I gave him the key. So I got caned. Instead of caning me on the behind, he caned me on the top part of my legs with my back turned. To prove it, I charged five cents for people to see the welts. Sick schoolboy society!

In a way, I got armoured at Upper Canada. I've always said that the best thing you got from your experience at UCC, if it worked out okay, was a certain kind of armour. You never had to feel jealous or invidious about anything. At the time, you were oblivious to the privilege you had being there, but later you came to understand it.

I remember the day in 1956 when a boy named Bela Fejer came to the prep. It was a big damn deal. We had all been hearing about the Hungarian Revolution and that a refugee was going to come into our class. He didn't speak a word of English. Boy, he learned fast. It was exotic having a boy come in from the headlines into our incubated world. I think that was my first awareness of cause and consequence in international events. It was very exciting. That's when I started reading newspapers.

BELA FEJER

1956–63

Lawyer

WE ARRIVED in Toronto on December 3, 1956. There was an article and a large photograph on the front page of the *Toronto Star* about my brother and I being the first kids out of Hungary during the revolution. In the picture, we're wearing Red Cross clothing. After living many years of great hardship and deprivation under the Communist regime, my family was able to escape to Canada. I was eleven years old.

A physician who knew my father wanted to know if the Fejers in the newspaper were the same Fejers that he knew. He told Ed Jackman, a UCC boy who later became a Catholic priest, about my family. UCC at that time had been trying to figure out what they could do to help the Hungarian refugees. So Jackman told our story to the principal, Dr. Sowby, and said, "Why don't we give these two Hungarian boys scholarships to UCC?" My father was making $800 a year as a junior intern at the Toronto General Hospital and my mother was working at the Toronto General as an X-ray technician. UCC at that time cost $2,500 to board, so there is no way we could have afforded it.

I had got my first orange in my life in Vienna from a distant relative. It was the first time I had seen a package of oranges in a plastic see-through bag. Wow! I saved my orange until we came to Canada. The first time I went to the UCC boarding house, I walked in wearing my nice little blazer. My tie wouldn't stay done up, so I spent hours trying to learn how to tie a Windsor knot. I still had my Austrian orange. My mother said, "You take your orange and you eat it when you want to. It will make you feel good. That orange will symbolize to you to have faith and that dreams do come true."

Laurier LaPierre was the attending housemaster. I couldn't speak a word of English. I had no idea about the boarding routine. Everybody was coming back from Christmas holidays, the first night, shuffling back and forth. I just followed. I brushed my teeth and had a shower because everybody else was brushing their teeth and having showers. The boys tried to talk to me, but people make a common mistake when people don't speak the language. They talk slower and louder to make themselves understood. When people talk to you slower or louder, you think they're giving you shit because you don't understand. It's totally intimidating.

I experienced total chaos for the first three hours. It was like watching a movie. All sorts of images kept going past – teachers, showers, kids going up to see the nurse, showing their hands, asking all kinds of questions. I didn't know what was going on.

A guy named Dickerson, the son of the mayor of North Bay, was the wild and macho guy in the dorm. Of course, he had to check out the new kid. He became a little abusive but basically I shrugged it off. Physically, I was a big kid. I had been swimming in Hungary. I was fairly athletic and bigger than average. Dickerson tried to pick a fight, but nothing happened.

Then I was shoved into a little cubicle. There were little holes in the wall and all kinds of graffiti and crap. When the lights went out, I had a

chance to reflect on the enormity of the whole situation. Remembering my
mother's words, I took out my orange, which was basically my security
blanket, my teddy bear, and I peeled it. I was starting to eat it when suddenly the lights were flicked back on.

Laurier LaPierre came in and started conducting a search. I didn't know
what was going on. Later I realized he had detected the nice, ripe smell of
my ten-day-old Austrian orange. I had no idea I had violated the rules of
UCC by having some food in my cubicle. Who was the terrible culprit?

Everybody had to stand at attention by their bed. There was a little curtain that he had drawn. I saw everybody getting up, so I also got up.
LaPierre was a big, tall, arrogant guy. He was standing at the end of the hall
with his hands behind his back, making a big speech. It presumably was
about, "Who is the boy eating oranges?" There was total silence. So he
repeats it again. Total silence.

Then Dickerson points to me. I have no idea what's going on. LaPierre
comes to me. I remember him standing in front of me with his hands
behind his back. He started to yell and point to the orange. Before I know
it, I was taken out to his room. I was wearing the polo pyjamas, grey with
little blue trim, which I had got from the wonderful Eaton's store. He
wanted me to pull them down, but I didn't understand what was going on.
I'm standing there and he's giving me hell. He pulls my pants down. Then
I had to lie over his chair and he proceeds to cane me. He gave me three big
wallops on the butt.

I didn't cry. Things crossed my mind as he was caning me. I thought, I
took somebody else's place. Now they hate me. What did I do wrong? I had
no idea why I was being beaten. I had no idea that you couldn't have an
orange. Being totally innocent, I figured I was beaten because I was a Hungarian. I was beaten because these guys were cruel. LaPierre was working
on his M.A. in English at the U of T at that time. Being from Quebec, he
of all people should have understood that not everybody is born with the
English language on their lips.

Years later, when I watched him on his TV show, "This Hour Has Seven
Days," I couldn't stand the guy. I just couldn't cope with him. When I
became a lawyer and I was doing some work with the National Bank of
Canada, I had to go to Montreal. LaPierre was a keynote speaker and I had
a chance to be with him on the dais. Of course, he remembered me as the
Hungarian refugee from UCC.

I said, "I want you to know that you are the biggest son of a bitch I
have ever met in my life. You are inhumane. You are an animal." He said,
"Why?" I told him the story. He said, "There must have been a mistake." I
said, "You must have known that I was coming into boarding as a new boy

who didn't speak a word of English. Dick Howard, the housemaster, made a big deal out of it. He would have said this kid does not speak any English and maybe he should get the benefit of the doubt. Then you have the audacity to cane me in the first three hours of our acquaintance because I have broken a rule that I couldn't have understood. It wasn't as if I had killed somebody." LaPierre said, "See, it taught you a great lesson. Look what a great success you have become as a lawyer. Maybe you should be thankful to me."

If the prep was like boot camp, the upper school was like going to West Point officers' school. I loved the upper school. I went into Seaton's House as a boarder. It was a phenomenal experience. My roommate was a guy named Barry Hill, a Mohawk Indian and a brain. It is amazing how difficult stereotypes are to overcome. Now my stereotype of an Indian is Barry Hill, who was getting 90 per cent. To me, Indians are smart people. They just don't get the chance. He was a Mohawk from the Six Nations Reserve and he looked like one. He was there on scholarship and he actually became head of Seaton's House. So here was a Mohawk and a Hungarian at UCC. We got along great.

Back then, I had a tremendous amount of insecurity and inferiority about the way I spoke. I was ashamed of my parents. I was asked by my friends to come to their homes. I went to Chip Barrett's beautiful house in Forest Hill. When I stayed at their house, I would have my own bedroom. Then we would go downstairs and there would be maids. They had a driver and cooks, which blew me out of the water. It was a fascinating period for me.

Years later, I was driving to a board meeting through Forest Hill. My son was at UCC by this point. One of the biggest moments in my life was when my son was accepted at UCC. I saw a Bosley Real Estate For Sale sign for the Barretts' house on Forest Hill Road, which was a huge house. I lived in Thornhill. When I saw the sign, I could hardly wait to phone the agent. I bought the house within a day. I totally gutted the place, renovated it, and moved in. That point was a watershed in my life.

Besides becoming a trustee and helping in fundraising at the school, my crowning achievement at UCC was in 1991. I was asked by the Tory government to work with the Hungarians establishing a blue ribbon commission to assist in the transition the country was going through in 1989-90. It was a fascinating experience. I worked with Cyrus Vance, who was representing the American side. It was really a tremendous opportunity for me to be able to go back to Hungary with some official status and meet quite a few of the politicians. It was like a homecoming.

In Hungary, I met Dr. Göncz, who is now the president of Hungary. At one point, Göncz had been sentenced to death. His life sentence was commuted three or four times. He's a lawyer and an incredible author. He learned English the way I did – with a dictionary. He was in jail and he couldn't get any books, so he found a dictionary and learned the language the same way I did.

I said to Göncz, "When you come to Canada, you must come to my school, UCC, to talk to the boys." When he was invited by UCC to make a speech, it created a tremendous security problem. The Canadian protocol people wanted him to go to a limited number of events, but we insisted. I said, "The president has to go to UCC. I have spent a lot of effort getting the guy into this country. I helped him to get his position."

Picture this: I'm standing on the front steps at Upper Canada College on a beautiful October morning. My son is beside me in his steward's jacket. My brother, the Eatons, the board of governors, and the principal, Doug Blakey, are all there. As I look down Avenue Road, rush-hour traffic has come to a dead stop. Nothing is moving. There are cops everywhere. Way in the distance, I see the flashing lights of the OPP. We see another light, then another. All of a sudden, we see about twenty police motorcyclists coming up through the gates of UCC, followed by a long cortege of cars. Traffic has been stopped. People on the streets are wondering what the hell is going on. The cortege moves up the front drive at UCC. Finally the presidential limousine drives up. Doug Blakey opens the door and I say hello to the president of Hungary.

We have breakfast and then the president is taken on a tour of the school. Then he goes to the morning assembly where the UCC band strikes up the Hungarian national anthem. I'm on the dais with Blakey, with the president of Hungary, and with my son. I had tears in my eyes. Blakey asked me to introduce Göncz. It probably was the most impressive event in my life.

My memories of Laurier LaPierre and all the years of suffering and hardship disappeared. My brother and I, refugees who were taken in by this school as equals, were allowed to play with them on a level playing field and achieve results which maybe others weren't as fortunate as we were to achieve. Canada gave me the ability and the financial resources to get my son into UCC and to arrange for the president of Hungary to visit the school. The highest ranking politician in my old country is now at my school. I have the incredible honour to introduce him to six hundred kids, who are totally impressed. It was an incredible moment. I had tears in my eyes. That day, everything came full circle in my life.

ALAN "MONK" MARR

1958 – 64

TV commercial director

IN EARLY 1964, our Grade 13 English master, Wilf Gallimore, came into class and said, "I'm taking orders for tickets to the world premiere of *Hamlet* at the O'Keefe Centre. I think it would be a good idea if you all went." The play was starring Richard Burton and was directed by John Gielgud. This was big, big, big. You were nuts not to go. For five dollars a ticket you get to see an incredible performance, and besides, you wouldn't have to read the play.

We all brought in five dollars each and Gallimore sent the order form off to the O'Keefe Centre. When he announced that he had received tickets to opening night, light bulbs simultaneously went on in all of us – hmm. Opening night? We met later that day. It was like a meeting that didn't need to be called. Scott Hall, Mike Royce, myself, and a couple of others met in the Jackson's House prefects' room. We said, "This is too good a chance to let pass. Why don't we make an entrance?" I knew I was going to be the centre shot because I had a quasi, half-assed rock band called the Clergy Reserves that had been performing at the boarders' shows and dances. By the time I was in Grade 13, I was definitely BMOC [Big Man on Campus], but very much the back alleyway, as I had a terrible academic average.

We knew there would be a big opening-night crowd at the O'Keefe Centre with all sorts of grand people, so we decided we would just sashay into it all. What could be more comical than to have a quasi-ersatz celebrity from among our own ranks trumped up into the man of the hour? Monk Marr, the famous New York satirist and rock singer, would make a spectacular celebrity entrance.

We had about a month to prepare. We realized that we had to have a front for calling meetings, so we got everybody organized to come into a lunchtime meeting in one of the classrooms. Pretty well everybody in our year came into that classroom without questioning anything. It was just, "Be there. There's something we want to talk about." We didn't even marvel when *everybody* showed up. There was that sort of brotherhood.

The whole stunt was led by the head steward, Scott Hall, a very powerful, influential, brilliant, rebellious guy who is now a lawyer in Victoria,

B.C. He chaired the first meeting with Mike Royce. The two of them were best of friends and easily the leaders of the class. They basically said, "We're going to pull a big entrance at *Hamlet*. Are you guys in?" We operated under the guise of the curling club, as there was no curling club at UCC. Anytime there was an announcement in morning prayers for the curling club, it meant there was going to be a secret meeting.

It was so slick. The future captains of capitalism and industry showed their stuff in stunts like this. The whole class was divided into five or six groups under group captains. There was a group in charge of putting together a motorcade and a signals unit responsible for alerting people how the motorcade was proceeding. Somebody actually went out and measured off the streets. They put a diagram up on the blackboard. Each group was told to be at a certain section of the O'Keefe Centre and each guy was supposed to bring one or two girls with him.

In those days, you could book a Culliton limousine in Forest Hill Village for eight dollars an hour. Everybody kicked in fifty cents. Everyone rented tuxedos. We recruited a guy named Mark Philips who had a motorcycle. We smuggled a battalion uniform out of the armouries for him to wear on his motorcycle. The UCC cadet uniform was virtually identical to a Toronto cop's uniform. Mark Philips had a crash helmet with the initials "MP" on it. One guy's father owned a funeral parlour, so he brought in two of those little flags that they use on hearses. So we just took some blank adhesive tape and put "MM" on the flags for the limo.

To set me apart, I wore a red tuxedo with black lapels. I was sitting in the back seat of the limo and Scott Hall was up front with the driver. I had two of the biggest guys in the school acting as bodyguards sitting beside me. We also smuggled out of the armouries one of those great big military walkie-talkies, a huge, oversized old black phone with buttons all over it. Rick Bell, who a few years later played piano for Janis Joplin and currently plays for the Band, was our signals guy. He stood on the traffic island at the corner of University Avenue and Front Street where the motorcade would turn towards O'Keefe Centre.

Everything was synchronized right to the T. An old white-haired chauffeur from Culliton's arrived with the limo at Mike Royce's place at 7:00 P.M. We called the chauffeur "sir." Typical, right? We said, "We're having a little fun tonight, sir. We'd like you to bear with us." He thought it was all a bit of a lark, so he was on board. We worked out the route with him.

As we started down Avenue Road, we were scared shitless. We had agreed that the motorcycle would come from behind the limo up to the front of the motorcade at a predetermined point. Just before we made the turn onto Front Street, we hear *rrrrrrrr* and Mark Philips, right on the money, pulls up alongside us on his big fucking Harley. All of a sudden, we had a collective adrenaline rush. We all just looked at each other and said, "Show time!" There was no turning back now. There were suddenly no negative thoughts any more.

Dozens of other guys meanwhile had been working the crowd outside of O'Keefe Centre for about half an hour, going up and down saying things like, "Is it true Monk Marr is coming?" People said,"Who the hell is Monk Marr?" They'd say, "He's a famous satirist and rock singer from New York …" They really primed the crowd. When you've got about forty people with one basic message working a crowd for half an hour, you start to get a buzz happening.

By the time we rolled in, the crowd was just fucking primed, to say nothing of the journalists. We had no idea there would be journalists from all over the world out in force. We had no idea opening night was going to be as big as it turned out to be. Who would have known back then that Richard Burton, fresh off the movie set of *Cleopatra*, had just taken off with Elizabeth Taylor. They had left their respective spouses and children and were balling their way across the continent towards Toronto, of all places. Liz and Dick were an infamous, scandalous couple living in sin, hounded by the world press.

So a cavalcade of black Cadillac limos with those big dopey fins – remember those babies? – is rolling into the front of the O'Keefe. By this time, Rick Bell, the signals guy, had caught up to us. He was the first to scream out, "It's him! It's him!" He looks into the limo at me and yells, "It is him!"

People went berserk. Mark Philips was just beautiful, revving up his motorcycle in his battalion uniform and helmet. He had sunglasses on in the middle of March, for Christ's sake. Here's this *rrrrrrr* and this limo with "MM" flags and all hell breaking loose. Limos stacked up. Flashbulbs popping. People screaming.

Scott Hall's door opens up. He gets out holding his hand under his lapels as if he has a gun. He shuts his door and looks at the crowd. They're all yelling, "Monk Marr! We want Monk Marr!" He just stares at them. Everything starts to quieten down. He then taps on the rear window. It hums down – *zzzzzz* – and they hand him out the big bogus battalion phone. The end of the cord was dangling in my lap, for Christ's sake. He says loudly into the phone, "There's too many people here. He's going to get mobbed. You've got to send over more bodyguards."

He throws the phone back in. Up goes the window – *zzzzzz*. He takes out a handkerchief and dusts off the door handle and opens it. My two bodyguards get out. He slams the door and they stand at either side of the door. He shouts, "Make way, make way! We're going to bring Mr. Marr through now."

They open up the door and I get out. Cigarette holder. Red tuxedo. The whole bit. I say, "Hello! Hello!" I'm scared shitless by this point. Then all hell breaks loose again. Guys are now making a wedge for me through the crowd. I see hands coming towards me from out of nowhere. I see the faces of little old ladies poking through the crush of people. It's pandemonium. Screaming. Flashbulbs. Photographers were holding their cameras up over other people's heads. Girls were screaming, "I touched him! I touched him!" It was unbelievable.

So I waded through, signing some autographs, but I kept going. Deeks was inside the door and he grabbed my coat. They cleared a path for me right through to the escalator. By the time everybody else got through, I was up at the top of the escalator. Then I got on the next escalator, which nobody expected, because we had the cheapest seats in the house, two or three rows from the back of the theatre, way the hell up.

We all sat there for the rest of the night wondering, What have we done? I was having second thoughts. We had pulled it off, but what had we pulled off? All we wanted was to make a splash, but what kind of splash did we make? The reaction was far bigger than we ever expected and the stunt went off like clockwork. We weren't prepared for absolute total perfection.

All the Toronto newspapers wrote it up. They found out the truth because they saw the UCC ties. All the boarders had to wear school ties, so the newspapers put two and two together. Afterwards, I got a lot of calls at my house from reporters. There aren't a lot of Marrs in the phone book.

The next morning, I was dreading going to English class because Wilf Gallimore was really a difficult and arrogant man. He was a tank commander in World War II. We called him "Big G." He walked into the class and I'm sure he knew that we would be on pins and needles. He got to his desk, turned and looked at us with an inscrutable look on his face. Then he began applauding, very, very slowly. "Congratulations," he said. "You boys made some very stupid people look even more stupid than they really are."

WALLY SECCOMBE

1957–63

Professor of sociology
Ontario Institute for Studies in Education

I WAS A SOUTHPAW, so the school shifted me over to become right-handed, which was part of the pedagogical theory of the day. I had gone through a period of months where I was stuttering, which I think was mentioned in my initial interview with the prep headmaster, Alan Stephen. So in the interview, Stephen did a delightful thing where he said, "It's not very often that you get to shoot the headmaster." He pulled out a toy gun, laid it on the desk, and said, "At the count of three, we're going to reach for the gun and see who can shoot the other one first. One. Two. Three."

He wanted to see which hand I would grab it with. I can't even remember what I did because he went into guffaws of laughter. I can't even remember if I grabbed it with my right hand or left hand. I think I grabbed it with both hands and then pointed it with my right hand. I remember this as an absolutely delightful experience with somebody who had a creative way to figure out which hand I would use quickly and instinctively. So over a period of time, I had to learn to write with my right hand.

I went through a very tough time when it affected me verbally. I was stuttering. There was a direct link between the changeover and my speech. A few months later, I pulled it together on the right side and I've been right-handed ever since. I seem to be able to use both hands with equal strength. I have faint residues of left-handedness, but I could no more write with my left hand now than fly to the moon.

I was very happy right from the word go in the prep. I ended up being the head boy of the prep. I was a jock. There was a fundamental cultural cleavage in the school between the jocks and who we would now call the intellectuals. As jocks, we looked down our noses at them and called them the brown-nosers or browners. We were more independent from the masters and we didn't need to suck up to them. Homophobic terms like "kiss ass," "suck up," "brown nose," etc., were a part of our adolescent vocabulary.

We would carry our books on clipboards under our arms and the browners had what we called "brownie bags." They were in the chess club and we were on the hockey team. The best they could play was the house leagues. They could never make the school's teams. They were uncoordinated, which subjected them to ridicule by us.

I think in retrospect it was a very unfortunate culture cleavage because we could have learned a lot from them. Within the school as a whole, the jocks were undoubtedly the dominate cultural group which generated the school leaders. The disdain for the intellectuals was part and parcel of the jock culture.

I remember that John Bosley, who later became a Tory politician, was a socially inept kid who was a target for scapegoating in the prep. We used to set up a wild man, Greg Dekatenzaro, as the persecutor of Bosley. Dekatenzaro would sit in the desk in front of Bosley and get ready to give him a judo chop. As soon as Bosley would cringe and go to one hand, Dekatenzaro would fling his hand around and chop him. Bosley would dissolve into tears and frustrated blubberings. We all thought this was a great lark. That kind of scapegoating was very much a part of the jock culture.

Dekatenzaro obviously had bully qualities but he wasn't acting on his own. If we had not encouraged him, if we had not laughed uproariously at his persecution of Bosley, then this stuff would have stopped. It was very much a part of the pathology of class culture rather than an individual act of bullying. I can't remember if I did any of that stuff myself. I know that I judo chopped Dekatenzaro at one point, which caused him to piss blood. He had to go to the infirmary. I can't remember the context. I guess I blocked it all out.

John Fraser, who later became the editor of *Saturday Night*, was not a big or intimidating kid, so he couldn't throw his weight around. But he really enjoyed darting around and mischievously stirring up trouble. Fraser would slash ink splotches with his fountain pen on everybody's books. He liked to orchestrate a high-energy repartee among the kids that always had an aggressive and conflict-oriented underside to it. He'd get everyone worked up and running around, which he thought was a great lark.

Fraser never really got caught because he had the immunity of the tongue. He was the kind of kid who was adept at working his way out of tight situations by being verbal. He was a shit disturber in his own way but he was always around the edge of the circle. I think that's why he likes to tell tales. It's part of the same mischievous impulse in him.

Conrad Black was one year ahead of us. I remember him as a wallflower, skulking around, not in any way a high-status kid in the school. I remember when there was a flea market sale at the upper school to raise money for a charity, Conrad was there with a cheque-book. He'd be bargaining and then he'd take up his cheque-book and whip off cheques. I don't think I even had a bank account, or if I did, it was only a savings account. I wasn't writing cheques. He was already into money. There were guys at the school who you knew were from ruling-class families who were right up there in the stratosphere.

I certainly knew the primitive joys of violence at UCC. I relished the physical contact of sports and got into it in a big way. I was already competitive but the school certainly brought it out. I was captain of the football team in the prep and assistant captain of the hockey team and very much thrived on being a leader. The bonding of team sports and the competitive effort of the team stay with me to this day as really deep-seated, primitive pleasures.

In my senior years, those pleasures became connected with sex for me as well. The masculine rituals of symbolic violence became connected to wowing the girls. In our final year in the upper school, we asked the Lawrence Park cheerleading team, who were the previous year's cheerleading champions in the city of Toronto, to cheer for UCC. Of course it was totally *verboten* at the time to have girls cheerleading for us. But the girls agreed.

In secret, Ross Wilson's mother had a hand in getting them all outfitted with UCC cheerleading uniforms – blue-and-white sweaters, short skirts, socks, the whole bit. Our first Little Big Four game of the year was right in front of the principal's house up on the hill. At an opportune time during the first quarter, out danced the cheerleaders from under their coats.

It was electric. I can remember our juices flowing in anticipation of the game, but the girls added a whole new dimension. We knew that there was sexual capital to be made in being an outstanding football player. We knew that this would set up an aura around us, strengthening our attractiveness with the girls. We knew we could exploit it. The testosterone juices that were flowing into the football game tied right into the girls.

Probably the most ecstatic experience I had at UCC happened that day. During the game, Ridley was running an offensive play, trying to make an end run down the sidelines. I was notorious as a defensive end who revelled in nailing the quarterback before he released the ball. On this play, one of my teammates forced the ball carrier to turn back in towards the sidelines, which set him up perfectly. I had a perfect angle on him. I just creamed him.

We all went tumbling into the sidelines, which were chock-a-block full of cheerleaders, scattering them like ten pins. There were bursts of screaming and squealing. I have a clear memory of the raw power of the crowd's adulation as the cheerleaders and football players all fell into a heap on the sidelines.

I'm sure that that moment was connected with later meeting a cheer-leader named Helen. In the pecking order of girls, she was a cut above who I could expect to go out with. But on the team bus coming home from a game against Ridley in St. Catharines, she ended up sitting on my lap in her cheerleading outfit. I was ecstatic. I'm sure that moment was connected to the earlier erotic tumble on the sidelines. It's amazing how those primitive manhood rituals were eroticized. It was a very pure energy flow that combined the camaraderie of the male group in combat on the field with the seduction of girls. It really pumped us up.

There was also an emotional linkage at the school between authority and sheer physical terror. I remember a couple of instances where kids were caned for a flagrant transgression of a school rule. But I also remember an occasion when Ian Douglas was caned by a master who was new to the school. It was a totally arbitrary, sudden, unexpected singling out of a boy in a totally innocuous situation.

Whatever joke or face Ian was trying to make just set the master off. He viewed it as being too familiar or somehow transgressing some invisible line of authority that he was attempting to establish for all of us. The master singled out Ian and abruptly caned him. It was completely unjust. The arbitrary nature of that kind of authority I remember was really shocking. Ian was one of the least likely kids in the class who you'd expect to be caned. He was exactly on the opposite pole, the kind of kid the jocks would have seen as a brown-noser. Here he was being arbitrarily caned.

Another master in the prep, Walter Ruffell, would line us up in the locker room every afternoon when we were going out to play games. One by one, we had to pass him standing at the doorway in all of his authority. When your turn came, he would dig his thumb into the hollow of your clavicle and interrogate you. He'd ask questions like, "Have you changed your underwear?" You'd be squirming and giggling nervously. He was insuring that everybody had played by the rules.

Then he would suspect that some kid was lying because the nervousness would come out. It was almost as if you were trying to smuggle dope through customs. He imparted that degree of authority and fear of getting caught out. He'd say to a kid, "Go get me your underwear." Everyone would have to wait in line while the kid would go to his locker and he wouldn't have any underwear. When he came back, the kid would get punished. I remember thinking that if he looks away, I'll go home and change my underwear so I don't have to lie to the guy because I'm afraid of getting caught out. I felt distinctly repelled and angered by the degree to which sheer fear was an element of authority.

Those kinds of experiences sowed the seeds of my subsequent rebellion in the upper school against the cadet battalion. When I got to the upper school, the battalion became an intense focus of hatred. The only way that I could possibly pass the time was by rebelling by being the military slob. It was something not well understood and always responded to emotionally. The battalion embodied the repressive, hierarchical, authoritarian, conformist nature of the school, the point of resistance where I had to stand and fight.

Mike Gardiner and I would line up and march in a totally uncoordinated way, moving the same arm and leg up at the same time as if we didn't know any better. We would do left wheels and walk into the wall instead of doing the right wheel. We would think of any way that we could to create disruptions and subvert the order of the battalion. It had nothing to do with a pacifist consciousness which I would subsequently develop. I would later develop a very strong critique of militarism, but I couldn't define my own rebellion with those kind of lofty goals. It was much more a visceral, anti-authoritarian desire to disrupt the conformity of military precision.

What I found most striking was the degree to which my peers climbed the hierarchy of the battalion. Some handled authority with a great deal of grace and never broke my friendship, even though I was a militant private throughout my upper school career. There were other guys whose authority as officers or sergeants went to their heads. They took great delight in ordering us around and singling us out for humiliating lectures.

To me, they broke the fundamental bonds of peer friendship. An hour after battalion was over, these guys were walking home with me, wanting to be my friend. I wouldn't abide it. I'd walk on the other side of the street if the guy had chewed me out on battalion. To me, the officers who took great delight in enforcing symbolic deference and humiliation were contemptible. I was sickened by the degree to which some kids got turned on and were swept up in the power of the military hierarchy.

There was no doubt that if you cut yourself off from leadership positions, as I did, you could never become a steward. The most you could become was a prefect if you insisted on rebelling in battalion and eschewed progressing up the school hierarchy over the years. If you were still shit disturbing in Grade 11, it was pretty clear that by the time you got to Grade 13, you couldn't be a prefect or steward.

But you could still gain social status in the school through athletics, which could more than compensate. There was a begrudging admiration in the school for rebels who could rebel in a fairly creative way. But as far as the school's official hierarchy was concerned, rebelling cut you out of leading roles, which of course were not chosen by the boys anyway. It was a pretty powerful experience for me because I definitely cut myself off from the kind of status which I probably would have relished. I certainly was not immune to the allure of the perks of the leadership positions, but I was always on the outs with the school authorities.

Dr. Sowby, the principal, didn't have any use for me whatsoever. He would engage in his own humiliation rituals in class. At end of term, he'd go over our report cards and single me out for particularly demeaning lectures. He used to go through the report cards of every boy from the top of the class to the bottom of the class. He would have each boy stand up and come up to the front. Then he'd make a few condescending comments.

This ritual took maybe a minute and a half for each kid, so the whole thing took up the entire class. I would be left to the bottom because I was a lousy student. I was sitting sullenly in the back row beside Jamie Massie. Sowby peered over his half-moon glasses and said, "Is there a bad odour coming from the back of the room, Mr. Massie?"

When my turn came, I would slink to the front of the class very slowly. In my own way, I was making it known through my body language that I didn't appreciate this process very much and that I was a very reluctant participant in it. I wasn't going to snap to attention or in any way show deference to it.

Sowby had me tagged as a rebel whom he wanted to bring down a peg. There were a couple of run-ins where he made clear to me that I was close to being thrown out of the school over battalion. He said when boys get to Grade 12 or 13, it becomes inexcusable that they rebel against battalion. He'd say something like, "We don't need people who pervert their leadership capacities in such a pernicious way." I guess in an informal way I did have leadership qualities, but only as part of the jock star system. I had a reputation in football as "The Bear."

I was totally turned off scholastically at UCC, which is paradoxical because I am now a scholar. I am someone for whom the battle for ideas is supremely important, but there was no intellectual excitement in UCC whatsoever for me. Through my entire career in the school, I can never remember being excited by ideas or a class assignment that electrified me. I screwed off all term and then studied like hell in the last week. We used to pop wake-up pills and stay up all night cramming for exams.

I was a notorious crammer. To this day, I have an occasional nightmare where I'm trying to write an exam and I've drawn a blank. I'm so strung out from taking uppers that I'm totally fucked. I feel like I never studied all year long, I deserve to flunk, and I'm a fool and an idiot. Despite the fact that I have certainly excelled as a scholar in my subsequent life, these primitive early experiences are still there. I'm so relieved when I wake up and realize I'm not still a student. I tell myself that I'm okay. At UCC, I was a dull-witted and thoroughly alienated student.

You needed 540 marks out of nine subjects to go to U of T and that's exactly the number of marks I got, not a single mark more. I got a 60 per cent average. Unlike many of my peers, I didn't go to Trinity College, which was the beginning of my inchoate rebellion against the cultural narrowness of the school. I went to University College because I wanted a broader experience.

I played football for Varsity and was recruited to the Delta Kappa Epsilon Fraternity, so I partook fully in a cultural stream which flowed directly out of my Upper Canada background. At the frat house, there were a lot of UCC and UTS old boys, so I was immersed in the same kind of milieu as UCC. After playing a Varsity football game, we went back to the frat, watched a game on TV, sat around with our girlfriends, and quaffed ale. We were the big boys on campus.

It was basically a lost year, although it was the beginnings of my class awareness. I had first decided to become a youth worker when Jim Feltzner, who was a street worker in Toronto, came to speak to my Hi-C youth group at Timothy Eaton Memorial Church when I was in Grade 13 in Upper Canada. He electrified me. My parents report that I came home and told them that I now knew what I was going to do.

That's what I did do. At age eighteen, I went to the YMCA and volunteered as a youth worker in Regent Park. It opened my eyes. It changed my life. The liberal impulse from my background was married to my anti-authoritarian streak, which gradually radicalized me. The whole class nature of the system was wrong and needed to be deeply reformed.

I went through the motions the following year at U of T. I was culturally disembodied. I was falling out of synch, unable to relate back to my youth work experience of the previous year. I skipped classes. I drank too much. I flunked out. I was living out a set of social roles and rituals that were completely dissociated with who I was becoming. I was becoming split. I was a classic case of "reaction formation" against my sense of identity and personality. I was gradually becoming more vehement in the denunciation of my own privileged class background and the institutional experiences that made it up – UCC and my first year at U of T.

I remember being shocked and appalled by what happened with women in the fraternity parties. Guys got drunk and used the excuse of alcohol to sexually abuse and degrade women in the back rooms. Women were also lost and going along with it. It wasn't strictly a rape experience, but it was on the borderline. The women consented initially, but it got taken considerably further. There were incidents with the Varsity football team which absolutely appalled me. When I recently learned that both George Bush and Dan Quayle are members of my old Deke fraternity, I rolled my eyes.

Long before feminism came along, I was forming a sense of disgust with the abusive prerogatives of "us" and an identitification with "them" and with their experiences which were silenced by our rituals. I wanted some way to break out of it and I had nowhere to go. After one year at U of T, I went down to Sir George Williams University in Montreal, which was my fork in the road. When I went overseas in 1967, I had an enormously radicalizing experience. I had a classic New Left trajectory from there. Right from the word go, I became an unrepentant anti-Stalinist leftist and I remain one to this day.

I developed my own radical politics in a milieu of women who were becoming ardent feminists. Judy Rebick, the former president of the National Action Committe on the Status of Women, was a comrade of mine in a revolutionary Marxist group. My intellectual priority was to integrate gender relations with traditional class analysis. I wrote a piece in the early 1970s in the *New Left Review* called "The Housewife and Her Labour Under Capitalism."

My own family was a classic Freudian configuration. I had what I felt was an authoritarian father and a mother who I identified with like mad and with whom I shared her sense of oppression. I always wanted to stick up for her when she was being browbeaten by my father with his argumentative, vociferous selfishness and his sense that she served him and subordinated her own interests to his own. I felt a tremendous identification with her.

My mother had gone to BSS. I haven't talked with many old boys about their own recollections about the single-sex school experience. If you had asked us at the time, I think that you would have gotten two responses. One would have been a serious response that it was better not to have girls at UCC because there were fewer distractions. You could get on with taking classes seriously and you wouldn't always be looking over at the girls.

That idea is very much part and parcel of the idea of the "eroticized other." Girls were not part of our daily life, so we therefore regarded them as very alluring sex objects. The other response would have been premised on the same cultural value, that we should have had girls at the school because it would make our environment a whole lot more interesting.

What would be missing in both of those scenarios, which I can now maintain only in retrospect, would be that all the mundane activities of day-to-day life – swapping math assignments, talking about people's family lives, rubbing shoulders in daily life – would have demystified relationships with girls and opened up platonic friendships in a much easier way.

We could have developed respect for girls. Far from seeing them as the opposite of boys, we would have understood how much similarity there is between us and how much our society has created a polarized map of gender relations. In reality, the closer you are, the more you see the enormous areas of commonality. The more you break down the mystical and eroticized relations with the exciting "other," the more you open up a field for respect and platonic good relations. You can sort out the girls who you like and don't like on grounds other than sexual attraction. Denied that experience, we were much more oriented to look at girls sexually. The girls we didn't consider sexually attractive were all considered small change in the scheme of things.

Still, a critique of an all-male institution like UCC is one-sided if it doesn't understand the inherent goodness and purity of the emotional wellsprings of the male experience, which were then constructed on a foundation of exclusion. Why couldn't we have experienced camaraderie with boys and girls of all different cultures and races? Why couldn't we have had the jostling, kidding, kibitzing, and loyalty to one another that represents the best of those emotions? Why did it have to be forged among a group of privileged white males?

Very much a part of my rebellion against UCC was a rebellion against my father. In some way, my father embodied what I objected to in UCC. I remember when I was a youth worker in my mid-twenties, my supervisor, who knew my father, said to me that I had a lot of similarities to my father. I was totally insulted. I considered myself to be the opposite of my father. This was a moment of pure reaction formation in my own development. My father was a belligerent conservative and I was an equally belligerent socialist. Our values were antithetical, which put us in polar opposition in terms of our visions of social order, justice, and fairness.

Of course, I later understood that in fact I was in many ways a chip off the old block. In spite of our differences, there were many aspects of my personality which very much made me his son. I was tenacious, argumentative, and principled to the point of stubbornness. You stand up for what you believe in and you don't let the bastards get you down. You speak your mind honestly. You don't kowtow to power. You have to say what you believe.

What most grated about the humiliating experiences at UCC was not the "top down" system of power but the way in which we degrade ourselves when we cower. You debase yourself when you can't find the courage to be honest. If you did find the courage to be honest, you'd be thrown out of that school so fucking fast that it would make your head spin. It is a very debasing, humiliating, deeply scarring experience to quake in your boots and kiss ass. You can say that you didn't have any choice and that the guy is an asshole. You can say you just did what you had to do to get by and you're right. But there is a part of you that detests grovelling in fear. Those are deep experiences.

UCC was not a Dickensian institution where rule was upheld by fear alone, at least not in my period. That is not to say that those moments don't scar us – those moments of trembling deference, those moments of eating humble pie, those moments where a part of your brain is screaming, "You bastard!" and yet you kiss the guy's ass. Everyone knows that those are dishonest experiences. When you are being deferential, you're being insincere.

Class consciousness was never a part of my Upper Canada experience. In addition to devoting yourself to achieving a leadership position in a prestigious occupation, the Upper Canada experience included the notion of noblesse oblige, which had always been part of the school's British, imperialistic, Lord Baden-Powell, boy scout ideology. You were being trained to serve the less fortunate in society beyond the narrow sphere of economic self-interest. My own subsequent trajectory was simply to take that idea seriously. The liberal impulse was to take it seriously. The radical impulse was to overthrow the system.

My subsequent rebellion evolved into an opposition to the school from the standpoint of its role in reproducing class relations. But that was not what I was feeling at the time. My first impulse was one of compassion. The school certainly not only allowed for that but wanted to insist that that was part and parcel of what leaders were about. You do not forget the poor and those who are less fortunate. Genuine compassion was part of the obligation of leaders. This was how you held together a society based on self-interest and individual upward mobility, which of course UCC is all about. It was part of the school's ideology that not only would people become stockbrokers and go off and make a bundle, but that they would remember the poor.

My father always hoped I would take over the family business and he was bitterly disappointed that I didn't. My father, who was a UTS old boy, had a modest business as a publisher of professional magazines like *Modern Medicine in Canada* and *Quill and Quire*. But to his credit, he swallowed hard and didn't make an issue of it. He had a sneaking admiration for me. In subsequent years, when his golfing buddies would talk about his radical son, he'd stick up for me. I really give him credit for that.

For many years after UCC, I refused to go to any old-boy reunions. I was opposed to everything the school stood for. I felt that I would stand out at a UCC function as a left-wing pariah. I imagined somebody like Conrad Black starting into a tirade and me being the only socialist in the place. I imagined myself either rising to the bait or swallowing my tongue and selling out my own values.

At the height of my own political radicalism in the mid-1970s, I was part of a group handing out leaflets calling for a general strike at the time of wage and price controls brought in by the Trudeau government. When the Canadian Labour Congress called a one-day strike, it wasn't totally off the wall to think that it might become generalized.

I was assigned to the Toronto-Dominion Centre to hand out leaflets to secretaries and office workers on a day in Canadian history in which class tensions and conflicts were at their height. High-powered stockbrokers, including a lot of UCC old boys, were passing by. The degree of Red-baiting animosity we received was extraordinary. The image of veins bulging out of their necks sticks indelibly in my mind. If I was ever going to go back to a reunion at UCC, I expected the same kind of response.

I went back to my twenty-fifth year reunion in 1988. Initially, I had been very reluctant to go, but my cousin, Peter Turner, finally persuaded me. At the reunion, Pat Johnson, a former principal, was clearly moved to get back in touch with Wally Seccombe. It obviously meant a great deal to him that I would come back. He would collar some other guy who was my peer and talk about how I was an exemplary old boy. He was so effusive that it was embarrassing. Johnson said, "The school was meant to produce more Wally Seccombes. We have produced too many stockbrokers. Here is somebody who really took the injustices of this world seriously."

The reunion turned out to be one of the high points of my life. I loved connecting with the guys, walking across the playing fields with them, remembering particular incidents and laughing about them. Those who had some inkling that I had gone off in a different direction in life from most UCC boys were really curious to find out more just because I was so different.

It is a cliché that we repress painful and unpleasant experiences. But I was amazed to discover at the reunion how deeply I had forgotten, repressed, or excluded the warm, deep, friend-for-life boyhood experiences that I had at UCC because of my own hardening ideological opposition to the school and all that it stood for. I had repressed the very best of what Upper Canada College meant to me. I had become so vigorous in my opposition to the school as a ruling-class institution that I had completely forgotten how happy I was there.

PART
III

MICHAEL IGNATIEFF

1959 – 65

Author, broadcaster

I THINK it is very important for a boy, for a young man, to see male authority that he can believe in. I came to the prep with a very uncertain, indeed bad, academic record. My first winter, I remember receiving extra tutoring in math from a young prep master named Ted Stephenson. He sat smoking beside me in an empty classroom as he was taking me through my math. I still can smell the nicotine on his fingers.

It is an astonishing fact that I can remember the UCC teachers so well and yet can't remember my university instructors. Stephenson showed tremendous pastoral concern for a lonely, frightened boy and I've felt a great affection for him ever since. I also remember Alan Harris, the man who ran the first soccer team, had convincing male authority. A cardinal experience was when I was made captain of the prep school soccer team. I remember him taking me aside and saying, "You are doing too much shouting out there. You don't lead by shouting." I've never forgotten that.

The prep headmaster, Alan Stephen, was a different kind of authority figure, more of a pipe-smoking, tweedy, gentle man. I had a sense of understanding from him. I also remember Dick Howard, who was a thin, elegant, tall glass of water. I've had a great affection for him ever since because he stood for something good. As a young boy, you were drawn to figures of masculine authority.

But what I remember with deep anger was that the school did not take action early enough to stop the behaviour of one of the masters. I look back on it with real indignation. When you are a young, frightened boy in a boarding school, you think the world has to be the way adults say it is. You have no capacity for distance. You are in the middle of something you don't understand. Adults make the rules and they must be right. Yet the prep permitted a grade-B psychopath to prowl the corridors at night beating boys for no reason. That was another formative experience in my life. My dislike, not merely of him, but of the ways in which the adult world colluded in this weak, vain, stupid man's aggression, left a very bitter taste in my mouth.

So all my feelings about the school are caught up by that primal ambivalence. There is this wonderful man giving me math lessons when I was lonely and frightened. Then there is this awful man frightening, beating, and bullying the boys. I lived in fear of him and I don't like to live in fear. I'm now a father. I feel very strongly that children must never be made frightened in that way. It is a wicked thing. A school must never allow it to happen.

Needless to say, the bullying bred a wonderful network of resistance and a great deal of solidarity. We bonded much more closely together as we were oppressed in this ridiculous way by this stupid man. I learned something about the joys of rebellion. I learned something about the pride of being in a band of disobedient brothers. I learned something about taking punishment without bitching about it. I was caned by the same man, Ted Stephenson, who gave me the math lessons. He gave me six swats for taking part in a pillow fight. I was so proud of those swats because I was rebellious enough to challenge the system.

When I think of my images of Canada, one of them is being in the prep school dorm at night, lying in our cubicles in the darkness. Radiators covered with grey wire mesh ran down the central corridor of the dormitory. On top of one of them is a radio. It is the second period of "Hockey Night in Canada" and we are listening to the voice of Foster Hewitt call the play-by-play. Those are happy memories.

When I think of images of happiness, I think of the cloud of feathers bursting from a busted pillow during a pillow fight, rising above the radiators, blown up by the hot air, water spraying all over. All of us were in a delirium of happiness that the system had been beaten, that we had revolted. Children were revelling in their natural gaiety.

But I will never quite overcome my anger at the amount of fear and institutionalized cruelty I saw in that school. I never want to see myself as a victim of that school. I'm not and I never was. But let's never forget that there were people who were destroyed by the place.

I think the indictment that perhaps gets closest to what I really feel was that UCC was a school that put much too much emphasis on duty, responsibility, honour, and achievement, and not enough on spontaneity, joy, and fun. Still, we managed to find those things with pillow fights, short-sheeting beds, water fights, roping dental floss along the floor so that people would trip, the whole gamut of childhood lunacy. Some of the happiest moments of pure joy in my life were just busting the place down.

I'm now a writer. If I think about when that was first encouraged, I think of Dick Sadleir's and Wilf Gallimore's English classes. Two of my books have included long discussions of *King Lear*, for no other reason than Mr. Gallimore took us through that play line by line. Through one whole autumn, I don't think we did anything else than that play. We went to Stratford to see it. I didn't even like Mr. Gallimore personally, but he had a certain kind of dour, southern Ontario tenacity and respect for these old texts that got into my bones. The cadence of Shakespeare had an indelible effect on me.

In the chapel, I felt the cadence of the Bible. I was bored and felt that Anglicanism was sanctimonious and phoney at the school. I hated the principal, Dr. Sowby, who was an Anglican cleric, and I hated all the chapel stuff. I've associated religion with sanctimony ever since because of Upper Canada. Yet in prayers every morning, we would read from the Bible. I can still feel what it was like to read St. Paul's Epistle to the Galatians, the words coming out of me. As a sixteen-year-old boy, I could feel the power of the words.

I don't know what language is now spoken in the school because I have never been back. I have no particular desire to. I don't attend reunions and I don't donate money. But I would salute that language, which was the language my uncle George Grant heard. It was the same language that my great-grandfather, George Parkin, and my grandfather, Choppy Grant, heard and spoke as principals of the school in the early part of the century.

I feel a deep gratitude for that linguistic continuity, the way that language used to echo through the halls. People say it is phonily derivative of Britain, but that's to misunderstand it totally. It's in an institution like Upper Canada College that you can understand the way in which Britishness, even an ersatz phoney Britishness, was the fulcrum around which a distinctive Canadian identity was formed.

This is the paradox of Canada that is ill understood. I've always believed rather strongly that the loss of that Britishness, that strange, phoney cult Britishness of the 1950s in Canada, has been a real loss. It's not been clear what we replace it with as a guiding official public culture. It's one of the reasons why we all feel confusedly and ashamedly more American now than when we were children.

At the time, I was very critical of my uncle George Grant's lament for the Anglo-Canadian world in his book *Lament for a Nation*, which was published in 1965, the year I graduated from UCC. I thought it was reactionary in the worst sense of the word, that he was attempting to roll the clock back when it can't be rolled back. I now see, with hindsight, that he had put his finger on something very deep about the public culture of Canada. We haven't yet found the alternative language to ring around the walls of the public schools, let alone the private schools. I heard the language of Shakespeare, King James, and the houses of parliament as it was dying at Upper Canada. It shaped me irrevocably.

The UCC culture in my time was basically Tory, Anglican, and fantastically patrician. I think anybody who was at UCC has to wrestle with the anomaly and irony of a patrician education in an egalitarian society like Canada. The contradiction is particularly flagrant. The Toronto that I grew up in was ceasing to be a white Anglo-Saxon Protestant enclave where the sidewalks rolled up on Sunday. It was becoming a Portuguese, Italian, Haitian town, and Upper Canada was a relic of WASP Toronto that was very swiftly ceasing to be. I felt very much on the cusp of that change.

Carl Berger taught me as an undergraduate at the University of Toronto that those Canadians who most intensely articulated their British connection, and I'm thinking of George Parkin and George Grant, did so out of absolutely passionate Canadian patriotism. There was the feeling that the young dominion would find itself, express itself, and come of age only through the articulation of an independent, autonomous, freely chosen connection to the crown.

You tamper with this stuff at your peril. If you tamper with it without articulating something different, the country will fall apart. You hear the total meaninglessness of the British connection to a man like Pierre Trudeau. Yet he articulated passion and a sense of the country that was completely unrelated to the British monarchical connection. Our greatest statesman's sole vision of Canada had nothing to do with Britishness and it came alive for millions of Canadians, whatever their origin.

Brian Mulroney came up with the other alternative, an essentially continentalist vision of ourselves, which is about to be deeply, massively, totally, comprehensively rejected. That's surely an astonishing thing. We're rejecting what our geography and our lifestyle tells us ought to be natural to us and what Michael Wilson thought would be natural.

We have nothing in its place, however, so we're fragmenting into regional parties where we feel our identities very clearly. I think there is nothing wrong with that. I think there is an honesty in it. People will now only feel about this country what they can honestly feel. The old stories, the British story, the continentalist story, no longer carry conviction. But we can't get a national story going.

Recently I was talking to an Iranian taxi driver in Toronto. He has a clearer vision of Canada than any politican I've heard. He said, "This is a free country. This is a country of opportunity. This is a country where if I get sick, I can get a doctor. This is a country where if I have to go to law, I can get justice without having to bribe somebody. This is a country where politics doesn't destroy your life."

The Canadian elite must be an open, permeable elite which is colour blind, religion blind, and gender blind. There has to be an elite based not even on intelligence, but character. They will mostly come from schools that have no resemblance to Upper Canada. The Canadian elite have got to hear the music that's coming up from the ground. Upper Canada doesn't teach you to listen to it, but you have to. If the elite don't listen, the country is dead.

My argument about UCC being out of touch is not an argument that the school must either be fantastically contemporary or it must die. It's more an argument about whether the patrician values it chooses to stand for are the right ones. I'm not against boarding schools necessarily. I went boarding too young. I think the logic of boarding is basically to get puberty out of the house, to get boys away from their parents so they can become sexual animals alone. I think there is a powerful rationale for it if we could find a boarding system, possibly coed, that wasn't full of privilege, sado-masochism, and needless cruelty.

I feel my sexual life has been slightly corrupted by one of the odd effects of single-sex education, which is that you invest women with too much mystery. You make them too special and too different. You invest them with absurd categories of honour. You make them everything that you are not. Upper Canada encouraged the sense of the bestial male and the vir-ginal, fleeing female, none of which turned out to be true in my own sexual life.

I remember Upper Canada from age sixteen onwards in terms of the smell of hair spray and corsages, the absolutely delicious feel of young women's foundation garments pressed against your tuxedo, the furtive sex-ual explorations in school dances. There was a tremendous suppressed ten-derness – suppressed by the school, suppressed by the ribaldry of your peers – but nevertheless finding its object mysteriously in fragile, frightened girls, usually from Havergal or BSS. It's a miracle we found each other at all, but many did. I guess that's testimony to the tenacity of Eros. The total institution could not beat Eros.

I think also that the single-sex environment produced a certain homo-phobia, which I now very much regret. I have very strong emotional feel-ings towards men, some of which were cultivated by that environment. Often the only source of tenderness, comfort, and affection you got in that school was from fellow boys. Yet there was a tremendous anxiety about crossing the line into homosexual experience. I think it is very right and important and appropriate for men to love each other, and love each other physically. That was damn difficult in that school, and made more difficult than it needed to be.

To be frank, when you [James FitzGerald] wrote me, initially I thought, I can't stand this project. That is an interesting reaction in itself. I can't examine all the reasons for it. Now I think that this book is an amazing way to slice into the identity of Canadian society. But try to keep the big picture. Keep people aware that what you are doing is looking at one thing, but actually looking at something much bigger. I now realize that, among other things, I've been talking about the anthropology of adolescence, about what kinds of elitisms are defensible, about the identity of Canada.

I think my years at UCC were probably the most successful single period in my life. I was very conscious of being a scholarship boy and, needless to say, proud that I won it. I became a steward and editor of the *College Times*. But I think back to my successful adolescent self with a real degree of embarrassment. Although I am passing the buck, I feel that the school encouraged me to be an authoritarian prig. I hold it a bit against the school.

Things were was also complicated by the fact that my younger brother, Andrew, happened to be in my boardinghouse. I feel very angry at the school and at my parents for having levered us into a situation where I had direct executive authority over my own brother, which had a devastating impact on our relationship as brothers. I've regretted it all my life. I was seventeen years old and he was only fourteen. Had I had a little more maturity, I might have said, "This is crazy. I can discipline other children, but I can't discipline my own brother. It's not fair. It's not right."

I've often had cause to reflect on John Kennedy's wonderful phrase that the student leaders of yesterday are the leaders of tomorrow. You get caught in a time warp because you've had success as an adolescent – a success you can never repeat. I think that's often the nemesis of a school like UCC , a total institution that shapes you utterly. You learn a certain code and form of practice which is phenomenally successful within that environment. When you leave, you are at a loss. I feel I've gone on to do other things, but I've often been haunted by the memory of that success.

The school did create a sense of self-worth and self-respect, for which I'm grateful. But it was obvious by the end that I was tremendously restless. I remember my sexual life beginning at the end of Upper Canada and feeling in a confused, teenage way that it was ridiculous to be there. I had come to the end of what the place could teach me. I was dying to get to university, to get out on my own. The waves of the sixties revolution were beginning to beat against the doors of the old place. UCC seemed more and more out of touch. By seventeen and eighteen, I felt a kind of rage to be done with it.

CHRIS GILMOUR
1957–65

Former commodities broker

I ALWAYS HAD A FEAR at UCC that people thought I wasn't bright. Michael Ignatieff, for instance, was one of the people who was always implying that I was stupid. He thought of himself as being an incredibly intelligent person, and I suppose in one way he is. But I think it's a limited intelligence, a kind of phoney thoughtfulness. I used to dread seeing him because he was going to make some kind of put-down comment. The funny thing about Upper Canada was that, even though I was in the academic A stream getting A's and B's, it always made me feel that I wasn't smart.

My overall experience of UCC was essentially one of isolation and repressed fear. Not even repressed fear – just fear. I was basically out of touch with what I was feeling. I didn't really express myself. I was very quiet. I didn't scream. When I went home I wouldn't talk about things to my parents. I was more or less in a situation of having to go home to patch up the scene there. I was basically going from the frying pan into the fire. I was in a more or less traumatized, fearful, numbed state for a lot of the time.

I did well academically and athletically. I was on the football team and the track team. In 1961 I won the preparatory school track cup, the Somerville Cup. I still remember my picture in the *Toronto Star*. I remember the picture showed me smiling, and I remember my mother saying, "I never see you smile like that."

I didn't really make any close friends. I felt alone. I don't think I really trusted anybody. I don't know whether it was my goal to do well, or whether I was told to do well, but I certainly tried my very hardest. I used to go to bed at night before exams and try to cram in all this stuff in a high anxiety state and then spew it out on paper. Enjoying learning was never part of my experience. I just had to get through UCC and get a job.

Both at UCC and at home, I was basically struggling for survival. I don't think my parents really knew what kind of person I was and what sort of institution I would have been best at. UCC is an upper middle-class private boys' school where they instil a certain set of values which has a certain quality and aura. There was a kind of violence to the whole thing that I felt. I don't know really how to express it even now.

There was a sense that they were not really considering the individual as someone with his own potential to be realized, although they would pay lip service to that idea. I never felt there was a teacher who could contact me, who knew who I was or who I could be. In fact, I wasn't even aware of how bad the experience was until after I left UCC. It was like surviving a bad car accident and staggering around for a few years afterwards in a state of mild shock, not really knowing where you were, where you were going, or what you wanted. My whole experience, in the end, was like being put in a sack in the boxing ring and getting beaten up and not knowing where the blows were coming from.

UCC was so locked into being self-validating. The people were always trying to prop something up because they felt they might fall down into something they couldn't name and were very afraid of, which I think is the whole area of feelings. They weren't at all aware of the limitations of what they were doing, that life has very broad, limitless kinds of potential to it. The education was broad in a theoretical, cognitive, intellectual sense, but not in terms of the human heart taking in a lot of different things outside of their own cultural predispositions.

My basic grievance about the place is that it socialized me against my will as opposed to just letting me develop into whatever I am. I'm not saying it was done against everybody's will, but it was certainly against my will. I think those people were very afraid to give free rein to their God-given potentials or whatever you want to term it. Places like UCC have no idea what real spirituality is all about. I resent the place because they wanted to snuff out your divine spark at a very early age and they succeeded in many cases. I left the place feeling angry and fucked up. I still have problems relating to women.

Robertson Davies for me personifies the kind of mentality that comes out of that place. I couldn't finish reading his novel *Fifth Business*, which is based on UCC, because it had the same kind of anti-life feeling. Is it anti-life? It's hard to put my finger on exactly what it is about Robertson Davies that I don't like. I just recognize this thing instinctively for what it is. Whatever it is, it is extremely repressed. Part of it is not looking at women as real people.

I know how people from that background tend to think and behave socially at places like the Badminton and Racquet Club and Havergal College. There's just something very "private school" about them. It has a lot to do with sexism, racism, and a macho WASP mentality in general. People weren't trodden upon because of their race at UCC, but I remember the Chinese and the black kids became homogenized whites.

I still have a real phenomenal anger towards UCC that comes out occasionally. I know I haven't worked out that anger yet. I didn't do anything for years after UCC. I didn't start working until 1980 because I didn't know what I wanted to do. I had very good years in university, but it didn't really lead me anywhere. Again, I can't really blame the institution. But had I left UCC early on and gotten into a different kind of schooling, or travelled, or done something completely different, I don't think I would have been as out of touch with my feelings as I was. That's what I'm still trying to do now, which is realize that I've been living in my mind for a long, long time. At a certain point, you have to take a risk and open up and trust somebody. No man is an island and I've been living alone on an island for a long time.

In my family I was a responsible, patcher-up peacemaker, putting-myself-second kind of person, just for the sake of keeping harmony in the house. My family was alcoholic. Some people who come from alcoholic homes become very overresponsible. Unfortunately, putting yourself second for the sake of family harmony stunts your emotional growth. You go from being a precocious kid to being an emotionally undeveloped adult.

Having all these emotional problems at home, none of the teachers ever asked me what the problem was. From an early age, there was nobody I could turn to or fall back on at home or school, so I was really very lost. There was a lot of anger, stress, tension, and physical and emotional violence at home, which kept me uptight all the time. I've never really dealt with or experienced my feelings about either of those situations at home or at school.

As kids, my younger brother David and I used to play hockey a lot down in the basement of our house in Forest Hill. Then we grew apart. After Grade 12 at UCC, he went away to Muskoka Lakes College, and when he came back, he had grown about a foot. At that point I began to feel quite alienated and somewhat intimidated by his height. He also became very verbal and intellectual. He got into a whole academic, intellectual, literary kind of tradition and I really didn't know what to make of it.

He was reading Ezra Pound and T. S. Eliot, who really meant nothing to me at all. I tried to force-feed myself to understand it and please him, which I've continued to do throughout much of my life because of my own family situation. I felt like I needed a lifeline to my own family, which never really worked. It caused me a lot of grief for many years because I never really got the family connection that I needed. So David and I didn't get along for many years. Recently we've mended it a bit. It's still not particularly comfortable for me, but it's an improvement on the surface. I don't know how deep it goes.

Now I find David to be hyper and stressed and needing stimulation a lot. He has never been very calm or still. I think his experiences at home and UCC got to him in some fashion as well as me. It may have been that I acted as a kind of buffer between him and the rest of the family, which allowed him to do what he wanted more than I was able to. There was nobody in our family who had any peace. They were all terribly strung-out, neurotic, unhappy, violent people.

I think the people from my father's generation tended to repress even more than we did. I don't think they questioned nearly as much, and I think many people from UCC still don't question any of it. My graduation year, 1965, was a year when things began to go wrong in some ways. People were not quite growing up emotionally the way they were before. They were essentially remaining children. They were kind of lost. My father was grown up but he was repressed emotionally. My generation, beginning around 1965, didn't become adults the way my parents did. Something was wrong.

Sometimes I don't like the way I dress because it reminds me of a combination Yuppie and WASP that people move into in their post-forties. My internal aspect and external aspects are not quite the same. When I put on a jacket and corduroy pants and look like a post-forties, semi-successful private school kid, it's a part of me that I don't know how to expel. There's nothing wrong with being that if that's what you believe you are. But when I put those clothes on, I feel like I'm some sort of repressed Rosedale old boy. I just fucking can't stand it because it isn't what I feel.

While UCC was a macho, anti-female place, ironically it was also a very castrating place. The absence of feminine influence had the effect of making people incomplete, half people, which is a form of castration. Many so-called well-rounded old boys have in fact had their balls cut off a long time ago. At UCC, they wanted to tame and castrate any natural wild streaks in the boys. This mentality was so implicitly built into the value system, it just subtly seeped into our pores by osmosis. Guys just lost their rebel, animal nature. There's something really wrong with people who aren't angry about it because they have given up their lives to some degree. They don't even know what hit them.

One of the masters, I. K. Shearer, used to call me "Bay Street" because my father was a stockbroker. He was a very towering guy who used his height to intimidate and talk down to people. I always felt intimidated. I felt that he liked me in a way, too, but he had a way of dealing with people that was essentially violent, negative, and inconsiderate. I used to see him walking up and down the school grounds with his hands behind his back. He was a homosexual and he had troubles of his own.

I was flattered to some degree when Shearer called me "Bay Street." When I think of him now, he engages me and brings up my anger, not a negative anger but a constructive, energetic kind of anger. Maybe he was just trying to get my goat to make me go. Other masters were quite malevolent and nasty and so was Shearer, but when he called me "Bay Street," at least he didn't call me scum. At least there is some status to Bay Street, even though it's part of the WASP stereotype. I think he at least respected me. Dick Howard basically dismissed me. He told me I had a big chip on my shoulder, but he never told me why. Wilf Gallimore was another nasty, narrow man who was always playing favourites with Michael Ignatieff.

I still have a lot of anger towards those little, stupid, elitist, mediocre people who were making me feel like I was dumb. It was reinforced for the most part by the staff. Of course all your feelings internalized and then you project it onto people and they feed it back to you and so on. You get to feel that you are not liked very much and then people pick up on that and they reinforce it. So it becomes a case of how much is it really their fault? The cycle goes on and on and then you end up blaming the whole school for what happened. Where does one start and the other leave off? That's just life.

At some point you have to fight back because the way it works is that if you don't, they'll walk all over you. I haven't done enough fighting back in life. I tend to be too acquiescent. I get my shots in other ways by going after weaker people — verbally, never physically — and saying things I shouldn't. But I'm simply projecting part of my personality that I don't like onto them. In the past, I've had bursts of anger that have come up out of nowhere.

You have to spend a lot of time deprogramming yourself in order to restore yourself as a natural, primitive, free, spontaneous person. I think my adolescent self, my young rebel self, is still very much alive, but lying dormant deep inside me. I don't think that I've stiffened up and begun to decline into old age. It has just put me on hold for a while, keeping me in suspended animation. One day I'll open a door and the music will still be playing, just like it was when I shut the door. I know it exists right here and now, if I could only do something about it.

It's a common experience that people feel they are in jail — the "mind-forged manacles," as the poet William Blake put it. But your mind is simply making your experience constricted. The mind is essentially to be used as an instrument, not as a master. If you live in your mind as many people do, you simply can't have a happy life and go in all directions, whereas the spirit or the self or whatever you want to call it has no boundaries.

I'm reading a phenomenally interesting book about dysfunctional organizations. Many institutions are full of dysfunctional people, to the extent that the entire soul of a place is sick. The more you get into it, you think, Jesus, is this ever widespread. But it doesn't scare me because ultimately the truth will set you free. You have to look at it to get free of it. You just can't run away to Kenya. It can help, but you've got to understand where you come from and what has affected you. Some people don't want to do it.

My father wasn't able to do it. He lived in a shroud. Both my parents did, although my mother was more emotional and more expressive, but highly frustrated and very scattered. But she wasn't as barren as he was. My father was really buried. I think that many of the guys who go to places like the Badminton and Racquet Club have the same mentality now. I worked downtown as a commodities broker for a few years, but I quit. To be honest, I was not really comfortable in that world. I'm just not very interested in an atmosphere which puts down people.

My father was an alcoholic and alcoholics suffer from a certain kind of hopelessness, negative thinking, lack of self-esteem, depression, an inabilty to express oneself. He had a really hopeless, depressed, fundamentally pointless sense that life had no meaning. He had given up for all intents and purposes. That's why he sat in a corner with a drink in his hand. Doctors tried to hammer it out of him with shock treatment, but it doesn't work. In fact, it's barbaric. It's the direct opposite to what can actually help.

My mother hadn't given up. She was still struggling. Her mistake was that she was blaming other people too much for her own problems. If she was not happy, she should have basically gone out and gotten her life together. If you're not aware of the disease, you're not going to get well. People get sick at an early age and they get overwhelmed by it. They start to live it and it becomes a reality. Then they contaminate their kids with it. I know I'm still depressed. I'm just now able to admit it more.

My mother died in 1972 of a lethal combination of alcohol and drugs. It was like a gradual, unpremeditated suicide. She succumbed to the physical abuse, but I don't think she was a suicidal person. If somebody said she had committed suicide, I would have been surprised. But I'm not surprised that my father committed suicide. I still haven't had an emotional reaction to him shooting himself back in the sixties. I don't know whether that's bad or good. Maybe there just wasn't enough of a relationship for there to really be any grief. I don't know what is the appropriate response. I know I haven't done anything about it yet.

I haven't left home yet in some ways. I left home in 1966, but here I am walking around and I still feel I'm just a kid. I share this experience with other dysfunctional types of people. They wander around in a body which has a certain chronological age, but emotionally there are times when I think, Christ, I'm about fifteen. There's something called post-traumatic stress syndrome which a lot of children of alcoholics have, and I think I've got it. I think it was complicated and exacerbated by my experience at UCC which was essentially violent to the individual.

People remain aware of the lasting power of the conditioning they impose on children in these places. It takes a long time to learn that it is okay to be angry. I paid a great price for not responding normally in an abnormal situation. I was never angry when I was at UCC. I just passively took shit from everyone. I let myself be caned when I should have taken the cane and shoved it up the master's ass. But you're completely on your own when you're young.

I know a guy who is a classic UCC old boy. He is a very sensitive man who is very knowledgeable about music and books and has a great esthetic and philosophical sense. But he's a depressed alcoholic who has lost touch with his power. I think he has the UCC disease. I think he had his balls chopped off a long time ago. He's a good guy and I like him, but I think UCC boys have all taken a sip from the same poisoned chalice in varying degrees. It interacts with their own chemistry and their own personalities in different ways, but it generally has its way with them.

JOHN HUGHES
1955–65
Businessman

IN RECENT YEARS a former classmate, Chris Gilmour, and I would go through long talks about UCC. He'd get on a harangue about how terrible things had been at the school. I'd argue that given where I was at the time, I was willing to play the game. I was reasonably good at playing, so I don't remember an awful lot of emotional stress. I basically bought into UCC. They wanted convention, but convention seemed okay to me.

Chris talked about being on the outside looking in. I remember him being particularly good at track and being amazed when he first told me he felt like an outsider. I said, "But you were a good runner." He said, "Yeah, but I wasn't even made a prefect and you were a steward. That's because you sucked up to everybody and I just played it the way I saw it. They were a bunch of shallow jerk-offs." I'd say, "Chris, I cannot relate to it. That wasn't my experience." I felt an affinity for him and yet we responded totally differently. I think his not being able to open up to the school was probably a reflection of the trouble he was having at home.

My memories of UCC are all positive. I made fabulous friendships, surprisingly long-lasting. When you bond with people at a young age prior to the adult persona becoming developed, you can always reach back into the past with a sense of comfort. I knew guys like John Lownsbrough and Doug Hayhurst in a childish, pristine state before they adopted conditionally driven adult personality traits. Somehow I feel the early years are closer to a person's real character.

I was fast-tracked at UCC and I enjoyed it. I never felt the need to be at the top of the A1 class because we had decided fairly early on that the kids at the top – guys like Richard Reive and Michael Ignatieff – were the brown-nosers. At the time, I perceived Ignatieff as an egghead and a browner. But because I played first-team sports, being in the middle of an A1 class was just fine.

In 1970 I got a call from one of my classmates. I had not seen him since graduation in 1965. We started to get together in Latin class in about Grade 10 and took it through Grade 13. We always sat close to one another and had a thing going where I would design a golf course and he would draw the clubhouse. That would be our only contact. He was a boarder so I never saw him. He was a physically small guy who wore thick glasses and carried the little brown bag. You tended to pigeonhole guys like him. He was very bright and the guys didn't seem to like him that much.

In 1970, five years after UCC, I had a particularly dramatic dream about him. The dream took place upstairs in the lounge of the Badminton and Racquet Club at Yonge and St. Clair where I played a lot of racquet sports. There were curtains across a long window which overlooked a badminton court. Somebody said, "Hey, come here, look at this." I went to the window. Somebody had pulled the curtains to reveal a vast desert. Way, way out in the desert was a solitary figure. There was then a kind of telescopic experience of zooming up to him. It was the guy from my Latin class, who I hadn't thought of consciously in five years, sitting in a lotus position in the desert with a funny little smile on his face. He suddenly pulled out a gun, held it up to his temple, and pulled the trigger. He fell over and I woke up. I thought, Wow! That was so weird.

The next morning I was driving to Boston. At the time, I was using my parents' address for mail. I came back after four days and checked for my mail. They said there had been a phone call from somebody in my class at UCC who desperately needed to get in touch with me. It was the guy from my Latin class – apparently he called the morning after I had the dream.

I didn't think of it again. Six months later, he called me again. He said he wanted to come and see me. He told me that he had always been in love with me. I had been preoccupying him for years and he needed to tell me he loved me. All the way through UCC, I had been the object of his adoration.

That was really a weird experience for me, particularly because I had a whole thing about people being gay at Upper Canada. Later, a couple of friends had started to declare themselves. I remember this with some wonder because the only gay experience I ever had at Upper Canada was when I was in the upper school. A boy put a tag through my locker one day in Martland's House saying he wanted to meet me in the gallery of the swimming pool at 3:30 to suck my dick.

At the time, I was captain of the football team. I grabbed John Cottrell and a couple of other big football players and we went to meet him in the gallery. The indignity and outrage I felt was dramatic. We chased him through the school and finally caught him outside of Vern Mould's art room on the second floor. We got him down on the floor and made him eat the note and swallow it.

That was like "the big gesture," for whatever reason – a weird display of macho fear or something. That was the only contact I remember having other than the ongoing comments about Gibby Gibson, a master in the prep who used to stick his hand inside your shirt. Walter Bailey seemed to be a fairy and of course Fairy Linn was seen to be gay, but homosexuality really wasn't an issue in my mind at the time.

So to be confronted five years later by a former classmate professing his feelings was quite powerful. By the late 1960s, I had already gone through a fairly broad opening of my mind as an undergraduate at Princeton University. I remember having a discussion with the guy, saying, "I love you as a brother and I'm thrilled to see you." I really was thrilled to see him. I was into the whole psychic contact thing in those days. I told him about the dream. It turned out he wasn't in despair or suicidal. I said, "I am not homosexual to my knowledge. I don't feel any particular rush around men, but at the same time, I am very much into brotherhood, peace, and love. I hope you're comfortable with that." We got along well after that.

After Princeton I did a master's at York University. When I was doing my Ph.D. at York, I took a year's leave of absence after I finished my course work. I went to England and lived in a trailer. I had been involved with a Hindu guru named Sri Chinmoy at the time and I moved into his ashram in the City of London. One thing led to another. I ended up leaving my girlfriend there and living in Java for about a year and studying with some meditation teachers who were more secular in their approach.

There's a variety in the Buddhist tradition they call "the awakening of the bodhicitta," which is a kind of an energy that I think we would probably best describe as compulsive curiosity. Once you really start to question, you can't stop. It's awakened in you. You may have settled down or finally conformed, but it doesn't go to sleep. You find more covert ways of exploring because it doesn't work as well to wear it on your sleeve the way you did when you were in your twenties. Those are the guys from Upper Canada who I tended to gravitate to. Stewart Smith and Tony Wells would be examples, whereas with guys like Lownsbrough, Hayhurst, and Musgrave, there's not the same kind of bond.

I remember going to Stewart Smith's place in London, England, when I was in my Yogi phase. His father Arnold was a diplomat and a UCC old boy. When I had dinner with Stewart, I had been living in an ashram for about nine months, had renounced materialism, and wore white. I couldn't possibly advance on my spiritual path with all of the material encumbrances of the world.

His parents were out and the servants had laid out a big dinner. We started with vichyssoise. One of the traditions he had was to fill your soup bowl with wine when you'd finished your soup. He opened a bottle and filled my bowl. I told him that I didn't drink. But before long, I was swishing the wine around and drinking it down. By the end of the evening, I was perfectly prepared to seek a different path. I didn't have to renounce everything I had been renouncing. I had a great time with a great old UCC friend and felt totally attuned. He was a philosopher and had gone through a lot of the same questioning avenues as I had. He got me off my white-robe renunciation trip.

Then I came back to Toronto and got into education. For a while I taught at SEED, which was the other end of the spectrum from UCC. SEED, or the Shared Experience in Education and Discovery, was one of Pierre Trudeau's LIP grant programs. I loved teaching there. I still have a gnawing sense that I want to get back into education. If there was a way I could make lots of money, I'd do it in a flash. If I won the lottery, I'd get out of business tomorrow and go back to education.

My father, who is a UCC old boy, always hoped I'd take over the family business, Hughes Containers, and be a successful businessman. I wasn't allowed in his house for about two and a half years because of my sixties activities and my involvement in teaching. I had humiliated him at seemingly very deep levels because of the way I looked and because of my choice of friends and pastimes. He communicated this through my mother, not directly to me.

My mother would say, "Your father wants you to know that you're not welcome in this house any longer." She was pretty supportive, although she'd try to do a little influencing here and there. She'd say, "Couldn't you tone it down a bit? Your beliefs are your beliefs, so what does it matter what you look like? Why don't you just look the way we want you to look and we'll respect your beliefs."

My parents were focused on externals all the way. My father was a product of Upper Canada College in that sense, but probably not as bad as some. There were people who were much more focused on having the right address and the cocktail parties. My parents weren't really caught up in the social swing, but they were definitely very conscious of appearances. You were seen to be successful if you were in an acceptable line of work, frequented the right clubs, and played the right games.

It's very difficult to extricate yourself from family expectations. Going into the family business, you end up being a bit of a steward for something that someone else has done. You're not really laying it on the line so much as you're trying to preserve and build on something that somebody else has done. At a certain level, running the family business has the quality of being a nanny. There are guys like Conrad Black who are clearly cut out for it and take off on their own way. I haven't yet found the avenue to do that, so I'm still feeling the strains of looking after the business that was created by my father.

Even though I felt pressure to conform, I can't relate to the degree of family pressure that makes people break down or want to kill themselves. Terry Peever was a boarder at UCC who killed himself. In John Medland's case, he was a schizophrenic. In the case of Matthew Smith, Stewart Smith's younger brother, there was a manic-depressive quality, if not schizophrenia. Another guy in our year went through a major emotional crash. Therapy has salvaged him, but he's a shadow of his former self. His father was a prominent lawyer, so there was a lot of pressure on him to be a player in the legal world. I could see the pressure building. My wife's teenage love was Harvey Southam, a member of the media family. A few years ago, he jumped off a Rosedale bridge with a rope around his neck. I guess it was the pressure of being a Southam. I just can't relate to it. I can't understand why people can't say, "Fuck off. I'll do what I want to do."

My internal, spiritual growth is still the biggest part of my life. Resolving it with my business life isn't as easy as I would like it to be, but if all else fails, my internal resources are vast. Today I'm a Yuppie who harbours the feeling that the Aquarian Age has not disappeared. The hopes we had are not shattered but are just sublimated at some weird level, so that we're actually going to have a more promising world one day.

It was a big thing for me to have some sort of awakening and to find out that I did care about all people. I had the experience of universal brotherhood, that we are all one, and that we have somehow managed, through ignorance, to become caught up in a self-serving, ego-dominated world. I think a lot of UCC guys are caught in that world. But I believe my own awakening was a direct result of the confidence and self-esteem that I developed in my ten years at UCC – which, paradoxically, freed me to let go.

GALT KORTRIGHT

1960–65

Anglican priest

THEY DIDN'T KNOW what to do about homosexuality at UCC, although I don't think it's because they wanted to deny it. I think it's because if they had accepted it, they would have had to deal with the implications. How do we handle the parents' comments? That's a different kind of denial. As individuals, they might want to do something, but as part of a bureaucracy, they feel helpless to deal with the ramifications. So they put off making a decision, though they may realize personally that it needs to happen. Like a lot of other difficult issues, they decide to let somebody else deal with it, and it ends up never getting dealt with.

I was in Scadding's House for a year as a day boy and then my father forced me to go into boarding in Wedd's House, which still makes me very angry. He had boarded at TCS. I didn't like boarding. I was born with a hearing disability, so it wasn't easy to make friends. I'm partially deaf. The disability has emotional ramifications because a child really doesn't understand what's going on around him. Because I was different, I was a bit of a target. I felt really isolated.

When I had arrived back at school one September, I got into my room first. One of the guys who was supposed to be my roommate had not arrived yet. A guy who was in a bedroom across the hall manipulated me into being his roommate. He came over and said, "When the housemaster comes around, tell him you want me to room with you." I don't know why he targetted me. I didn't even know him.

I asked the housemaster and he said, "Oh, is he a particular friend of yours?" Because I was so easily manipulated, I said yes. That is another part of my anger, the fact that I got easily manipulated. I didn't know how to say no because I was so intimidated. I didn't know why he wanted to switch rooms. Before long, my roommate started to hit me. Maybe he realized that I was easy to manipulate and maybe he despised me for it. It's really weird. I had absolutely no understanding about it at all. I just didn't have the self-esteem or the sense of identity that I could be independent. A little while later, he made a sexual move on me.

I think that after a while people knew what was going on. But I wouldn't know because I couldn't hear any side comments due to my poor hearing. Maybe people were commenting about it. For all I know, my roommate could have gossiped about it. He could have said the opposite of what was happening. He was a manipulator, so he could have told people that I came on to him sexually. But I have no idea.

The housemasters must have been aware of the situation, but there was an inability to deal with it. No housemaster ever talked about it. I was bitter about that too. I can't believe that nobody knew anything. I suppose they felt the only possible way to deal with it would have been to expel the person. They didn't have any education about sexuality and there was a lack of clarity on the role of parents and the role of the school. Maybe the school felt that sexuality was the realm of the family and they had no right to get into it. They didn't want to stir up a fuss, so they just ignored it.

It wasn't until recently that I realized that I was physically and sexually abused in that situation. I have classic symptoms of abuse, such as passivity, feeling unable to do anything. Another thing I'm looking at now is the concept of codependency, the way other people passively allowed this to happen. That's also part of my anger.

This experience obviously didn't do anything for my self-esteem. It really knocked me down. I hadn't a clue about homosexuality at that point. I wish there had been someone I could have talked to. The abusive situation was really confusing to me. I sort of got into it, but I really didn't know what was happening. I was very confused by the sexual stuff, and he beat me up as well. The mixture of the two things was so confusing emotionally. You know this sort of thing happens in jails, but nobody ever talks about it. Part of me liked it. I hadn't been told that it was bad.

It took me a long time to understand. I didn't come out as a gay person until much later, partly because of the ramifications of the earlier confusion at UCC. I knew I wasn't attracted to women, but nothing happened at all. When I finally came out in my early thirties, I looked back and thought, Oh, this is what all this means. I didn't know before. Now I can see it going all the way back into childhood. After I was ordained as a priest, it all came together and I understood why I felt the way I did.

I have not gone back to any events at the school. I simply can't face it. It's really difficult for me. I refuse to enter into any kind of denial about what happened. One of the reasons I don't go back to old-boy events is that it's a very straight crowd. You bring your wife. It would be kind of nice if we could have a gay old-boy association. Maybe it's not just me. Maybe my theme of personal isolation is more common than I realize.

Despite the abuse experience, I can see the good in UCC. I feel very positive about a lot of things. I wouldn't write it off. It's really important to separate out the good and the bad. I have really good memories of the extra consideration by some of the masters who made sure that I could hear. My mother didn't have to ask to have me sit at the front of the classroom to ensure that I could see and hear. I don't think I would have got as far as I did in my life if I hadn't gone to Upper Canada.

I took piano all through public school. Then I took up the organ, which is pretty exceptional for somebody with my degree of hearing loss. I really enjoyed John Linn's music classes at Upper Canada, which helped me be sensitive to sound and helped me concentrate. I got to know him and took organ lessons from him. I practised in the prayer hall. The other kids made fun of me. I wasn't that good, but I do remember being allowed to play something one morning at prayers. It was exciting. I remember the principal, Dr. Sowby, acknowledged it. I remember sitting at the organ, feeling that this experience was so huge and overwhelming. But I managed to get through it.

Battalian was mandatory. After a couple of weeks of doing battalion drill on the field, the masters realized I couldn't understand the orders being yelled out, so they put me and another hearing-disabled boy in the orderly room. I actually got to be a sergeant. They seemed to value me for who I was, even though I was never on the field. They actually promoted me even though I was just doing stuff in the orderly room. I thought that was creative.

I'm volunteering with AIDS organizations now. Out of my work in the AIDS committee of Simcoe County, I'm also one of their delegates to the Ontario AIDS Network, a network of thirty AIDS organizations across the province. I'm now involved in helping organize a conference for people living with HIV and AIDS across the province. I'm working a little bit out of the

AIDS Committee of Toronto and I'm getting involved in holistic health care.

I'm liberal and progressive. I try to be outspoken. I find other Anglican priests tend to be schizophrenic about gayness. There are lots of gay people in the Anglican church and clergy, but they tend to be very upright and closeted. I was once in a meeting where somebody told a fag joke. I knew one of the guys was gay. He laughed harder than anybody else.

My whole life since UCC has been involved with the disenfranchised, even before I was diagnosed HIV positive. It's really important for the establishment to look at the disenfranchised without a charity mentality, to see them from the inside. Some people from UCC have. Dan Heap, the former NDP politician, is an old boy who is plugged into the world of the disenfranchised, as are Bruce McLeod, president of the Canadian Council of Churches, and Peter Dalglish, the founder of Street Kids International. It would be interesting to see how the Upper Canada experience spurred them into service work.

Personally, I think the UCC community, for the most part, is a collection of individuals who talk about the spirit of the community, but is in fact not a truly humane community. The old-boy network is really just a collection of superficial individuals who rally around a convenient, mythological common denominator. The myth of UCC forms a kind of quasi-religious bond. But in reality, like in many churches, there really isn't much real, deep, personal, and emotional interconnection of human beings, which forms a true community.

PATRICK CREAN

1961–67

Book publisher

UPPER CANADA was a very homophobic place, although I wasn't particularly aware of it at the time. Everybody was masturbating to a phenomenal degree. In Wedd's House in the upper school, we had an agreement that it was okay to go down to the can and masturbate. One copy of *Playboy* was available. Masturbation is an intensely private thing, but we actually managed somehow, without speaking about it, to arrive at an agreement that it was okay. I remember there was one poor deaf guy, Kortright, who wore a hearing aid. When he was going down to the can to masturbate, guys would sneak in and pour water over the cubicle on top of him.

There were some terrible incidents. In the prep, guys would go up and hump a boarder and he would let everybody do it. When I was a steward in Wedd's House, I remember coming across a couple of kids who were in bed together, but that was all I ever saw. Then there was a reverse thing in the boardinghouse where guys would knock on your door and stand in front of you stark naked. It was a big joke to pretend to be gay. It was a curious thing.

But Upper Canada became very important to me and remains important to me. It was like a third-rate hotel, but it was my home for six years. My father, who was an old boy and a diplomat, once said to me that he felt very badly that the only thing he hadn't given us was a sufficient sense of roots in Canada. Indeed, in a strange sort of way, although I feel very Canadian, I feel slightly nomadic.

It was heart wrenching leaving home and going to boarding school at the age of twelve. I remember saying goodbye to my parents at Union Station as they left on a train to go to New York to get on a boat to go to Yugoslavia. My first term in the prep was awful. I was homesick and cried a lot. I flew to Belgrade for that first Christmas, but after that, things started to settle down. I started finding my sea legs. I was strong enough if I got into any fights, so it started working out. It helped somewhat that I had connections to two of the masters. Ted Stephenson was my second cousin, and my father, who had taught at the prep for a term, had been close to Alan "Spud" Harris.

I remember caning incidents as something rather horrible, standing outside the master's door and knowing that we were about to be caned. It was the closest thing I can imagine to walking to your own execution. Three of us were caught having a rumble in the dormitory, so we each got three swats. It was really brutal. I don't agree with corporal punishment. But on the other hand, in boarding we had a sense of community, almost a ritualized tribalism, a sense of being with others. But there was an incredible loneliness about boarding school too. I remember Sunday as being an especially bad day. Time passed so slowly. Luckily, I was able to go to relatives from time to time. I have a capacity for solitude, so it was okay. I began to write a lot of poetry.

I remember Matthew Smith, who was definitely a mama's boy, left the school early on. I think he was pulled out after the first year in the upper school and then he went to school in England. Then I saw him again at

Queen's University. His father, Arnold Smith, was an old boy who had a very high diplomatic position as head of the Commonwealth. Among the diplomatic kids at UCC, there is a certain parallel course.

At Queen's, Matthew had gotten into the heavy drug scene and was doing a lot of speed. He was terribly affected by that whole rarefied world. I remember visiting him in London at his parents' place in Pall Mall where they lived a rather glorified life. I always had a problem with the way Matthew condescended to the servants. I always had a problem with class privilege. I'm too democratic. My father said, "If you treat the servants as equals, they get offended." Matthew did the whole Oscar Wilde bit, saying things like, "Don't bother, my man will see to that." Give me a break! He got into some weird shit. We lost touch and then I heard about his sudden death. It was very sad.

I think it is fascinating how UCC has always been a training school for power. In a country as small as Canada, there is virtually only one highly concentrated centre of training for power. You can talk about other schools like Ridley, SAC, and TCS, but Upper Canada as a school is incredibly muscular in the power element. I'm not sure that they train people properly for it. It's a very tricky thing to do.

Indirectly, the school certainly taught me a sense of class consciousness, an awareness of the haves and the have-nots. There were a lot of times in my life where I wanted to charge the barricades and bring down the system. It seemed totally false and unjust that the people in positions of power seemed so stupid and so unaware. People should have to qualify to hold power. Somebody has to deal with power because it will always exist. That's why UCC has to train people to deal with it properly and responsibly.

The school claimed to be elitist, yet it did not train boys to have manners or graciousness. They certainly didn't turn out chivalrous gentlemen, in the best sense of the phrase. Mostly, UCC turned out boors who could barely hold their knives and forks properly. For a school that prides itself on turning out elitists, most of them would be laughed out of an upper-class Italian gathering.

I thought the essential problem was that UCC was wrapped around wealth and money, which is one of my quarrels with North American culture versus European culture. Here, you are judged according to how much money you have. In Europe, it is what's going on in your head or your heart that matters. I think UCC could have been so much more if the latter viewpoint had been imbued. Maybe it's changing. But to have a school that exists for many parents simply as a status symbol is troublesome.

I'm not adept at Jungian analysis, but it's interesting that there is a lot of men's movement activity right now. Carl Jung said that there are four male archetypes – king, warrior, lover, and magician. The first two, king and warrior, predominated at UCC. UCC is definitely a warrior school. Today it is unpopular to defend the warrior archetype, but it exists as a fixed part of the male makeup and I don't think you can change it. There are more benign ways of accessing it, but at the same time, men shouldn't wimp out and deny their natural, healthy aggression.

Although this is an unpopular thing to say, it is quite useful for a male to experience some form of military training. That does not mean I espouse war, but I think it is a part of the warrior archetype and a certain sense of ritual. UCC was definitely a place where you were trained to be a warrior and hero in battalion and athletics. I really began to enjoy it because I was good at soccer and track and I was an officer in the battalion. Winning the Somerville Cup in track was a highlight for me in the prep. My father, who also had been a runner at the school, came out to watch. A story appeared in the *Globe and Mail*, "Crean wins Somerville Cup." Then a guy named James FitzGerald broke my record in the 220-yard dash the very next year.

I'm now learning about the Jungian concepts of *puer* and *senex*. There were some very interesting *senex* masters who taught at UCC, in many cases for over forty years – Skull Bassett, Willy Orr, Mike Bremner, Piff Biggar, Spud Harris, Tim Gibson. Some of these men actually taught my father, so I got a really strong sense of roots and belonging, which I didn't get from my family life. We changed homes every three years, so UCC really grounded me.

I don't know how on earth you sensitize rather than brutalize kids at a boarding school. I don't think people were necessarily brutalized, but there was a rigorous repression of emotions. I think men, and women, have suffered a great deal as a result. But, at the same time, UCC gave me a sense of self. I felt confident, which has helped me through life. The bedrock training helped me immensely, but psychological and emotional work has to take place afterwards. I think a lot of people really hate the school because they think it damaged them on those levels.

I see a number of UCC old boys, twenty years later, who seem to be emotionally arrested. No emotional development took place and the soul lay dormant. The influence of privilege and money is a very difficult thing. Even Mother Theresa says the wealthy have their own set of problems. It's too easy to condemn wealth, but I think wealth is really important. It's how we view it and use it that matters.

Certain wealthy American East Coast families try to embrace a sense of civic responsibility. I think there were a lot of people in our lives at UCC who had that sensibility, but I think we should have had more of it. I feel,

certainly in the last decade in our materialistic age, that many people at
UCC were saying, "What I really want to do is own a Mercedes and a house
in Forest Hill." I mean, what do you do if you have a lot of money? Are you
just a king who holds on to your money?

There were also a lot of boys who suffered who weren't wealthy, who
might have been at the school on a scholarship. But I had a rather nice situation in that my parents weren't around to bother me. I could see them on
holidays and Christmas, so I had a very positive experience. I changed a bit
in the last year because suddenly I became head of Wedd's House and one
of the law upholders. One of the ways I think a lot of the boys got through
the school was by being rebellious, which made for camaraderie.

My position of power caused divisions with some friends who weren't
prefects or stewards. The system of punishment was ridiculous. I wasn't
really simpatico with the housemaster, John Symons, so we had problems.
In the upper school, the prefects and stewards were able to hand out punishments like running around the field twice if you didn't make your bed
properly. There was a lot of brutal stuff, like the new-boy hazing.

At midnight, the prefects would turn on all the lights. The kids would
all be tumbled out of bed and have to stand on the floor while the whole
room was ripped apart looking for cigarettes, skin books, and everything
else that was evil. It was pretty brutal. It was like a Nazi raid on these poor
kids. There was a lot of cruelty and bullying. As head of house, my disposi-
tion was to hear people's different sides of the question, but the more dictatorial prefects put the fear of the Lord into the boys.

I have noticed that some kids went really sky high and accomplished
incredible things at UCC, and then bam – it just wasn't there in their careers
after UCC. I haven't been able to come to any conclusions about that phenomenon. Somebody who was head of the battalion, head boy, Herbert
Mason Medalist, or a big football star, peaks at age eighteen and then goes
kaplop in life. It's strange.

When I went to Queen's University, suddenly we were in a new environment with kids from all kinds of backgrounds. I quickly realized that if
I said I had gone to Upper Canada, people would slot me as a privileged
rich boy. It created barriers, so I just didn't talk about it much. I really had
trouble well into my thirties. I would be careful because sometimes when
you mention UCC, people react strongly. Power has a very strong aura and
energy attached to it.

The sense of being superior didn't really come directly from the masters.
It was almost like there was a powerful psychic energy field we absorbed
every day in Laidlaw Hall. Walking into the prayer hall every morning had
a strong, cumulative effect on me, looking at the large portraits of past

principals, the names of illustrious old boys on the walls, and the huge imperial UCC crest, the crown ringed by palm leaves, above the stage. The principal sat in a throne-like chair, like the Speaker in the House of Commons. There was something very authoritarian, grandiose, and symbolic about the physical surroundings.

I don't have a problem dealing with the idea of the power force of energy. I'm saying objectively that it's interesting that UCC emanates it so strongly. I suppose Eton and Harrow in England have it in the same sort of way, except that there is so much more depth in the history and culture of Great Britain. But in such a young country as Canada, it dwarfs everything. I'm not sure I can think of other institutions of learning, including Trinity College at the University of Toronto, that have this particular kind of aura.

But the overwhelming impression I have is that most UCC guys were either traumatized in varying degrees or became lobotomized servants of the system. There was a lack of rites of passage. Many of them just tunnelled their way through life and ceased to think critically of themselves or the world, if they ever did. Maybe they were adept at making money in business, but so many of them were primed as candidates for success in corporate culture, so zoom, off they went.

I was lucky because my father was a liberal guy who encouraged the arts. Living in Europe, we were exposed to a lot of art galleries and different people. I remember when I was a small boy, he would include me in small parties at home. I would listen quietly. I was very lucky that he was interested in broadening our minds and getting us to learn how to think.

He never pressured my younger brother and I towards a career. He said, "If you publish one book of poetry, I'd be so proud." However, he had such an incredible career that I always felt – phew! – what a tough act to follow! He was a diplomat doing all sorts of things. It turns out latterly he was involved in counterintelligence, which I never knew.

So I was lucky I could get away from Toronto and its culture during the summers and at Christmas. We would go to the Adriatic or Scotland or wherever it was. I acknowledge it was very rich. But then I wanted to go back to Upper Canada because I really liked the competitiveness. I was deeply affected by it, but I wasn't nailed to the cross by it. Others were consumed by it and stripped of any emotional life whatsoever. So why does this institution encourage certain traits to the detriment of others? What they are encouraging is going to be destroyed because it doesn't have the balance that the other does. It's very curious.

Many old boys come back, wearing their old blazers, telling jolly, sentimental stories of how wonderful UCC was. Why are they doing this? There is so little sense of continuity and context in our culture, it is nice to have a knowledge and experience of tradition. I acknowledge and honour it. There is nothing wrong with loyalty, but it's misplaced. It's like belonging to a club.

Robert Bly, the author of *Iron John*, says our patriarchy is not representative of true masculinity. It represents immature masculinity. Some of the old boys that I know are hollow guys who think everything is fine and who just operate on automatic pilot. Give me a break! They are clearly cut off from the real world.

I happen to believe that we're going through a major revolution in terms of the way we relate to ourselves, how we relate to each other, and how we relate to the planet. When you're in the middle of it, it is very difficult to measure it. But I think we are in the eye of the storm now. The system isn't working and it is changing. I think we have gone off the track because we have not paid enough attention to the spiritual and intuitive side in nature.

But we don't know everything and we never possibly can know everything. I'm not sure how that idea will be translated into education. But there certainly is some very, very interesting stuff being written and talked about right now, a really cutting-edge, new way of thinking. A lot of it is coming out of North America.

We are now experiencing what looks like the feminization of our culture, but I think we have to be careful as males not to wimp out. It's interesting that if a man has emotional difficulties, he generally talks to a woman, not another man. If you talk to another guy about sex, it's usually bawdy, locker-room talk, not talk about deep sexual emotions and vulnerabilities. It's exciting to see some males now who are really maturing and doing a lot of this work. The last year or so, the most exciting thing in my life has been finding male friends that I can really talk to. I find it quite incredible. For many, many years, I had no men friends at all. There is a loneliness about being male that we've suffered for so long. We've been bludgeoned by the feminist cause. I think it's a time for healing and a time for celebration.

I think men really have been affected by women so much that when we try to define what it is to be a man, the only thing we can say is that we are not women. I think self-definition is much easier for women. They have their cycles and their reproductive lives, so they just are. But we have to define ourselves in opposition to women. It will be very interesting to see how UCC meets the challenge of coeducation. I think the school has the ability to change and grow from within.

At Queen's University, I hung out with old boys, including my two best

friends, Bob Blakely, whom I knew at Upper Canada, and John Hunt, who
went to Ridley. But when I went into book publishing, a social division
took place because there's no money in publishing. I was not an up-and-
coming young lawyer, accountant, dentist, or doctor in the professional
UCC mould. Book editors' salaries were modest and they remain pretty
modest.

I always remember Jack McClelland calling me at Queen's and offering
me a summer job. That was a really big thing. Jack didn't go to Upper
Canada, but he was from that private school world. He was an important
figure in my life. I began hanging out with publishing people, writers, and
the arts community, which was a whole different world. Book publishing is
vastly stimulating. Every book is a new project. I love the joy of being
involved in the act of disseminating ideas through society. But it really was
a very different world from UCC. I found it harder and harder to relate to
UCC people.

I find latterly that I'm encountering people from UCC again. I am working with a woman, Jane Somerville, whose husband, David Caspari, was a
schoolmate. Our lawyer, Brian Rogers, went to Upper Canada. The
woman who is doing a book on puberty for us is married to Ian Urquhart,
who is the former managing editor of the *Toronto Star* and was in my year
at UCC. So was Brian Johnson, an editor at *Maclean's,* and Rob Prichard, the
president of University of Toronto. David Gilmour, the novelist, was a year
behind me. It's amazing. The list goes on and on.

BRIAN JOHNSON

1957 – 67

Journalist, film critic

I N GRADE 12 I wrote an essay for Mr. Ainsworth about the time I
nearly drowned on a canoe trip at summer camp in Temagami.
Ainsworth was an uncharacteristic master for Upper Canada because
he was modern and humorous. He was an entertainer. I remember he
allowed us to bring a Bob Dylan record, "Masters of War," into class and
play it. He said, "It may be interesting, but it's not poetry." We all looked
forward to his classes.

The incident happened on the first day of paddling out of camp. It was a bright, sunny day, but there was a very strong wind. A tail wind is always much trickier than a head wind. We were having a great time sliding down the backs of waves, surfing them like you can in a canoe. Chris Giffen was sterning, Dan Lang was in the bow, and I was in the middle. We were all UCC boys. We went sideways to the waves and tipped. It wasn't really a big deal. These things happen and we were okay. We hung out of the canoe and another canoe came along. We got the packs and stuff out of the canoe and into the other canoe so that we could right our canoe.

Then I swam upwind to get a paddle, only about two strokes. I grabbed the paddle, turned around, and the canoe I'd been hanging on to was twice as far away as it had been. I started swimming towards it and I realized that I couldn't catch it. I was stuck out there in the middle of the bay with my shoes on. I started to panic because I wasn't that strong a swimmer. I didn't know how I was going to get to shore. I know that I went down twice. I went down a third time and I knew I wasn't going to come back up. The old cliché is true. Your entire life flashes before your eyes. Your mind fills up with regrets about things that you wanted to tell your parents, all the little undone things in your life.

Dan Lang pulled me up, but then he got into trouble too. So the two of us were out there almost drowning. Then I think Chris Giffen came out. This is where it gets foggy. I think he got into trouble too. Eventually, the counsellor managed to paddle his canoe upwind to get us. We just hung on to the back of the canoe and went ashore. We came very close to drowning, not just me but Dan as well. I was quite scared of the water for a while after that. I love the water now, but looking down at the blackness, it scared me for a few years afterwards.

I wrote a lyrical description of the experience when I got back to UCC. My essay was the first real indication that I could write, as far as I was concerned. It was a different kind of piece, a more rhythmic piece. Ainsworth said, "I showed it to a publisher friend of mine and he said he thought you had a real talent." His encouragement really had an influence on me. He said, "If you want to write, what you have to do is write every single day. Spend half an hour writing and half an hour revising what you wrote the day before." I started practising that and it was good advice. It's still good advice.

Jack Schaffter also had a fabulous influence on me in the prep. Because I had come from the English school system, I was a much more advanced reader than everybody else in my class in my first year in the prep. The English system is more advanced. Schaffter, an Englishman, got me on a program of signed reading where you read every night. Your parents sign to say that you've done the reading. I don't think I've ever read quite as much as I did in my first three years at Upper Canada. I became editor of the prep magazine and I won a *Roget's Thesaurus* for a prize in an essay-writing contest. I wrote an incredibly florid, badly overwritten descriptive essay about the sea.

I just devoured everything Schaffter gave me to read, mostly war stories. After a while, it was no longer compulsory for me. I think I read every single Douglas Bader story. I read all the British World War II literature, all the submarine stories, all the Murmansk convoy ones, all the bombing ones, and all the infantry ones. I just devoured them. Then I went on to Hammond Innis and Alistair MacLean. I probably developed bad reading habits because before I knew it I had glasses. I couldn't see the blackboard. I would lie on the floor with a book in front of me.

My best friend early on was J. T. Pepall, who even back then was an eccentric. He hasn't changed at all, to his credit. We walked around pretending we were military officers in Europe. I have very strong memories of Charlie Hulton, who in the early years of the prep organized an anti-Semitic, fascist group of boys. It was all just play acting, but in hindsight, it's frightening when you think of the implications.

Even then, we knew this was not right. I remember Charlie was going around glamorizing fascism and popularizing the idea of anti-Semitism. It was done in total ignorance. I didn't know what a Jew was when I was in the prep. It took quite a while before I knew what a Jew was. I don't remember there being any Jews in the prep, although there were one or two in the upper school. There were just enough token Jews that they really stood out. They seemed that much more different because there were so few of them. I think the only thing close to a black guy we had in the prep was a kid from Bermuda.

When I got to university, there were a lot of amazing things that I realized I had been missing out on. But I enjoyed Upper Canada because it offered a lot of things that I could do as a bit of a nerdy kind of guy. I joined the radio club and learned the Morse code and all the kind of stuff that you wouldn't do at most schools. We created a group of ham radio enthusiasts and strung an antenna from the prayer hall tower to the clock tower. VE3UCC were the call letters. At seventeen, I think I had the honour of being the first person to get a ham radio licence for the school.

I ran the signals platoon in the battalion, but I was a real spaz when it came to marching people around. I'd be marching them along and all of a sudden we'd come to an embankment and the platoon would split off. I was never very good at disciplining the ranks. I think I only got that post because I knew the Morse code.

Regardless of whether you are gay or straight, there is an inevitable homosexual subtext to social behaviour at a boys' private school. You see girls occasionally later on at dances and parties, but basically you're with boys all the time, especially in the early years. Young children have sexual fantasies. It's not as if they start at age fifteen. So at places like UCC, many of your sexual fantasies inevitably are geared towards boys because they are the only people around most of the time.

Tim Gibson was a notorious prep Latin master who probably was a pedophile. He'd openly fondle kids in the middle of class. It was just like "The Boys of St. Vincent," although I don't think he went beyond fondling. I remember his classic phrase that everybody mimicked was *"Quid nunc?"* which means "What now?" He would go around and stick his hand inside kids' shirts or fondle their hair. As kids were declining Latin nouns, he would be sucking up sensual pleasure from the children in the class.

He didn't do it to me, which I had a funny reaction to. I felt an element of envy when I was not one of the favoured ones. He chose the cutest kids, so if he didn't chose you, it felt like you weren't one of the cutest kids. To some extent I was relieved he wasn't doing it to me, but on the other hand, I didn't really understand the implications of this inappropriate behaviour. Kids of that age today probably would. In my day, there was no propaganda or education about that kind of molestation. Nobody said a word.

I remember a lot of cliques and ritual intrigue. In my year, there was an "in crowd" of guys like Brian Boxer, Mike Sainsbury, and Ian Urquhart, who were mildly rebellious, up to a point. Ian Urquhart, who later became the managing editor of the *Toronto Star*, was the editor of the *College Times*. I wasn't one of the cool guys, but I think I was considered a nice guy.

In the prep, I remember a ritual called "pink belly." A gang of boys would grab some kid, strip him to the waist, and repeatedly slap his belly hard until it got pink or red. A ring of twenty-five kids would gather around the kid like some kind of strange African humiliation ritual. There were various types of reactions. Sometimes the kids cried and sometimes some of the kids seemed to get off on it. This stuff was quite hidden from the authorities in the sense that it looked like the kids were just outside playing. There would always be a huddle of kids doing something to someone.

When I later saw films like *Lord of the Flies* or *If...*, the depictions of similar rituals had very deep resonance for me. I don't think it's any accident that a film like *If...* really played up animalistic kinds of behaviour at a boys' school, showing scenes where the main character turns into a tiger.

It was part of the totemic nature of the private school ritual. Beneath the hymn-books slamming shut and all the traditional Anglican rituals, a lot of pagan primitivism runs quite deep. Luckily I didn't have any particularly bad experiences myself. I was usually an observer.

Some of my fondest memories of the prep are getting on the football team. I got to go out to parties and meet girls, which really changed things. Status was linked to athletics. All through school, girls were just people you met at football games. We'd go to parties, play Lettermen songs, slow dance, and neck with the lights out. It started with the football team in the prep. All of a sudden, a whole social world opened up to me that hadn't existed before. I never had a steady girlfriend for years, but there were a few nice evenings that I remember making out.

I remember I went to the Battalion Ball with a girl from Etobicoke, where I lived. I didn't know her very well, but she was really beautiful. I really wanted to go out with her. I was amazed when she accepted my invitation. Only now do I realize that going to something as posh as the Upper Canada College Battalion Ball was probably a big thrill for her. She wasn't really interested in me personally.

When I said goodnight to her in my battalion uniform on the doorstep of her house, I remember she gave me a big French kiss. This had never happened to me before. I thought, This is fabulous. She loves me. I'll be seeing a lot of her. But she never wanted to go out with me again. I guess that was my reward for taking her to the UCC Battalion Ball.

Writing was something I was interested in all the way through UCC, so in the end, I decided I wanted to go into English at U of T. I wanted to get published quickly. When I was in university, a professor told me that he thought I should go on into literary criticism, publishing or academics. I ended up working for the *Varsity* student newspaper and then short-circuited into journalism.

I had the marks to get into Victoria College or Trinity College, where a lot of UCC boys went, but my brother Howard persuaded me to go to University College, where I met Jews for the first time. He thought that would be good for expanding my horizons and he was right. It was great. The *Varsity*, where I spent a lot of my time, was also heavily Jewish. It was only when I got out of UCC that I discovered what sort of effect it had had on me in terms of social class, perceptions of society, and what the world was all about. The school does insulate you incredibly from the rest of society.

Coming from ten years of Upper Canada College, slamming into the sex, drugs, rock and roll, and politics of the late 1960s had a tremendous impact on me. Part of the sixties was an attempt by a lot of people, from

UCC and elsewhere, to become déclassé, to try to shake off our socialization as spoiled, upper middle-class white kids. Having been to UCC, there was even more to live down in a sense.

Following again in the footsteps of my brother, I joined the fraternity Alpha Delta Psi at U of T, but I was only there for a year. Once I got involved with the *Varsity* and New Left politics, there was a lot of work to do. I had my adolescent rebellion late in university. I was never a rebel at UCC at all. Then I became an intellectual rebel and a rebel in every sense and every way. My angry-young-man phase was part of a fairly rational, very controlled, and very political sixties revolt against my UCC background, and against my parents to some extent, although it wasn't their fault at all.

I wouldn't call myself a Marxist now, but I probably wouldn't have become a Marxist if it wasn't for Upper Canada College. While I was working at the Montreal *Gazette* as a very left-wing labour reporter, I was involved in a Trotskyite group affiliated with the Fourth Internationale. In the early seventies, in the middle of the James Bay crisis, a man named Duhamel caused millions of dollars of damage with a bulldozer in one night at James Bay and stopped the project, something they had tried to do through the courts for ages without success. Shortly after that, the *Gazette* published a big exposé of union corruption in the construction industry, which was the first stone thrown in what led to the whole dismantling of the Quebec labour movement. But the article drew no attention to the fact that it was part of a triangle of management and government corruption.

Being the labour minister's confidante may have something to do with the fact that I eventually cracked up. He'd take me aside for brandy after the press conference one minute. Then I'd be in with the union leaders and the strikers the next minute, my Trotskyite meeting the next minute, then writing my stories for the *Gazette*. I had my finger in the whole pie. Although I thought I knew who I was working for, ultimately it got pretty confusing.

When I saw what was happening, my whole conspiracy theory came together. The shit hit the fan. I held a press conference, went on live television, and denounced the newspaper. It was covered in all the papers. They thought I was sane when they put me on live television, but I wasn't. I was quite mad. They had to cut me off in mid-sentence. I think my last words as they were trying to cut me off, as I was pointing to the cameraman, were, "What about the technicians? Don't they get a say in this?"

Journalism has a very short memory, though. I was back working for the CBC as a freelancer a year later. I had done my "I'm as mad as hell and I'm not going to take it any more" routine out of the movie *Network*. I was feeling quite crazy. I had what I guess would be called a nervous breakdown for a year or so.

So I went to Italy and wrote poetry and became a musician. I played congas and percussion in a Latin band full time for about five years. After that, I wrote a column in the *Globe and Mail* called "Hanging Out," until I was hanging out so much in bars where I was playing music that I didn't have enough time to write the column. After turning down a Canadian record contract and holding out for a U.S. deal, the band fell apart and we went bankrupt. I went back to freelance magazine writing, which led to my current position at *Maclean's*.

One of the things that I like about having gone to Upper Canada was the fact that because I was surrounded by money and wealth and class, I was never impressed by it. I think that is one of the best things that you can get out of an institution like UCC. You aren't lusting after wealth because you see, among other things, that a lot of the really rich kids are not very interesting or happy. You see what wealth does to people. They can be ass-holes and they can be snobbish. I realized there are more interesting things in life than money.

PERRIN BEATTY

1963 – 68

Former Progressive Conservative cabinet minister

I REMEMBER when Prime Minister Mulroney asked me to be minister of national defence. My experience in the military was limited to five very unhappy years in the battalion at UCC in the sixties, which was a very anti-military period. I hated it. The stretcher squad was where they would put the worst cadets. My mind would drift off when we were on parade. I'd be thinking of other things and I would despise every minute of it.

So when the prime minister wanted me to be the minister of national defence, my first response was, "You're kidding, aren't you?" He said, "No, I'm perfectly serious." I said, "Thank you very much. I'm very honoured. You realize I was the worst cadet in my high school." I used to kid about it afterwards. I'd say, "The prime minister knew that with my distinguished career in the UCC battalion, the only post in the military I could hold was as 'Minister Without Doing Serious Damage to the Security of Canada.'"

I came into the experience as minister of defence with deep suspicions of what I was getting into. I came away from the experience with an enormous respect for the men and women in the forces. I had a much better understanding of the way in which the military in the course of centuries has used discipline as a means of shaping character and drawing the best out of people.

I came away absolutely sold on the military. They are outstanding people, patriots in the best sense of the word. What I admire about people like George Grant and Donald Creighton was their sense of unabashed Canadian patriotism, which is also one of the things I admire about the men and women in the military. They have a pure love of the country and they are prepared to literally put their lives on the line.

The other thing that fascinated me was to discover that the best military officers are the ones who are the most liberally educated. The military has a side within its schooling that you are a better military officer if you know about more than simply ballistics. It's not remarkably different from the philosophy that animates Upper Canada College – the belief that your best citizens in government, business, law, or anywhere else will be those who have the broadest possible education and who are well trained as human beings. That experience in the military was very useful for me in setting into perspective my own thoughts about the college.

I've thought many times about those formative years. My father had died when I was ten, so my mother thought I should have some male influence in my life. There's no question UCC left an impression on me. Ironically, when I was at UCC, my personality was such that I tended to resist anything that I was expected to do. So much emphasis was put on mandatory participation. Battalion and the cross-country run were required. You were expected as part of your personal development to be involved in everything.

I tend to be resentful of being required to do things. As a consequence, I didn't take advantage of a lot of the opportunities. There's no question that the resources were second to none. I think about friends who did throw themselves into things and had wonderful opportunities. When else do you have five years during which so much of your personality and capabilities are being developed? You have the ability to sample, to stretch yourself and challenge yourself.

But in my particular case, I tended to resist being involved in things because it was required. Then, when I went to Western, I reversed 180 degrees because I was not required to do anything. At Western I got involved with everything, whether it was student politics, the student paper, having a program at the radio station. Looking back, I might well not have thrown myself into things at university if it hadn't been for the influence of UCC where, in spite of my resistance, I think I came away with the feeling that people should be involved and try things out, test themselves, stretch their wings and make a contribution as best as they can. I'm not sure I would have done that if I hadn't gone to a high school that put a premium on involvement.

UCC had another impact that was very real. Jim Biggar, my housemaster, asked me to help him with some work he was doing matching kids up for Visites Interprovinciales, which was a summer student exchange program. A UCC student would stay with a Quebec family for two weeks and then have the French-Canadian student stay with the UCC boy's family in Ontario.

Then in Grade 11 or 12, I exchanged with a young chap down on the north shore of eastern Quebec, past Quebec City. I had been taking French lessons since Grade 9 and saw French as an instrument of torture to be used by French teachers on their students. I came from an area of Ontario where people spoke English exclusively. French didn't seem very relevant to me.

Suddenly, in making this student exchange, I became aware for the first time that somebody could be born, educated, grow up, work, live, and die without speaking a word of English. For the first time, French had some relevance to me. For the first time, I had some understanding of the complexity of Canada. One of the dangers of growing up in southern Ontario is that it is very easy to grow up oblivious of the rest of the country.

My Quebec experience was the first time that I really became aware of the fact that there were other Canadians who lived lives very different from mine, but they were every bit as Canadian as I was. I realized that the French that I was learning on an academic basis had some practical application as well. That experience has been very useful for me in public life, helping to motivate me to have a better understanding of my country and to speak to every Canadian in their own language.

Graham Fraser, who is now a journalist with the *Globe and Mail,* was a steward in Seaton's House when I first came to the school as a new boy. Graham was a great gentleman even then. I don't think he has changed remarkably, other than he has matured. He's a very nice, thoughtful man. What I remember very much about UCC was the great separation of the older and younger boys, but Graham was much more open. I just instinctively liked him.

John Bosley, a future Speaker of the House of Commons, was in Seaton's too. Bos was very young for his peer group but he was very successful. He was involved in the battalion and I remember him playing *Little Mary Sunshine* in the Little Theatre. He still has a lovely singing voice. I remember Michael Ignatieff was a very bright guy. It's been fascinating for me to follow him since and to read pieces he has written and to watch him on TV. Mike was one of those people who you knew was certainly making a mark.

My closest friend, Ross McLean, was in Wedd's House, although we weren't close at the time because he was very much involved with athletics and battalion and I wasn't. We bumped into each other on the main street of my home town, Fergus, fifteen years ago when Ross was living in the area. We struck up a close friendship and we have maintained it ever since. It's not by coincidence that Ross is now one of my closest friends. Even after many years out, you really do feel a close bond with people because of shared experiences at UCC.

I suspect my interest in debating would have happened whether or not I went to UCC. I found that the discipline of organizing your thoughts, being able to analyze an opponent's argument, and knowing how to do research was all very useful. Coupled with my experience working for the student paper when I went off to university, that experience helped me to research and write in a coherent way. Both of those skills were very useful for public life.

I remember I debated together on the same inter-house debating team with David Gilmour, who has gone on to become a very distinguished writer and broadcaster. He's a very brilliant person. He was a great person to debate with, although I think I took our house down to defeat for the eighth straight year in house debating. It meant that I had all the attributes that were required for the House of Commons.

I was David's roommate when he went out the window one night and ran away to Mexico. I don't think any of us really expected that his escape was going to be quite so successful. When he came back several weeks later, I was helping to promote the publicity for the boarders' show. David liked to be a drummer, so we created a band which we called "David Gilmour and the Runaways." We put pictures and posters all over the school saying "He's back and he'll be at the boarders' show." I can remember meeting David many years later on Bloor Street in Toronto. We got talking about UCC and I mentioned that I had seen Michael Ignatieff, who had been in Wedd's House a few years ahead of us, on the cover of *GQ* magazine. I remember David said, "What's *GQ*?"

I believe the ethic that underlies Upper Canada is a belief in excellence and a belief in service, which in the 1990s seems very old fashioned. But if you look at the qualities that are most needed, whether in Canadian public life, business, or whatever sector, those two values are needed today perhaps more than ever before. At UCC, there is a desire to create the very best, to achieve and to make a contribution that uses all of your talents to the fullest.

The interesting thing is that only when you get away from the school do you really begin to realize what an impact it has had. It gives you a common bond with people whom you bump into at different points in your life. UCC can have a very profound impact, something that perhaps you can set in perspective only some years down the road.

DAVID GILMOUR

1959–67

Arts journalist, novelist

I RAN INTO Perrin Beatty at a Christmas party in 1993 after he had just been defeated in the federal election. His wife turned to me at the party, after she'd had a cocktail or two, and said, "You know, enormous damage was done when Perrin went to UCC. We have spent over twenty years trying to undo some of the damage – the closed-offness, the defensiveness, the stiffness – that came from his years at Upper Canada."

Then, after a couple of cocktails, Perrin himself said to me, "I hated every second of UCC." I was just amazed. I thought I was the fucking rebel, and here I am the one with the good memories of UCC. It's like, "Wait a minute. I'm supposed to be the one saying these things." Yet I'm the one who has softened over the years. It's odd. My older brother Chris was a model student and yet was permanently traumatized, both from the pressure of our family, which he calls a "Vietnam-like" experience, and UCC, which he calls a *"Lord of the Flies"* experience. I was the black sheep and yet I enjoyed it and emerged relatively unscathed.

At the cocktail party, Perrin Beatty said, "I hated UCC. When I graduated, I had a recurring nightmare that lasted for a number of years. It took place in the summer after I graduated." It's a wonderful dream archetype. He said, "I had a dream that I got my report card and I passed and I moved on. Then, late in the summer, Upper Canada phoned me and said that there had been a mistake marking my exams. I had in fact not passed and all my plans for university were ruined because I had to go back and do Grade 13 at Upper Canada all over again." He said that he had this recurring, disturbing dream for some time. Isn't that wild?

I was Perrin's roommate in boarding. I remember coming to my room one afternoon and seeing him with a pair of scissors, snipping out an article about John Diefenbaker and pasting it into his scrapbook. I remember thinking, What a lonely little boy he must be. This is not what a boy should be doing on a Saturday afternoon. The rest of us were out running around. I remember having one of those epiphanies you have when you are young. I suddenly thought, God, what a dreadful life that must be.

Later, I revised my interpretation of him. When I looked at his life and thought about it, I realized he was happy. He enjoyed it. He was actually doing something that gave him pleasure. Then, at the cocktail party, when he remarked how much he hated the school, I realized I had got it absolutely right the first time, in the way that children do.

I had started as a day boy in the prep. When I was in Grade 12, I had an unhappy breakup with a girl. I went to my parents and stupidly decided that they were going to put me in boarding. For someone who was going to two or three parties each weekend in Forest Hill, to suddenly find himself in an institution where the lights were turned off at 9:00 P.M., where you were allowed out for three Saturday nights a term, it was like being sent to prison.

I was absolutely devastated and heartbroken by the breakup with the girl, who was my first serious sexual relationship. My father by then had lost a lot of money on the stock market, as well as his confidence. The following year, he shot himself. At this point, my parents had just sold their house in Forest Hill and had moved up north. On a train ride back from their house, I saw a picture of Florida. I remembered Florida as a child and I was filled with this extraordinary longing to go back there.

I went back to my dormitory and said to Perrin Beatty, "I think I'm going to run away." He said, "Don't tell me where you're going because I don't want to be responsible." To cover my tracks, I told him I was going to British Columbia and I told another fellow down the hall that I was going to Florida. The assistant housemaster, who was on duty, walked in at 11:30 at night and found my entire suitcase packed. I told him I was just unpacking and he walked away.

The long and short of it was I ran away. I ended up at 8:30 the next morning, a cold October day, standing on the Peace Bridge, the wind blowing like crazy, looking over at the United States. Over the years I had been led to believe that boys who were expelled from UCC didn't go to other schools but rather fell off the earth and died. They landed in a little white pile of bones of boys who had been kicked from the epicentre of the universe. I always had a sense about UCC of living under God's umbrella. If you flew off the wheel, your life was over.

But when I successfully passed customs in the U.S., nothing happened. There was no giant heel descending from the sky or a feeling of eternal damnation. I had broken the cardinal rule and absolutely nothing happened. It was all smoke and mirrors. There was no substance to the threats at all. Life just went on. I never had the same institutional repect for UCC again because I had literally stood on the bridge and thought, I'm free. It's over. Nothing has happened to me.

I had eleven dollars in my pocket and had never been away from home. The house prefect heard that I was going to run away from school and collected eleven dollars for me. The deal was that if I stayed away for three days, I could keep it. If I was returned to the school before three days, I had to refund the money.

I ran away for two months and ended up living with a prostitute in Mexico named Gloria Garza. She was twenty-three and wore a patch over her eye. I met her wandering for days through a little town called Nuevo Laredo. I had hitchhiked to Florida and then crossed over to Mexico. This kind-hearted prostitute introduced me to a certain kind of real sex as opposed to Havergal sex. They did things very differently in Nuevo Laredo.

I then went to California and sent my mother a letter saying where I was. My mother was herself an American. The long and short of it was that she flew me back and sent me to see the principal, Patrick Johnson, the following day. He said, "Well, you've been on one hell of an adventure." I thought it was an extraordinarily generous reaction. One has to remember that there was a whole lot of decency at Upper Canada, even then. Apart from the raging homosexuals who never set foot outside the institution and the masters who were repressed, angry, violent, frustrated, and thwarted, there were also decent people who understood.

Johnson brought me into his office and, with an unmistakable tinge of admiration in his voice, said, "I hear you've been to South America." I said, "Well, no, actually I only went as far as Mexico." He said, "Three or four days after you left, another boy ran away. When we caught him, we asked him what he thought he was doing. He said, 'I'm doing a Gilmour.' I don't want this to happen again, so I'll make you a deal. I'll let you come back, but I don't want you telling anybody about your adventures. If you start telling people that you were in Florida, Mexico, and California, we're going to have a whole lot of kids running away next weekend." Very generously, he allowed me to come back.

I had said to my mother on the phone from California that I wanted to go back to Upper Canada so badly that I could taste it, because I intuited it then – it took me another twenty years to completely understand it – that I love institutions. I despise the repressiveness of them, but I love to survive them. Years later, after I graduated from university, I used to live every summer in Trinity College at the University of Toronto for the same sense of weight, history, institution.

In any case, I was allowed back to school. Over the months, my friend Bill Milne used to come and knock at my window at midnight and we'd go out into the playing fields just simply to get out of my room at night. I later wrote a novel about my relationship with Milne called *An Affair with the Moon.* I met him in my first year in the prep. When he was in his thirties, he served time in jail for shooting and killing a guy while under the influence of drugs.

Some time after Mexico, I met a girl named Scarlett Page from Bishop Strachan. She told me which room she boarded in at BSS. I went over one night and snuck in through a window of the principal's office that was left open. After two or three times, I became reckless and started to take other boarders with me. By the end, I was taking parties of two and three guys over to BSS in the evening.

Once, when we were visiting one of Scarlett's roommates, a teacher came into the room. We all hid in the cupboard but the teacher knew that we were there. She left the room and waited at the end of the hall and saw us escape down the stairs. Then she went into Scarlett's room and said, "I want the names of those boys or else you are all expelled." Scarlett immediately coughed up our names.

The next morning at UCC, the old decrepit messenger came around to class and said David Gilmour was to report to the principal's office. I didn't have the foggiest idea what was going on. I walked to the office and there was one of my cohorts. Pat Johnson said, "This is very serious. I want you to go to Bishop Strachan right now and show them how you got in, what your route was, who you talked to. Anything less than this and you'll be out of this school this afternoon."

I heard later that he could barely contain his laughter while he was talking about us. In fact, it was something he had to pretend to be quite serious about. Later that afternoon, he called me in and said if I took one step off the school grounds before the end of the year, I was expelled. But there was no question for the principal that there was nothing morally wrong with me for going over to a girls' school. In fact, he said breaking into a girls' school seemed to him more of a university prank than a high school prank. There was no suggestion whatsover that I was a degenerate, rather that this was the sort of thing that was slightly more mature than the kind of thing that ought to be going on at Upper Canada. This was an immensely flattering thing to hear for someone who was in the kind of shit that I was in.

Soon I got another girlfriend from Havergal College who started to visit me late at night, sneaking out of her house. I would meet her down at one of the lower playing fields where we used to roll around in the leaves. This was after I had been told that if I left the school grounds, I was finished.

I remember our housemaster, Piff Biggar, a harmless, sweet old man, often gave a little speech in our evening meetings with the boarders where he would say, "It is a proven fact that all well-educated people are virgins when they get married." This was a stunner. I was having my first sexual intercourse during these days. I remember thinking, This is bullshit.

One night near the end of May, I was coming back in through my window covered in leaves to find the assistant housemaster, Sniff Ainsworth, waiting for me. He said with a smile, "I want you to know that if I were the principal, you'd be packing your bags and leaving the school tonight. But I'll tell you what I'm going to do. I'm not going to tell anybody. All I'm saying is, don't do it again while I'm on duty." Again, this was extraordinary. These people weren't afraid to endorse rebellious behaviour. They wanted to make you understand that it was inappropriate at the school, but that in a larger world, it was really quite okay.

I got my report card at the end of Grade 12. They passed me, but there was a little letter from Pat Johnson saying in effect, "It's over. Don't come back for Grade 13. There are many other schools where David would be a lot happier." He was absolutely right. It was a wonderful piece of teaching because I was in fact sent to Muskoka Lakes College, an experimental school. My marks went up 20 per cent and I got into the University of Toronto, which I probably wouldn't have qualified for had I remained in Upper Canada.

The housemaster sent me a little goodbye letter in which I remember he said, "Don't shoot the piano teacher. He's only doing his job." Even at the time, I remember thinking it was an awfully generous goodbye letter because he really was saying, "You don't belong here any more. But don't hold this against us morally. We're only trying to run the institution. It's nothing personal." There was no moral condemnation whatsoever, so I bear no scars at all. I left Upper Canada at the end of a boot, feeling like a hero.

ANDREW IGNATIEFF

1962–69

Community worker

B EFORE I STARTED in the prep at age twelve, our parents sat down with my older brother and I. They said, "Michael, you're the big brother and Andrew is going to UCC for the first time. It's the first time he has ever been away. You have to understand you have to be good to him." My brother had just left the prep in a blaze of glory and gone on to the upper school.

Michael was very sweet and he told me how wonderful UCC would be. Then we went to my aunt Helen's house and again he was very sweet. My aunt Helen again impressed on him the importance of him looking out for me. Then we went to the school and he introduced me to all the masters in the prep. The next morning he came down to see how I was doing. I still remember the front steps and railings of the old prep Peacock Building. He said, "How are things going? Did you sleep well?" I said, "Yes, I slept well." He said, "How's the food?" I said, "It was gross." He said, "Do you want to go for a walk?"

We went for a walk and he said, "I want to make one thing absolutely clear to you. When we're at Aunt Helen's house or Aunt Charity's house, you can say whatever you want to me. But if you ever see me on the school grounds, you're not to talk to me. You're not to recognize that I'm your brother. You don't exist as far as I'm concerned. Do I make myself clear?"

One of my main themes about Upper Canada is what it did to interpersonal relationships. That my own brother would do that! Everybody bowed and scraped when Michael passed. He assumed ever greater glory in the upper school. Then this fat little prick, who had been his curse all the time he was growing up, pursued him from around the world to join him at school. He didn't want me around. I wasn't any better: I didn't want him around. It wasn't until many years later that we could sit down as equals and talk issues out, acknowledge our differences and respect them.

My first year at the prep was great. I was away from my parents, on my own and doing all sorts of exciting stuff. I remember realizing the boarding-house had been built by my great-grandfather, George Parkin. But in the second year, the prep became a disaster for me. I hurled myself into puberty in a big way and became increasingly resentful of authority. I resented the canings and the paddlings and the increasingly sinister relationships we had with those creepy teachers at the prep. I felt incredibly homesick and out of phase with the teachers.

I recall one teacher who was a loathsome little man. One night, we were all waiting to go to bed at some ludicrously early hour. We were all sitting around the dorm, enjoying our only fifteen minutes of peace in the whole day. He was flicking on and off the lights and I screamed, "Would you please fuck off!" He came in and said, "Who said that?" Of course, it being Upper Canada, the boys all pointed at me. I said, "It was me."

He took me into this room, deep in the bowels of the place, and caned me six times. Being an idiot and a Canadian, he didn't know how to cane properly. He caned me six times and said, "Did you enjoy that?" I said, "No!" So he caned me six more times. Pat Johnson, who was English, used to do it properly – six absolutely perfect parallel blows, an inch separating each blow. But when this Canadian jerk caned me, he drew blood. I peed my pants. I remember feeling profoundly degraded. I wept with rage.

Another time, a master was completely drunk while he was on duty. We had committed some minor infraction and he called us in and presided over a mock trial. I remember thinking, What I am doing with this drunk? After this stupid trial, he slippered us. It was just pathetic. I was so angry. I remember feeling deep resentment. Another old jerk, Tim Gibson, used to rat-tail naked boys in the locker rooms. He wet a towel, rolled it up, and flicked it at our butts. It can really hurt. I can remember just feeling repulsed.

A feeling of being trapped was my principal emotion for my seven years at UCC. I kept feeling: Get me the hell out of here! But I did not know where to go. My parents lived in Europe and even then I realized there was no place else to go. Consistently through my time at Upper Canada, I felt caught in the grasp of people who I knew even then were mediocre. There was nothing I could do except take abuse from people for whom I felt nothing but contempt.

The food at the upper school was never great, but at the prep it was revolting. In the second year, as a senior boy, I had to serve some shit called boiled mince in an aluminum bowl. They took cheap chuck, boiled the bejesus out of it, and made beef broth, which they then made into vegetable soup at lunch. Then they boiled the shit out of it again in the afternoon and out came a grey gruel filled with grisly buckshot. It had a particularly putrid smell that made the bile rise in my throat. The cinnamon toast was soggy Wonder bread caked with cinnamon and sugar. The cinnamon was of such industrial quality that it was utterly bitter.

Turnip wedges are now served in nouvelle cuisine. Count me out! The prep served us turnip cubes about an inch square, pressure-cooked so they were always cool and crisp in the interior. They were a very, very pale cream colour with white veins in them. We had to go and pick up the food. The maids would slap margarine up and down the bowls. There would be a tepid turnip with an acid, spongy quality swimming in margarine in this aluminum bowl. Margarine for me is forever cursed.

When I was having all sorts of problems in second year at the prep, they decided I needed a psychological examination. So they brought in Nicky Laidlaw, who was one of the great sweet people of the world. The Laidlaw family has strong ties to UCC. He starts showing me Rorschach inkblot tests. Then he looks at one and asks, "Andrew, can you tell me which way the toilet flushes in the Southern Hemisphere?" I said, "No, Dr. Laidlaw." He said, "I don't know why I'm asking you these things. You're just fine. How's your mom, by the way?" I said, "Oh, she's great." Then he said, "She was just the cutest girl. I remember she played hockey on the UCC rinks."

Then we just had a lovely talk. He said, "I'm just going to say you're fine. You're just having a difficult time here. I can really sympathize with that because I had a difficult time here too as a boy. Look at me, I'm now a psychiatrist." Nick was one of the very few people from Upper Canada whom I met continuously through later life. I had a tremendous feeling of affection for him because he was the only person who said that what I was going through was perfectly normal for an adolescent boy, that I wasn't rebellious and antisocial by nature. He realized that I was just having trouble adapting to a perverse situation.

After two years in the prep, I went up to the upper school. The whole psychology was that you're now out of the slum. The whole prep was like a slum. So there I am, a new boy in Wedd's House in the upper school. My uncle had been a master of Wedd's House. Wedd's was named after Uncle Basil Wedd. Where else could I go but Wedd's House? And who was the steward of Wedd's House but Michael Ignatieff!

These people always told you what great educators they were, but they violated Psychology 101. I clearly had difficulty in a competitive relationship with my brother, but what do they do but consistently put me in a situation where I was competing with a person whose stature I could never attain. I was never a sports person and Michael always was. He never had difficulty writing and speaking. He was ardently competitive and my way of doing things was not to be competitive.

But for five years they consistently tried to force me into a competitive situation with my brother. They said, "Is this all you can do? Your brother was the school valedictorian, your brother was the editor of the *College*

Times, your brother was the captain of first-team soccer, your brother was the debating champion for the whole of Ontario, your brother was the head of Wedd's House." It went on and on and on and on.

They forced me to be in the academic A stream because my brother had always been in it. For five years, I was twenty-seventh out of twenty-seven kids in our class. It would have been better to put me in a lower stream and let me excel to give me a sense of confidence. But, no, my brother had been in 1A1, 2A1, 3A1, 4A1, 5A1, so that's where I would be. The whole experience at the upper school was Sisyphean, the feeling that I would always end up a failure no matter what I did. They just never twigged. UCC always trumpeted endlessly about how much better they were than the public school system, how they had the finest teachers around. As far as I'm concerned, the school set false standards, academically, socially, and psychologically.

One of the principles of a good education is the uniqueness of each child. Upper Canada encouraged conformity of the worst sort, as well as intergenerational conformity. The Conachers were jocks, so for five generations the Conachers will be jocks. The Eatons are dumb but will go into trade, so it doesn't matter. The Grants will succeed and be academic, so there had to be brains.

The school of course was also full of family history, which I didn't need to be constantly reminded of. Every morning when I went into Laidlaw Hall, I would see the portraits of my great-grandfather, George Parkin, and my grandfather, Choppy Grant, both of whom were former principals of UCC. I'd see my uncle's name on the golden boards. I'd see my brother's name on the golden boards. I'd see Grant House. I didn't need to be reminded my grandfather, Choppy Grant, built up the school in the twenties and thirties with Massey family money. Vincent Massey's wife was my mother's aunt. That's how all the Massey money came into the college.

My heart goes out to my uncle, George Grant, who was a most tormented and conflicted individual. He and my mom were very close. He had very dismissive attitudes to women, but he felt my mother was great. Canada's great philosopher and my mother used to phone each other from anywhere in the world, saying, "Oh, my God! I watched Bette Davis in *Juarez* last night." My mother would start singing. They would recite whole pieces of dialogue from movies when they had been kids down in the flea palaces at Yonge and St. Clair. They had a very tight bond from their childhood. He also lived with my mother during the war.

Each year at the school had its new fiasco for me. A group of us were caught shoplifting when we were in Grade 10. Five of us had been shoplifting together since Grade 7. We had been through the prep together and we shoplifted together in a casual way, a chocolate bar here and there. A boy from Ottawa was the ringleader. He decided he wanted to go big time, so he animated the rest of us. Peter Tovell, myself, and the ringleader, Simard, were the inner core. The height of our glory was around the beginning of November. I had to buy something. My mother had given me twenty dollars, so I paid twenty dollars for a standard church-going raincoat.

Then we just walked through the whole of downtown. Peter, Paul, Cameron, and Robbie were picking stuff up and I was the bagman. I ended up in the basement of Simpsons with a shopping bag full of stuff. I mean, how stupid can you be? I thought because I had a raincoat on top of the shopping bag, no one would ever notice. Suddenly, someone grabbed me from behind and put their arm around my neck. I looked up and it was a huge woman. She said, "Come with me, sonny." They dragged me off. Other people had caught the other four guys.

They took us into a room and started cross-examining us. Every time I pass The Bay, I look up and see if that office is still there. The woman who had captured us took her wig off. It turned out to be a man. I wasn't born yesterday. I lived in Europe, but I had never seen anything like this in my life. When I saw this huge hulking person taking off an auburn wig to reveal a 1965 crew cut, I was ready to confess everything. I had shoplifted one of those swivel-top pen sets which had Canadian maple leaf pennies embedded inside the plastic base. I just wanted it so badly. It was like forbidden fruit. To me, it was like real grown-up stuff. Even thirty years later, when I see one of those pen sets, it brings up a psychological reaction. I think, I can't touch it. I can't even handle it.

In 1964, my first year at the upper school, Pat Johnson was a wonderful housemaster. I still see his wife Eleanor quite a bit because she and I sit on a board together. She's exactly the way she was then as she is now – loud-mouthed, terribly affectionate, exaggerated, outrageous, but very warm-hearted. You could imagine her as your mother. In his peculiar, rather reserved way, you could imagine Pat as your surrogate dad. He was a great big, athletic, handsome guy.

When I see him now, he's one of the many UCC people I wish had just gotten away from the place. I had a good relationship with him at the school. He made no secret of the fact that he just thought Michael was the greatest thing that ever happened to his school, but he never made me feel small. He's the only one who never said, "Why aren't you like Michael?"

Then in 1965, when Johnson became principal, horrible John Symons became our housemaster. After the shoplifting, he put us in different rooms and pulled KGB tactic stuff. He said, "Confess, confess. The others have confessed. Are you going to confess?" I was crying and begging for mercy. He was saying, "No, you have to confess. You're going to get the maximum penalty. You're going to be thrown out of the school." I was ready to kill him. It was completely blown out of perspective. We were kids.

After the shoplifting, which was on a Saturday afternoon, the five of us were brought in, heads down, and made to sit at different tables for dinner. They said, "These boys have been caught shoplifting." We were publicly humiliated, which was completely unnecessary. On Monday morning, the principal, Pat Johnson, took us in one by one into his office. Talk about the fear of God! I knew he didn't fuck around.

He said, "You've done something absolutely unpardonable. You will receive the maximum punishment. Simard is being expelled because he has been caught many times before. This is your first offence, so you boys are going to get six strokes and you're going to sit down and write a letter to your parents explaining everything. You will hand it in here by the end of the afternoon. Then we will never talk about this again."

Down come my pants and I got six exquisite strokes across my legs. Unbelievable pain! I was sure I was going to be expelled, so I was ready to kiss his feet. I didn't realize his caning was artistry until afterwards. I still remember looking in the mirror at the welts and seeing six absolutely perfect parallel lines. He had been educated at a British boarding school, starting at age five, so he knew what he was doing. We went back to the study room on the fourth floor at Wedd's and wrote the letter to our parents. Then we took it back to his office at the end of the afternoon. He read them, sealed them, and mailed them. As far as he was concerned, that was the last we heard of it. He never mentioned it again.

But John Symons flogged it for everything it was worth. We weren't allowed off the grounds. For five consecutive weekends, he made us build a woodpile. Then he would kick it down. We would build it up again and he would kick it down again. We would have to endlessly write lines. I just remember thinking, You shithead! As I got older and a little bit more knowledgeable of the world, I thought: What the hell are you doing here? You are a miserable, lower middle-class Englishman who hates and resents the rich for very good reasons, because you come from an ironclad class system. You put yourself in a situation where you were tortured and now all you can do is torture the people who tortured you."

A lot of my life has been given to community development work in which the promotion, training, and equality of women in society is important. At Upper Canada, I remember the horrendous way that we talked about the maids. Not only were they women, but they were low-class scum. As adolescent boys, the whole humour was based on sexual innuendo. That is not unique to Upper Canada because it goes on everywhere.

But the thing that really concerned me in retrospect was the severe distortion of interpersonal relationships. It was impossible to ever have a normal relationship with a woman because it was so put into your mind about how women are stupid, inferior, and fickle. It's difficult enough for people to have normal relationships as coworkers and friends, let alone as partners and sexual partners.

Once, on a Friday night before a Saturday night boarders' dance, we were taught how to dance. I remember identical twin boys from Barrie, who were members of the Acne Hall of Fame. They had the sort of acne you don't even see any more because of changes in diet and lifestyle. I had to dance cheek to cheek with one of them, which was like being asked to dance with a leper. I remember feeling physical repulsion coming close to him.

For the dance the next night, the girls were bussed in separately. While we were kept under lock and key in our rooms, the girls were herded like cows into Mr. Brennan's classroom between the front entrance and the masters' common room. The windows were all papered over. Hazel Flynn, the matron, and the principal's secretary, Mrs. Carrier, who had the wonderful nickname "Aircraft," would stand in the doorway while we were lined up in parallel lines, the Seaton's boys on one side, the Wedd's boys on the other. Aircraft Carrier and Hazel would call out our names. When you got up there, they would say, "Ignatieff, this is Cathy McLean. Have a good time." You'd grope around for something to say, like, "Well, would you like to look around the college?" Then we had to walk the gauntlet. Everyone started barking and growling, making dog noises at the girls. Really positive, right?

Women are treated with such contempt in that system. I don't know how the few female teachers at UCC survive. Miss Barrow, the nurse, was completely sexless. Our matron was a very nice woman, but she always reminded you of your mother or a robot like Barrow. There were never any positive female role models for us, except for Mrs. Paichoux, a woman who was treated with respect and affection.

Her husband, Louis Paichoux, the French master, was very spontaneous. They weren't all over themselves, although that's what we fantasized, because they were French. They had the kind of joshing relationship that reminded me very much of my parents' relationship. But that was the only good relationship that we ever saw. Once Eleanor and Pat Johnson had gone over to Grant House in 1965, we really didn't see them very much.

The other big issue at UCC was physical appearance. I got it coming and going for my physical appearance and so did my friend Harry Underwood. I'm sure that's why we were quite good friends through Upper Canada.

People would call me "fatty," "piggy," "slob," "big ass," or "spaz," for which I had no patience and no forgiveness. When the revolution comes and I'm at the gateway of hell, I'll make sure that those who bullied me are the first to go through the gate. I will push them. I was persecuted the whole time I was at school in an unmerciful way.

I have spent a lot of time reflecting on that period of my life. Through my own life quest, I'm trying to achieve a sense of inner peace in which all that stuff moves to the periphery. I try to forgive the things that were done, and not done. So I don't say, "My life was ruined by a bully and I'm a failure." I just say that I really wouldn't care to see that person again. I don't feel permanently embittered by the experience. My principal emotion is what a fucking waste it all was.

When my brother and I talk about Upper Canada now, I get fairly heated about it, but at the same time, it's not such a tremendous weight on me any more. I've been through therapy, so I've already analyzed a lot of these situations. I'm fascinated by my brother's recollections of Upper Canada. His memories are of never-ending martyrdom too. He has a lot of resentment. And he achieved! Pat Johnson still asks me, "How's your brother?" Well, he's just in a rage. His resentment is equal to mine.

Michael had a shelf filled with golden books which my father had placed in a position of pride everywhere we went. They just infuriated and enraged me because they symbolized my problematic relationship with my brother and everything that I had aspired to, but had never attained, at UCC. Towards the end of his life, when my father retired, he kept on saying to Michael, every time he would come back to Canada from England, "Why don't you take the books back? Now you have your own home. I'm sure you and Susan would like to have the books." Michael would say no.

Then our father died. When Michael came back, I said, "Get those fucking books out of here!" He said, "I don't want them." I said, "Then send them down to Crippled Civilians because I'm not having them in here." He said, "But they are nice." I said, "I don't want them in here. Get rid of them." But they stayed in a box. Finally, a couple of years ago, he took them. It was interesting psychologically. Every time I would ask him about it, he would say, "Oh, I have a bad back. I can't carry them." So we all have our psychological baggage to carry around.

A few years ago, I met Barbara Barrow at a Boxing Day party held by my aunt, Charity Grant. Barrow and I always had a rather prickly, tense relationship. She died recently after spending over forty years at UCC. She always used to say, "Come back to the college." She was famous for being at the centre of all the old-boy shit and keeping track of everyone. I would always act up, the rebellious old boy, saying stuff like, "Oh, back off, Barrow!"

After the party, she phones me up one day and says, "Oh, hello, Iggy." She always called me that because she knew that it's one of the things that I cannot abide. My nickname for seven years was "Iggy." She said, "One of your classmates, Andy Pringle, is going to South America and he wants to know the names of some hotels." I said, "Look, Barrow, I'm really busy right now. I don't have time to meet him, but why don't you just get him to phone me. Here's my phone number and I'm in the book."

He never phones me, of course. A month later, I got a personalized letter from Andy Pringle, who is the 1969 year representative for fundraising. He is a Bay Street type married to the TV journalist, Valerie Pringle. I tore up the letter and threw it in the trash, like I've done with everything else I get from Upper Canada.

A month later, I get yet another letter saying, "We're deeply disappointed that we've been out of touch with you." So I sat down and I wrote a letter. I basically said: "I responded to an information request from the school nurse. I now find that this information is being used inappropriately for a fundraising letter. You must understand that I have done my utmost since leaving Upper Canada to remove myself at a great distance from the college and what it stands for. At the time, and upon further reflection, I found the education both elitist in theory and mediocre in practice. I would be grateful if you would remove my name from any correspondence, information list, or mailing list related to Upper Canada College. Yours sincerely, Andrew Ignatieff."

UCC's idea of community service is paternalism and noblesse oblige of the worst sort. It is against everything that I stand for in terms of my own experience of community development and community organization, to which I've given my life. I remember the school's attitude to the lesser orders came out in one particular incident. There was a huge UCC party in which people had jumped naked out of windows and been taken off to jail. A master in Grade 13, a very tight-lipped guy, gave us a lecture. He said, "You behaved no better than people who live in places like Regent Park."

He said it with complete contempt as he was sitting in front of the class. He said, "Boys took a Harley-Davidson motorcyle, put it on the diving board of a swimming pool, and drove it off into the pool. The pool had to be drained and cleaned. Those boys never even thought of the inconvenience to everybody." I just remember thinking, God! Why didn't I think of doing that? It opened my eyes to a form of conceptual art.

There is a conspiracy of silence through the generations about the dark side of UCC, which I find fascinating. I'm not saying, "Let's blow the roof off the school." In the end, it doesn't really count for a whole lot. But it is fascinating that, year in and year out, old boys constantly sentimentalize the place. No matter what distance I get from the school, it was a formative experience in my life. The other night driving up the Avenue Road hill, when I saw the clock tower, I found myself suddenly bursting into the school song:

High on a hill she stands,
Her tower a landmark clear,
Her colours bright are blue and white
To all of her sons most dear!

Sons of a mighty school,
Proudly the palm we bear,
Striving to merit more and more
The colours that we wear!

Like, get a grip! If I had the opportunity to live my live again, I would have lived it somewhere else. But I don't think of myself as terribly marked and irrevocably changed by the experience. You have to believe in your own heart to change your life and set it straight. But the school had such a significant effect on me that it took me a long time to get myself back on track.

Mercifully, I didn't have a nervous breakdown like my friend Peter Tovell, who is gay, or suffer the humiliations of my friend Peter Meltzer, who is Jewish and physically handicapped. I went through UCC for seven years with Peter Meltzer, watching him be humiliated because of his physical deformities and because of his Jewishness. His grandfather had been the chief justice of Quebec. His mother was the most wonderful, cultivated Jewish woman. When we went to Peter's house, she would serve us watercress and smoked salmon sandwiches when we were twelve. Mrs. Meltzer would take me around and show me their Picassos. We're talking class. I'd grown up in embassies in various countries, so I know what I'm talking about.

I remember watching how he was martyred by UCC. I used to watch him crying. People called him a kike and a Jew and then derided him because of his wooden leg. He was born without a lower limb. He struggled to get ahead and play sports. He had no choice but to buy into the whole place. Now he's a loyal and grateful old boy.

In Grade 11, I roomed with David Molson, who was a really gentle, sweet-natured guy. His parents, Hartland and Lucille Molson, had been very good friends of my parents. When his parents split up, David and his brother Peter were put into boarding. It was always clear that David was very, very fond of his mother. What people said in the school was that Mrs. Molson had been playing around on her husband. At some point in the family drama, Mr. Molson ended up killing himself.

During this period, David started to unravel in front of us. What a martyrdom! We roomed with a guy who was a spaz, a complete retard, and all the things that Upper Canada prided itself on calling people. David's favourite thing to do to our roommate was to force him behind a door and hurl himself against the door, squashing him. The poor guy would stand there screaming in pain. There was no way to get out. David just hurled himself against the door and it would go on and on. People would just say, "Shut up. What are you, a girl?"

I still remember the horrible feeling of trying to drag David Molson off him. That year, I was in a three-bedroom. I was at one end, our roommate was in the middle, and David was by the door. David would get up in the night and persecute the boy. He'd wake him up, pour water on him, or lie in the dark and throw lighted matches at him. David was just unbelievably angry. He'd refer to his mother and father with a string of obscenities. When he got letters from his parents, he would tear them up and scream and shout.

The next year, he signed out of the boardinghouse one weekend and shot himself at another UCC boy's house. Everybody said, "Oh, what a tragedy!" I remember a terrible feeling of sadness about the whole thing. It was awful. When I look back on it, part of me asks, Why didn't I do something? I should have done something, but part of me says I was only a sixteen-year-old boy at that time. Where the fuck were the teachers? Where were the counsellors? Where were the advisers? Where was the housemaster? What the hell was going on?

I remember only one moment that whole year when there was any intimacy or solidarity among the three of us. I was lying in my bed in the dark at some ridiculously early hour on a Friday night. There was a very strong smell of gasoline and then suddenly I heard an explosion right outside our window. I looked out and some boys had draped the centennial tree with a gasoline-soaked blanket and lit it, right outside our window in Wedd's House. A tree had been planted that morning in front of the whole school to commemorate Canada's hundredth birthday. Three boarders were dancing around a huge pillar of flame, singing wildly.

My roommates and I just sat on my bed, looking out the window. I remember thinking, That's the most wonderful thing I've ever seen in my whole life. I was impressed by the beauty of a huge fire, but also by such a magnificent act of defiance. I haven't seen the boys since I left the school, but they are still my heroes.

CRAIG SILVER

1963–70

Used-car dealer

J UST BEFORE the final provincial exams in the spring of 1967, there was a big deal about Canada's centennial celebrations. Everybody was doing centennial projects and Upper Canada decided in their great wisdom that they would plant a commemorative maple tree. In the prayer hall, Patrick Johnson announced that everybody had to go out behind the tennis courts for a tree-planting ceremony.

The whole upper school, which was about five hundred guys, stood around as some grand Pooh-Bah planted the tree. It was about twelve feet tall with a two- or three-inch diameter. It was a puny little thing. I don't really remember the speeches because there were so many little stories going on among the boys. I remember hearing one guy say, "This is so stupid, making a big deal about a scrawny tree. Let's dig it up and plant it in front of Pat Johnson's house." Another guy said, "Let's dig it up tonight and plant it in the middle of the football field."

My friend John Best and I said, "These guys are coming up with some good ideas. We've got to do something and we've got to do it first." I don't think we decided right then and there to burn it down. It wasn't like we spontaneously came up with this idea. The seed was planted by the older guys.

Within the next hour, we had come up with the inkling of a plan. The planting was on a Friday, so we did it right away that night. I remember we met up at John's house. It became a big military operation for John. He got his father's dark-blue navy greatcoat and I had a pea jacket on. We both wore caps. We didn't want to get caught, so we took soot out of the fireplace and blackened our faces and hands, camouflaging ourselves like commandos.

We said, "How are we going to burn this thing? Let's get a gallon of gasoline!" What did we know? I mean, a gallon of gas! It's not like we were experienced pyromaniacs. We borrowed his folks' car and drove over to Guy Purser's gas station in Forest Hill Village. John was fourteen and I was sixteen. We bought a gallon tin of gas. We thought we better take a blanket. His folks didn't know anything because they were away on a trip.

In our naivety, we had no idea what a gallon of gas was capable of doing. But we were pumped. We hadn't told anybody, except your brother Mike [FitzGerald], a friend of John's. So it was just our gig. We were tickled pink, giggling about it like a bunch of schoolgirls. We got to the school around 9:00 P.M. when it was dark. We came in the gates across from Frybrook Road on the west side of the school. The tree was planted between the tennis courts and Wedd's House, a boarders' residence.

I had the gallon of gas and John had the blanket and a Zippo lighter. Mike was there too, but basically just out of curiosity. He waited out on Frybrook Road and didn't come in with us. We skulked along the edge of the tuck shop and tennis courts and got to the tree. There were lights coming on and going off in Wedd's House. It was shower time for the boarders. We couldn't see exactly who they were because they had their curtains drawn, but we could see the light.

The school had put up a wrought-iron grill to protect the tree. The tree had wire and rubber clasps attaching it nice and straight to the metal. The whole thing was stupid. Here was this la-di-da presentation making a big fuss over a sapling. There was no centennial memorial or plaque, just a lot of hooey over a tree.

Through the bars, we wrapped the blanket around the tree. Then we poured gasoline all over the blanket. John accidentally clanged the gas can into the metal bars that surrounded the tree, and it made a loud noise. One of the curtains in Wedd's opened and a face peered out. He had red hair. I later learned his name was Graeme. We froze and just hunkered down, trying to imitate a lump of shit or a rock on the ground. We waited about five or ten minutes and finally the guy's face disappeared from the window. We splashed the rest of the gas on the blanket.

I'll never, ever forget as long as I live when John pulled out the Zippo, lit the flame, and touched it to the blanket. The noise just about blew our eardrums out. The explosion sucked the breath out of both of us like napalm. Holy shit! The tree was about twelve feet high and it went up like a Roman candle. I swear to God, a forty-foot pillar of flame shot up almost as high as the fucking clock tower. The fire was so bright that I remember seeing three or four guys and their girlfriends in the very far northwest corner of the cricket fields, having their own little party. They were one hundred and fifty yards away and we could see them all making out as clear as day.

I said, "Holy shit! Let's get out of here!" We ran out south of the tennis courts, behind the tuck shop, and onto Frybrook. The flames were so bright, we cast about thirty-foot shadows as we were running away. We tore down Frybrook at about eighty miles an hour and hung a left at the first intersection. We were burning down Dunvegan Road like Ben Johnson.

Before we were even off the school grounds, we could hear the commotion behind us. We heard a car door slam and a car start up. We just went screaming down Dunvegan. I don't think my feet had touched the ground. We were trying to wipe the soot off our faces as we ran because we were sure a teacher was coming after us. I think I. K. Shearer happened to be out patrolling in the neighbourhood. But we were gonzo! We never said a word to each other as we ran. We were just making tracks.

We weren't running anywhere in particular, we were just running. At one point, we passed Mike, who had a head start on us. When we got down south of Lonsdale, we figured we better duck in somewhere. At that point, John said, "Let's got to Fike's place! Mike lived at 75 Dunvegan Road. His nickname was "Fike." So we went down the side of his house and up into the top floor of his coach house in the backyard. You [James FitzGerald] and a couple of your buddies, Dave White and Mike Albery, happened to be in there playing snooker. For the first half hour, we were terrified. We were sure that Mr. Shearer or whoever was following us was going to find us. I remember getting to the coach house, but that's the end of my memory for the rest of the weekend.

I remember being nervous going to school on Monday morning, but not as nervous as I was five minutes after we got into the prayer hall. Pat Johnson was wild. I don't remember all the words that he said, but he was livid up at the pulpit on the stage. He knew that two ucc boys had burned down the centennial tree. I think he knew it was me and John right from the get go, but he wanted the culprits to come forward and turn themselves in. At that point, I sat in a different house than John in Laidlaw Hall, but he was looking back at me and I was looking at him. I was sitting right beside Ian Roberts. He said, "What a great stunt! I wonder who did it?" Sweat was literally streaming down my face.

Our first class was double gym. On our way to gym, John and I basically decided that we were not going to say a damn thing. When we got back from our cross-country run, somebody came to John with a note to report to the principal's office right away. I remember he went ghostly white and off he went. I remember sweating through the rest of the gym class, wondering, What am I going to do?

After my gym class, I figured, John is my friend. I can't let him go on his own. Nobody had brought me a note. I thought, Screw it. I'll go take the heat. I'll turn myself in. I went to the principal's office and told the secretary that I wanted to see Mr. Johnson. I had been in his office at the very beginning of that year when he read the riot act to me after I failed Grade 9. I had never really paid attention to his office before. The one previous time, I sat across the desk from him and listened to a lecture about being a good boy.

I remember waiting in Johnson's office sweating bullets for about twenty minutes. Then he opened the door and said, "Come in." Where was John? I didn't realize at that point that the principal's office had one entrance in and another way out. It turned out they had locked John upstairs in the nurse's office. His folks were in the middle of the Atlantic Ocean on the liner *France*. They had a lot of money and they were constantly away on trips, so we did a lot of partying at John's house.

When I went in, Johnson was apoplectic. He could barely speak. There was a wild, demented look in his eyes. He was literally shaking with rage. I was shaking with fear. He was doing everything he could to keep from going ballistic and physically launching himself at me. I know he wanted to come right across the desk and beat me senseless. Johnson was wild about the fact that he couldn't reach John's parents. He could only reach John's sister, who was only in the twelfth or thirteenth grade at BSS. He went after her like he wanted to chop her into little bits. He had to scream at somebody.

The Bests had an old housekeeper, but she was a half-assed schizophrenic who could barely speak. I think she had Alzheimer's, so she didn't really remember anything. She knew how to clean the house, but she didn't know how to do anything else. There was really no one supervising the two Best kids most of the time. John's sister was in fact the one in charge. John was fourteen and his sister was probably seventeen. Their parents were alcoholics, but it wasn't a big deal. The Bests lived in Forest Hill, which is a safe neighbourhood. In those days, kids were old enough to look after themselves. You didn't have to worry about your house being broken into because crime wasn't such a big deal.

When Johnson called my dad, who is a cosmetic surgeon, he was in the middle of an operation. Johnson wanted him to get his ass up to the school. My dad called my mother and said, "You better get up there. Who knows what the little bugger has done now."

I was so scared that I don't remember a damn thing Johnson said to me, except that he did drum into me the fact that I had really fucked up. I had been nothing but trouble since I had been in the school. I had been given a second chance because I failed Grade 9. I had been doing just fine and dandy my second time around in Grade 9 and then I had to go and blow it.

Then I went off to Nurse Barrow's office. I was put in a little infirmary room which had little tiny glass holes where you could look out. I was in there looking out, wondering where John was. I was up there in holding until my mother could get up to the school. When my mother arrived, Pat Johnson ripped her to shreds and reduced her to tears. The man was temporarily psychotic.

Unbeknownst to us, guys in the upper grades had apparently been planning a panty raid on BSS the same time we burned down the tree. I think that Pat Johnson had been out patrolling the area between Upper Canada and BSS in the hopes that he was going to catch someone in the act. Meanwhile, Kingsley Graham, Roland Cardy, and Peter Szatmari had been letting off cherry bombs around Lord Seaton's statue in the quadrangle. Guys were up to amazing shit. We were all on the same wavelength, that's for sure. I later learned that some boarders came out and started dancing round the tree after we torched it.

Johnson was getting a little schizo with all this adolescent rebellion. He must have felt like he was facing some kind of coordinated mass insurrection, but we were all acting independently. In some ways, he had invited it, but we were now putting him over the edge. When he was screaming, spit was flying out of his mouth. He was close to literally foaming at the mouth.

My mother got a complete dressing down. He went at her brutally. When she collected herself later, which was very much later, she was fairly pissed off. At the time, Johnson was just shrieking at her. He was off the deep end at this point. Maybe they should have put him in a rubber room in the infirmary himself. I think the board of governors sent him off on a little trip down to Bermuda shortly thereafter.

I remember sitting up in the infirmary for hours. John was probably just next door or down the hall a bit. That afternoon, Alan Stephen, the kindly old headmaster from the prep, came up and talked to me about it. He was the complete opposite side of the coin from Johnson. It was almost like I was set up for the classic good cop/bad cop scenario.

This nice old guy comes in and sits and talks with me with civility, humour, and love. I was crying my eyes out. I was scared to death, but not about Johnson any more, because I figured my ass is cooked. I'm expelled for sure. But now I'm seriously worried about going home. I didn't know how upset my mother was going to be, but I knew my father would be upset. We did not know that this harmless prank was going to turn out to be an atom bomb.

Burning down the tree wasn't the brightest of ideas that we've ever had. I'm certainly embarrassed about our total brainpower on this stunt, but it was just meant to be a prank. We weren't trying to burn the school down. But it was a real personal thing for Pat Johnson. It never crossed our minds that we were doing anything criminal. I guess it was an act of vandalism, but we never meant anybody any harm by it. All we thought was, We're toasting a ten- or fifteen-dollar tree. Big deal! They can replace it and have another stupid ceremony. But it turned out to be the crime of the century.

Johnson would have loved to have flayed us with a cat-o'-nine-tails and thrown us out of the school right then and there. Luckily, old Mr. Stephen got the message through to him that he could not just cane us and throw us out. We were only a week or two away from final exams and John's parents weren't even in town to take responsibility.

So they came up with a plan that when we went home, John and I were not allowed to communicate with each other. We were suspended until October 1, which was like getting an extra month of summer holiday. We would be allowed to come back and write our final exams, but not with our classmates. Our parents had to pay one of the teachers to supervise us taking our exams up in solitary confinement up in the nurse's office. It was like we were lepers in quarantine. Tim Gibson, an old prep master who was notorious for fondling kids, was one of our supervisors. He fell asleep.

It was beautiful. They took the beds out of a little two-man room in the infirmary. It was June, so we had a nice, cool breeze blowing through the windows. We were just a few feet apart. Old man Gibson was sitting in the back reading the newspaper and nodding off. If we had wanted to, we had the perfect opportunity to pass notes back and forth. We didn't cheat, although we certainly could have. They even forgot to give us half our French exam.

I didn't dare screw up any more now or my old man would have flayed me. I know if Johnson had picked up a cane, he would have killed us. I knew what a caning felt like. The previous year, I had skipped a lot of gatings and detentions, so I was caned by Willy Orr, the vice-principal. He was an ancient little Latin master with a hearing aid and whistling dentures who had been at UCC for about a century. He said, "Bend over the chair." He caught me with six good ones, two on the leg, two on the butt, and two on the back. Orr was so old that his aim wasn't very good. Even though I took the precaution of wearing long johns and corduroy pants, it really hurt. He went red from the exertion of caning me. My ass looked like a zebra. I didn't dare tell my parents.

The very next morning, it was announced in prayers that the old bugger had had a heart attack and died that very night. The news made me feel a lot better for the pain on my ass. So I was the last guy that Willy Orr caned, and he probably caned thousands of guys over the years. Everybody in my class who knew I had been caned by Orr were giggling away. I gained a little notoriety.

I also got a little notoriety for the tree burning, which actually made the bloody national news on TV. Lloyd Robertson always ended the news with some little funny item, so there was a clip about a couple of Upper Canada College boys who had burned down the school's centennial project. We got our fifteen seconds of fame.

I settled down after the tree burning. I got increasingly more fed up with UCC, so after Grade 12 I went to Jarvis Collegiate for Grade 13, and then took landscape architecture at Ryerson. A few years later, in 1974, I was driving a cab for the summer. I used to meet some guys at UCC on Tuesday nights, play a little baseball, and then swill some beer at the Ports of Call. As we were playing baseball on the UCC field, somebody came over and told me that, earlier that day, John Best had accidentally driven his Volkswagen off a mountain in B.C. He died a few days later. He was only twenty-one. Ironically, I was standing near the spot where we had burned down the tree.

KINGSLEY GRAHAM

1963–70

Criminal lawyer

P AT JOHNSON announced in prayers one morning near the Victoria Day weekend in 1967 that under no circumstances were we to light off firecrackers on the school grounds. Well, telling me you couldn't do something was like waving a red flag. So Peter Szatmari, Roland Cardy, and I crept onto the school grounds that night loaded down with firecrackers.

It turned out that by complete coincidence, two other guys had decided to burn down the school's centennial tree, which had been planted earlier that day in front of the whole student body. Unknowingly, we were lighting off firecrackers in the quadrangle some time after the tree had been burned down. We got nailed by a master, Ike Shearer, who was out on highway patrol for the tree burners.

Pat Johnson went nuts. He got up, put on a suit, came into his office at eleven o'clock at night, and screamed at Szatmari and me for about an hour. He told us that he was going to throw us out of the school. He was convinced we'd burned down the fucking tree as well as setting off the fire-crackers. He was trying to get us to confess. He said we should get it off our chests. We didn't know what the hell he was talking about. I'm now a criminal lawyer and Peter Szatmari is a child psychiatrist, which may not be a coincidence.

Johnson had me into his office again on Monday morning and he must have whaled me about eight times with that cane of his. He really, really let me have it because he was still convinced I'd burned down his tree. Boy, that was the worst caning he ever gave me, and I had had a few. By then, everybody knew it was John Best and Craig Silver who burned down the tree, including me. But no one ratted on them, initially at least.

At UCC, my history of defying authority just fed on itself. Once, the vice-principal, Jim Coulton, caned me for whatever it was I was supposed to have said to the gym teacher. I had no idea what it was that I'd done. Then people started handing me gatings left and right because they'd pegged me as a discipline problem. So, if I was going to be pegged as a discipline problem, I was damned well going to be one.

They started caning me so much that I started to dread Monday mornings. The first couple of times, I didn't realize how bad the canings were going to be. They left welts about eight inches across my buttocks that were open and bleeding and scabbing. I've still got scars on my ass to this day. I must have been caned at least fifteen times, maybe more. I lost track. Coulton was a methodical caner, but Johnson was a real pro, a real master of caning. He'd take a real long wind-up.

I started driving a motorcycle. I got my first one when I was fifteen, a little Suzuki. Then I got a BSA 650, which was a huge motorcycle in those days in Grade 12. That really set off alarm bells in all their minds. I drove it to the school. It was okay to park a wimpy Yamaha 80cc moped in the school parking lot. But when I started showing up on a big black and chrome BSA 650, it drove them wild.

The BSA was a real "hood" motorcycle. But what could they really do? On the last day of Grade 13, I tore up the entire back soccer field on my bike. I started gunning it, doing wheelies up and down, just tearing up the northwest field. Some master came out to say, "Please stop tearing up the field on your motorcycle." I was trying to blast the windows of the school right in. I took the baffles out of the mufflers so the thing would sound like a B-52.

I would rebel against authority in all its forms. On weekends, I wore black jeans, black boots, a broad black belt, and a black shirt. I was part of an "in crowd." Pretty much every Saturday, there was a party at Jennifer Jeffrey's place. So doing that and playing football, I never felt ostracized at

UCC. By the same token, when I would go to Saturday night parties in Forest Hill, everybody else was would be wearing Bass Weejuns and slacks. My image of myself was black boots, black jeans, and Camel cigarettes. Upper Canada fed and heightened my rebellious self-image.

I used to have big parties at my house on Saturday nights where I'd have a mixture of Upper Canada guys and North Toronto and Northern Secondary School guys. I still knew guys from the public school system, some of whom became real juvenile delinquents. Two of them died violent deaths. I used to get caned a lot for having those parties too. Beer would be flowing and women would be attacked. Pat Johnson would somehow find out and whale me for throwing the party.

I remember another guy had a huge party and Johnson found out about it. He was ready to expel everybody who was at the party. He methodically went about an inquisition, pulling out every single guy who had been at the party and asking him what had gone on. I gave my typical reponse: "I didn't see anything. I didn't do anything. I didn't see anybody else do anything." This infuriated him.

When you're sixteen or seventeen, you drink beer. But if you're sixteen or seventeen and they found out you were drinking beer, they expelled you. They threw out some guy a year ahead of me who was a punter for the first football team for drinking beer. That was pretty unjust, considering I was smoking pot and hashish and drinking beer. I was going up to Collingwood and getting looped. Somehow the school would find out about these things. It was as if we were all under surveillance by MI5.

Johnson had my father in at one point. My father, who was a judge and an old boy from the class of 1940, basically mollified him. As we left Johnson's office, my father said, "Stay out of trouble. You can't just keep doing this." On the other hand, he sympathized. He figured I was getting dumped on, going in for gatings every Saturday. He was saying to the school, "What do you expect? How many Saturdays do you want this kid in school?" A battalion major in the morning and a double gating in the afternoon would kill my whole Saturday. It was just such a waste of time.

For the gatings, you'd sit in the classroom and some master would sit there supervising you. He'd write on the blackboard incredibly complicated long division, like 156,328 divided by 4,785. If you had a double gating, then you had to do it for two hours. You had to finish them or you couldn't go home.

I kept banging up against these people because the more they did stuff to me, the madder I got. I adopted the attitude: Take your best shot! If you think you can break me, forget it. The more you dish out to me, the more I'm going to give it back to you. There was never an issue that I might leave the school. The more they did it to me, the more determined I was that I was going to finish, because I made a lot of friends by the time I was in Grade 11. Half the masters weren't on my case at all. Some of the younger, more progressive masters had absolutely no problem with my attitude. The other half was constantly trying to break my spirit.

For example, I never cut my hair. My hair today is longer than it ever was at Upper Canada., although it's relatively trim and neat for a criminal lawyer. But I didn't really want to wear what was almost the equivalent of a brush cut back when I was a teenager, so I was always growing it too long. Wilf Gallimore would go out of his way to make sure that he spotted me every morning and told me to get a haircut, which I wouldn't do. So I got caned.

Then I was told that I could either cut my hair or leave the school. Johnson had absolutely no hesitation in giving me ultimatums all the time. But I didn't want to leave all my friends. I thought I was getting a pretty good education, all things being equal. I really did have it pretty cushy. By time I was in Grade 12, I didn't have to go to battalion because I was a sergeant in the colour party. I didn't have to turn up for half the stuff because I was away playing football. Or so people thought.

In Grade 13, every Friday afternoon, I'd go down with a group of guys, who will remain nameless, to the men's room at the Ports of Call and we'd drink lunch. I would come back, pass out, and sleep through class. No one noticed that I was juiced every Friday afternoon in Grade 13 for my double math periods.

After Johnson had the heart-to-heart talk with my dad in Grade 11, I backed off a little bit. I'd seen them turf out my friend Malcolm Albery and I didn't want to get turfed. So I just went more underground, as opposed to Rob Barlow, who became more and more overt in his rebellion. Midway through Grade 11, he was expelled for publishing a highly irreverent weekly paper. They basically threw Barlow out for thinking too much. He's now a lawyer in a big firm downtown.

Another guy in my class became a white-collar criminal. I first became acquainted with Steve Axton in Herb Lacey's Latin class. We had to learn the poetry of Catullus and I couldn't understand a damned word. Even if I could, I didn't want to. This fucking faggot Catullus was writing stuff like, "Canary, my girlfriend bird, how I wish it was me sittin' there strokin' ya." I thought, This guy has got to be a class-A wimp. Who the hell wants to read anything by this jerk?

So, Axton, realizing the mood of the class, obtained translations of Catullus, printed up copies, and sold them to us. Like Conrad Black, Axton was a budding entrepreneur in high school. When called upon to translate by Herb Lacey, we'd each stand up, put a copy of the English translation right beside the Latin book so that Lacey couldn't see, and in a very halting voice translate Catullus into English. Norm Campbell, now the actor Nicholas Campbell, was the only exception. He would always do it with an Italian accent.

When my turn came, I would haltingly say, "A ... canary ... my girl-friend ... bird ..." The art was in not letting Lacey know that you were reading directly from the hidden translation. Occasionally we would pur-posely bugger it up so Lacey could give you the right word and feel like he was teaching you.

Axton turned out to be the greatest swindler to come out of my class. He got his law degree from the University of Ottawa, came back to Toronto, practised law, and then started a firm. I had a family law case with one of his partners, who was bankrupted by Axton's actions. Axton became more and more involved in large real estate transactions, to the extent that he had enough money running in and out of his firm that he was able to have sufficient leverage to actually buy a trust company. He bought a trust company with funds that really shouldn't have been in his possession in the first place.

He went further out on a limb in terms of the operation of the trust company. Its margin was far too narrow to meet any standards, and through the auspices of this trust company, he increased his real estate transactions on his own real estate holdings, through flips and that kind of thing. The end result was that somehow, somewhere, a number of people were out five million dollars, which found its way into Axton's pocket. The money was spent in various interesting ways. His father became the recipi-ent of a Rolls-Royce and a large mansion in Forest Hill.

Axton was caught, disbarred, charged with a series of frauds, and sen-tenced to five years. I think he served one and a half or two years. I assume he went to Beaver Creek, where another UCC white-collar criminal, Harold Ballard, served his sentence, because it's a nice comfortable jail. White-col-lar criminals get a real kiss from the criminal justice system. Axton's out now and nobody knows where the five million dollars went.

There was a great deal of bullying at UCC. I also thought the boarding-houses were a breeding ground for faggotry. Happily, I was exempt from the bullying because half the school liked me and the other half was basi-cally scared of me. There were always several classes of guys. The bottom of the food chain were the guys who everybody picked on. Then there were guys who blended in, who had their own friends. Then there were the gleams in the eyes of the masters, athletic guys like Rodger Wright, who is now headmaster of TCS. Then there were guys like me who had it pretty good. I was at the top of the food chain. I had a lot of friends. I never had a problem. I was always big enough physically and I had a bit of a reputation, what with the motorcycle and the gatings and the canings, that nobody ever wanted to fuck with me.

The worst case I can remember in my year was a poor fellow named Bob Jones. He was called "White Rat" because he had very fair hair and skin. He was almost an albino. Ironically, he was too white, even for UCC. This poor guy tried everything to blend in, but for some reason, the bullies in the school had it in for him. One day in Grade 12, I saw a gang of boys in the front yard chasing Bob Jones, who was the brunt of everything in my year. I don't know what it was about him that upset people. I never found him particularly disturbing. I guess he was easy prey.

A crowd grew and grew until there were about sixty or sixty-five boys chasing him across the yard at lunch hour. They finally caught him and held him down. He wore a Beatles haircut and they literally shaved his head. No one intervened. I didn't see a master anywhere and it was really noisy. I don't recall anybody being disciplined for it afterwards.

I think, in my own teenage way, that I was appalled by it. But on the other hand, I had also developed a very strong sense of TCOB – Take Care of Business. *My* business. So when I saw sixty-five guys chasing this poor fuck, I thought it was not my problem. It was his problem. I watched with some detachment. I didn't participate, but I certainly didn't step in. I might well have been able to prevent it, but I just didn't care enough about the guy to be bothered.

The ringleaders were in fact friends of mine. Gary Slaight, who now runs a radio station, was the guy that led it and actually did it. He and I were friends. I could have said, "Gary, fuck off. Leave him alone." But Slaight was a class-A bully. Perry Beadon was also a bully. He went out of his way to try to pick a fight with me. I can remember in the prep, there was a lot of bullying by Beadon, who was a year ahead of me. In the prep schoolyard, rings of boys would form, screaming, "Fight, fight, fight!" while some poor kid got the shit kicked out of him by one of the class bullies.

I remember one thing that I never really could understand. I was friends with Dave Molson. He had a Honda 90 when I had the Suzuki 80. We used to hang around because we were the only guys with these little rinky-dink motorcycles. He was part of the Molson beer family. When we were about seventeen, he sat down in front of the furnace in a friend's basement, took out a double-barrelled 12-gauge shotgun and blew his head off. God, if I owned Molson Breweries, the last thing I'd want to do is kill myself. Owning Molson Breweries would be my dream. I'd say, "Just fill up the swimming pool, will you? Bring the truck around back. I just have to get my straw."

Despite all the hassles, I'm glad I went to UCC. I'm going to a party on Friday night and I would guess that half the males at the party are UCC old boys. Most people don't have such a high quantity and quality of connections over twenty years after high school.

They beat the shit out of me at UCC but I got straight A's in university. That's why I got into law school. I'm not overly bright. In fact, I'm lazy. But UCC instilled in me the idea of getting my work done. You have to be tough in this world, and UCC made me tough. If the school had been coed, I would have spent my entire time drooling at the blonde two rows over. I'm convinced girls would have been such a distraction that I wouldn't have learned a thing.

I feel strongly enough about UCC that I gave them five thousand dollars. At my twentieth year reunion in 1990, a guy hit on me, pointing out that I could pay it in installments over five years. I'm not married and I don't have any kids, but if I had a son, I'd certainly send him to UCC. I like the old-boy network. It works. Sure, UCC is a bastion of privilege and oligarchy, but I'd rather have that edge than not. For my first job as a lawyer, I was hired by a UCC old boy, John Jennings, who is now a judge. I was the only articling applicant who had gone to UCC, which I know was a swing factor in hiring me over other applicants. I don't feel I have to make any apology for it. At your twentieth class reunion, it's nice to look over and see a judge sitting in front of you at his thirtieth reunion.

I understand an increasing number of visible minorities are getting into UCC. There's probably a lot of Hong Kong money. Who else can afford $12,500 tuition these days? There is still a WASP power base on Bay Street, but UCC is slowly becoming diluted. If I ever have a kid, they bloody well better let him in instead of Who Flung Dough. Who does the school get their money from? Guys like me! The old-boy system let me in because my dad went to the school. It should still count for something.

If I start to see too many towel-heads or Chinese wandering around the halls of UCC, I am turning the tap off. I'm dead serious. I believe in looking after my own first. How many Chinese or black friends do I have? Zero. I would stop giving UCC money if I walked in there one day and it looked like a normal high school.

I'm too old to care if I make politically incorrect statements. Rich, white males run the world. So what? Somebody's got to do it. Who is better equipped to do it than us? Can you suggest an alternative that makes sense? You can't divide up the pie too much because you'll have too many chiefs and not enough Indians. Some people are just born to be Indians.

ROBERT PATTILLO

1958–68

Vice-president of communications, CBC

I HAVE OFTEN WONDERED how Dick Howard, who later became headmaster of the prep, became such a legend at UCC. When he was a prep master, everybody thought he was such a great guy. I thought he was a nasty, mean-spirited man. After having him as a form master for a year, I remember not wanting to go back to the prep the next year. I hated Dick Howard. I hated being constantly humiliated by him.

I can remember being called a dirty little boy by Mrs. Milsom in Junior Form at age six, and never forgetting it. As a result, I was forever pathological about being clean. To this day, I still change my clothes completely twice a day. I do it even when I travel, and I travel constantly. I think it's a result of that miserable woman accusing me of being a dirty little boy.

In Form 1, Jack Schaffter was a good man. Ted Stephenson was an incredibly interesting man because he was struggling with so many personal problems which were so apparent to me as a boy. He seemed to overcome them by dealing with his own issues, which always impressed me. Stephenson always seemed fairly unhinged himself.

I can remember George Karrys and I were arch enemies, as boys can become for such silly reasons. I can remember Alan Stephen, the headmaster, being in a state of great frustration, obviously having dealt with George Karrys' parents who had come in to talk to him. I was a typical little prick. I'd always get a couple of boys to participate with me and make life miserable for George Karrys. He later drowned underneath the sail of a boat in Georgian Bay.

Alan Stephen summoned us to his office one day. I thought, This is it. I'm really going to get in shit this time. But he gave us an interesting lecture on how human beings had to get along in life. If I thought it through, I could almost repeat everything he said. It was a watershed moment for me about how human beings just had to get along.

The prep headmaster's office looked out over the playing fields, north, towards the upper school. Stephen gave us one fifty-cent piece. He asked who wanted to hold it. I said to George, "Take it." Alan Stephen said, "I'll watch you both walk up the field to the tuck shop. You may each spend twenty-five cents. Then I'll watch you both come back. I would like you to share whatever it is you bought with the other. I want you to talk with each other the entire time you are walking." That effectively ended the row between George Karrys and I. There just didn't seem to be anything useful to row about any more.

Alan Stephen and Ted Stephenson were the only masters who didn't talk to me like I was a child. My father didn't talk to me like I was a child either. I've always hated it. My father was the senior partner at Blake Cassels for years, then went on to become chairman of the Securities and Exchange Commission in Ontario. He died early of cancer in 1978. We weren't a close family. If I had to reflect on why that is, UCC had a role in it. We travelled in packs and created extended families. For some of us, our friends became our family more than our families.

I've never really been into all of this male-bonding crap. I've never understood why the school spent so much time on it. I had to box in the first round one year with my friend Tim Aikenhead. The two of us didn't want to fight, so we just pranced around. Dick Howard, who was one of the judges, stopped the fight and called us over. He said, "If one of you boys doesn't hit the other and turn this charade into a boxing match, I'll climb in the ring and hit you myself."

I can still remember turning my back, walking back into the middle of the ring, thinking, What an asshole that guy is! I touched gloves with Aikenhead and then belted him. Aikenhead burst into tears and that was the end of the fight. Unfortunately, I immediately moved into the second round, which I also won. Now I'm in the semifinals, the only time in my life I had to get into an actual boxing ring. We moved from fighting inside ropes loosely hanging around four metal chairs into a real, professionally constructed wooden ring. For the semifinals and finals, the school would invite the parents and the entire student body to watch small kids bash each other around.

I ended up having to box Steve Axton, who was subsequently incarcerated for fraud. I saw him years later having dinner with two very lovely women. I was sitting quietly at Prego with a couple of film people during the Toronto film festival. I don't think he recognized me. He was wearing a moustache, but I recognized him from all the newspaper clippings. In the fight, he knocked the shit out of me. My friend Mike Grant actually physically climbed up to my corner between rounds. I can still remember Mike saying, "For God's sake, don't start to cry!"

I said, "I've got to get the hell out of this." Mike said, "Just fall on the mat." So the next time Axton hit me, I fell on the mat. I got up. They made you wipe your gloves when you fell. I thought, I'm not going to go down just like that. I knew that I had lost. Axton was getting quite cocky, so I just slammed him. At least I gave him a bloody nose. That was my last fight at UCC because then I got braces on my teeth. I was free, free at last. Lord almighty.

I had no preparation for the upper school, which was a whole new environment. In the prep, I remember the whole class had to trek up to the swimming pool at the upper school in the middle of winter and swim in the nude in cold, cold water. Muzz Greatrex used to call me an "old woman." Around puberty, things changed. Our balls dropped and we became "men."

Then we ended up in a very competitive environment in the upper school. People were starting to evaluate each other based on their possessions, measuring people's successes and failures by what they saw externally. They didn't understand much. Everything changed at that point. The boys who were given prefecture and stewardship were models of something out of World War II. They certainly weren't models of anything that I remember happening in the sixties.

Around 1966 or 1967, I was totally convinced that the upper school faculty were collectively uninspired and not very bright, totally unaware of how we were all struggling with radical social changes. If there was value in that change, they certainly were busy trying to denude it and struggling to hang on to what they remembered to be their right of authority. In the 1960s, the school was trying to hang on to values that no longer had any application. As young men, we were being exposed to so many more influences than the teachers in the UCC environment. A lot of us had lost our virginity by the time we were at the end of Grade 9 in the upper school. Of course, there was a lot of bravado talk too.

In the upper school, I was beaten by Pat Johnson when a bunch of guys cut Bob Jones's hair, although I really wasn't directly involved. Gary Slaight, who was older than all of us, instigated it. A bunch of us dragged Bob Jones into a bush and snipped off his bangs. He kept driving everybody nuts. Today, I couldn't imagine a worse thing to do to anybody. But I had become a pretty bad bastard at that point. I had repeated Grade 9. Three boys were directly involved, although there were countless boys who saw what was going on and could have intervened at any time.

Pat Johnson hauled us all in and caned us one by one in the office. The only inspired piece of verbiage that ever came out of his mouth in my years in the upper school was the incident about Bob Jones. In the prayer hall, he talked about how men just didn't do this kind of thing. But Pat Johnson was someone I did not respect. I couldn't have cared less one way or the other about the caning. I wasn't embarrassed by it and certainly not humiliated. A person you don't respect can't humiliate you.

I did respect Terry Bredin, an eccentric Brit whom I liked jousting with in Latin class. His nickname was "Bump" because he had a big permanent bump on his forehead. After he had just bawled the hell out of me one day, he asked me why I was smiling. I said, "Well, sir, it doesn't really matter." He said, "No, I want you to share it with all of us." I said, "Well, sir, it doesn't really matter." He said, "No, I insist you share it with all of us." So I said, "Well, there was a rumour that when you get very, very angry, the bump on your forehead would swell. But it hasn't." The class burst out into laughter. He said, "And it shall not." It was a very funny moment. He was one of the few good men at UCC.

I raise dogs now. I sometimes walk my dogs at Upper Canada College in that part of the school. As part of the rite of passage of arriving at school in September, we'd roll in the leaves and smell them. We were enthusiastic about it because we knew that the autumn was coming, that the leaves would be falling, and the compost heap would start to grow larger. Those were wonderful times. I remember the janitor, old Tom, who ran the showers down in the prep basement every day after games. There was nothing confusing about your life. It was all very straightforward. The prep was the only rarefied time in my life, the only time when things were really rather sweet.

Personally, I didn't feel the least bit unbalanced for the lack of girls at UCC. But by Grade 10, I had started to seriously alienate myself from the place. I was more uncomfortable with society in general than I was with women in particular. Certainly, we didn't have a lot of respect for women. As Upper Canada College boys, we thought we were better than just about everybody else, including the women that we spent our time with. I guess it's true that I had some trouble in my early life getting over that. I lived with a very strong woman for a period of time who basically shook the shit right out of me. Perhaps she helped change me.

My entire senior management at CBC are women. I don't have any men working for me, other than my own executive assistant. I prefer to have women working for me because they are more focused, they are better managers, they are broader thinkers. They tend to be more compassionate and have better instincts.

I've chosen the kind of life that I now live largely in reaction to the people that I met at UCC and the values that the school was encouraging them to pursue and protect. They weren't values that I shared. Upper Canada College never asked any of us to love each other, to believe in each other, to overcome the shortcomings of one person with the strengths of another. They seemed to believe that we were going to become something important because of Upper Canada College. The implicit attitude was, "You bastards had better recognize that a lot of great guys have left UCC and done well. Don't fuck up on their behalf." There was always that kind of tension at work.

The evil that can be found in school faculties is not unknown to me. When I taught briefly at a Catholic high school in Halifax, I'd listen to teachers talk about boys and girls and completely write them off. They'd say, "He's an idiot. You're wasting your time with him." That's exactly what those fuckers at UCC constantly did: "Never mind him. He is a waste of time." You might just as well be cattle on my brother's 47,000-acre ranch in Alberta. You might just as well watch him take out the cattle that are no good and shoot them.

I don't want to paint a completely grim picture of UCC. But some days I do wish I still had the feeling of warmth and freedom of those few years in the prep. But of course, you have to grow up. One's burdens become defined by the experiences you have, which help you to bear them. I suppose my experiences at Norval, the school's country property, were good stuff, but the upper school wasn't an important institution in my life.

We all became privy to what the hell was going on with Walter Bailey and Ken Shearer, and all those other clannish weirdos. Homosexuality has never been an issue in my mind. I'm surprised that I have that attitude. There will always be boys having sexual activity among themselves. There was in the prep. How can anybody be surprised about it? There will continue to be. You just have to embrace those instincts.

I can remember there was talk about individual boys who had obviously been seeing too much of each other. That happens at the CBC too. If I go to lunch with any of my staff, there is constant talk about, "Oh, well, he's probably sleeping with her." The CBC environment today is very similiar to the environment of UCC in the 1960s – emotionally and visually charged. Substance doesn't really matter. People deal in and of the moment. You work very hard on a program, it comes to air, and then it goes away. It's very instantaneous. Everything was visceral and instant at UCC too.

I'm at the CBC to change it. Change, of course, is not a well-received commodity at the CBC. There has been a lot of nasty stuff going on lately. Dealing with the controversy surrounding the film "The Valour and the Horror" was very difficult. I don't think that my experience at UCC helps me with working at the CBC. I wish it did.

One of the things that makes me most disappointed is no one in the upper school ever asked me to reflect upon the prep and what I liked about it. We were never asked to reflect on our pasts or think about our futures. The prep and upper school were worlds apart. You couldn't have put the Atlantic Ocean between us and got them any farther apart. I always thought the lack of continuity and perspective was a bit of a tragedy because there were so many good things that happened in the prep.

I did not encounter one goddamn person at Upper Canada College who encouraged me to search into the world of words and books, being sensitive to the ideas inside human experience. We weren't asked to freely think about anybody's writing. What does the author mean? What do you think he is trying to say? I think those goddamn masters were afraid of all of the hidden innuendo. They didn't want to talk about a book that might contain sexual connotations because they didn't want the students walking around saying, "I think he's gay."

UCC is like the priesthood where certain personalities are attracted to all-male environments. At King's, a housemaster admitted to me, a couple of years later at a lunch, that he was gay. He had moved up to London, Ontario, because he couldn't stand seeing so many naked boys every day. If you have difficulty looking at naked boys, your gayness isn't the problem. I would suggest the same to a heterosexual male who had trouble seeing naked nine-year-old girls. If this is provocative for you, you are in deep shit.

But when these people remove themselves, they remove themselves from all the issues that are most important for students to know. Particularly in the sixties, there was so much we needed to know. We needed to know about sex and drugs, but no one wanted to talk about sex and drugs because they didn't want to be implicated. Johnson couldn't manage a five-car funeral, let alone a school. I can't imagine anything worse than being principal of Upper Canada College. It would be a very tough job. It would be a little bit worse than being president of the CBC.

I thought it was utter bullshit that I should have to repeat Grade 9 because of my poor mathematics, so I immediately started to plot a strategy to get out of UCC. I thought, What are my options? I know I have to get a degree. The old man is going to insist on one and so is society. I knew it had to be in history and English or history and economics. I've always liked economics, but hated math.

So I basically sat down with my dad and said, "I want to leave UCC. I'd like to see if I can go to Nova Scotia where the high schools only go to Grade 12. If they accept me out of Grade 10 into their Grade 11, I could get early acceptance to Dalhousie University and skip two years." My father said, "You'll never do it." But I did. I left UCC at the end of 1968 in Grade 10 and completed Grade 11 at King's College School, where my father had gone to school. I got early acceptance at Dalhousie and graduated in 1973. We have such a stupid education system in this country. All the other poor bastards stayed at UCC until Grade 13.

It was a brilliant strategy which made up for the years that I'd lost. It got me the hell out of the system earlier. It also changed my life because I got my first apartment that year. I went to tellers' training school in June, worked as a teller at the Bank of Nova Scotia in July and August, and then went back to school in September when I turned sixteen.

I was quite an active old boy of King's for a couple of years when they were having difficulty raising funds. A teacher of mine in the prep, Benny Cole, an Englishman, resurfaced in my life several years later as a teacher at King's College School. Cole was quite a little nut case at that point. In 1983, I ran into him on the street in downtown Toronto, unshaven and obviously a derelict. So in the space of two decades, I saw him go through several incarnations. I had him as a teacher in Form 4 at UCC prep, then I saw him as a teacher of other boys at King's College. Then I had to personally fire Cole on behalf of the board of the King's Old Boys' Association. Then a decade later, I find him a street person in Toronto. Our lives are such cyclical things.

My father thought that I would go on to Dalhousie law school, where he had gone. At that point, I refused because I had got a contract with the film board as a writer. I was going to do some voice-overs for CBC and I was going to work at the Halifax shipyards to make some money. From the day I left Upper Canada College until today, I have always paid my own way. I've always had a job, in the evenings or weekends, and every summer. I never took any time off.

In 1975, I travelled with friends through Europe and Asia and worked for Hawker Siddeley. I came down through Bulgaria and the Eastern bloc countries, then went across visiting all the Hawker Siddeley sites on behalf of the international chairman. I went out through Turkey, across India, down to Bangkok, then into Cambodia and Vietnam. I was in Vietnam just at the end of the war, which was pretty hairy.

When I came back over a year later, my father basically said, "Now it is time to go to law school." I had a degree in history and economics. Much that I had seen and done had changed me. I had broken my back skiing earlier in 1973. Many people said I wouldn't walk again. When I came back, I wanted to teach school because I didn't want to go to law school.

In 1976, I graduated with an education degree. I was asked to speak in response to an after-dinner speech by Premier Gerald Regan. The guy who was going to return the speech fell ill at the dinner, so I spoke instead. Regan offered me a job. I became special assistant to the premier in 1976 and then went on to become executive assistant to the minister of development and did the Waterfront Development Corporation Act.

Then I went on to become executive assistant to the minister of education, who did the Student Loan Act and the Adult Education Training Act.

That's where I met Pierre Trudeau. I joined the CBC and went into television news. After my father's death, I moved to Fredericton, New Brunswick, to do the 6:00 to 9:00 A.M. morning show.

In 1981, the CBC went on strike. A member of Trudeau's staff called me and invited me to Ottawa. I ended up leaving the CBC and working for Trudeau for two years in various occupations, all in communications. I was appointed to the McDonald commission. Then I became head of public affairs at Scotia Bank. In 1990, I was a consultant for CBC and then they hired me full time.

I wonder what would have happened if I hadn't broken away from all the stuff that I thought was so mediocre. Frankly, I believe that if I had stayed at UCC, I wouldn't have achieved anything in my life. I honestly believe that I've achieved a great deal. I have a body of work behind me now that reflects nothing of UCC. So I'm sorry that my father spent so many thousands of dollars on sending his three sons to UCC for so many years. I wish he'd had it to leave it to me!

Having said that, I'm glad of my association with my friend Michael Grant. I have very, very few friends. I don't go back to old-boy reunions. I see old boys from time to time. If I can help them, I do. But I do it simply out of an early friendship that doesn't have anything to do with the UCC old-boy network.

I know people who have denied going to UCC. I have two old boys who work for me. I had an executive assistant, who was a head boy at UCC, when I was in Ottawa. He's gone on now to practise law. He is married and divorced, about to remarry. I don't know what it is about old boys from Upper Canada, but their marriages never last very long.

I was asked back to speak at a Career Day at UCC when I was vice-president of public affairs at the Scotia Bank. I told the UCC boys, "If you think you are going to come out of here as something, you are wrong. You have to find something inside yourself. You have to decide what you want to achieve. Then you have to fight for it. This bullshit institution is not going to contribute to your getting it."

I have a great sense of missed opportunity at UCC. If I was any of those masters, I would feel a great deal of sadness and regret that I hadn't given those boys something that they needed. I think of the young men who have been lost to us now, like David Malthouse, who jumped off a Rosedale bridge. They are a number who are now dead for ridiculous reasons – drugs, alcohol, sexual identity, confused state of mind.

A number of guys crippled themselves with drugs. There was a chap at UCC whose brother was found out to be gay. The boys were pretty nasty to him. I understand he tried to commit suicide. Another guy, Jamie Morden basically committed suicide through prolonged self-abuse. I liked Jamie a lot because he had a funny kind of influence on me. I trace many influences back to those early days.

A lot of our guys in the 1960s were terribly passionate, sweet, sensitive guys who wanted to do creative things. Who has to take responsibility for what happened to them? Maybe it's nobody's fault. Maybe you just say to yourself, Well, it's like the CBC. It's just tough to change things. But someone has to take responsibility. Is it the board of governors? Is it the headmaster? When I think of Pat Johnson and Willy Orr and that coterie of assholes on the UCC faculty, I couldn't even visit their grave sites and be civil.

People often ask me, "Why do you think you became such a reclusive person?" I'm convinced that it is a result of my years at UCC. Frankly, I didn't like very many of the boys there. They didn't like me. We were competitors. I wish some of the sweetness of the prep could have been instilled in us as upper school boys. I wish to hell we would have been taught to respect each other and to believe more in each other. We simply weren't. Often I would get very depressed. There was no counselling. There was nobody to help you. You didn't want to show a weak side because of the viciousness of the boys.

Frankly, this is the first time I've talked about the school since I left it. Talking about it, I feel like a veteran who survived something. I remember what it was like being in Bangkok in 1975 talking to soldiers who had come out of the Vietnam War, kids eighteen, nineteen, twenty years of age. I felt that I had shared something with them, but at the time I didn't really know what it was.

Now, all these years later, I look back on UCC as having been something I would rather not have done. Having said that, the environment forced me inside myself. As a result, perhaps I'm more in touch with who I am. It's likely that many old boys, the stockbrokers and lawyers who married and had children, who surround themselves with the high-velocity life that is generated in UCC's culture, don't reflect on their lives or get in touch with themselves. At some point, much later on, they say, "What the fuck am I doing here? Who is this woman I'm married to? Why am I here?"

I have lived alone for years. I have a home in Nova Scotia on the coast. I have two dogs. I listen to music and I collect art. I try to surround myself with a quality of life that is so distant from those years. I would like to be a better person. I would love to be able to be more accessible and friendly. I would like to be more comfortable around people in certain situations, but I'm not. I blame UCC for it.

RICHARD MEECH

1965–72

Filmmaker, anthropologist

I N MY YEARS in the prep, there was an archaic quality to the rite of passage that was taking place among the young boys. When I compare the prep to the anthropological work I completed recently on the "Millennium" documentary series, there are striking parallels to the Xavante tribe of Brazil.

When the Xavante boys are very young, they are allowed to play and interact with little girls in a coeducational environment. Then, at a certain age, which can be between nine and thirteen, they have to leave the girls. They are pulled away from their mothers and go into what is called the bachelor-age set, away from all female contact for a period of seven years.

They then go through a series of rites of passage, after which they are proclaimed to be men, even though they may not feel like men themselves. They are seen as men and they have the right to marry and have children. During the bachelor years, they cannot interact with women, although they must have the highest respect for them. There is a separation of the sexes on the verge of adolescence. All through puberty the tribe maintains distinct social groups.

The boys have to do many things during the time of separation. They learn to be a warrior, a hunter, a leader. That period of liminality, on the threshold of society when you're no longer a boy and you're not quite a man, was similar to what we were all going through during the prep years and early upper school years. It is the time for the highest concentration of education. Probably the strongest time for me at Upper Canada was from Grade 7 through to about Grade 10 or 11. Then I was ready to interact once again with the outside world. I missed the company of women by the middle of high school.

In the Xavante tribe, certain elders are assigned to look after the bachelors. Some of them become the figures who helped you in your advancement. You never know who they are going to be and they are not assigned to you, just like at the prep. It was never said to the masters, "You have to look after Meech, you have to look after Grant." But somehow you found them. This was not necessarily the case in the upper school, which had different dynamics.

I felt like I was in a wonderful cocoon in the prep. After I got over my initial fears of fitting in, making friends, and being liked, I began to connect very quickly to the other boys. I had the feeling that the prep wanted to open up so many different windows into my world and life. For instance, everybody in the prep in the upper years had to study music appreciation. I couldn't sing a note and probably still can't hum a tune. But I had to go and listen to music – classical music, jazz, whatever it was. The teacher, Herbie Sommerfeld, loved the boys best who were musicians or singers, but he insisted that everybody appreciate music and understand that it is one of the arts that make us human.

Similarly, we had to go to art class with Vernon Mould. I hadn't done anything like this before. One day, he went off on a tangent about the importance of art in society, talking way beyond the intellectual level of our class. I got frustrated because I wanted to get going on my mask. But the longer he talked, the more I listened. I realized that art wasn't just a case of making the mask. Art was about how you looked at the world and how you interacted with the world. I learned that the esthetic dimension of life was all around us, including right there in the classroom at that very moment. I've lost the mask but I've never forgotten his lecture.

I relished going into the theatre. I wasn't a great actor, but I enjoyed participating in the prep productions. I played the harlequin in Robertson Davies' *The Masque of Aesop*, a play he had written specifically for the prep boys. You always had a sense of a cocoon, a warmth around the prep, the sense of everything in you growing, yet at the same time protected. At that point, you were trying to understand your own soul, even though you didn't know you were. You were finding out all sorts of wonderful things about yourself.

Anytime somebody said, "Here, try this," you would try it because you were just a little guy. Usually there were wonderful things that you learned about yourself. The prep was in some ways a magical place where you existed outside of normal time, before you had developed self-awareness, before you would even consider the critical distance between the development of yourself as a person and who you might be publicly in the school.

I really liked Jack Schaffter, who taught me history and geography. He went on to do wonderfully progressive things as a headmaster at private schools in Winnipeg and Victoria. He taught well because he loved his subject. Kids are so sensitive at that age and they know who loved what they taught. That was one of those things that stayed with me throughout university – find somebody who loves what they are teaching. You learn from other people's passion.

There was a lot of passion among the prep teachers. Bruce Littlejohn's passion was the outdoors, the school property at Norval. Unfortunately Norval disappeared from the vocabulary when we got to the upper school, and yet it is a great opportunity to tie in urban education with nature and environmentalism. We would stay up there for a day and night and walk around the acreage, go down to the river, take samples of the water, or look at the leaves or the structure of the riverbed. But my main memory is actually just playing and wandering through the woods, getting lost, not having something that we were supposed to do. I thought that was a very novel concept.

Of course, the word "gay" was not in our vocabulary yet. We used the words "queer," "fairy," "fag," "queen," "homo," or "homosexual." By about Grade 11 or 12, I would talk about it to some of my friends. We were trying to second-guess it because it became something to talk about quietly, but with a certain amount of derision.

It actually interested me, to tell you the truth. I wanted to know more about these characters. Who were they? Why were they different? In the upper school, we began to realize who they were among the faculty – Walter Bailey, Ken Shearer, John Linn. Linn's nickname was "Fairy." He was the most out of the closet of all. I'm sure there were many other gay masters.

At first, I didn't know what those words meant. I'd say, "What do you mean, he's a fairy?" Somebody would say, "It means he's a homosexual." I'd say, "Oh, what does that mean?" He'd say, "It means he sleeps with other men." I thought, Oh, that's an odd idea. To me, it didn't bother me one way or the other, it was just an odd idea. Then it became more apparent.

When I thought about it at the time, I realized the homosexual masters were actually some of the nicest ones in the school. I hate to be stereotypical, but generally the gay masters were the more sensitive and caring ones. The words "pedophile" or "pederast" hadn't entered my vocabulary yet. I didn't necessarily even suspect that they would want to have relationships with the boys and that's why they were there. I thought they did it amongst themselves.

Still being a virgin, I didn't know what sex was anyway. It was just a whole curious world. There was probably not much homophobia at the time, at least amongst the students. There may have been amongst the masters. The students didn't know what it meant. It was just coming to be a discussion by my Grade 13 year in 1972.

Interestingly enough, I had two experiences with teachers by my Grade 12 or Grade 13 year. They were not sexual, but when I reflect on them now, they were expressions of sexual interest. One of them was with Walter Bailey, who was an alcoholic math teacher. I liked the guy a lot because he was very funny and taught math quite well. He would come in reeking of cologne because he would be covering up his booze.

At the end of Grade 12, I got a good mark in math. He invited me to go to a movie with him. I said, "Okay, sure." He was a guy I liked. Kids are like that. So I said I would bring along my friend Paul, because Paul and Bailey got along well. Bailey said, "Oh, so you don't trust coming with me alone, eh?" I said, "Sure, but Paul would like to come." He said, "Well, that's fine. Bring Paul along then."

The three of us went out to some little place for dinner and then we went to see *The Manchurian Candidate*. At the end of the movie, that was it. We said good night and nothing ever happened again. I only realized much later that he was trying to show a personal interest in me. I don't know if anything would have happened if he had been with me alone.

Another teacher was a charismatic guy who befriended a lot of the boys. He was one of the guys. I was certainly one of the guys too, having won the Herbert Mason Medal in Grade 13. The summer I graduated, I went to Europe, where we happened to meet up and travel together. We were in a motel one night. I didn't know what was going on. My teacher was in his bed and I was in another bed. He reached over and put an ice cube in my belly button and held it there. I laughed at first, but his hand stayed there. He said, "What would you say if I seduced you?" I said, "Well, I wouldn't be very comfortable with that. It's not my style." I was just shocked.

That's when he told me that he was bisexual. I had known a couple of BSS girls he had gone out with. He said, "I like boys and girls equally. Double your pleasure, double your fun." Then he told me he had slept with about ten or fifteen guys in my class. At least, he claimed to have slept with them. We continued talking and I said, "I feel really uncomfortable about this. I really like you as a friend." When you say those things, they sound awkward at the time, but you mean them.

His longest-term lover was a contemporary of mine at UCC. My personal theory is that the guy probably just went along with it. I imagine it was like the adolescent sex that happened very openly and very lovingly in ancient Greece or ancient Rome. Alexander the Great had a sexual relationship with a friend who accompanied him on all his military campaigns.

In those cultures, an older man personally introduced adolescent boys to sex as part of their education. This teacher would always make reference to male bonding in our classes. From what I've heard, when the guy he was living with decided to get married and have kids, it was very hard on him.

That night in the motel room, the teacher told me the names of some of the other guys he had sex with. In a way, I think he was trying to convince me that it was okay because everybody did it. That was a real shocker for me. I never knew that our male camaraderie would go to that level of physical expression. I stayed friends with him for another year or two. Then he went on to another school.

I know the teacher had relationships with a few of the boarders because they were among the ones he named to me that night. I thought, No! Not him! I'm not implying any value judgement. At the time, I was just so shocked. Homosexuality wasn't something that went totally against your record in those days.

From the perspective of the 1990s, my teacher may have abused his position of influence. But back then, we wouldn't necessarily have said so. We would have said that that is just who he is. I believe that even at that adolescent age, you do have a choice to get involved or not in a homosexual relationship. By the time I had that experience in the motel, I was in Grade 13, so I was already eighteen and I already had had a sexual experience with a woman. I had already bitten the apple, so to speak. But I think if he were to get you before your first sexual experience, it might well have been a difficult ethical question. In the context of a friendship, the kid wouldn't necessarily know what he was doing.

Sex was all part of the liberation of the late sixties for me. Sexual experimentation or sex itself was a taboo to be broken through. A lot of people explored their sexuality at that time without any value judgements. It was innocent, but it was also about learning about your body. The girls that I was meeting at that time were also interested in the same thing.

Sex was actually quite free and open. To be able to "go all the way" was no longer a sneaky thing. You actually did it. I was at many parties in Grade 12 or 13 where there would be great music and people would be smoking grass and rolling around on the floor making out. If they were going to actually make love, they would disappear somewhere and go do it.

I was part of that scene. So the fact that there were some guys who were also exploring it amongst themselves seemed all right. It was a time of openness. Then the conservative era returned and things began to close down in the late seventies and early eighties. I still think the biggest single thing the WASP culture has to get over is its fear of the body. The Protestant body has no blood and no sperm. We have to put our minds back in our bodies and vice versa. Old boys like Robertson Davies personify that split-off, bloodless WASP sensibility.

Nowadays, the school would presumably know if a teacher was gay or not. Actually, I don't know how they would know. Perhaps it is now more out in the open. Maybe some of them live with lovers now. I certainly hope it would be more open and accepted these days at UCC. I think all that the school would demand is that you don't fuck with the boys. If they felt that your character was such that you're not that kind of a person, gay or not, they will go for you. They have to watch out for the guys who go after the young girls in the public schools too. I hope they look for character more than sexual preference.

There are instances in many tribal cultures where a form of ritual homosexuality is part of the coming of age. During the time that they are separated from women, boys are introduced to sex with men. After the ritual homosexuality, they are not to engage in it any more. Like that teacher's long-term UCC lover, they are supposed to get married and have kids.

Some anthropologists will say it even applies to women in their groups, not in terms of active sexuality, but in terms of exploring their emotions and their bodies. Past a certain point, however, all societies basically want to replicate the society. They want people to come together to have children to carry on. That's why, in the end, most societies don't advocate ongoing homosexuality. They allow it only as part of the threshold or shadow time of your life. Then you go on.

MICHAEL MACMILLAN

1967–74

President, Atlantis Films

MICHAEL CARVER, an Englishman who taught in the prep, was a great influence on me. One day in a Grade 8 art class, we had a little mounted super-8 camera. You could take pieces of cardboard or coloured paper, put them on the page and move them around. Everytime you moved them, it would expose a frame of film. If you moved them enough times, you were in fact animating the image. You could play it back the next week and see what you had done.

I remember thinking it was foolish, but it remained with me. Later, in Grade 10 English class, Mr. McCord gave us a media project to do. A couple of friends and I decided to do a film. My only reference to it whatsoever was that day in art class in Grade 8 doing the animation. We made a short film entitled *The Upcan File.* This was around the time of the FLQ crisis in Quebec when Pierre Laporte was abducted and later murdered. Our film was about how "Le Front de Libération de Battalion" had abducted the guy who used to run the UCC cadet battalion and was holding him for ransom. The protagonists had to uncover the kidnappers, save the hostage, save the battalion, save the school, and save Western civilization.

Throughout our project, Michael Carver offered encouragement, advice, and support. He was still teaching in the prep and I was now in the upper school. Based on that experience, I got interested in film. All through the upper school, after this one media project, I spent a huge amount of time making films. I made dozens of films. I spent a lot of afternoons down at the prep instead of in the upper school, where I should have been. For a couple of years, there was a film club. The Arts Festival was just starting in the early seventies, and we had a film section which I ran. I spent at least fifteen hours a week, evenings and weekends, making films. Michael Carver went above and beyond the call of duty to be supportive.

I was on sports teams and in other clubs, but film was the one outstanding thing that I was involved in. To the school's eternal credit, they never caused me any problems. Film was not exactly an activity that was going to lead to a safe, traditional UCC profession. They might have asked why some kid would waste his time, but I got nothing but support. By the time I graduated from UCC, I knew I wanted to make films for a living. Film has remained an absolute focus ever since. I'm doing exactly what I want to do and I'm very lucky for it.

After UCC, I went to Queen's and got a B.A. in film studies. I made a 16-mm film about Queen's called *The Academic Cloister.* I was the director, producer, cinematographer, and editor. Friends helped me edit and shoot it. The film showed scenes of university life, ranging from Orientation Week through the study environment, the lecture environment, the exams, and the social life. The thesis of the film was that the university and our institutions in general were all about stuffing information into the heads of students and then demanding its successful regurgitation. They weren't encouraging original, creative, or contrary thinking.

Even if it was unspoken, conformity and uniformity was the goal. Students acted like trained seals during Orientation Week, being forced to conform under the guise of tradition. In the lecture halls, professors blabbed away at three hundred people who are all writing down the same stuff with little chance for personal interaction. Then five thousand kids are stuck in the hockey arena to write exams, spewing out the same stuff. On the social scene, the kids are all wearing the same red or yellow leather jackets, hoping to fit in by doing the very same stuff. At all levels, uniformity permeated the academic cloister.

When I was corunning Orientation Week for the fall of 1976, every student who went to Queen's had to come out and listen to my speech about why, in fact, Orientation Week was crazy. They had to watch the film and listen to a dose of my rhetoric. I said, "Don't always accept what authority is telling you. Don't even believe what I'm saying right now."

It went over like a lead balloon. We were severely chastised by the Faculty of Arts and Science. I said, "We're just telling one side of the story. If you want to hire us to tell the other side of the story, we'll think about it." So they hired us to make three promotional films for the university, which showed all the positive aspects of Queen's. It's a great example of the co-optive powers of institutions.

The whole experience worked out quite well, because the next year we made a film about juvenile delinquents in Kingston. That so annoyed a few people in the Ministry of Corrections that the federal ministry in charge of juvenile delinquents hired us to make a film about a special juvenile diversion program in Kingston. So a trend was started. It was at this point that I thought, Hey! This is working. I'll keep making films.

Some of my fellow film students and I incorporated Atlantis during our fourth year at Queen's. We began working on getting our first post-university contract. By the time we left Queen's in April 1978, we had a name, business cards, and a couple of contracts which came through shortly afterwards. I've never had a real job in my life.

Seven years after I left UCC, we had a class reunion. We had all graduated from university and most of us had jobs. There was a recession at that time, but it wasn't too bad. Probably fifty old boys from our year showed up for the reunion. For three or four years afterwards, my wife, my partners, and anybody else who could stand to listen would hear me bitch and moan about what I encountered that evening at UCC. Everybody was either a stockbroker, an investment analyst, a banker, a trust fund administrator, a lawyer, or an accountant. There were no coffee-cup manufacturers or shirt designers. There was nobody making stuff. They were all defending capital, not creating it. I found it absolutely shocking.

In 1989, when I went back for my fifteenth reunion, it was better. The majority were still on Bay Street, doing the same types of jobs. But some more guys were doing different things, and curiously, almost all the ones who've done something different are in the arts. Out of one hundred kids who graduated from UCC in 1974, about fifteen or twenty of us are now in the arts, including Jim Cuddy of the rock group Blue Rodeo. Paul Toyne owned the Santa Fe Restaurant and invented the board game Balderdash.

Richard Charteris is the editor of *TV Guide*, Dave Fleury and Gord Sheard are musicians, and Peter Meech is a screenwriter. It was really weird how we polarized. One group of us went way over here and everybody else was way over there. There was not much in the middle.

The school encouraged me to think that the world was there to conquer. If I wanted to do something, I should be able to do it. There were no barriers. It's a terrific attitude to have and it was very much encouraged at UCC. I believed it then and I still believe it. So far, at thirty-five, owning and running a decent-sized film operation, it has come to pass for me.

EVAN THOMPSON

1963–73

Business writer

C OMING TO UCC at age eight, there was quite an adjustment from the public school system. I missed the gentleness of the female teachers in the public school environment. In fact, I missed female company for my entire ten years at the school. I found it very unnatural that I would be with boys and be taught by men, with very few exceptions. Throughout the piece was a sense of being a little bit off balance competitively, socially, and emotionally because of the lack of female influence. Actually, I have never been able to articulate it until now.

By the same token, there were a lot of things in the prep that were very good. Jack Schaffter was an excellent history teacher, as was Dick Howard for English and Ted Stephenson for math. Alan Harris came as close to perfection as one could imagine for a teacher. He had a good sense of humour and a great rapport with the parents. He did not portray math as rocket science that could only be learned by slavery. He tried to make it fun.

But generally, I saw shoulder-to-the-wheel, long-suffering individuals. Looking at my classmates, I was never struck by their illustriousness or their brilliance or their sense of vision. The ones who excelled were just a little bit older, just because of the luck of the draw of the birth dates. Besides being gifted with physical attributes, and in the odd case a photographic memory, no leaders emerged to me. They were carried by their drive and their parents' wish to see their children cast in their image.

I had great respect for Tom Creed at that time. I knew who the Creed family were. Tom's father, who was an old boy, would take us all out to the Inn on the Park for swimming parties. But trying very hard to look at it through a ten- or eleven-year-old's eyes, no one really impressed me as someone who was ultimately going to lead the country. Other classmates may have felt that there were potential leaders, but I do not think it is possible to identify leadership qualities until you are well into your adolescence. Some people, like the late Roy Thomson, do not really come into their own until they are sixty, or later. I happen to be one of those people.

I thought the forms of discipline at UCC were basically demeaning, like marine boot camp. The really inhuman forms of punishment were not physically violent, just demeaning. Ever since UCC, I have been extremely conscious of avoiding humiliation, not embarrassing myself. One of the tendencies of an all-male private school system is to not put any velvet over the hammer. You just come down hard. If someone cannot do their arithmetic timetables, you just work them like a Camp Lejeune drill sergeant. You humiliate kids to the point that they break down and cry. That happened to me a few times.

This is where I keep coming back to the lack of female influence. Why do you think the nurse, Miss Barrow, is so lauded as the Mother Theresa of UCC by so many old boys? Because she was, in some instances, the only female influence on the boarders and the day boys. She was a good person, but that is why she was so excessively revered.

But humiliation was used pretty consistently, either to push further, do better, run faster, be smarter. I suppose we gave as good as we got. Certain kids were bullied more frequently. Boxing was the essence of public humiliation. There were three rings going simultaneously and we fought for three rounds, one minute each round. Muzz Greatrex was the emperor of the games. If he saw something getting too out of hand, he would ding the bell and the match was stopped.

I remember I was boxing Keith Milne, a really wiry, good boxer. By the third round, my white-crested T-shirt was like a red tie-dyed shirt, something out of Peter Max. The mucous membranes in my nose had gone. At first, I thought, Shit, a little blood, no problem. But it was bad. When I looked down, I just went to pieces. It was just like fucking Vimy Ridge. Blood "R" Us.

So Muzz dings the bell and stops the fight. I think my nose was bleeding for another twenty-four hours. But I cannot say that experience was humiliating because I had some good matches. I was more embarrassed for having been beaten up so badly. Boxing was a blood sport. I do not quite know what I learned from that situation or what I was supposed to do with that experience in later life.

The social pecking order of UCC became more visible in the upper school, where you saw the boys who champion UCC. I call them the poster boys, who were obviously destined to follow in their fathers' tracks, who did all the right things and set the tone as to what was acceptable and what was unacceptable.

Unfortunately, the same values that the boys learned at UCC, the private school girls learned. The girls learned what was desirable in a boy from UCC – external, physical accomplishments, like playing on the first football team. I am not being acerbic or bitter. I participated in athletics, I was editor of the *College Times*, and I was drum sergeant major in the battalion, the guy who carried the ceremonial mace. I did quite a bit, but I was not a true champion of the school in terms of the true UCC role models, who were the jocks.

I remember some of the first football team parties were just like the last days of Rome. I saw UCC faculty members literally rolling under the tables with teenage BSS girls. Nobby Noble was into that in a big way. Those parties were bacchanals, wild celebrations of alcohol abuse. I do not know how I got home behind the wheel.

There was a lot of drinking that went on in Fran's Restaurant. Approaching graduation in June 1973, there was a big celebration at the Crown Room. A lot of our Grade 13 class were down there whooping it up, just getting absolutely hammered. I almost accepted a ride in the car that night with Dack Allen, Stephen Jeffrey, Ian Whicher, and Jim Wright. I almost was going to hop in with them. The car was driven by Dack Allen. They were driving south on Mount Pleasant and they hit the railway bridge at Whitehall Road in Rosedale. Jim Wright was thrown out of the car and killed instantly. Ian Whicher was badly hurt and the others got banged up.

I remember the *College Times* was going to press almost the next day. I was the editor. Patrick Johnson, the principal, called me into his office to talk about putting an appropriate message on the inside front cover dedicated to Jim's memory. Johnson could not even speak. He was just absolutely devastated. He had written out something and then torn it up and then written out something again. We finally worked up a little message and put it in. He was just a mess.

The whole thing was just awful. Throughout the next twenty-four hours, two or three classmates came to my house with revised captions for their leading class photos, so I had to get on the phone to the printer and make the changes. Stephen Jeffrey made a revision in his caption, which was something to the effect, "When a rock hits the pond, the ripples go on forever."

Pat Johnson was already under a lot of pressure as principal in those years. He was under pressure from the parents to produce winning ball teams and curb rebellion, among other things. In 1971, he banned something called "The Peoples' Notice Board," where a lot of guys were putting up inflammatory slogans like "Johnson is an imperialist lackey of the board of governors." There were a lot of different factions – parents, old boys, students, faculty, the board of governors – pushing and pulling him every which way. One of my vividest memories is of him chain-smoking near the end zone at football games. He was a nervous wreck.

Jim Wright had been a steward and a big man on campus. The accident was extraordinarily traumatic, casting a real pall over the whole graduating year. It was a nightmare. The communal mourning was incredible. There were hundreds at the funeral. Today, it would have cost thousands of dollars. Many people attend these things for their own purging, especially when it is a contemporary who died.

There was so much alcohol abuse. We literally had drinking contests between the parents and the students. There were some major parties at the Harvie house, which is now part of the Cohon compound at 110 Forest Hill Road. Andrew Harvie's father used to have kegs brought in and the kitchen floor would be literally awash in beer. The parents would put on their old blazers and relive their youth. They would become adolescents again, socializing and mixing it up with the girls. Everyone was so drunk. There was no stigma or boundaries attached. It never got to the state of being an orgy, but the alcohol consumption was just amazing.

The adults did not participate all the time, but God, compared to accepted parenting styles today, it was quite something. I never saw any concern for drinking and driving. Only when the driver fell down, threw up, or passed out, did I see any acts of intervention. I saw drunken guests coming and going from these events, myself included, all evening. People would think nothing of driving to another bar when they were drunk. The Morrissey Tavern was not yet in favour for private school types in the early 1970s, as it is now, but the Jolly Miller and the Crown Room were popular.

On occasion, guys would rent rooms in the Sutton Place Hotel for drinking or stag parties which would go on for eighteen hours at a time. Bathtubs were filled with beer, ice, some hard stuff. Hard stuff was not very popular because it was considered an old person's drink. It was seen as sort of sucky, even though it is ten times as lethal as beer. But beer was the dominant social currency, straight from the bottle.

Some of the girls and boys got so sick, I thought that they would die in their own vomit. I would just step over them and just keep going. Sometimes the girls would help each other. I remember a party in which a girl had a concussion from being thrown into the swimming pool. The behaviour was generally not violent, but it was basically the gridiron removed to the drawing room. This sort of role playing has probably screwed up a lot of people.

When I graduated in 1973, I realized alcohol and material status went a long way in determining an individual's self-worth and worth to his or her peers. In the brokerage community and in big business, you are judged by what you drive, where you live, who you date, where you holiday, or what you wear on your wrist or your finger. I was never overly materialistic. I did not have the available cash or flashy cars that would have put me on the "A" team with people like Tom Creed.

Latterly, community outreach has became fashionable at the school, but before that, complete self-absorption and status-consciousness dominated. To me, this set of values became something to aspire to as an adolescent and as a young man. It is only recently that I have come to the realization that it is not what you have, it is who you are and what you accomplish under your own steam that is important. Maybe it is a case of delayed adolescence. My maturation process was probably retarded by ten years by my ten years at Upper Canada.

Recently I was on a first date with a woman from Vancouver who is very pleasant and well adjusted. We were having a wonderful time. Then she said, "You went to UCC, didn't you?" I was not wearing a UCC blazer or tie. I said, "Yes, as a matter of fact." She said, "Yes, you smell of it." I think that she was trying to be funny, but there was a little bit of an edge to her remark. "How does that smell?" I asked. She said, "Oh, don't worry about it. I can just tell." I pursued it. I said, "Is it because I stood up when you came back from the bathroom? Because I held the door and took your coat?"

She said, "No, no, I like all that." She could not isolate any sort of reason for it, but she just knew that I was from UCC. This is nothing new. It is something that I am constantly reminded of. So, unless I am with a group of old boys or private school types of any age, I do not start a conversation with, "Oh, I remember when I was at UCC." I really try and back away from it.

No one can help the fact that they were educated at a private school, but I think that there is a real public prejudice against UCC. In some ways, there is a malevolence ascribed to private school education because we are deemed to be the homophobic, sexist, racist old-boy network which keeps the glass ceiling firmly in place.

Admittedly, I get a lot of business from fellow UCC old boys. In fact, I now work in an office with two UCC old boys, Dave Kingsmill and George McNeillie. There is a real comfort level, a built-in bond, and a trust among old boys that is played out at UCC events and at fundraising time. Some of us have the advantage of having an inheritance and a financial net to catch us. Some of us do not, especially after the rigours of the market over the past few years.

Over twenty years after leaving UCC, I realize that I have gradually come into my own, having taken the best out of the place. Maybe it's a bit of selective memory, but I find that I am socially adept, that I do have good connections, and it does look good on my resumé. I just let that enhance rather than carry the whole situation. A lot of people who trade too heavily on their UCC tie are just stricken when people do not immediately leap to their feet in their presence. Just because you went to UCC does not mean that you are the second coming of Ted Rogers or Conrad Black.

My parents' attitude to my education was: "Do not rock the boat. We will take care of you. Do not get expelled. Do not drink. Do not get caught. Do not impregnate someone. Do not embarrass the school or your family and things will take care of themselves. Because you come from an illustrious Toronto family and went to UCC and Queen's, everything is just going to be fine."

Bullshit! I woke up five years ago. After being married, I was still under the impression that if you just wait long enough, good things will happen because you are a member of the lucky sperm club. That is not true of all UCC students. Some were pushed to the point where they just cracked. Some became alcoholic, overly competitive, or insufferably aggressive.

I almost went the other way, taking the path of least resistance and doing what I was told. I was told, "Be a good soldier and you will get your stripes." I woke up at age thirty and asked myself, Where are the fucking stripes? I can just see that phrase printed in your book: "'Where are the fucking stripes?' asks Evan Seton Thompson, Toronto nobility."

When I busted out of UCC, I just followed my nose to Queen's. I soon discovered my aptitude was for pussy, to be quite honest. I was completely engulfed by coeducation. It was like being in a candy shop, although Queen's was a little bit like UCC and BSS in Kingston. There was still a lot of that competitiveness, but there was such a large base that I could meet new people who were not completely reflective of private school culture. In my later dating life, I became involved with people from different backgrounds outside Rosedale and Forest Hill. I do not know if that is good, bad, or indifferent.

I married outside of my class. The marriage ended about four years ago. We have gotten on with our lives and everything is just fine. She was blue collar from Montreal. My parents were against it, although they did not openly forbid it. They could foresee disaster. They thought that this was a morsel that was interesting for the time being, but that it would not stand the test of time. It got pretty messy.

In a way, my marriage was an act of rebellion. I wanted to prove to myself and to my partner that I was not a UCC addict, that I could stand on my own two feet – and "Watch this! I am going to marry a Catholic!" Coming from a Protestant family, that was not acceptable. Had she been a WASP from Lawrence Park or Rosedale, who knows if the marriage would still be intact. But the ramp-up phase certainly would have been smoother.

When you are raised within a family and a school that celebrates sameness of class, religious, and racial origins, you are almost preconditioned to follow in that vein. It is almost instinctive that you will marry a woman raised in Forest Hill or Rosedale, someone with whom you will share an ease of communication, a comfort level of what is expected and what is appropriate. When you step out of that mode and get challenged by remarks like, "Oh, you went to UCC? You must think that you walk on water," there is something within you that makes you want to prove otherwise. You say, "I am a person. I like to go to the Legion or the Elks. I drink beer out of a bottle just like anyone else."

I found myself – I will not say "slumming it," because that is a very snobbish word – but gravitating towards people whom I felt accepted me for who I was, indifferent to the fact that I went to UCC. I'd rather sit in a beer hall with my ex-father-in-law as opposed to sitting in a den in Rosedale with a WASP father-in-law, looking me up and down and saying, "Yes, yes, Spadina House, yes. Would you care for some more port?" In other words, you are "in." You might be an asshole, but you are in. So, right now, I do not know where I am exactly. Click.

When you marry within your own class, when you marry a BSS or Havergal old girl, the chances are better that the marriage will work, only because of the pressure exerted by both families to keep it together, regardless of whether it is a living hell. The parents say, "No, we simply cannot have a divorce in this family. They are only two docks down the lake, you know. We will make the necessary arrangements, but stay married." So, you have all of this flying around. But when there is no social or family pressure to keep a failing marriage together, you resolve to end it before it gets worse.

I no longer date Havergal or BSS old girls, which may be self-defeating in some ways. There is nothing wrong with marrying the private school girl next door. Some old boys I know are in very good relationships because of the class similarities with their wives. Their parents play a very large role for two reasons. First of all, the parents control or maintain the environment in which their childrens' relationships grow – the houses, cottages, properties, clubs, vacations. You know, the nummies.

Then there is an ease of access. They feel comfortable sharing ideas or dictating to partners from the same background because they essentially see them as children. Often the strangest thing occurs when people from the same class and background marry. The young married couple become almost like friends or siblings in the eyes of both sets of parents. They are like brother and sister, two kids to be looked after and set up at their summer cottage in Muskoka, the ski lodge at Osler Bluffs, and the condo in Florida.

The male loses his maleness and the female loses her femaleness. The couple becomes almost androgynous because they are just an extension of the suppliers, Dad and Mom, who continue to call the shots. The BSS old girl says to the UCC old boy, "It's Thanksgiving. Let's go. It is their fucking cottage, so we are expected up there this weekend. Do not drink so much again. Dad said you had too much to drink last time."

They remain like children until their forties and fifties when they finally bury the parents. There is a lot of hanging around for the inheritance. You do not want to piss off the inheritance lawyers either. Do not drink too much up at Muskoka. Do not make it look like you would piss away five million dollars if it came your way. So history repeats itself. The parents put up with all sorts of shit from the in-laws and all of this is lovingly called "the UCC family." You cannot cut your nose off to spite your face by totally rejecting all of it, although it has happened in rare instances. One of the DuPonts gave away hundreds of millions of dollars because he just could not stand the emotional baggage.

David Thomson, the son of Ken Thomson, is a troubled soul. He was a couple of years behind me at UCC. Both he and his father would rather be collecting art than running their media empire. I know Ken Thomson, and I have heard him say as much. Ken had greatness and responsibility thrust onto him because he was the son of Lord Thomson of Fleet, but he is really a very sad sort of individual. My late father knew him. Ken wanted to buy Spadina House to house his Krieghoff paintings. So my dad struck a deal with him, saying that he would consider it, that he would talk to my granny, if Ken would get me on a newspaper apprenticeship in England, which he did. I worked without pay for a year for the Merther Tydfil *Express* and the Reading *Evening Post*.

God, it was great. On a non-UCC footing, I lived and died by my own abilities as a reporter and a writer and I did extremely well. There were no UCC strings or net, other than the fact that people thought I was the son of

Ken Thomson – especially the unions. They thought that I deliberately added a *p* to my last name to avoid detection. I finally had to come home because the NUJ [National Union of Journalists] thought I was a plant. I was scabbing. I was crossing the picket line to put out the newspaper in Wales.

After his father Roy died, Ken Thomson told me he would rather collect art than manage his father's media empire. When I interviewed him in 1975 when I was a journalist with the *Mississauga News*, he said basically that it was a lot of work maintaining the house in Mississauga where his late father lived. He was of the view that there were a lot of people sniffing after him, wanting a piece of him, which is inevitable. After all, he is worth over six billion dollars.

DAVID THOMSON

1964–67, 1970–75

Deputy chairman, The Woodbridge Company

WHEN I first started in the prep, I was cycling along a bridge with another little seven-year-old UCC chap. He said to me, "My mother is so happy that we are friends because you are going to be able to do so much for me later in life." I remember thinking, I wonder what it is that I am going to be doing for this chap? Then I grew up and realized: So that is the way it is. That is what people expect.

The prep was a traumatic time for me. My father had a set routine to work every morning. I was driven to school in a limousine, one of those great big black Fleetwoods with the huge double doors, so I felt very isolated. I would spend my recesses with another chap, hiding in washrooms and trying to avoid my fellow classmates.

At the end of the day, the boys would hold the doors of the limousine shut until the driver came and parted them, like Moses with the Red Sea, and rescued me. I felt pretty miserable. When I did have friends, it was because I had a lovely little racing car that we raced on what we called Magoo's Highway, which was a little yard in front of the steps of the Peacock Building, the prep boardinghouse.

I can remember talking in Junior Form one day, chatting to the fellow beside me. The teacher, the only female teacher in the school, said, "Silence is the golden rule. Thomson, will you please stand outside the classroom." So I stood out in the hall. I could hear her saying to everyone, "You know, Thomson seems to laugh a great deal. He enjoys laughing. Why do we not all go and laugh at him?" She had a group of students come out and laugh at me in the corridor. It was really a shameful act. I was only seven. There was a very bitter approach to things.

I did not really like sports. I played those silly games like British Bulldog that children play at intermission, but normally I would be the last one to be picked. Then everyone would jump on me, so I tended to veer away and spend time in the library. The years went very quickly. I actually still have a lot of my early drawings of aircraft and Hallowe'en, so art class was a haven of great excitement and anticipation.

The prospect that gave me the most pleasure was looking north towards the upper school, across the wonderful piece of green field and the beautiful rows of tall elm trees. I remember when I played hockey in the winter on the makeshift outdoor natural ice rinks, there was a sense of physical distance and freedom from the prep itself. When you crossed the main avenue past the headmaster's, Dick Howard's, home, you got away from the school, which was a great relief.

After three years in the prep, I left and went to school in London, England, for three years because my father took over the chairmanship of the *London Times*, the newspaper that my grandfather had purchased from the Astor family. The organization also owned other newspapers, book publishing companies, and information businesses.

When I left Upper Canada, I felt there had to be a system that was somehow more conducive to the growth of the spirit, something inspiring beyond the literal, rational process of learning and study. England was a completely different world. Things were never the same again. I still came to school with a chauffeur, but it was accepted. It did not at all impinge upon me as a person.

Unfortunately, I had deficiencies. I could not play soccer well so I had to play with children two or three forms lower. So I worked hard every night and every weekend, back and forth, left foot, right foot. Over time, it fostered in me a tremendous work ethic and I came to play for the school and play for my house. I was working towards a goal, exceeding my own expectations and having people realize that my capability was of my own making, not a social inheritance.

I was ten when I left the prep. When I came back to the upper school at age thirteen, the same children were now young men. We cohabited, again, in classrooms and on soccer teams, but again, I had very little to do with them. In the upper school, I found the physical property and amenities to be marvellous and there was a great variety of characters. There were the conventional, staid, dull academics who taught the A forms, who were almost ritual in their movements among their groups of colleagues and friends. Then there were the peripheral madmen who had very little respect for the system, the controls, and the whole pattern of protocol which seemed to pervade our lives.

When I came back from England, I really could play soccer fairly well. I remember playing with my form at recess and a master said to me, "You should really try out for one of the school teams." But I knew that when you played on a school team, you took long bus journeys and you lost your Saturday. The girls from BSS would turn up and watch you like a physical exhibit. Your craft was almost incidental. So I played for Martland's in the house leagues.

I was really small because I did not really grow until Grade 9. But the larger fellows in Grade 13 on Martland's gave me some protection, particularly against the boardinghouses. I used to get three or four goals, which was wonderful. We went to the finals against one of the boardinghouses, who were always the strongest house teams because they practised and used tactics of intimidation. I thought when I was in Grade 13, I would like to do the same thing and lead the younger and smaller chaps who were in Grade 9 or 10. One is a little reluctant to dash down a wing when a Grade 13 boy from Wedd's is about to take your feet from underneath you or bash you in the head.

House leagues were so much more interesting than playing for a school team and losing your Saturday and feeling terribly uncomfortable in front of all sorts of people. I also played for a while in a summer soccer league against some of the Catholic schools like St. Michael's and De La Salle, but it was uncomfortable listening to the defencemen covered in black body hair calling you a WASP in Italian accents. That was no fun. But in the UCC house leagues, it was great to see the pride that forms with colleagues, peers and youthful fellows, that have been chased out of the locker room by the housemasters.

I have to say that I felt that Patrick Johnson was a very fine principal. I really thought he was fair and greatly in touch with the boys of the school and the parents. He made very fine addresses and he had a marvellous, wry sense of humour. I certainly admired his poise, integrity, and approachability. But I must say that I was terribly isolated. I cycled to school, parked at the far end, and locked up my bike. I spent my time reading books in the library or in the art room. I really had very little to do with the mainstream because I was not a real sportsman.

The prep certainly shaped an awful lot of my character. I lived, for so many years, feeling a sense of helplessness. Now I am extremely self-sufficient and rather overly aggressive. I'm not mean, but I do not hide any more from anyone. In fact, I seek out places where I can go straight on in situations with people. I love it. In fact, it is almost sick, to the point where it has driven a lot of my learning. Probably I was driven too hard. You accepted the challenges and you won the game, but you lost so much in the process. The process itself was gone. There was no enchantment.

I feel that the sad legacy of the school is that it focuses people in the completely wrong areas of life. The rigidity and authoritarianism of the environment should have been loosened somewhat, not completely erased, but blended with a looser culture. Individuals should have been encouraged to blossom. Instead, there was almost a formula that was applied. Basic areas were seen to be important. They spent all our money to build a hockey arena and no one used it.

To me, that quality was systemic in the school. When it came to raising funds, they would always be writing to my father. They would be terribly critical when my family did not give any money. They'd say, "This is not right. How can this be? You have enjoyed your time at UCC. We just assume that you have. We have given you so much. Now is your time to give it back." Yet, there were no customer advisory boards. No one understood the competitors' product. No one even understood their own product. UCC was terribly isolated in their own skewed idea of what they had given everyone.

Walter Annenberg, the American billionaire who published *TV Guide*, recently gave millions of dollars to his old prep school. But there is a point at which you can destroy the very organization you're trying to promote with too much money. You might as well just blow it up. There is a lot to be said for directing amounts of money that are commensurate with the metabolism of the organization and the abilities or the vision of the people running it. You really have to be terribly, terribly sensitive to situations.

I have encountered such odd behaviour from many ex-UCC chaps. I went to a dinner party once with my wife and a UCC old boy proceeded to tell me how much of a miser my father was and how he symbolized all that was really bad in old boys. He thought it was a great embarrassment that someone with so much gave so little.

My wife had to hold me back because he was an older man in his sixties. I thought, It is precisely because of people like yourself that we have very little to do with Upper Canada. There is always something that people want, and I have not figured out why. There is an expectation that is part of one's psychic inheritance which says, "You have made a pledge. You now are a secret member of a secret order. You owe society."

I was never part of the UCC brotherhood. I kept to myself. I had very few friends in school. Even today, I know a few people, but I do not go to any of the reunions. I should not be, but I am, somewhat suspicious of the motives of the various people. Even at seven years old, I was judging people's every action and response. In the prep, when my father gave me a pennant, I turned around to a boy and said, "I suppose you are jealous now?" He did not know what to say.

David Rae, Bob Rae's brother, was a fine fellow who I knew at UCC. It was really very sad when he died of leukemia at only age thirty or thirty-one. I was running Simpsons at the time. He worked for GE Capital and we tried to meet several times for lunch, but he kept on having to go back to the hospital for his chemotherapy treatments. I remember going to see him in hospital. No one was there so I just left a letter on his bed.

I suppose I was not really terribly close to him. I knew some chaps at UCC but we were not terribly close. But after UCC, I kept touch with David Rae through other people and I was really quite impressed with how he seized opportunities that presented themselves. He would go down to New York and work through the system. I admired what he made for himself.

I suppose the lessons I learned at UCC are very much like the lessons I have learned in business. I think the greatest lessons in life are not necessarily the passages of time that you derive the greatest pleasure from, but the passages that are very difficult, when you feel awkward and out of sorts. But it enables you to isolate yourself. It affords you the time to reflect and to decide upon goals of your own. I often felt that a lot of my contemporaries at UCC had a lot of pressure on them to get good marks. They were asking, "What will my father say?" I still remember a colleague telling me about how a father ran out to home plate during a baseball game and started to beat his child for striking out.

I think that one of the difficulties in an environment like UCC is that it is very hard to be frank, honest and open. People were hiding so many things. There were many good things about UCC, but there was a sense of unreality. So many things were done for the wrong reasons.

You frequently encounter an attitude in business where it is considered a sign of weakness to show any emotion or passion for something. If you are not a very cold, analytical, rational person who can cut the shit out of expense, you are not a true man. When you try to live a more balanced life, traditional businessmen think that you are not a real man.

But who is not the real man? You are telling me? You have not taken a weekend with your wife, you have no spare time that you use constructively, you do not have any hobbies. You do not know how to spell Mozart and here you are telling me that I am weak? It is pathetic. You cannot get upset at these people. You just feel horrible. The reality is the opposite. The reality is not about control but about feeling and about passion. Without it, you will not build up your businesses or your people and you will never understand your customer or your marketplace.

The same was true of UCC. There was never a humility, openness, or frankness in coming to terms with reality as it constantly changes. You are fixated in a culture that is trapped in a time warp. It is a very debilitating thing for young people to be trapped in that kind of world during their formative years.

I always ask businessmen I work with about their greatest regret. They tell me about a marketing tragedy or that they did not buy a company at a certain point. Then some would say, "At the basic human level, I completely missed the early years of my family. Did I have a choice? I did not, but I did. For the quality of time that I spent, I could have accelerated my learning curve. I could have driven harder." I saw that very early on with my grandfather. I saw, later in his life, that he was a lonely man despite his accomplishments. He had his grandchildren, but they were not close to him.

I said to myself that in my lifetime I would be a success, but on my own terms, not Upper Canada's terms or my grandfather's terms or anyone else's. Probably, I would be more successful because my own values and goals are a lot higher and I valued myself. But I would never, ever place all of the material things that I had as a priority.

My own father has been a wonderful father to me. Whenever I have driven towards an objective, he has wanted me to do my utmost. My grandfather was the same way. His advice to me was, "David, whatever area that you enter and drive towards your goal, you just have to try to be the best. Whatever you accomplish, just do that." My grandfather put his hand out. I shook his hand and I said, "I will. I absolutely will, and I will do it on a balanced and reasonable basis too. When I have to fight, I will." You do not have to have great brawn and muscle. You just have to have tremendous will and determination, and just be absolutely emphatic.

When you [James FitzGerald] wrote me your letter about this book, I was fascinated. I realized what you were doing. There have been official histories that just recount events rather than getting to the guts of the experience and having people open up about things that have been subconscious and undisturbed. You troll under the surface and you find that although there are some marvellous passages, there are also some tremendous lost initiatives and directions. Even if only one person reads this book and is able to influence change, it will be a great achievement.

JEAN-GUY BRUNELLE

1968-75

Banker

WHEN I was in the prep, I used to take my $1.50 allowance and go to the tuck shop and spend it on a box of junk food. I wouldn't eat any of it. I'd bring it back to the boardinghouse TV room and sell it to the boys for twice the price. I would take that money and buy and sell more junk. Now I had enough money to buy a pizza. I needed capital to buy a pizza.

On Sunday night, I would buy a pizza and sell the slices. I'd start the week with more money than my $1.50 allowance. I did that many, many weekends. When I went home, I'd buy a case of pop at Loblaws for next to nothing, better than the UCC tuck shop. I would take it back to UCC and sell it. I used to do that a lot.

Ever since I first played Monopoly when I was five years old, I wanted to go into business. Maybe that's one of the things I liked about UCC. As I started learning about the history and the people there, I learned there was business involved. But even before that, I always knew I wasn't going to law school, med school, or engineering. I was going to be in business.

I'll never forget the first day of my Grade 10 year. In Grade 10, you are still on the new-boy floor in boarding with the Grade 9s. The Grade 10s knew the routine. You get there early, grab the better bed, grab the better dresser, get into the study hall first, and grab the desk you want. Of course, I had figured this out quickly. Upper Canada taught me how to work systems really well.

John Symons, an Englishman and our senior housemaster, walked into the study hall to make his speech to try to put the fear of God into the new boys. I was doing what I normally did when he was speaking, which was not paying attention. I was staring out at the tennis courts. I had strategically placed my desk in front of the window, so I could ponder the goings-on outside. Symons said, "Take Mr. Brunelle over there, for example. We have a mutual understanding. He hates my guts and I hate his. As far as I'm concerned, he can go stick his head in the mud and leave it there."

That sums up the relationship that I had with John Symons for my five years in the upper school. I did everything possible to avoid him, yet I wasn't going to avoid him at all costs. I would be double gated every Saturday, all through Grade 10 and 11. Symons just rode me. For five years, we hated each other. I don't think anything would have made him happier than if I were to quit or convert. He would gate me for having round-toed shoes, if my hair was too long, if I looked at him the wrong way. It just didn't matter. He never instilled in me a reason to change, so why change?

Symons kept threatening to take me to see Pat Johnson, the principal. I kept saying, "Okay, let's go." Pat Johnson and I got along well. We still do. People kept asking me, "How do you put up with all of this crap from Symons?" The rest of the school was great. I got along famously with the rest of the masters.

It got to the point that on Fridays it was a bit of a joke, because I'd routinely come back from breakfast to get a gating assignment from Symons. I'd go see Nobby Noble and he'd say, "Okay, what's your homework for the weekend?" I'd say, "Latin." So he'd make my gating assignment Latin instead of something punitive or non-productive. I was double gated every Saturday, but I'd get my homework done in the process, because Nobby would always give me my homework as a gating assignment. Of course, nobody knew that except Nobby and I. So it worked out well.

To my knowledge, I was the last student at UCC to be caned. I was caned by John Symons on the last day of school in June 1972. I had no exams that day. I only had one exam left for the year, which was my French exam the next day. Being French Canadian, I wasn't paying too much attention to it, so I took the day off.

I had a lot of friends I wanted to say goodbye to before taking the train home to Montreal the next day. I thought it would be a good day to screw off and see everybody, which I did. I got back to the school about 8:30 that night. I had missed a couple of meals and the roll call, but I thought because it was the end of the year, they couldn't gate me.

Predictably, Symons went crazy. He hauled me into his study and yelled and screamed at me. He pulled his cane out of the corner, which was surprising because I had never seen it. He yelled, "Bend over!" I said, "No!" He was screaming and waving the cane in the air. I think it was hickory. Again, he yelled, "Bend over!" So I bent over and he came down hard with it. I put my arm back to deflect the blows. He whacked me again.

I was getting a little mad at this point. The third time, I half turned around and somehow grabbed the cane away from him. I said to him, "Here, do you want this?" I offered it back to him. He just stood there. He was much bigger than me. I was in Grade 10. Then he yelled, "Get the hell out of here!" I challenged him all along. My attitude was: Go ahead and gate me. I don't care. I'm still going to do what I want.

I got along beautifully with Louis Paichoux, a Frenchman who was the housemaster of the other boardinghouse, Seaton's House. Louis and I were buddies. I used to take weekend leave from Wedd's and sleep at Seaton's. Of course, nobody knew. I had a brother in Seaton's. I can't remember if the issue ever came up of being transferred to Seaton's. Obviously it would have been a lot better for me being under Paichoux than Symons. Part of me would have said that I had given in. Also, I got attached to the guys in Wedd's. It's not only a slap against Symons, it's a slap against your buddies in Wedd's.

Louis Paichoux was French and the French attitude towards life is very different from the British. We just don't take life in the same way or at the same speed as English Canadians. I remember when my younger brother went out with a friend of his from Forest Hill. The kid's parents had gone, so they raided the liquor cabinet. My brother was only eight or nine years old. Apparently, they found him drunk in a ditch.

The school's attitude was: What's the worst punishment we could possibly give these two children? In the prep, Mr. Hearn thought the worst possible punishment was to make the boys phone their parents and tell them they'd been drinking. Marc, who is the only one of my four brothers not to have graduated from Upper Canada – he flunked Grade 12 and went into Grade 13 at TCS – couldn't believe it.

He said, "All I have to do is call my father and tell him I've been drinking?" We'd been drinking wine with meals for years. My father laughed when Marc called. He said the fatherly thing – "You shouldn't do that" – but he was laughing his head off. The whole thing was hugely ironic because we had seen a number of masters drunk from time to time.

At that age, you are just finding out about things. You begin to realize, yeah, the parts don't all fit. I knew that one of our housemasters was a drunk. I spent a lot of time at Yonge and St. Clair – you are either there or in Forest Hill Village – and I'd see him walking back to the prep boardinghouse with his brown bag from the liquor store.

Being French, I maybe viewed it a little differently. Drinking to us is not an issue. To me, if somebody drinks, so what? I was used to my father coming back and helping him unload the booze into the house. I had seen people who had gotten drunk, but a person who was a drunk was not something that I had been used to seeing.

We created the "Rat Pack" in Wedd's, which really pissed Symons off, but it made life a lot more bearable for us. We were allowed to smoke in master's residences. We used Mike "Pooh Bear" Miller's living room like it was our club house. We would walk in there when we wanted to and put pop in the fridge. We had a colour TV and we pitched in and bought cable. We paid the first month but Pooh Bear had to pay for it after that.

It was like our own room. There were about twelve of us, along with most of the seniors from Grade 12 and 13. We printed "The Rat Pack" on our ball hockey team sweaters. The Rat Pack and Pooh Bear's residence room made life in Grade 12 and 13 much, much easier. It used to just piss Symons off. He'd walk into the room and see us all there eating pizza, watching TV, and doing all the things that he didn't want us to be doing.

If there was a tie hanging on the doorknob, that was a signal that Pooh Bear had a date with a woman and we were not allowed to use his room. The guys who would smuggle in the girls were not the guys you would suspect. I remember Munson McKinnie, who was in the Rat Pack, was a quiet type. He's a close friend of mine now. He told me he smuggled his girlfriend into his room one night. Here I was breaking all the rules, and here was a rule I just never thought of breaking. I never dated a girl long-term at Upper Canada, but I had dates almost every weekend. I was always out with girls, but I didn't bring them into the rooms.

I was involved with Interact, a worldwide volunteer organization like a junior Rotary Club. We would work at different places around the city, like Bloorview Children's Hospital and the Crippled Children's Centre. I used to take kids swimming up there once a week. We brought BSS girls into our group. We had one of the bigger Interact groups in the world actually. It was a valuable experience.

But I'll be honest. One of the reasons I got into it was because Interact was off campus and I'd grab any excuse to get away from the school. The second reason was to meet BSS girls. But it was fun doing some of these projects. I had a lot of memorable experiences with the crippled kids. I probably didn't go into it for all the right reasons, but I continued for the right reasons for two or three years.

If you make anything mandatory, then you get people like me reacting against it. For example, in Grade 13, I never went to battalion the whole year. I got away with it. Like I said, I had a lot of friends. I got along well with the staff and a lot of the students. My sergeant was Gary Davis, an ex-officio member of the Rat Pack because he was in Seaton's House.

So I said, "Gary, I don't want to go to battalion. This sucks." I purposely flunked my battalion exams in Grade 10 to make sure that they could never consider me for sergeant. So we worked out a deal that when he called out roll call, he wouldn't call out my name. It worked beautifully up until the annual full-dress battalion inspection.

Frank Brennan, the master in charge of the battalion, happened to be looking over Gary's shoulder during the inspection. Gary came down to my name and he didn't know whether he should call it out or not call it out. Obviously if he called it, no one was going to answer. Brennan was looking at him. Gary thought, Maybe he's just staring into space.

So he didn't call my name. I was sitting there, watching battalion inspection, talking to other masters. Nobody ever asked me, "How come you are not in battalion?" I would normally leave the grounds and go do some other stuff. So I never went to battalion once in Grade 13. The whole thing was disbanded at the end of the year.

Sometimes I would get called "frog" at Upper Canada, but I could tell if it was in jest or not. It hurt more when it was meant to hurt. But it still hurt a little. You're at an age when you don't really want to be different. That may have had an influence on me. I know when I was in Grade 12 and 13, I was very different. I liked being different. At parties, everybody was smoking drugs, but I'd go with a twelve-pack of beer.

There were a lot of drugs. The drugs I saw were marijuana, hash, and hash oil, although in residence you don't see the stuff much. It's a lot easier for high school students living at home to wander around and do drugs. It got to be the thing that if there was a party, everyone would be smoking pot and I'd be drinking beer. It was my way of being different, plus I did have a thing about the law. You push the system only so far. I could have got tossed out of the school and I didn't want that.

I was too small to fight. I was always a better talker than a fighter. Today, in my job, I spend half my day negotiating. So I never fought. In fact, I assimilated into UCC very well. There were no religious problems. People were jealous because the Catholics got to go to a different church, so the masters never went. Of course, none of the Catholics ever went to church. We'd go to Forest Hill Village, have coffee and a danish, and come back an hour later.

As I say, I learned to play the system at UCC. I remember doing a book report for Terry Bredin. My friends kept asking, "How are you going to do it? You haven't read the book." I said, "I'll figure it out." So we get into the class and Bredin hands out the paper. Bredin knows me to be a terrible student who does just enough work to get by. My motto was "Never work, but never fail a course." So I sat there thinking, I've got to make like I'm writing. I started writing some story. My friends were looking at me as I'm writing like crazy and getting into this story. They're wondering, What is he writing? He hasn't read the book.

I got an idea halfway through. Terry Bredin was looking at me and thinking, What's Brunelle writing? He probably hasn't read the book. Every time he'd come by, I'd lean over so he couldn't see what I was writing. But he saw that I was writing something. When the bell rang, everybody got up and handed in their papers. I took mine, tore it up, threw it into the garbage, and walked out. He never saw me do it. He thought I had handed it in. Two weeks later, I said, "Mr. Bredin, what about those in-class exams we wrote?" He said, "I can't seem to find yours." I said, "But I was there. You saw me."

At Upper Canada there was a way to break the rules and yet not upset the apple cart. You see a lot of that in business and in life. There are things you just don't do and there are things you can get away with. You have a certain control, but don't push it too far. So you say, "How do I get what I want?" You've got to go out to left field, wander around, think about it, and say, "Hey, it looks different from out here."

For the past five years, I was the head firefighter for Banque Nationale in Montreal. Now I've taken on a new job as vice-president of syndication and financial advisory services, which takes about 10 per cent of my time. The rest of my time is spent as an in-house consultant. I'm either hired by a division of the bank to do something for them or outside companies will hire me to help them.

I am the bank's representative dealing with any major problems. For example, I did all the negotiations after the problems with Olympia and York erupted. I did Campeau. I've done Red Carpet. I had to do that deal. The big problem loans or the big problems that the bank has, I'm the guy who has been putting out the fires.

UCC was a real challenge and we had a lot of fun. All in all, my years there taught me that you can't fight the system or change it overnight. But you don't necessarily have to accept everything at face value either. You just have to learn to play different games with the different people.

PART
IV

PETER DALGLISH

1969–75

Founder and executive director
Street Kids International

S OMEONE recently asked me, "Why would you, as a lawyer and someone with other career options, end up working with raga-muffins in the street?" I trace it back to Upper Canada College, and Taylor Statten Camps which had strong UCC connections, where I had my first leadership experiences. We had the benefit of extraordinary teachers at UCC. Robertson Davies once wrote that the advantage of private schools is that they can keep a few cultural eccentrics on staff who don't have to answer to the authorities. I'm sure he was thinking of Upper Canada.

I came to UCC from a conservative Catholic choir school in London, Ontario. My father started one of the first Volkswagen dealerships in Canada. For me, UCC was an exotic place. The school had the *Globe and Mail* delivered to the boardinghouse every morning before breakfast at 8:00 A.M. I distinctly remember Grade 7 boys fighting over the Report on Business section. That's when I realized this was a different kind of school.

As a boarder, the school was your home. In the fall and in the spring, I loved walking up the avenue and experiencing the incredible canopy effect of the magnificent row of elms. I loved having the use of the facilities. Every night in the winter, we used to skate at the artificial ice rinks and come back and have hot chocolate. I used to love to jog around the school every morning. It was all part of the ritual, part of the mystique.

We did things that were quite innovative. In 1969 we had a whole pollu-tion week organized by the chemistry teacher. I remember marching to city hall in protest of pollution, wearing a gas mask at the age of twelve or thir-teen. We had an options program, including filmmaking. I was interested

267

in piano and we had Glenn Gould come to the school. The school was a workshop for ideas, the prep even more so than the upper school. Intellectually, it was an exciting place to be.

I remember being told in Grade 7 that the reason we had to work so hard was because we were going to be holding positions of responsibility in society one day. I remember being told many times that we were the future leaders. I know that approach works. If you tell kids enough times that they're going to be leaders, they will be. If you tell them enough times that they're pieces of shit, they will be.

The debating, theatre, and community service programs at UCC had a huge impact on my life. I must have been volunteering ten hours a week, maybe more. I had a burgeoning social conscience. I also had a sense that the purpose of education was primarily empowerment, that you acquire a technical skill that you can use to change the world. From early on at Upper Canada, I knew that I wanted to use my education to change the world.

For some boys, UCC is an extraordinary experience which helps to engender natural leadership abilities. Others can be severely damaged. There was a significant amount of physical abuse of the boarders. One master, a German guy who used to read us the *Communist Manifesto*, used to hit us with his cricket bat. It would really hurt. In tears, we had to sign the cricket bat, which was highly bizarre. I don't know why we had to do that. He was hard. He used to beat us regularly.

There was a lot of that in the prep. I was a good kid, but I got beaten at least once every two weeks. Some kids were beaten pretty regularly, for minor things like not having your shoes shined properly, coming back from leave late, or not having the proper leave. Those were the days when boarders needed leave to go anywhere. You had to wear a jacket and tie, even to go to Forest Hill Village or down to St. Clair Avenue.

The youngest kid in the dorm was only eight or so. Some kids had clearly been dumped by their parents. I remember one kid barely recognized his parents when they came to pick him up at Christmas. A lot of these kids essentially had been abandoned. I was one of those people who'd break up fights and look after younger kids. I had a pack of kids around me all the time.

Some of the teachers were real bastards who singled out kids and basically destroyed them. Of the kids in that dorm in 1969, I know of at least two who have committed suicide. One guy from Chicago, who was quite brilliant, went all the way through the prep and upper school. He blew his head off with a pistol. There is a veneer that these kids come from nice, affluent families where everything is going fine. In reality, a lot of them are from seriously dysfunctional families. In a society based on consumerism and materialism, parenting skills aren't something people have a lot of time to invest in.

There wasn't a lot of supervision in the prep. Many of the masters lived lives of quiet desperation. One of them was drunk a lot of the time. We used to spy around the corner and see him coming up from Yonge and St. Clair from the liquor store on Fridays. He had LCBO stock in a grocery bag and he'd put some vegetables on top to cover up the booze. Of course, he never cooked because he was a bachelor and didn't have a kitchen. We always listened for the clanging of the bottles. You had to be particularly careful on Friday nights, because that was the night he'd usually get sloshed and be more apt to hit us.

I was first soloist in the chorus with a boy named Booth, who later died of AIDS. Booth and I were expected to preserve our voices for the annual carol service, which was on Sunday, December 6, 1969, my first term at the prep. I was twelve. I remember walking up to the prayer hall behind a master. It was snowing and he was carrying an umbrella, which struck me as an English, not a Canadian, thing to do. He was walking in a rather odd way. I knew something was wrong.

The master was a reserved man who did not like making speeches. He had very few social skills and not a lot of confidence. He was a good classroom teacher, but he never should have been entrusted with the care of fifty or sixty crazy little boys in a boardinghouse. He was a lonely bachelor, not good with women at all, who wanted to be left alone to read his books and smoke his pipe. Instead he was stuck with us, and we weren't angels.

At the carol service, they had a series of different readers. First a prep kid reads, then a prep master reads. I remember the upper school principal, Pat Johnson, announcing in his very British way, "A master from the preparatory school." The master got up and walked down the aisle. As he went up the stairs to the stage, people realized something was awfully wrong. He couldn't climb more than the second or third stair. He collapsed and fell into the orchestra, right on top of the musicians. Suddenly the nurse, Miss Barrow, came running down the aisle saying, "The poor man fainted!" I remember her words. I remember saying to the kid next to me, "He didn't faint. He's sloshed."

And he was. Imagine – all of 1969 high society was out for the carol service. A lot of non-UCC people go to that service, too. Here was a master, in front of everyone, falling down drunk. Patrick Johnson took over the reading while the master was taken out and ministered to. We never heard another word spoken about it. You would think someone would have asked, "Does this guy have a drinking problem? Is it appropriate that he have the care of fifty-five young boys?" But it was never addressed.

There are strange contradictions at UCC. In many ways it was a very progressive school. A lot of people came out of the prep filmmaking program. The people of my generation who have distinguished themselves are not the business people, the lawyers, and the Michael Wilson clones, but people like Michael MacMillan, the president of Atlantis Films, and Richard Meech, who produced the "Millennium" film series with another old boy, Michael Grant. Rob Quartly, who makes videos for "Much Music," was very involved with music and film at UCC. The actor Geraint Wyn Davies, who I boarded with, is a star at Niagara-on-the-Lake and the Stratford Festival and has his own TV show, "Forever Knight."

But in some way, the school has an inflated notion of its presence in Canadian society. I don't think it has ever succeeded in playing the kind of central role in Canadian society that both Exeter and Andover have played in the United States. Half of the leaders in America went to Exeter or Andover, which are not much larger than Upper Canada. The Andover and Exeter admissions staff fan off every spring to visit inner-city schools in the worst part of Harlem and the south side of Chicago. I know some of these "diamond" schools now myself because it's in my line of work to track them down. The admissions people sit down with the principals and say, "Who do you have for me this year?" They look at kids going into Grade 7 and offer them a full scholarship.

Upper Canada has never thought of doing anything like that. I have to fight to get inner-city kids into the UCC Computer Camp. I think a prime failing of Upper Canada and many other schools is that they still have no sense of being part of a community within the city or the country. UCC still sees itself as set apart, which is a concept from another age. The school has to change.

Eric Barton, who was the principal at UCC for only a couple of years in the late 1980s, made huge strides forward, but he met with considerable resistance from the parents and faculty. The parents were complaining that they were paying $20,000-tuition fees and he was having kids dish out food to rubbies down at the Salvation Army. There's still a lot of anger directed at Barton, who only lasted a couple of years. Once he turned off the plumbing in the school to simulate Third World conditions. Apparently at least one parent said, "I don't want my kid to go to Bangladesh, I want him to go to Harvard."

There is a lack of imagination in terms of how UCC works, based on a rather restricted idea of their natural community. The school is still very upper middle class. There are Asian kids at UCC now, but most of them are richer than the white kids because they are from the Hong Kong establishment families. The school still sees its mission as providing an adequate education to the male progeny of the Canadian elite. We haven't taken it a step further.

One of the reasons I went to Stanford University after Grade 12 was because, after six years at Upper Canada, I wanted to meet the other half of the human race. All of Seaton's House wanted me to stay on to be head of house, but I thought I'd made my contribution to the school and I didn't need all this prefect and steward shit. I knew I wanted to do something involving words and ideas and leadership, perhaps working with youth.

Stanford was a place where women and men were on equal footing. Here was a place where you were accepted as an individual and your ideas were prized. It was a much more democratic place. I did well, but I had to bust my ass. I had Jane Goodall for anthropology, Paul Ehrlich for population biology, and Ken Kesey for creative writing. It was an incredibly exciting, intellectual experience.

UCC is often called the "Eton of Canada," yet it has never produced a prime minister. Eton has produced nineteen British prime ministers. UCC tends to produce very conservative mainstream figures, usually in financial services. The vast majority of the students I know who've come out of the school have gone into the towers of Bay Street as lawyers, stockbrokers, and accountants. It surprised me that so many of the students I knew who had such creative ability ended up in such mundane professions. I think it's a tragedy.

The school is a common reference point for so many different people. For people who are mediocre it's awfully sad because it's clear that Upper Canada was the high point of their life. Their social lives centre on it even now. Many Upper Canada old boys socialize with each other. They're best men at the others' weddings and they play ball hockey and tennis together at the school. A lot of them have never left the school. Even the term *old boy* suggests this continuity. These people can be very narrow and conservative, spending their lives drinking beer, partying hard, and making a lot of money. For a lot of guys, UCC was the peak experience in their life. It's almost like hearing people talk about the war.

Old Times, the UCC alumni magazine, is a pure propaganda vehicle for the myth of the school. The people that *Old Times* appeals to represent a tiny bit of the spectrum of graduates. When I read *Old Times*, I feel that I'm excluded because it's meant for the conservative old boy in the office tower. A lot of us aren't in those offices and I'm really glad. I'm not saying that what I'm doing with kids isn't respected. I'm saying that if the magazine is indeed a banner publication of the school which goes out to the whole old-boy community, then it is perpetuating a limited reality.

In 1985 I ended up being a camel driver in the Sahara Desert. I was in charge of relief operations right on the border between Chad and the

Sudan. It was a nightmare. Everything went wrong. A lot of children died who never should have died. The trucks had virtually no medicine or food. Eventually we traded in the trucks for some camels, so I became a camel herder to help move food around. I wrote a letter about it to *Old Times*. Of course, my letter didn't get published because it put forward an unacceptable image of an old boy.

Few Upper Canada old boys have given me any money for Street Kids International. I don't really ask, but I get almost no support from the people I went to school with. Ken Thomson, an old boy, is the kind of guy who epitomizes what's wrong with the bloody Canadian Establishment. The Jewish people are much more unified in their generosity. The WASPS are so tight. Thomson, who is a billionaire, gave us exactly one hundred dollars. I sent it back.

Eventually I want to start an Upper Canada College for the street kids in Toronto. I want it to be a coeducational, non-denominational, 100 per cent scholarship school in the worst part of the city. I'm talking to David Latimer, the head of Royal St. George's School, who is very interested in the idea. I believe that inner-city kids, girls and boys, have the right to the same vision of Canada that I believe in. It all begins in education. I'd like to build on everything I learned at Upper Canada and maybe avoid some of the mistakes.

Stanley Milgram, of the University of Chicago, did a study on the power of institutions. He arbitrarily assigned two different sets of students to play the roles of either prisoners or wardens to gauge the effect of a prison environment upon inmates. They even wore uniforms. They had to actually stop the study three days into it because of the amount of violence that was breaking out. The designated wardens were beating the shit out of the designated prisoners. Previously well-behaved people had now adjusted to the role of warden. Because of the power of the rules of the institution, they were beating the shit out of the other kids who had been randomly assigned the role of prisoners.

My cousin, David Callaghan, who left UCC before graduating in the early 70s, had a similar experience. He was a brilliant guy who is now a medical doctor. He left the school because caning was so prevalent. The repressive institution turned some masters into monsters, against their better nature.

Recently I was talking with Patrick Johnson. He was talking about the terrible events at Mount Cashel in Newfoundland, where boys were sexually abused by Catholic priests. I said, "Patrick, it's not just Newfoundland. It happens everywhere. You were principal of Upper Canada College when there were some pretty bizarre things going on." I told him about the cricket bats and all the sadistic stuff. He opened up a bit and talked about the master who used to fondle little boys at the prep and the masters he had to fire in the upper school in the early 1970s.

During the Easter break of 1992, there was an incident when some UCC boys went on a cricket tour in Barbados and one of the kids was caught buying marijuana. A headline in the Barbados newspaper read something like, "Toronto schoolboy in jail for dope." A lot of vacationing Toronto families read the paper, so that's why the school was really upset.

The school invited me in to talk to the kids and advise the school on a course of action, so I spent a week with the boys. One of my recommendations was that there be a full-time counsellor on staff. If there had been someone like that at the school in the sixties and seventies, they could have prevented some of the suicides. But there's still no counselling service at the school.

It was very interesting talking to the kids about the Barbados incident. Kids are very perceptive about the hypocrisy of adults. They went to Barbados knowing that school trips have been basically an excuse for students to get stoned out of their minds. It happens all the time. They said they were much better behaved than a lot of previous school trips. They said that some of the teachers got stoned with them. They said the only reason the school was upset was because one of the kids happened to get caught. As one of the kids said, "Peter, the school isn't really concerned about our reputation. The school is worried about its reputation."

One of the reasons the school doesn't have a counsellor is because the school doesn't think of itself as a place where kids need counsellors. In fact, some of these rich kids have it worse than the poor kids I work with in Bogota, Colombia. They don't have much of their parents' time. A lot of these kids just need to be loved and there's very little love at home. One of the UCC boys told me, "My parents are totalled every night by 6:00 P.M., so why can't I have a little toot on a school trip?" There is a serious problem now with alcohol and drugs.

The mythology of UCC is more of an enemy of the school than the actual administration itself. The administration is not against the idea of having a counsellor for kids with emotional problems. They really aren't. No conspiracy exists. The current principal, Doug Blakey, is certainly not against it, and most of the faculty wouldn't be against it either. You can't really put your finger on the reasons for the inertia. I just hope a UCC boy doesn't have to kill himself before the school wakes up.

Recently the school invited me to talk to the boys about the environment. In the student parking lot, I counted six Jeep Cherokees, two BMWs, and a Jaguar. So I said to the kids, "You guys are environmentalists, right?"

They all nodded. I said, "Okay, who owns the Jeep Cherokees? Stand up. Who owns the Jaguar and the BMWs? Stand up." They'd say, "Oh, Daddy owns the car." Sixteen-year-olds were driving to school in a Jaguar!

I said, "None of you guys can call yourself an environmentalist until the student body passes a resolution saying that no kid who lives within twenty miles can drive to school. You ride a bicycle, you walk, or you take public transit." Do you think they'd pass a resolution like that? The question I have for Upper Canada College is: How do we instil values in children growing up in a world which is overwhelmingly materialistic and consumer-oriented? I think that's the true mandate of the school, which it hasn't even thought of addressing.

JOHN COLAPINTO

1972–77

Journalist

I N ONE of my first classes in Grade 9 in 1972, I remember Mr. Biggar referring to Christopher Columbus as a "wop." I don't know if it was meant to be funny or ironic. I remember feeling a kind of embarrassment. I got my own back five years later in Nigel Barber's history class, in the exact same classroom. Mr. Barber was an eccentric Brit who used to wear white Oxford cloth shirts with his bare elbow sticking out. Nigel Barber was definitely odd.

He was talking about how the British thought of Napolean as a "greasy little wop," how some people thought Napolean was Italian, not French. I couldn't believe it! It was circular, like the sled Rosebud in the film *Citizen Kane*. It was just perfect. At the beginning of UCC, I had been given the wop treatment and now, at the end, I was getting it again in the very same classroom.

As Barber repeated the word "wop" over and over with the adjective "greasy" in front of it, he triggered my memory of Mr. Biggar five years earlier. I couldn't resist. I put up my hand and said, "Sir, I just want to be sure of one thing. I understand that people thought he was a wop. But are all wops greasy? I'm of Italian descent. My grandfather sweats a bit, but I wouldn't say he was greasy."

Barber – an ironic name, given that my grandfather was an Italian barber who had a shop at the Bloor and Yonge subway station – turned scarlet. He was really embarrassed. He was fumbling around trying to explain himself. It was a little sadistic on my part, but it was probably five years of feeling like an outsider at UCC that made me grill this guy. By Grade 13, I was becoming known as someone who tweaked teachers and was a bit of a pain in the ass.

I think a lot of my personality was formed at UCC. Maybe that "wop" anecdote is indicative of something about my passage through the place. I began as someone who was frightened, nervous, shy, afraid of authority, and likely not to speak up. When I graduated, maybe I had overcompensated because I had become brash and rebellious.

In my Grade 9 year, I did what a lot of semi-miserable people did, especially in that era. I started to smoke dope very heavily. My brother Ted, who graduated from UCC three years ahead of me, and I noticed that the names of most UCC boys were always WASP names like MacDonald, MacIntosh, Fitzpatrick, Wilson, or Scott. It's not as if those were entirely alien names because my mother was Irish-Scottish, but somehow having the name Colapinto really seemed to stand out. We used to sit around smoking dope and making up bland, flat, Michael Wilson-ish WASP names. We'd try to make them as bland as possible. We'd gradually get more and more stoned and laugh our asses off. I guess in a way we had a thing about our WASP compatriots.

I was on weekly report because my marks were so bad. On weekly report, the teacher would check your homework. You had to go up and have your report signed each time. All your friends could see that you had to go up and have it signed. You would never have done your homework because you were the sort of person who had been on weekly reports or you would have failed a test. That would be written on the report and you would thus get a gating.

So at the end of week, the hall porter would come around and announce who had gatings. My friends always knew that I had the double gating because I had failed a test or not done my homework. I eventually pulled my socks up the next year because I simply could not stand to be on that humiliating weekly report any more. Public humiliation was a brilliant tactic on UCC's part.

In Grade 9, I was probably one of the few UCC guys who was getting regularly wasted. In Grades 10 and 11, I smoked with guys like Peter Mettler, who is now a filmmaker. I would make him laugh in class. He kept smoking dope for too long and eventually got caught doing it. He went on the famous school field trip led by one of the young English masters, Marshall Webb. The excursion gave new meaning to the word *trip*.

Everybody had become free and easy in some kind of rural setting outside Toronto for about a week. In a way, it was the final blossoming of that dope era at UCC. All of a sudden, everyone was overstepping their bounds. The students suddenly felt comfortable to let young Marshall Webb, who was probably all of twenty-six and an old boy himself, know that they were smoking dope.

The shit really hit the fan when they got back to UCC. Webb had seemed to tolerate it, or at least had said, "You guys really shouldn't be doing that. I'll get in trouble." They knew he knew, but everyone had the feeling that Marshall was going to be cool. This really typified Marshall's problem. As a young master in his twenties, he didn't quite know what side of the line he stood on. He was caught in a terrible middle position. He discovered that hanging with the boys was not going to be possible. The dope field trip was where Marshall Webb learned a lesson. We students did too. Webb got back and reported it, as he professionally should have. If it had gotten out any other way, he would have lost his job. When he reported it, a whole slew of students were expelled, which wiped out a whole group, Mettler included. It was a bloodbath.

By that time, I had stopped smoking dope because it started to make me feel bad. I was starting to know people at UCC, some of whom were not dope smokers, who were engaged in school life in more productive ways, which influenced me. Music became important to me. I remember in Grade 11, I saw Dave Fleury perform at the Arts Festival. He played "Tubular Bells" and got a standing ovation from the UCC boys and BSS girls in the prayer hall. I remember thinking, I want to be up there doing that. So I started playing the piano on my own, without taking any lessons. The next year, I was sort of up to speed. I auditioned in the Arts Festival, which was really exciting. In Grade 13, I closed the show. I played songs that I had written, but I also played James Taylor and Elton John songs, which helped attract the girls.

I started school in Grade 11 wearing big, outlandish Elton John glasses. If you look at the 1977 *College Times* leaving-class photos, you'll see them in all their glory. They were stolen from my friend Bob's dad's garment store. They were a pair of women's Christian Dior sunglasses with stain-glass frames and plastic lenses, which I knocked out. My mother let me put in candy blue lenses with my prescription in them. It was exciting anticipating what the teachers would make of these glasses because technically they passed the dress code. They could say things like, "Cut your hair. Don't wear shorts. Wear a school tie." But they couldn't really say, "Don't wear those weird glasses." They got a little easier with the hair thing as time went by. A lot of guys started to refuse to cut their hair.

My brother Ted had started off at UCC as a golden boy. Teachers said, "This guy is brilliant." But then he also started to fuck around. Ted became very different. He acquired John Lennon style glasses and grew his hair really long. I remember turning to look at him in prayers. His hair was like a huge pyramid down to his shoulders. I don't know how he got past the dress code. It was almost like the school realized that Ted was going through something, so they were letting him go through it. But then he started to really fuck up. His grades fell into the 50 per cent range. In his final year, he smartened up long enough to get the marks to go to university and eventually become a neurosurgeon. He now lives in the U.S., as I do.

Perhaps not making the first teams opened up another side of my brother. His artistic side was extraordinary in that he made wonderful super-8 movies that starred me and my friend Bob. At that point, I had an obsession with the film *A Clockwork Orange* because it tells the story of a wild, violent teenager who is tamed by a brainwashing technique called the "Ludovico treatment." I totally identified with the main character and saw UCC as trying to brainwash me, so we made a film, a parable of our life at UCC, inspired by *A Clockwork Orange*.

I eventually found a niche for myself at UCC in all of the available artistic pursuits. I was in Mr. Tompkins's creative writing classes, an after-school activity which we had started together. In my final two years, I just flowered. It was extraordinary. I met some great people, including Peter Dako, who is a very good musician and visual artist, and Jim Searle, who is now a clothing designer. There were a lot of guys who have gone on to do really creative things. It was an exciting time.

One of our mentors was Milt Jewell, the art teacher, who had a lasting effect on us. He brought in nude models. He started with "Fat George" and then brought in some fat women. Then, I think to be mischiveous, he brought in a couple of drop-dead gorgeous, beautifully formed young women. I think he delighted in watching horny teenage boys sweat out these classes, trying to be artistic. It was a scream. He had to cover up the windows in the doors to prevent the guys in the halls from peering in.

Milt was important to me in many ways. He always wore cowboy boots and smoked home-rolled Drum tobacco cigarettes. He looked like Jackson Pollock, a rugged, cool, hip guy with buzzed-off long hair. He was a fantastic character. He would often come in announcing he had a hangover, sit in his beanbag chair with Stevie Wonder songs blasting from his ghetto blaster, light up a cigarette and say, "Just draw amongst yourselves, boys."

I remember one time he had his boots off, smoking a cigarette, filling the room with what to Dick Sadleir, the new principal, would have smelled suspiciously like dope. Milt had Fleetwood Mac's album "Rumours" blasting really loud. All of a sudden the door opened up. It was Sadleir taking some parents on a surprise tour of the art class. It was brutal. Milt scrambled to his feet and Sadleir was absolutely covered with confusion. You could see that he just wanted to turn around and hustle the parents out. I'm sure Sadleir thought we were all having some kind of bohemian opium party.

I think it probably led to Milt leaving the school two years later. It was a pretty good gig for a visual artist, so I don't think he would have given it up voluntarily. It's a shame if he was given the axe, because he was a real artist, which was a very good thing for us UCC boys to be seeing. Art class was an amazing, fertile place which made a huge impression on all of us.

At that point, I was at my most outwardly eccentric or rebellious stage. People couldn't figure it out. My uncle Chuck is six feet six inches, and I used to wear his big rust-coloured corduroys. I'd use the school tie knotted around my waist to cinch it up. I wore funny women's glasses and my hair was rather long. In some way, I guess I was unconsciously trying to feminize myself in an all-male environment.

I was double gated pretty much every weekend. I was known more than anyone in my year to be the guy who just hated the school. I don't feel that way now. I'm sure a psychoanalyst would say it was all transference, that the school represented my father. My father, who was a doctor, ruled at home. Over the years, I went through a stage of serious headbanging to final resolution, acceptance, and mutual respect, not unlike what I went through at UCC.

At one point, Mr. Coulton, the vice-principal, thought he would get me under control during my rebellious stage. I was kicked out of the cadet battalion and put on the stretcher squad. Even that wasn't working well. I had to rebel. It wasn't like I was yelling and screaming. It always seemed impossible to take seriously the idea of older students being my sergeants. It seemed impossible to take seriously some of the intellectual mediocrities we had as teachers.

I would arrive late, often because I was exhausted, having been up late smoking dope. I was missing prayers for really no good reason. I would get the early-morning detention, which I would then miss. I would then get the afternoon detention on Friday. I wouldn't go to that, so I would get gated. I might miss the gating or commit some other infraction, and therefore get a double gating.

Thank God corporal punishment was just ending by the time I arrived at the school. When you're a teenager, I almost would have rather been beaten than have to go into that school on Saturday gatings. At that point, I hated the school so much. It was a real punishment to have to go in on Saturdays. They really had it figured out. It was brutal.

I was at UCC from 1972 to 1977. A whole wave of old-guard teachers left in 1975, when Pat Johnson, the principal, retired. Maybe that was why the school started to feel so good after 1975. The 1970s were amazingly difficult growing pains for UCC, but out of those growing pains came a great creative flowering, from which I benefitted.

Pat Johnson epitomized the terrifying Brit, who in a way was the best thing about UCC. There was something about him. You had to love the guy because he was so extreme. He was direct from central casting as the British headmaster at a boys' private school, saddled with God knows what unsavoury repressions that were forcing him to smoke sixty cigarettes a day and drink like a fish. To go for that knee-quaking, nerve-wracking inter-view with the headmaster when you are trying to get admitted as a Grade 9 student, you would be disappointed if a Canadian academic like Dick Sadleir was sitting there. Pat Johnson, with his pack of Silk Cut and his Oxford accent, was so much more appropriate.

Jim Coulton, the vice-principal, was the man you reported to during recess for your punishment. A long line of boys would snake away from Coulton's office. If I ever made a movie of UCC, I could just picture the way that hallway looked. At recess, you would join the line. You'd shuffle up and quickly smoke your cigarette. Of course, Coulton could smell the tobacco reek. We would line up in the sickly light that filtered into the cor-ridor, shuffle around with our fellow fuck-ups, waiting to go in to see Coulton.

The thing that was exquisite about Coulton was that he was so good at it. He did it so well that he never stopped seeming creepy and scary, per-sonifying raw authority. You couldn't charm him. I would go into his office and he would say, "Now, I notice that you've missed your early-morning detentions and your after-school detention as well. Colapinto, what are we going to do with you?" I'd say, "Well, sir, I don't know. I better start trying to make those detentions. I really do have to do that." He would say, "Yes, I think you do. Gated one hour."

My mother suddenly realized that I was ungovernable because I was hardly going to school any more. She tried to send a signal to the school. She finally wrote one time, "Please excuse John's absence. He says he is feel-ing unwell." Coulton picked that up immediately and phoned my mother. My mother later told me that he had chuckled about it, so he did have a sense of humour when dealing with a parent. He actually admitted to my mother that he rather liked me, which amazed me because he didn't show it. What was very odd about that place was that even Gallimore and Coulton, who had to deal with the discipline-problem boys, actually liked the boys who pushed beyond the limits.

That became something that I became aware of when the older authority figures were no longer there. When Mr. Coulton stopped being vice-principal, it made a huge difference. All of a sudden, we had Mike Adamson as the vice-principal, who was just a very witty, neat guy. He would laugh when I would come in.

One day in Grade 12, he said to me, "Look, please don't do anything too bad. I'm not going to give you any more gatings. Have fun, but don't get into too much trouble because you'll make me look bad." It was very weird. It felt like a weird kind of triumph, I felt I had broken the back of the disciplinary system. I guess I was gated so often that they were just bored with gating me. They called me John "Beat the System" Colapinto in the *College Times* in my final year.

When I say that I broke the back of the disciplinary system, obviously I didn't. But ultimately I got my own way. I finally had the vice-principal, who was in charge of handing out punishments, say to me, "I'm not going to do that to you any more. I'm going to let you just be." But he was only able to say that because he realized I was more amenable to abiding by the rules. I was working hard and participating in a lot of school activities. I wasn't miserable any more. I felt good and I liked the place.

My behaviour improved immeasurably. I started getting quite good marks and attended classes more regularly. I entered the life of the school in a big way. I remember I ended up singing in the choir for the National Ballet School. I was participating in all facets of the Arts Festival and I was doing well academically too.

I remember doing an advertisement in prayers for the Arts Festival. There were some guys who played really harsh electric guitars who worked out a really funky, crunching riff. I wore a girl's one-piece skintight bodysuit and my stupid glasses. I was going to be the lead singer. When the curtains parted, I yelled into the microphone, "Let's beat ass over this hellfire terrain." I remember yelling this throughout Laidlaw Hall as we went into a crazy jam.

After prayers, I was running to class. I was late because I had done this advertisement. Mr. Adamson stopped me and said, "Colapinto, you're a man of many talents. Be off with you." I remember hurrying away and thinking, What a great guy! He made my final years great as well.

Many aspects of my personality and creative life were shaped at UCC and later merged into my professional career. I've got to hand it to UCC. They were old pros. I even had an odd sense that they liked me for being a rebel. We were locked in some kind of battle, but they weren't hating me for it. I ended up having a tremendous amount of respect for the very men who were being so hard on me.

In the 1970s there was still massive conformity at UCC, but they were losing ground to the rebels. It was a time of real change. We really felt we were getting the upper hand on the straighter guys, who were suddenly looking ridiculous. But that's not to say that the conformity wasn't pervasive. I remember one master, Boog Powell, locked his class in his classroom one day. He was walking up and down the rows with a plastic bat, hitting desks and lecturing about how UCC boys musn't conform any more. He said, "UCC is not everything. You must live!" He literally had a complete nervous breakdown in the class.

I was milling around outside in the corridors, waiting for the next class, aware that something was going on. No one was coming out. We became aware that the doors were locked. Only the very courageous people got up and left. Jeff Kofman was always ridiculed as being a wimp and a jerk, but he was one of the few guys who had the courage to stand up and say to Powell, "You're talking bullshit. I'm out of here." And he walked out. He's now a journalist with CBC-TV.

The people who came out were saying, "You wouldn't believe what's going on in there." All of a sudden, Mr. Coulton arrived to defuse the situation. I thought, I have got to stick around for this. He somehow got access to the room. The door opens and in goes Coulton. It was quiet and then we heard some murmuring voices. Five minutes later, Coulton comes out and says, "It's okay, boys. You can all go to your classes. Everything is fine."

What was hilarious is that Coulton was carrying a big toolbox full of tools and machinery. I said to my mother, "It was the weirdest thing. It was as if Boog Powell had been a robot and Coulton had taken him apart and put him in pieces into the toolbox. It was like the real Boog Powell was tied up in the basement somewhere and given the *Clockwork Orange* lobotomy treatment. A robot had been substituted." Boog was gone the next day. I don't know what happened to him.

In Grade 12, I remember, I met this amazing girl from BSS. I didn't quite understand it at the time, but her family was a connected old-Toronto family with money galore. Her parents were divorced. There was some incestuous business that had made her a highly sexualized creature. She was very sexy and precocious in only Grade 9 or 10 at BSS. She had shortened her little flannel skirt, designed to make a frustrated UCC boy go to pieces.

We met in the basement of Grace Church on-the-Hill, next door to BSS, and became boyfriend and girlfriend in a big way. I lost my virginity with her in Grade 12. She introduced me to variations on a theme. We were going for it. She was astonishingly beautiful. She looked like the French actress Isabelle Adjani, only better. She was wonderful, although also a mess, as it turned out.

We'd meet on Spadina Road waiting for the bus to school. She'd joke around and say, "I'm going to take my skirt off." She would hold it in front of her as if she was still wearing it, although anyone walking behind her would see that she was only wearing underwear. She was really an unhinged maniac, a real femme fatale. But it was very potent for me. It was like a dream come true.

I had a feeling that some of the guys at UCC had been affected in some way in their relations to women. It's not to say they were sexist, but there was a lack of ease about them, some way in which they just were not socialized properly with women. It wasn't true of all of them, but it was quite remarkably true of many of them.

I remember being very thankful that I had socialized with, learned about, and made out with girls at Forest Hill Junior High before going to UCC. I was fortunate. There were definitely boys who were damaged by having no contact with women. Personally, I valued the all-boys aspect of it. BSS was down the road. In the summers, I had had girlfriends. It worked for me. But if I was a woman looking at UCC, the place would appal me.

There were a lot of gay guys in my year. One guy, Eddie Sheng, came out to me, which was very courageous. He knew that I had girlfriends, so I don't think it was that. He just wanted to talk about it. I bummed a cigarette from him. He said, "I've got some in my room." That was his way of getting me up into the boardinghouse alone, away from everybody. We were sitting there smoking and he just started to tell me about it.

It was my first time talking to a guy who was coming out. It was one of those moments. It was almost like a great training to be a reporter. You have to be poker-faced a certain amount of the time. You could be sitting with a criminal, a drug addict, a maniac, or someone you just think fatuous, and you can't reveal what you're feeling. I remember freaking a little bit, but getting through it. I was able to be his friend in a kind of nice way.

That was another good thing about UCC, how the jockishness was delightfully undermined by the gay subculture. Jim Searle, one of my best buddies, eventually came out. We probably became friends because I must have recognized that he didn't have any of what you stereotypically think of as that UCC maleness about him. I didn't know he was gay at the time, I just thought he was a gentle guy. All of a sudden, it was clear that there were gay people there. Eddie Sheng said, "There are others, and some of them are teachers." I was rebelling against the patriarchy, both at home and at UCC, so it was good to realize that there was another reality. It made UCC a more congenial place.

EDWARD SHENG

1973–77

Architect

B EING GAY was a bit of a problem at UCC, especially in boarding. I arrived in Grade 10 on a scholarship. People used to taunt me and make fun of me. I never really denied the fact I am gay. On the other hand, I didn't think I was so obvious. You had to live with these people in the same house. I got it mostly from other boarders. They called me "fag" or something like that. I wasn't very good at sports.

I came out outside of the school. I met gay people through the local community. I made some friends and I usually spent weekends hanging around these people. Actually, because I boarded, I had a lot more freedom than I would have had if I been living at home. How much leave you got depended on good behaviour and marks. If somebody was acting up, then they would be restricted to the school grounds for the whole weekend.

Since my marks were pretty good, Mr. Paichoux, the housemaster, was fairly generous with me. I used to take overnight leave, usually every weekend. That's something that probably never would have happened if I lived at home. The first time I had overnight leave, he didn't know where I was or who my friends were, so he asked for a phone number where I could be contacted in case anything happened.

After the first few times, he never asked any questions. I would just stay with a group of friends who lived together in a house. I usually hung out with them. Then I met somebody from UCC in Grade 11, so I used to stay over at his place. People obviously knew, because somebody put up a poster on a bulletin board showing two pairs of feet, one person on top of another, one pair of feet facing the wrong way. Somebody wrote my name with a bubble to one pair and my friend's name with a bubble to the other pair.

I used to borrow books from the library by homosexual authors like E. M. Forster and Jean Genet. Sometimes on the covers there might be a little blurb where homosexual words might appear. I didn't hide the fact that I was gay, but I didn't broadcast it either. People pick out mannerisms or physical traits that gay people have. Even if I have them, I didn't try to change them. It was extremely irritating and I got angry when people made fun of me, but it never got to where I'd get really upset and cry.

One time Marshall Webb, an English master, was going to read out one of my stories to the class. I wrote a one-page prose piece about lying in bed, drifting off to sleep and starting to dream. It was clear from what I had written that the person I was lying in bed with was a man. Marshall asked me if he could read it out in class. He thought it was well written. Of course I said no because everybody would have known what I was writing about.

In Grade 12 or 13, I had a sexual encounter with one of the closeted masters who lived on campus. It happened on campus on a weekend. It was an okay experience. I think it was a mutual feeling between us. I was in some of his classes and I liked him. We had a basis to our relationship, a friendship outside class, so the sex was based on that. After the fact, I asked him why he had approached me. He said it was because he thought I would have been discreet. Obviously, to do something like that with the wrong person would mean the end of your career. The weird part is that he was one of the teachers who was really in the closet. I don't think he had any experience with men, or very limited. I felt more sexually experienced than he was.

When you hear about boys and masters sleeping together, people don't always take into account what each person feels. A lot of times, it is the younger person who initiates it. In my case, we both knew what we were doing. There was mutual consent. We weren't using each other. I told my best friend about it, but nobody else at the school knew. My best friend was really freaked out. I didn't really think about the consequences.

One time, the ucc boy that I was having a relationship with went to get a vd test. He must have had asymptomatic gonorrhea, so he suggested that I go and get tested too, which I did. He was all upset and paranoid that in case I did have something, I would have to go to the nurse and then Miss Barrow would find out about it. He was afraid there might be a big scandal. I didn't have anything, as it turned out, so nothing came of it.

I don't remember there being any sex education at Upper Canada. It was such a set environment. But if I had lived at home, it might have been even more difficult. My parents, who live in Taiwan, still don't know I'm gay, although my brothers and sisters know. I don't think my parents would understand. Not only is there a generation gap, but there's a cultural gap.

I really had no idea which ucc boys were gay. They didn't really come out until they were in university. Just a year or two ago, I met Alan Cornwall, who was in Seaton's House. He's gay, but I didn't know it at the time. He said that he used to admire the fact that I didn't take any shit from people. I never really thought of it that way. I just tried not to let it bother me.

I guess the most horrible part about being at school was being in love with my best friend, who was straight. I told him absolutely everything. He's a loner type of person. He doesn't share things. I think that was what was the most frustrating. I opened myself up to him and he wouldn't reciprocate.

In Grade 13, I wanted to write a little clipping from a poem to have under my leaving-class picture in the *College Times*. In the poem, it just happened to have the word *gay*. When the poem was written, *gay* didn't mean homosexual. When I submitted it, the guy got all anxious and concerned. He called me down to the prefect's room and asked me why I was putting it in. He asked if I was gay or not. When I said I was, he said he wouldn't put it in.

I've had a recurring dream the last few years. I've finished my university degree at Cornell University, yet I'm going back to UCC for Grade 13. At the beginning of the semester, I look on the board for the room assignments in Seaton's House. For some reason, I've not been assigned a room. I've had that dream a lot, where I'm back at UCC and there's no room for me.

BORYS WRZESNEWSKYJ

1972–79

President, Future Bakery

I N MY FIRST WEEK in the prep, in the locker room, one of the guys called me "Bore-ass." I turned around, pushed him over a bench, shoved him into the locker, and locked it. I'd grown up at Queen and Bathurst streets in Toronto, so that seemed like a completely normal reaction to me. The whole class was stunned. I pretty quickly learned that was not the way you did things in that school. It was not Queen and Bathurst.

But every little boy has a bit of a vicious streak. In Grade 8, there was a big phase of putting thumbtacks on people's chairs. I thought it would be great if we did it to one of our teachers. I found one with a really long end on it. I stuck the tack on the English teacher's chair. As soon as I did it, I thought, Shit! Why did I do that? He came into the class, pulled his chair out, and sat down.

Nothing happened. I was thinking, My God! Either he's pretending not to feel it or he's wearing a girdle or something. After a while, he got up to write something on the blackboard. It was pretty hilarious. The tack was right in the middle, so he hadn't felt a thing.

We did all sorts of stupid things. In Grade 10, the English teacher used to antagonize us by writing his test questions on the side blackboard through glass doors. We could see through, but we couldn't see exactly what he had written. So I got the class together outside the classroom window and built a human pyramid. I got up on the top and I was writing down all the questions on the windowsill. Then all of a sudden the pyramid started to collapse and I grabbed on to the windowsill.

The teachers wondered what the hell was going on. They saw everyone running away. As I'm looking over, I could see all the teachers looking out of the teachers' common-room window. Our teacher leaned out of the window and said, "Borys, what the hell are you doing?" He came into the class and opened the window. I came in through the window. I remember I had to spend the first half of that test writing an essay on why what I had done was wrong. I had to write the test afterwards.

There were a lot of little pranks. There was a boy named Hindsmith who was a little bit on the gullible side. We passed a message around the whole class that at a certain time everyone would simultaneously stand up, turn around, and sit down again. We were always playing jokes on teachers, except this time the joke was on Hindsmith. We had passed around a second note to everyone except Hindsmith that the joke had been called off. Sure enough, when the minute hand of the clock clicked, Hindsmith gets up, turns around, and sits down, all by himself. The teacher said, "Hindsmith, get out of the class." We used to pull pranks like that a lot.

I still can remember thinking in Grade 7, Why are we studying English history and not Canadian history? I later understood it was because of the very WASPishness of the school, which still exists in some form. But by the time I graduated, a lot of the English traditions had been tempered. In the 1970s, the battalion, boxing, and caning were eliminated. There was a better understanding of the cultural makeup that Canada has taken on, although at UCC that realization took longer. Most teachers in the public school system would be more aware of it.

At the same time, there was a whole social structure built around the school. There was a feeling among a number of kids who were of non-English background that they felt a need to be WASP. It was almost as if the anglicizing process was done subtly with white gloves. The WASP culture was implicit in the curriculum, in the morning prayers, in the cricket games, in the green-hills-of-England stuff. You understood very quickly. You would see boys' parents applying to be members of the Granite Club. I remember I harrassed an Estonian guy and a Bulgarian guy when they anglicized their names. I thought there was no reason to think that the fact a guy was Bulgarian or Estonian made him any worse than anyone else.

Being of Ukrainian background, I was used to parties where everyone danced, sang, and drank. The first couple of UCC parties that I went to were very strange for me because they were so stifling. Nobody seemed to be enjoying themselves. At one party, one of the UCC teachers came in. I walked up to him, slapped him on the back and said, "Hey, how are you doing?" Everyone just stared at me. As a kid, I quickly realized that there's a strong element of aloofness and control in English culture. Being from a culture that is very colourful and warm, the coldness was something I noticed quickly. I also noticed that a lot of the guys at the school had no real understanding of what life is about. Most of them really were born with a silver spoon in their mouths and hadn't seen the rougher parts of life.

I remember feeling almost a little bit sorry for the boys at Upper Canada with their lunch bags with peanut butter and jelly sandwiches on this terrible stuff that they called bread. I'd have my Kolbasa sausage and garlicky sandwiches on a big, hefty chunk of rye. It didn't bother me whatsoever if somebody said, "What a horrible smell."

Being from a politicized Ukrainian family, I was very aware of my heritage and history. I went to Ukrainian schools on Saturdays. My knowledge of European and especially Eastern European history was always better than most of the teachers'. I was constantly correcting them. Some teachers appreciated it, others didn't.

The name calling, such as "Bore-Ass," stopped very quickly. Most kids sure wouldn't say it to my face. After all, when it came right down to it, my grades were very good. During high school, most of the time I was on the Principal's List. I ended up being one of the captains of the track team and set records in the decathlon. In terms of sports and academics, there was nothing there to really pick on. I was quite confident in myself.

UCC had a competitive environment, which I enjoyed. It didn't exist in the public school system. It was probably one of the reasons why even in Ukrainian school in Grade 2 they were going to kick me out. I was difficult to handle. Once I'd been accelerated several times, when things got more academically interesting, I was a lot more attentive in class. It might be difficult for people to admit it according to today's social mores, but the competitiveness was probably one of the healthier aspects of UCC. It prepared people for the real world, because the real world isn't always nice.

All the "correct" people were chosen to be prefects and stewards for my final year in Howard's House. I was different from the rest. My last name, Wrzesnewskyj, was very different. Throughout UCC I didn't hide the fact that I was Ukrainian. Initially, my attitude was almost like, "Yes, I live in Canada, but who I really am, the way I define myself, is Ukrainian." As I began to understand Canadian society, I started to define myself as Ukranian-Canadian. I guess certain parents expected their kids would become prefects because they had been to UCC or because their families were known in the Canadian Establishment.

Our year was the first time that prefects were elected by the students and not the masters. Being captain of the track team and doing a lot of athletics, a lot of the Grade 9 and 10 boys looked up to me and liked me a lot. I wasn't an aloof-type person, whereas some of the older boys wouldn't talk much with the younger boys. On the Monday following the voting, they announced the names of the prefects who'd been elected for all the houses except Howard's House. They said that because of some problems, Howard's House would still use the old voting system. That was quite odd. All the "right" people were ultimately chosen. Maybe they lost the ballots. But I had a sneaking suspicion that maybe, according to the school, all the wrong people were chosen by the younger students. That's what I mean about a lot of things happening with white gloves.

Other things happened of that sort. One summer, several other students and I went to Europe for a coeducational course led by one of the UCC masters. By the end of the term, everything had fallen apart on him. Nobody was paying attention. It was almost total anarchy in his class. He couldn't admit to it when he came back to UCC. Because I had absolutely no respect for him, I did everything to undermine him. I was the ringleader of it all that year.

We had a curfew, but each night we all went out on the town. Most of these boys had never been drunk before in their lives. There was a whorehouse, so we went and bothered the hookers. They were yelling at us to leave, but we kept singing at them out in the street.

One night I was talking to one of the girls in the class and she seemed pretty shook up. She said she had been molested by the UCC master. When she told a few of the other girls about it, another girl said the same thing had happened to her. Before you knew it, a whole bunch of girls said they had been molested by this teacher.

Gradually the whole course fell apart. We would arrive late at night and wouldn't bother going to classes. I would chuck mini-bombs and they'd explode. It was very embarrassing for the teacher. But everyone got very good grades, which was almost like a buyoff from the teacher. I got an excellent grade even though I did nothing.

When we came back to Toronto, the parents of one of the molested girls told the principal of UCC. Three of us got called in to tell the principal what had happened. The other two guys got scared, so they didn't say anything, but I did. I know the teacher was scared of me. I used to run laps through the school stairwells. If he saw me coming, he would literally hide.

Everything that had happened abroad was hushed up and covered up, and the master is still teaching at UCC. A number of years later, I was walking down the street with a classmate. The teacher was walking by and he was really shook up when he saw us.

But no institution is perfect. On balance, I come out with a very positive outlook on the school. UCC is one of the more valuable educational institutions in Canada, steeped in a type of rational, WASP tradition which shouldn't be dismissed out of hand. The processes of the school reflect Canadian society, although perhaps in a delayed way. The school reflects a certain type of cultural background, which I think is very valuable. At UCC I became aware of a different culture and a whole different approach to the way you go about understanding life. That's an education in itself.

ALLEN EAGLESON

1974–80

Lawyer

SOMEBODY SAID to me recently, "Did you know you're famous around UCC?" Over ten years later, I was remembered as the ringleader of a prank in my final year. On the night before our last class, we scrounged some bricks and mortar from construction sites and Canadian Tire. We had a master key to the upper school building for quite a while. We could get into any room we wanted. We had illegal access to absolutely everything in the whole school.

That night, we went downstairs and grabbed all the baseball gear in the prefects' rooms. We put towels over our heads so we couldn't be identified and dragged all the stuff into the building. We bricked up the doorway to the masters' common room from the bottom to the top. Then we wrote with spray paint "The Wall," because that's when Pink Floyd's song was out. Then the security guard caught us. We had baseball bats and stuff, so we said he could either sit down and mind his own business or we could tie him up. He decided he would sit down and mind his own business. We bragged about it the next day to our classmates, but there were no repercussions. Nobody found out that we did it.

We did some shit disturbing in a big way. I remember dropping dummies off bridges on the Sherbourne Street walkway in Rosedale. After our parents had gone to sleep, we'd sneak out and ride around town on our bikes. Initially we dropped a dummy on a rope, but the drivers were not seeing it. It was a very well made-up dummy with a wig, shoes, and clothes. Then we started dropping it onto the side of the road. It actually would fall one hundred feet or so onto Rosedale Valley Road. We always dropped it when there was a car in sight. We didn't want to hit the car, so we'd have to drop it early enough.

One time when we dropped it, it got caught in the lights as it came down. The guy smashed right into the guardrail. The car screeched to a stop. About five minutes later, there were cop cars, fire trucks, and an ambulance on the scene. Then somebody turns it over and sees it's a dummy. The cops were coming up through the ravine looking for us, so we left our bikes and ran. We ended up in the basement of an apartment building on Bloor Street, blindly trying to hide ourselves. They never found us. This little group booting around town were all UCC guys.

I was definitely a hyperactive, talkative, shit-disturber type kid. I think it was a result of trying to be overly clever and the centre of attention. I had a thing about being the centre of attention. My father started the NHL Players' Association with Bobby Orr in 1967 and in 1972 he was part of the first Canada-Russia hockey series. My last name raised people's awareness of me, because the kids knew all about Alan Eagleson.

The best thing that happened to me in Grade 8 was when John Bassett, Jr., came to school. He came to the upper school halfway through the year. His father's name was well known, so everyone started picking on him instead of me. Everyone called him "John John" in a kind of whiney voice. I thought he persevered quite well in the circumstances. It would have been tough for him. I went through what he did for the first part of the year and then he went through it for the balance of the year. Their attention was shifted away from me.

There were other people to pick on as well. One guy, who had a bad case of acne, was nicknamed "Zit." It was just like a movie of a typical

British public school. Kids can be really, really cruel to each other at that age and not aware of the damage they are inflicting. It is almost a *Lord of the Flies* scenario. Once the wedge of the group mentality opens a crack, it seeks out and attacks the weakest person.

I remember my first day at UCC. One big fat guy and one skinny, greasy guy took me into the washroom. They didn't really beat me up but they tried to scare me. I remember the scrawny guy was on the rowing team and really didn't have many friends anywhere. One of them dropped out or was kicked out and the other went through the upper school for a while. The way time reverses people's circumstances is quite interesting.

I'd give it back to the guys who picked on me, but you tend to avoid confrontation when you're one against a group. You don't do it by direct confrontation but by subterfuge. It's no good fighting five guys at once, so you take them on one by one, but underhandedly, so they don't really know you're doing anything to them. That's the way I approached it. You plant seeds in other people's minds that certain guys are losers. There was a definite suspicion that the two guys who tried to intimidate me on my first day were doing it to each other sexually in the bathroom. That was one of the major rumours in Grade 8. Whether it was true or not didn't matter. The rest of the kids in boarding were just looking for an opportunity to get back at these two bullies, and the way to do it was to call them fags.

I was always jabbering in class. I was probably kicked out of every class I was in. In Bump Bredin's Grade 10 history class, there was Alan Cornwall, Alan Cooper, and Allen Eagleson. The three of us sat back to back because we were alphabetically arranged. Alan Cooper had a funny laugh. Once I started laughing at his laugh, then Alan Cornwall would start laughing too. It would be a domino effect because we also thought Alan Cornwall's laugh was funny. So we'd be expelled in groups. I wasn't too keen on Bredin because he was a very mean and degrading teacher. If you didn't have the right answer, he would strip you down right on the spot, which in retrospect I don't think is a valuable way to teach. There were other teachers in the school who were equally effective without taking that approach.

The school was highly competitive academically. I'd always compare my marks with other people in the class. The really smart guys you'd forget about, because they were in their own world. I was in the tier below the brilliant guys academically. I had a fuller itinerary of daily activities. Rather than just books and computers, it was a little of books and lots of house sports.

Sports was fiercely competitive. The school song was called "UCC Is Supreme." That says it all. If you think of the words, it is pretty egotistical and competitive: "UCC is supreme. We'll never die. Ever by UCC, we'll lift the banner, lift the banner high." We'd scream, "U!. ... C! ... C!" afterwards in unison. The guys would come in from the first football game and do a little skit, which would conclude the pep rally.

That spirit spilled over into the house leagues. I played house soccer, house volleyball, house basketball, house everything. The competitiveness among the houses was even fiercer than UCC versus other schools. McHugh's and Scadding's Houses had distinct rivalries in those days. McHugh's won the Prefects' Cup when I was a new boy in Grade 9 and the housemaster chose me to go up and accept it. They wanted someone representing the new people coming through. In Grade 13 we won it again, so it was a nice beginning and end to my UCC career.

The house system built a terrific esprit de corps among the five grades, 9 through 13. It helps people coming in in Grade 9 to associate with a distinct group, wear a house tie, and pull together. You set an objective as a group and you try to move towards it. You don't get anywhere by tearing people down within the group. It's a positive thing. You want to build the other people up so that they perform and carry on your tradition.

It made me into a team player. As an individual, I would say I was average. Competing just for my own benefit I wasn't half the competitor I was when playing for a team of some sort. Even just at a level of playing tennis, I'd be far more effective as a doubles player because I knew somebody else was relying on me and we're moving towards the objective together. You can't screw up because you'll feel that you've let your half of the obligation down. Then you can extend that to soccer or baseball. Wherever there is a team involved, I'd perform much closer to my potential.

I had a great time. The harder I worked, the harder I played. A prime life skill I got out of UCC is time management because I tried to squeeze so much into the day. You have a house game or your classes at such and such a time. You want to get home for dinner, do your studying, go to bed, listen to music, watch TV. I'm still trying to squeeze too many things into too little time. It's a great skill to have, although it's a bit of a drawback because I don't feel happy unless I'm doing something. I don't like sitting around watching TV on a Sunday if it's sunny out. I'd rather be playing tennis or golf or swimming. Maybe it's just that I'm hyperactive.

Should UCC go coed? That's a tough one. I guess the question is, coeducational in what sense? If you admit three women, why bother? That serves nobody's best interests. If you go 50 per cent, it's a real issue to be discussed. I think UTS and Lakefield initially had a few girls, but they didn't have a lot. If UCC did it that way, it would screw up the whole balance of the school. You'd have the 80 per cent of men running after the 20 per cent of women. Your only goal when you're in high school is to get women. But it's not the distraction that would concern me, because there will always be distractions, women or otherwise. You can find women anywhere in the world. You don't have to be in school to find them.

If UCC were fifty-fifty, I would think there would be distinct benefits because I think that the UCC graduate definitely has a warped sense of what women are all about. It gives you a warped sense of reality in that you don't have to respond to somebody else's needs. I definitely had that viewpoint, but I think I grew out of it. There are other people I can think of from UCC who took a lot longer to get out of that philosophy. It's a very difficult thing to correct because it is not something you do purposefully. It just becomes ingrained in you.

Coeducation would be a definite advantage at UCC because if there are women around you day in and day out, you have to be answerable for your actions. In a male-only school, you don't have to live with your actions the next day. If you dump somebody and start going out with somebody else, you don't have to see those two people the next day. In a community, you are made to think about how to treat somebody responsibly.

I came out of UCC at age eighteen with sexist attitudes. The corollary of that is upon entering university, you get a heightened awareness of feminism. I remember being very sympathetic to the feminist movement when I was in first year at McGill. I could definitely understand what these feminists were pissed off about. They were pissed off about guys like me.

BLAKE HUTCHESON

1977–80

Real estate developer

I CAN THINK of a good example of the old-boy network in action. When the Ontario NDP budget came down in April 1991, I actually phoned Floyd Laughren, the finance minister, at home at about 11:00 P.M., the night after I watched the news of the budget. His executive assistant picked up the phone and didn't let me speak to him. I said, "This won't be the last time you hear from me."

I wanted to say, "Historically the highest annual deficit we've ever had is $3 billion and you slap a $10-billion deficit on us in the first year. The accumulated debt of the province is $34 billion. You're projecting $10

billion a year for the next three years. You are going to match what it has
taken us since Confederation to accumulate. You have no right doing that
to this province." So I organized a few rallies. My architect said, "You
should speak to so and so." So I phoned him and we had dinner. We said,
"Let's pick a date in our diary. If nobody wants to come out to a rally
against the NDP budget, we're in the wrong country. If we can get a good
response, hopefully it will have some effect."

I've never seen the old-boy system work so well. Of 110 in our leaving
class, about 50 guys were involved. It was mainly a fax campaign. It was
fantastic. I put together a one-page fax and faxed it to about 200 people,
who then in turn faxed it to 10 people minimum, but probably 20 or 30.
The word got out.

In no time, we raised about ten thousand dollars to pay for banners,
paper, stationery. We manned every Blue Jay game and every subway in the
city for three to five days. I can tell you that good comes from Upper
Canada guys. I wasn't prepared to speak because I'm building for Ontario
Hydro. But just by putting the word out, I got four people instantaneously,
including two old boys whom I didn't know, who were prepared to speak.

The rallies were covered in the newpapers, one on May 17, another on
June 24. In two weeks, just by faxing and talking to friends, we got about
5,000 people on the front steps of Queen's Park for the first rally. For the
second rally, a month later, we had a bit more time to organize, so we got
about 7,000 or 8,000 people. Then we had a bunch of follow-up meetings
with Floyd Laughren, myself, and two other guys.

Actually, a rally of elitists was not what I wanted to achieve. A picture in
the *Globe and Mail* showed a guy standing beside his Rolls-Royce with his
driver on the front steps of Queen's Park. It said, "With the NDP coming
into power, it's amazing how you create a new class of malcontent."

That experience proved to me that the system worked. I've never been in
a sales profession where I've sold my UCC friends things like life insurance,
but I'm sure for those who have businesses, there is some leverage from the
old-boy network. But clearly with that political event, I knew people who
were of like mind. I knew that they would come through, and they did.

I don't think UCC should accelerate and stress elitism, but I sure don't
think they should apologize for having a strong tradition, a great academic
background, and tons of wealthy people lining up to send their kids to the
school. You can politically correct yourself about everything. You shouldn't
wear it on your sleeve, but I don't think they should apologize. That's why I
wouldn't mind UCC staying an all boys' institution. Let it be. It's working.

If I learned anything at UCC, I learned that everybody puts their pants
on the same way. I grew up in a hick town, Huntsville, Ontario, with a

distant perception of what these people would be like, not having a lot of contact with a lot of wealthy kids. What you learn quickly is that we are all human beings and it does not matter what your last name is.

Maybe the old expression "To whom much is given, much is expected," is true. Maybe there's more of it in the Upper Canada crowd than elsewhere. There are clearly huge expectations placed on the boys. I'm not sure if conformity or expectations or family pressure is a negative thing. One of my dear friends from my class, Tom McMurtry, is a film sound editor. He's got short hair now, but for the last three or four years, he had hair down to his ass. He's from a completely establishment family. We played football together. We were interchangeable up until the time we left. I got into the politics and economics stream and he went off another way.

Our differences were so subtle prior to that. He'll probably be as successful as anybody or more so. He'll do great things because he is following his passion. In some people, their passion is lost, irrespective of their conditioning. It's what they really wanted to do. For me, real estate development was something I grew up thinking about. It's second nature.

A guy in my year, Mark Yakabuski, had strong family influence and pressures. He was a great debater in my year. He's a great character and a dear friend of mine. He's scary smart. At UCC, everybody called him "Prime Minister Yakabuski." People genuinely believed Yak could be the prime minister of Canada. I think he will be political and he will probably be a cabinet minister. He came out of school with nineties, but he has since done a lot of flip-flopping. Now he doesn't know what the hell he wants out of life.

MARK YAKABUSKI

1976–80

Government relations consultant

DURING THE MUNICIPAL ELECTION in Toronto in the fall of 1976, my first year at UCC, the candidates for alderman of Ward 8 came to the college to speak. Anne Johnston and David Smith, who later went on to be a cabinet minister in the Trudeau government, gave their speeches. As is customary at UCC when a speaker comes, there is always a short question period in Laidlaw Hall.

I was very conscious of being a small-town boy arriving for Grade 10. I had a double adjustment, coming from a town of fifteen hundred people in the Ottawa Valley, and coming into such a different sort of educational environment. But I had been politically initiated from a very young age, so I was not at all shy. My father was a Tory MLA in Queen's Park for twenty-five years.

I put up my hand. Dick Sadleir, the principal, recognized me and I got up and asked my question. John Robarts, the former premier of Ontario, had been commissioned to do a report on adjustments to the Metropolitan Toronto government. I said, "Mr. Smith, I know that you've come here as alderman, but I have to ask you what you thought of certain features in the Robarts Report." Everyone turned around because I was a new boy who had only been at the college for two or three weeks. They were thinking, Who is this kid? He asked a pretty darn good question.

David Smith waffled. He said, "The Robarts Report has to do with Metro government. I'm running for the City of Toronto." I didn't wait to put up my hand again to ask a supplementary. I said, "Now, Mr. Smith, that kind of response might go over well at city council, but I'm sorry, you said nothing about the Robarts Report. Certainly your concerns in government are a little broader than the concerns of Ward 8. You're potentially a Metro councillor yourself."

He turned red in the face. Hundreds of guys in Laidlaw Hall turned around and looked at me because, one, who was this kid, and two, how brash of him to stand back up and ask Smith a supplementary. I think people were taken by me just standing up, but I also spoke fairly eloquently. After that day, I was noticed. People would talk to me in the halls. A couple of English teachers came up to me and asked, "What is your name? Where do you come from? What has been your schooling?"

The next two or three speakers that came to Laidlaw Hall, I would put up my hand and Dick Sadleir would very purposely not recognize me. But the die had been cast. I was at UCC to do the sorts of things that I did in life, like asking penetrating and sometimes embarrassing questions. I immediately got involved in debating and became the resident gadfly. It took a while for people to get comfortable with the fact that I wasn't there to make a farce out of assembly or to attract undue attention to myself. I was earnestly interested in public debate. The people who came to Upper Canada to speak had better be interested in it too.

As time went on, I became fairly well known around the school. Speakers would make their speeches and then ask if there were questions. Everyone would turn around and look at me. In my last two or three years, I was known as Yak Yakabuski. In prayers, boys would turn around and start chanting, "Yak, Yak, Yak!" They would call on me to pose a question. Sometimes I would simply demure. I wouldn't give in because you can't be perfectly predictable. I enjoyed a little gamesmanship. You've got to have fun too.

One of the most memorable incidents was when Stephen Lewis, who had just given up the leadership of the Ontario New Democratic Party, came to UCC. Michael Cassidy, who was an old boy in the prep, had been elected the new leader. Lewis, who had a son, Avi, at the prep, was invited to speak in Laidlaw Hall. I remember him saying that he couldn't help but notice it was only after he had given up the leadership for the Ontario NDP that he was invited to speak at Upper Canada College.

The time for questions came. A few people asked questions and then, of course, people started wondering whether Yak was going to match Stephen Lewis, a well-known political figure renowned for his oratory. Everyone was turning and looking at me. I was seated near the back of Laidlaw Hall with the Martland's House boys. The chants started, "Yak! Yak! Yak!" I slowly got up from my seat. The applause was thundering.

Lewis had been going on about plans for development in Northern Ontario. I said, "Mr. Lewis, I've definitely got great interest in your plans for Northern Ontario. But I can't help noting that in the last election, the NDP didn't manage to get a seat up in Northern Ontario." I asked several other questions as well.

After prayers, I met Lewis personally in the principal's office because I was a member of the Focus Canada Committee which had invited him to the college. He said to me, "I know your father from the legislature. I see you've inherited the gift of the gab from him. I have to say that I've given many speeches in my day and been asked many questions. People have often been applauded for their questions to me, but always after they posed them. I've never been in a situation where someone is applauded before they've asked the question!"

UCC has always been perceived as a bastion of Toryism, but it's not. Far from it. It has produced NDP figures like Dan Heap and Mike Cassidy and a large number of people from various political persuasions. The Liberal clique at UCC was represented in my years by a few people in the debating society, including Larry Grafstein, Peter Singer, Tim Endicott, and Denys Calvin. In 1976, the Liberal guys were definitely the dominant ilk. They got a rude surprise when I arrived because the Tories now had a spokesperson. There are a lot of old Establishment families at Upper Canada College. I'm not of that ilk, but my father was a member of the Ontario legislature and I was an unabashed Tory. I characterize myself as a real Tory, which I think is a Red Tory.

When the Parti Québécois was elected on November 15, 1976, it was a real shock to the country. We had to face the reality that Quebec independence was no longer just a figment of some warped imagination but a real force to be dealt with. It led to what in my time was one of the happiest developments at the college. In 1977, a group of masters got together and said, "Upper Canada College was founded in 1829 to form the governing class of the province of Upper Canada. There is still something of that function that we must honour today." They formed a committee of several masters, along with an equal number of students, to better sensitize the student body to the real issues facing Canada by planning debates and seminars and bringing in speakers. Early in Grade 11, I was asked to become a member.

Much of the student body came to look upon us as an elitist clique, but I thought of it as a tremendous exercise in real collegiality. Masters were inviting students to help them design a whole program of activities focusing on Canadian issues. I constantly brought up a move to invite a more representative group of students to be part of our activities. I set up an ad hoc student representative committee, serving as a liaison between this group and the rest of the committee. For me, the Focus Canada Committee was a wonderful exercise in what I call collegiality.

By Grade 12, I had certainly been a candidate in everyone's mind for head steward, but I wasn't elected. Instead, I was appointed secretary of the board of stewards. I remember on Prize Day in Grade 12, the guest speaker was the attorney general of Ontario, Roy McMurtry, who was a colleague of my father's at Queen's Park. Roy had gone to St. Andrew's, but his brothers and son had gone to UCC, so there were connections. McMurtry is now the chief justice of Ontario. I had won more than my share of awards and my father had taken great heart. When people get awards, there is applause. I think I was genuinely quite popular around the college and Roy McMurtry pointed that out to my father.

When Prince Philip came to the college, I gave the speech inviting him to open the quadrangle named in his honour. It was the principal activity of his visit to the college. I prepared a speech of my own. My father was not able to be there because he had a public commitment in the riding, but he was immensely proud.

Grade 13 was a year when I could begin to relish some of the things I had accomplished. I noticed that I had more fulsome friendships with some of the guys. We did more partying. I now was very conscious of my role as someone capable of speaking and, in many ways, representing a large group of the college that cut across the literati, the jocks, and all the other subcommunities.

I recall vividly my English teacher, Wayne Tompkins, coming up to me after my having been announced as the winner of the Herbert Mason Medal in Grade 13. Wayne Tompkins was thought of by many of my contemporaries as a bit of an oddball, but as an English teacher I found him immensely supportive and encouraging. I did my best work for him. I think he saw something in me that other teachers did not.

I wanted to downplay winning the Herbert Mason Medal. That's why I took no heed when he said, "This is really quite an accomplishment. You've done a lot of things at this school, but, in retrospect, I think you will see the Mason Medal as one of your greatest because you've been selected, Mark, by your peers. Up until now you've had lots of accolades, but this is more a recognition of who you are as a person. That will be more lasting than some of the other forms of glory."

The Herbert Mason medallists are selected by secret ballot among the students in Grades 11, 12, and 13. Some of the criteria are "unflinching truthfulness," "cheerful submission to authority," and "independence of character," which some people might see as a contradiction. I just see it as a pretty accurate description of life. Life is filled with all kinds of contradictions and yet it's an organic whole. That's really the Tory vision of the world. There are times to wilfully submit to authority and times when you know you've got to strike out and do something different. When to make those judgements is a function of a well-formed character.

Interestingly enough, I was not the valedictorian of our leaving class. I accepted that, but there was a certain disappointment in that I was known for being as eloquent as any of the members of the leaving class. I think Dick Sadleir took it as a bit of a surprise himself. He asked me to introduce the leaving class, so I did. Mr. Sadleir introduced me by saying, "Mark has just won the Greville Smith scholarship to McGill, of which we are very pleased and proud. He is on his way to Montreal after a very illustrious career at Upper Canada College. I'd just like to tell René Lévesque – René, I think you've more than met your match!" He sent me off to Montreal with those words.

As a Catholic, what was very meaningful to me about Upper Canada was that it was consciously chosen to be a non-denominational institution when it was founded in 1829. Religion was the great cleavage of the nineteenth century. People didn't do anything if they didn't do it as an Anglican, Presbyterian, Methodist, or Catholic. To establish a school to educate the governing class of Upper Canada, and to establish it forthrightly as a non-denominational school, was revolutionary in many respects.

I would say that going to UCC only made me more sensitive to my Catholicism because it was not the school's orthodoxy. I saw it as difference, never as opposition. I think UCC very much complemented my own

Catholic spirituality. I loved choral music, which is not something which is well developed in the Catholic church. Every morning, I loved bellowing out the hymns. Everyone in Martland's House knew that we were going to sing the hymns the way they were supposed to be sung. I just loved it.

As part of ucc's sesquicentennial celebrations in 1979-80, because I was secretary of the board of stewards, I took the initiative to invite a number of people. I discussed it with the principal, Dick Sadleir. I said, "I think that we should invite Cardinal Carter, the cardinal archbishop of Toronto, to celebrate ucc's sesquicentennial year." The principal was in agreement, so I wrote to Cardinal Carter. He responded immediately saying he would be more than delighted. We fixed a certain date and then something happened so that he was not able to come.

It so happened that he was not able to come any time during my Grade 13 year. However, he wrote to me that summer saying, "I very much regret not having been able to honour our original engagement, but I'm really interested in coming to speak at the college some time soon." I relayed the message to the principal. We agreed that Cardinal Carter would come the following semester, the fall of 1980, when I was at McGill in my first year of university.

The principal asked me to come back to Upper Canada to introduce Cardinal Carter. I remember getting a letter from Mr. Sadleir saying, "His Excellency, Cardinal Carter, has agreed to speak at the college." Of course, you don't address the cardinal as "Your Excellency." It's "Your Eminence." I called Mr. Sadleir just before Cardinal Carter's arrival and said, "Cardinal Carter is a very relaxed sort of fellow. I think it should be noted that he should be addressed as 'Your Eminence.'" Later I learned that the day before Cardinal Carter came, Mr. Sadleir announced in prayers that the archbishop of Toronto, Cardinal Carter, would be coming to speak and that if you got a chance to speak to him, you should address him as "Your Eminence."

As it turned out, I introduced Cardinal Carter. He gave a masterful speech in Laidlaw Hall. In essence, he said, "ucc is a great school. You boys are imparted with tremendous gifts of scholarship and training that few others in our society will gain." He can often speak very colloquially. He said, "Guys, don't let it go to your head. You are here to go out and work for the glory of God. You have been given a great deal and more will be asked of you." He spoke with an authority that I have seldom seen matched. Frankly, I took great heart. It was a moment of great personal accomplishment that I was associated with his visit to Upper Canada.

ucc was a great place for me. They were probably the best four years of my life. I strongly believe the school should remain a single-sex school, which can open the way to more powerful forms of bonding, which are important in adolescence. The college is sound. To my knowledge, there aren't any ghastly horror stories about the place. UCC has never descended into *120 Days of Sodom*, which is what can happen when patriarchy degenerates into a climate of domination where sexual and other perversions can take root. That just isn't the way UCC is.

AVI LEWIS

1976–80

CITY-TV reporter

I WAS IN GRADE 3 at Deer Park Public School in Toronto and I was going slowly insane. The academic program just wasn't challenging or stimulating me. The principal's idea of gifted education was to give me a balsa wood rubber-band boat project. So my parents, Stephen Lewis and Michele Landsberg, reluctantly and against all of their tastes and proclivities, got me an entrance test at UCC when I was nine. The school was very kind and gave it to me in the middle of the year.

When I arrived at UCC in 1976, the prep offered me the choice of skipping one or two years. They obviously felt that I could handle it, but I'd never been in a serious learning environment. I was very green, knowing only that I had never had a peer group. I'd always felt quite alien from kids my age. I felt like an adult trapped in a kid's body, probably partly because of my home environment. Apparently, when I was three, my mother found me at our neighbour's fence with my diapers around my knees, trying to convince the neighbour to vote NDP.

I didn't have any idea of how to tie a necktie. I couldn't write. I was still printing, and very poorly. I'm left-handed with severe mixed-brain dominance. One of the explanations for left-handedness is that normally the left- and right-brain functions control the opposite sides of your body. When those messages get crossed, it's one of the theories to explain left-handedness. I think that is why lefties are lunatics and geniuses.

My dad is one of the success-without-college stories. He went to Harbord Collegiate and then he either dropped or flunked out of four different universities, emerging unscathed by a degree. It's a story he likes to tell at convocations when he is given honorary doctorates. He has a dozen of these things now, but he never legitimately earned one.

My parents' feelings about my going to Upper Canada College were mixed because, for them and for me, the school was then, as it is now, a symbol of the Canadian Establishment. UCC is a breeding ground for "the big boys to be." Socially, we had no interest at all in the UCC world. We were looking for a place where I could learn.

And I found it. I got some of the most valuable academic education in my life at UCC. I also learned a tremendous amount socially. I saw the people who run this world in their purest and most undiplomatic state of childhood and adolescence. I saw the thrustings and boastings of power in their most naked form. I saw the savage cruelty of those with power exercised against those who are defenceless. The school yard is an archetype for what people do to people when they get to the boardrooms.

I found that the people who came from the most wealth and power – the Thomsons, the Burtons, the Turners – were the most ruthless. Even at that young age, they carried with them the greatest sense of entitlement. They felt they deserved everything they got. They would be first in the natural order of things. People with power believe that everything in the world unfolds as it should. They believe that only the strong survive. The UCC environment, which they create, control, and perpetuate, is a perfect microcosm of social Darwinism.

I learned early on that the most dangerous boys were not the thugs who were actually beating me, but the quiet, reserved, and honoured star pupils who never laid a hand on anyone. The ringleaders, the guys who called the shots, never dirtied themselves with the business of enforcement. But they were responsible for more suffering than anybody else, and that's something I can see now in the world at large. They let it be known that someone was undesirable and they had boys carry out their wishes. Some boys were so desperate to receive approval and status that they would happily prove themselves by punching out, or stuffing in a garbage can, whomever was deemed undesirable.

I was doubly undesirable. First of all, I was Jewish. There's no question that there was a great degree of latent and explicit anti-Semitism, all inherited views from the breakfast table. I was also a socialist. I spent many an hour in the prep school locker rooms in heated arguments, insisting that there was a difference between socialism and communism, which they did not accept. The arbiter of those arguments was always the fist. I wouldn't call these fights, because fighting conjures up the notion of two people facing off on roughly equal terms. I was abused regularly, and by crowds.

I've never been in any atmosphere where there was more petty criminality than when I was in the embrace of the privileged class. No one's possessions were safe. It didn't matter if it was a jockstrap, textbook, a notebook, or a calculator watch. Some boys had collections of calculator watches. It was theft for the thrill of it, pure and simple, because there was no material need for it. I also saw more drug use in Grade 8 at UCC than I saw in Grade 12 at Jarvis Collegiate, which was known as a drug school. Many UCC kids had anything they wanted. They had the ready cash, so they could buy or sell high-quality drugs. I remember one kid, who was too young to drive, had his own collection of antique cars.

The homophobia was virulent, continuous and unchecked. I'm quite sure there was plenty of homosexuality going on, adding further intensity to some of the scenes of abuse. The school, in my opinion, encouraged it, particularly teachers of the "old school." For example, boys were forced to swim naked at a very vulnerable stage of their sexual development. In a group of ten- or eleven-year-olds, the boys are sexually developed to varying degrees. Some of them are real babes who don't know anything and others are already sexually active. When you throw them all together and force them to be naked, it's a scene of intense embarrassment, humiliation, and sexual pressure. I found it disgusting.

But it was enforced with military completeness and time-honoured tradition. The old phys ed teacher, Muzz Greatrex, who was almost the regimental mascot, was a nineteenth-century hangover. I remember the year they sent him away to "modernize" him. It sounded like having your plumbing refitted. It wasn't enough to try to tell him, "You know, you can't make the boys do 'eyes right' and 'stand at attention' any more." They had to send him away and have him remodelled.

I found the whole military motif in the phys ed classes quite scary. I think that the borderline between hard-core establishment capitalism and fascism is really only a difference in degree and facility of disguise. Whether they do it with all the appearance of a genteel tennis game or a naked power play is only an expression of the relative quality of their social disguise. An overt fascist simply doesn't have the necessary restraint and social facade. The military strain and tradition is an encouragement of that facade, which I have always found ominous.

The damaging effect of all-male environments cannot be overstated. I believe that almost all of the things that are wrong with the UCCs of the world could be mitigated by desegregation. Only in an all-male environment can the degree of savagery which I experienced flourish unchecked, and in fact be considered a proper and desirable way of living. The all-male microcosm is really one of the great challenges that the world has to overcome. Despite the successes that feminism has brought, everywhere in the world where you find serious injustices, men are in power. I'm not saying that women are better, but a lot of the brutality could be mitigated by feminization. Women are the key.

I was at UCC during the school's sesquicentennial celebrations in 1979–80. Prince Philip, the Duke of Edinburgh, visited the school, as he does on occasion. George Dube and I were chosen to give him the tour of the prep. Because Dube was French Canadian and I was Jewish, it was quite clear at the time that we were chosen to represent "the ethnic diversity" of the school. The token Frog and Yid represented the multicultural diversity of UCC.

I already had proper contempt for the monarchy, but I didn't refuse the assignment. I remember admiring the way Philip cultivated a professional look of interest when it was clear that he had done it a billion times and couldn't have cared less. But he was playing his part and we were playing ours. I was impressed with the skill with which he personalized things. He made a point of asking boys when they got up in the morning and how they got to school. He made a point of talking to a kid at each stop and appeared to be interested. It was a painless little ritual that unfolded as it should.

Academically, the school was an absolute flowering for me. The teachers were, with only a couple of exceptions, committed, creative, and supportive. They were joyful about learning and communicated it without barriers. It was really a revolution for me to be in a place where intellectual achievement and commitment were praised, regarded, and encouraged. Previously, my interest in learning was a problem for the teachers to handle. When I got to UCC, it was a joy for them to have someone who was so interested. With a number of teachers, I just took off.

In an English history course, an Englishman taught us the Arthurian legends. The first thing the teacher said was, "There are a lot of myths about King Arthur." Then, with a glint in his eye, he said, "Come here, I'll show you." He led us down the hall to the English room. He put on the record "Monty Python's Holy Grail," which was our introduction to Arthurian legend. What more can you possibly ask for? That's the spirit of joy and delight in history that cannot be imparted in any other way.

Another teacher, Bruce Litteljohn, was severe and strict. He reminded me of the Dr. Seuss character, the Lorax, a lumpy, environmental relic who watches the world turn into a factory around him. But he had a strength of commitment and seriousness which infused our studies. He made our trips to Norval, the school's country property, seem important and crucial.

So the only reason I put up with being stuffed in every locker, garbage can, closet, confined space, and reeking corner of the building – literally running for my life on a daily basis – was because I was just exploding with learning. I was having incredible mutual relationships of respect and intellectual seriousness with great teachers.

One of the teachers, Doug Brown, saved my life. He tried to teach me when to shut up, which was an invaluable lesson. I still haven't learned it, but I've made a lot of progress since I was nine years old. He tried to help me save my own butt by teaching me restraint, to understand what provoked people, to know where to make your stand. He said, "If you're going to take a fall for something, make sure it matters. Make sure it's not over some irrelevant or trivial issue." He taught me a really valuable lesson.

I think all the teachers were aware that I was being persecuted, but any intervention on their part would have made me even more despicable in the eyes of the crowd, and the teachers knew that. I've seen it in the CITY-TV newsroom. If the boss treats you with any kind of special attention, it can be a curse and an additional burden which you may never live down.

The teachers knew that there was only so much that they could do. In fact, one of the nastier lessons of this world that I learned was that it was only when I finally fought a boy who was dying to fight me that people stopped beating me up. I realized how disgustingly simple it was. Not fighting back branded me as a – fill in the blank – Gandhi fag. That was my burden, but I didn't realize that I'd been choosing to bear it.

I don't deny that I was an obnoxious, mouthy little shit. I was smarter, I was Jewish, I was socialist, and I was two years younger than everyone else in my class. I didn't know my place. When I felt someone was wrong, I told them so, which made me insufferable. I was completely the other, in every respect, at a place where there was absolute intolerance for any variation from a norm which is mythological and destructive in the extreme. No one person actually embodies the norm, but any deviation from it is punished, physically and psychologically. It's a strict and brutal world where the lessons of life are taught in no uncertain terms. I've always found it quite bizarre and paradoxical that such enlightened and magnificent teachers, the ones I had in the prep, could live in that kind of world.

I learned that I needed to perform that one act of macho assertion – to fight this kid – before they would finally leave me the fuck alone. By the time I realized that, and did it, I knew that I would not go to the upper school under any circumstances. The prep had been described to me as a "safe, sheltered environment." If this incredibly predatory and threatening jungle was safe compared to the upper school, I knew I wasn't going to go there.

I also started to get interested in girls, who of course didn't exist at UCC. My family and I had always been uncomfortable with the idea of segregated education. I never believed in it and they certainly don't believe in it.

Around the time I started hitting age twelve or thirteen, I was eager to go to a place where the whole human population was represented. My educational decisions were always my own. My parents gave me options, but I chose. I chose to go to UCC and I chose to leave when I did.

I went to Jarvis Collegiate. My learning more or less stopped after UCC, and resumed at university. Jarvis has a good reputation, but there's just no comparison with UCC. I didn't regret the decision to leave UCC, though, because I spent those remaining four years in high school learning about all the other things life has to offer – sex, drugs, and rock and roll, and everything else. I think I changed at the right time and I don't think I really lost any ground. By the time I got to university, I was starting to get bored and frustrated, and I was ready to do some serious learning again. The timing actually worked out quite well.

At CITY-TV, a fellow reporter, Colin Vaughn, told me the only thing he didn't like about me was that I went to a private school. The simple fact was that UCC met my needs as a gifted kid. I didn't hobnob with the elite. I'm not a champagne or silk-stocking socialist. I'm a socialist who paid his way, literally, in nose-bleeds. The fact that I went to an establishment private school is a favourite detail of *Frank* magazine and that whole journalistic crowd. Being seen as the son of Stephen Lewis and Michele Landsberg, and having gone to UCC, is a burden I'll carry to the grave, but I don't regret it for a moment. I learned a lot about the world in my three and a half years at UCC – a world which I lament, and which I will spend my life trying to change.

EVAN JENNINGS

1978–85

Student, Trent University

I MANAGED TO SURVIVE most of Upper Canada without really ever doing anything that people wanted me to do. I wasn't consciously rebelling. I just didn't do it because I was too busy doing something else that turned me on.

If you think of yourself as an outsider, Upper Canada College is great. You can just be yourself. I feel a real benefit to being an outsider, which is something I learned at Upper Canada. It's part of the whole struggle to become human. If your parents are willing to fork out the cash, you have access to as much information as you really want. You have relative freedom to spend your time as you wish. You really don't have to do the assignments. You have freedom to organize your day and show up when you want. As long as you toe the line enough, they will give you a lot of latitude.

You're also subjected to weird patriarchal conditioning, but by doing what comes naturally, you can become feminine and therefore fully human. You learn how fucked up a lot of the patriarchal conditioning is. The only price you pay is that you exclude yourself and deny yourself. Even at the time, I think I was intuitively aware that this process was happening to me at UCC.

I wanted to be an outsider, but I didn't want to have an us-and-them situation. It wasn't us and them, it was all of us. Some of us are being conditioned and some of us are trying not to be. I figured that whatever it was that I figured was human about me had to be human about everybody else too. So I ended up walking around saying all kinds of stuff at Upper Canada that really tripped people up. I'd say things that everybody agreed with but that seemed to undermine what they were doing. I knew that if I learned how to drive a car, it would make me more of an insider. I carried around a leather wallet as a symbol of participation. I tried to make sure that I wasn't an asshole about the subversive stuff I did. Sometimes I could go a little overboard.

I really liked the outsider perspective. It resonated with a lot of what they were teaching us, because Canada is an outsider country. I learned to have a sense of humour about it all. To me, it was marginal to actually read the stuff that they were telling us to read, then write about it the way they told us to write about it. To me, academics wasn't all that important. I liked what they were giving us to read. I loved following the ideas, putting them together and thinking about them.

This outsider thing is the privilege that we have as Canadians. I think fewer Canadians understand that now than at one time. We have perspective. We have the privilege of being able to say we didn't buy the American Revolution. A lot of us left and came up here. Some people didn't particularly like what started to happen to communism, so they came to Canada and tried to create their own brand of utopian socialism.

We really have to drum into people's heads the idea that the Canadian conservative tradition is in fact anti-capitalist. Come on, wake up! The refusal to idealize capitalism is not an exclusively left-wing perspective in Canada. George Grant's book *Lament for a Nation* was about Canadians adopting the drive to empire through technology. We're losing one kind of imperial system and deciding to opt for another kind of imperial system. We didn't have to do it, but unfortunately it's too late now.

I saw arrogance and elitism at UCC, but I basically laughed at it. Paradox is the law at UCC. The problem is the frame of reference. The school has set up something *important*. It's only recently that I've started to really perceive their worldview in any kind of coherent, comprehensible way. I'm sure UCC forms a part of my conditioning, but I never really took it all that seriously. I said, "Okay, we all get to be elitists."

But I was excited by so many other things, like making computer programs, writing poetry, making all sorts of satirical, Dadaist tapes. People would put on art exhibits and I'd staple newspapers to the opposite wall and give them really pretentious names. Then I'd sit around in the hall. People would walk along, look at the art, then look at the newspapers and say, "Oh, wow." We'd have an amazing laugh.

There was a little group of weird, marginalized guys I identified with at UCC. They all had a hard time. One friend of mine, who was brilliant, did a lot of drugs as a strategy of resistance and eventually left the school. I used to babysit people on acid a lot. Another friend of mine killed himself a year after he left the school. He hung himself at his parents' place. An amazing proportion of kids were from divorced families. Almost every one of them had a shrink. It was a weird pattern. Some guys would have to skip games after school because they were going to see their shrink.

To me, the "in" group of UCC guys were crass, insensitive, and anti-intellectual. I saw the offbeat things as beautiful and funny. My dad, who is a judge, went to UCC in the 1950s and was in the same year as Michael Wilson, who is my godfather. My father wasn't a serious intellectual but rather a subtle, witty, wry Stephen Leacockish kind of guy. The mainstream UCC guys can't deal with wry. Wry is not part of the game. I'm not trying to say I was too cool, but I felt that I enjoyed so many other things. I couldn't figure out where they were coming from.

They spent a lot of time being really sexist. I didn't know what the motivation was. I felt like I was an actor. I'd sit there and think, What's my motivation here? I couldn't sit in the locker room with them and say, "Hey, she's got big tits, eh?" I would just get all squirmy. I would think, They're going to think I'm too good for them, but I just don't understand it.

I never had a girlfriend until I was eighteen or nineteen. I just spent a lot of time with friends who were girls. A lot of guys at Upper Canada, when they decided to go out with girls, they went as a pack. My relationships with girls were not organized the same way. At Upper Canada, if you had friends who were girls, you were considered weird. You had to be from Scarborough to have friends who were girls. It was a real Scarborough thing to like heavy metal bands and hang out with chicks on the weekends and not want to fuck them. Still, I can't help treating women as something other than me, which was part of the subtext of being at Upper Canada.

It was liberating to discover at UCC that the conditioning of homophobia, sexism, and patriarchy is a two-way street. Throughout society, women and men both play their roles, consciously or unconsciously. Guys from Upper Canada push all the right buttons to bring that kind of situation about. They treat women like porcelain objects, which is part of the brand of puritan patriarchy we have in North America. A lot of the feminists like women to be educated by other women for a while so they learn what they are about, and the same with men. There is something good about that, too, because at UCC there was a certain part of my childishness that I didn't abandon in order to act like a man around women.

When I used to row at UCC, a lot of the women on the Canadian Women's Rowing Team would row with us. They would coach us and they would completely smoke us. A lot of them were friends of mine, and still are. So the whole set of stupid sexist attitudes about women just didn't hold up to what I knew. I rowed with a lot of women who were the best in the world. I aspired to be like them. So I didn't get into the whole macho scene in a big way, which I think has served me really well.

Rowing was great because it was very basic. You work hard, you go fast, you win, and that was it. You had to be a fanatic and get up at 5:00 A.M. and train five hours a day all year just for a little string of regattas. We were one of the best teams in the world. We went door-to-door to parents to raise the money for ourselves because we didn't get any money from the school. We got land from the city down on the waterfront and built up the program ourselves.

Rowing was initially a self-organized, volunteer activity. Allan Lamport, a UCC old boy, had started rowing at the school in the 1920s and then it was discontinued for many years. Some boys started it up again in the 1970s all by themselves as a marginal activity. When I was there, the school was just beginning to incorporate the rowing team into the mainstream of the school's culture. They were starting to say, "Wait a second. You guys are really good." We said, "Damn right!"

I was fairly non-athletic in the traditional sense. I ended up getting a first-team tie, which was kind of cool. I liked the rowers because they were the guys who never were very good at any other sports. They suddenly fell into this one sport and were totally carried away by it. We had coaches who we'd smuggle into the country from Eastern bloc countries. One amazing coach wanted to come to North America, so we worked a deal where he came and worked for us. Suddenly we had training that was putting us on an international level. He's now the head coach at the University of British Columbia. A lot of Upper Canada guys now go out to UBC to row.

I was attracted to rowing because it was self-organized, fanatical, and weird. Canada has a long, weird history of this funny, highly refined, traditional sport of gentlemen oarspeople who trained really hard and had mystical experiences. Ned Hanlan was one of the first international athletes in the world. We were totally tapping into a magical world. It was so non-bullshit. You work hard and you do well. It's simple. You felt the power of working together as a team. You didn't have any of the baggage of being a star jock in the public view competing against the Little Big Four private schools. We were in our own world, quietly taking on the Soviet bloc. It was just so unreal.

Initially, rowing was part of the whole outsider mentality. We would be walking around in the school and people would be saying, "Yeah, the football team kicks ass. We're going to take on Ridley." We'd say, "Great, good luck." Meanwhile, we're taking on the evil empire and, out of pride, we didn't even tell anybody. It was like a secret society.

If you turned up at prayers dripping with Lake Ontario water, Mr. Bredin would say, "What's wrong with you?" You couldn't say you were down rowing at the waterfront at 5:00 A.M., so you said, "Sorry, sir. I fell in the water coming to school." But we would never mention rowing. It was already something that was weird and marginal and had a very tentative existence. We couldn't afford to get bad publicity, so it just never came up.

As elite athletes, we didn't eat red meat or refined sugar. We did weird experiments on ourselves, changing the chemistry of our cells, having mystical experiences as a result of pushing ourselves to the limit. It was perfectly suited to the people who were doing it, who were the self-actualizing humans at Upper Canada.

The year Canada won the rowing in the 1984 Olympics was also the year UCC swept the Henley Regatta in St. Catharines, Ontario. I got elected to be one of the captains in 1985 because I was in the lightweight boat at Henley in 1984. The year I was captain, everybody and their dog suddenly wanted to row. Suddenly it was like, "Wow, Canada won the Olympics!" Rowing suddenly became stylish and people wore rowing shirts all over town.

Suddenly the team grew like mad and got very institutionalized. I'm actually glad that was my last year of association with it because it lost a lot of its allure. Suddenly the school was trying to administer it and the parents were taking a bigger role. We owed our existence to the parents' generosity, but we were the ones who had organized it. Suddenly, all the parents were scrambling to get on the rowing committee.

When I became one of the captains of the rowing team, I got incorporated into the establishment. When some of my outsider friends became validated as insiders, there was a real break. My cousin, Linc Caylor, became a steward. Immediately it was like I was persona non grata with him because he was a huge "Mr. Society." I don't think it was entirely me. I think a lot of us got pissed off at Linc at that point.

The same thing happened with the Arts Festival, which had been founded by the boys in 1970. It gradually became institutionalized the same way. Kids came up with "The Jam" as a response. The Jam was the arts festival for the kids because everything else had become too institutionalized by the school. The Jam was like Woodstock, with photographs, music, plays, the whole bit. It was an arts festival for the people of the people. When it became institutionalized in turn, somebody invented "The Peanut Butter." Similarly, the *College Times*, the first student newspaper in Canada, was founded by John Ross Robertson in 1857 as an anti-establishment rag. It wasn't long before it got institutionalized too.

Canada is a volunteer society in many ways. UCC was like a microcosm of Canada. All the things started at UCC that really went anywhere were autonomously organized by volunteers. I learned that at a certain point, whatever you started will be co-opted by the institution and itself become an institution. I decided that once that happened, you had to let it go.

Upper Canada College is a perfect postmodern idiom, a weird jumbling of different things. Like the Ralph Lauren houses you can buy, it's a postmodern patchwork which markets tradition. You buy tradition from it, but everything else about it is modern. It has labs, computers, physics, BMWs, baseball, drugs, all sorts of weird things going on. But they are simply trappings which hang like ornaments on a traditional infrastructure.

As soon as you did something truly eccentric or creative at UCC, people didn't value it. They thought you were trying to be different. There was a pervasive fear of anything different. A lot of people did get away with weird stuff, especially in the boardinghouse, but you had to understand the boundaries. As a joke, I used to carry a briefcase to school every day full of strange things like rubber duckies, rolls of mints, gummy bears, rulers, pens, and pencils. As long as people laughed, everything was cool. One day a guy came over and said, "You just do that because you want to be different." There was real anger behind it. It really bummed me out. I realized, from that point on, it was going to be difficult to keep doing it. I said, "No, no, don't worry about it. It's supposed to be funny. It's not a big deal. I'm not trying to be different."

One of the teachers, Paul Illidge, was a really funny, free-thinking guy who pointed out a lot of things that needed to be thought about. But the only way people could appreciate him was by laughing. They couldn't bring themselves to actually join him and do something constructive, creative, or different. For example, Illidge would give us a test with nonsense questions. Guys would try really hard to write the test. They'd say, "Are we getting marked on this? How many marks are these questions worth?" Illidge would collect the tests and say, "I'll be giving these back tomorrow." The next day he'd give them back. Each one would have some esoteric rubber stamp marked on it – a duck, a star, or a wave. He'd say, "Well, I marked them." People just laughed and said, "Excuse me? Excuse me?" They'd go down to the locker room and say, "Fuck, Illidge is really weird!" Some guys would say, "You're right, but I see what he means. Marking tests is arbitrary." Some guys would get it, but for a lot of guys it was frightening and subversive.

Illidge was just trying to get kids to think. Some teachers really tried to get us to realize that independent thinking was valid, that we could actually use it. We could use the school as a method for discovering and exploring things that we were interested in. After a while, Illidge must have felt he was banging his head against a brick wall. He was eventually forced out by the administration and went on to teach at a public school.

My brother went to Upper Canada too, but he was kicked out fairly early on. He was angry at my dad. There was some weird shit going on. He did something which I thought was really smart. He knew the teachers were privileged to know everything about us. They could talk about your bowel movements, your medical problems, the things you've done, the fights you've had, the people you know. Because of the interlocking nature of social circles, they could also find out about shit you did somewhere else. They were privileged to know about personal information and keep records on it.

So my brother thought: Well, it works both ways. We know their wives and children and husbands and daughters. We know all that stuff too and we can find it out. It's just that we're not privileged to keep that information. It's only rumour for us. So he decided to put together a newspaper with dossiers on the teachers. He would talk about teachers' marital problems, where they had their cottages, what they did, or how much money they made.

It was a great idea but it got so out of hand that one of the teachers decided to sue him. The teacher called up my parents and said, "Your child is expelled and I'm going to sue the pants off him because of the libellous things he wrote." I don't know why it doesn't cut both ways, because there are libellous comments about us in our school records.

You know the card game called Asshole? You deal out the whole deck to four players and then you take tricks. You try to get rid of your cards. If you get rid of your cards first, you're the President. The next person is the Vice-President, then the Vice-Asshole, then the Asshole. The Asshole is the last person to get rid of all their cards. Then you switch seats. The President sits at the head of the table, the Vice-President sits at his right hand, the Vice-Asshole at his left hand, and the Asshole in the remaining seat.

It's a hierarchy. The President can tell everybody else what to do, but especially the Asshole. Everybody else can tell the Asshole what to do. You can just completely rail on the Asshole. The game brings out the weirdest conditioned responses in people. Everybody starts telling the Asshole to wipe up the beer, go get another beer, shuffle the cards.

Once you become President, everybody else has to give you their best cards. If you're the Asshole, you have to give most of your best cards away and everybody else gives you their worst cards. So it's a self-perpetuating system. It's very difficult to get out of the Asshole position. You have to be really good at playing cards. But also you've got to get people to not give you really harsh cards, so you've got to suck up to them. It's an amazing microcosm of our social system played out in a card game.

When I was at UCC, a large majority of the guys were just putting in time. There was a crowd of preppie guys who made T-shirts and called themselves "The Beautiful People," believe it or not. I think they all ended up going to Queen's together. They hung out as a team and they wore really preppie clothes. They would get wasted all weekend, come back and talk about how wasted they got. They would lie and cheat to get through the courses. They wrote all their essays, but they would do it at the last minute, usually by copying off each other. Everything they did looked good, in a way. It was mediocre, but they didn't care.

They got through. They realized that they had the privilege of buying into a certain kind of game early on, not unlike Asshole, and that they could play it for the rest of their lives. That's why more than half the UCC student body still flocks, sheeplike, downtown to Bay Street. They subvert themselves because they are lethargic. They don't realize that they are being given freedom.

LINCOLN CAYLOR

1980–87

Lawyer

I NEVER HAD an academic bent at all, nor did the guys I hung out with. I was always in the B forms at UCC, right from the start. I never did homework. I just had a blast! From Grade 9 on, I lived with my best buddies in Seaton's House. In Grade 9, on the third floor, there were four of us – Jim Hayhurst, Greg MacMillan, John Maloney, and I. We had a great time.

Greg and Jim would go out at 4:00 A.M. and sneak slurpees or panzos at St. Clair and Bathurst. They'd come back, jump on us, and wake us up. When we were new boys, the senior guys used to do it to us all the time. They would randomly burst into a room, yell and scream, pull our blankets off, jump up and down on us, and then just bail out. We would be lying there wide awake, wondering, What the hell is going on? We'd be terrified that they would come back.

We used to do it to each other all the time. We used to run on a couple of hours sleep. I was sleeping through half my classes. It didn't matter because I seemed to always get about 65 per cent in my sleep. It bothered my dad that I wasn't putting out any effort, but we were having so much damn fun. I was quite a shit disturber, a tough kid to crack. We all thought we were indestructible. We thought we could do anything we wanted, cool boarders from Upper Canada College. That was the way we lived. All we did was drink a lot and hang out. It was lucky that I could keep up my marks without doing any work.

In Grade 11, I was suspended for two weeks. A number of things led up to it. I'd been in trouble for stuff like drinking and being late. During the Stewards' Dance in the upper dining hall, girls were seen going into the boardinghouses. Of course, one of them was my date. We were up in my room on the second floor. No girls were allowed past the visitors' room on the first floor. We'd all been drinking.

There was a bang on my door. I opened it and there was Jamie Procunier, who we called "Tough Guy." He's still at the school as one of the housemasters. He said, "Linc, where's your date?" I said, "Well, actually, sir, she's in my closet." He said, "Fine. I think you should leave."

I ended up getting suspended. The school said to me, "You can still go to classes, but you can't live in the boardinghouse for two weeks." My mom thought it was okay because I lived at home during the suspension, so she got to see me more. But my dad, who was an old boy from the class of 1958, wasn't too happy.

By Grade 12, I was rooming on the first floor with David Turner, the son of John Turner, the former prime minister. Jim Hayhurst and Greg MacMillan were on the floor above us. About ten of us would leave at lunch, skip our afternoon classes, go right across Oriole Parkway to Charles Field-Marsham's house and drink beer all day. We would stagger back to the boardinghouse late at night.

One time we had extended leave to go see a late movie. We told Doug Blakey, who was then the housemaster of Seaton's, we were going to see *Commando*, an Arnold Schwarzenegger movie. Instead, we went to a huge party at some girl's house in Moore Park. In the spring in Grade 12, we had friends who were girls in Grade 13. They had afternoons off and their parents were away, so we went to their houses and drank all day. Staggering back around midnight from this one girl's house, we said, "We've got to act sober and make it look like we actually saw the movie."

Dave Turner came up with a great idea. We were going to burst into Blakey's office and pretend to fire guns and show him how cool the movie was. So Dave bursts open the door and yells, "*Columbo* was the best movie!" Blakey said, "Don't you mean *Commando*?" All four of us are standing there, reeking of beer. Then Dave and I went to the bread-and-milk room on the first floor to make peanut butter sandwiches. Blakey walks in and says, "This room smells like a distillery." We said, "I guess we had a couple of beers."

We'd get letters from Blakey whenever we got in trouble. This incident provoked about the third or fourth in a series of letters. The letters would say stuff like how disappointed he was. We'd post the letters above our beds. We had a competition to see who got the most letters. I was leading the pack. The younger kids would come in and read them and say, "Whoa! That's so cool! Look at what he said here."

I remember Rodger Wright, who's now the headmaster of TCS, came to us in Grade 9 after our final exams in the spring. We did very badly at Christmas. He said, "Okay, guys. What did you fail?" Greg MacMillan said, "I think I failed English and history and maybe math." I said, "The only one I think I really know I failed was English, but there could be others." He said, "Who teaches you these courses?" We gave him the teachers' names, Terry Bredin and the others. Wright said, "Fine, don't worry about it." Sure enough, we got fifties in all the things we thought we had failed. Bredin gives you 51 per cent or 52 per cent when it's a sympathy pass.

Once we had a scavenger hunt and ripped off one of those yellow blinking construction lights off the corner of Yonge and St. Clair. We put it in the back of Jim Hayhurst's mom's Cherokee and parked on Forest Hill Road. As we were walking away from his mom's car, we realized the whole car was lit up by this blinking light.

So we walked back into Seaton's with the thing on my shoulders, going blink, blink, blink. We were forty-five minutes late. We'd all been drinking, except Jim who was driving. We walked in right past the master, who was Tough Guy. We said, "Good night," and kept going. He said, "Whoa! Get back here. What the hell is this?" We told him about the scavenger hunt and how we had won. He said, "That's great, but you have to return the light."

So we went with him back to Jim's car. The whole back of the Jeep was full of empty beer cans, so Jim ran ahead and said, "Linc, why don't you hop in the back and clean up a bit?" I said, "Good idea!" I threw newspapers over the beer cans so Tough Guy wouldn't see them. You could hear them rattling around, but Tough Guy just ignored it.

We drove back to Yonge and St. Clair. Tough Guy looked around and said, "Okay. No cops. Grab that thing and stick it back on the road." I put it back. We were just driving away when a cop pulled us over. Tough Guy was saying, "Oh, my God! Now I'm going to get fired. Now you guys have got me in trouble."

I was starting to laugh in the back seat. The cop pulls over Jim. Before the cop could say anything, Tough Guy says, "Excuse me, officer. I'm a master at Upper Canada College and I was just ensuring that these boys took this light back." The cop says, "Uh huh." Then he takes Jim's licence. Tough Guy was still talking. The cop says, "Would you like me to take your licence as well?" Tough Guy said, "No, no, it's okay." The cop comes back and says, "You'll make sure you get these boys home safely?" Tough Guy said, "Yes, yes, of course." As soon as the cop drove off, Tough Guy said, "If I hadn't been there, you guys would have been in jail." That was the kind of stuff we did. We just thought we could do anything.

One time in Grade 13, we were walking up Yonge Street after we left the mall. We were always at the mall or the Morrissey Tavern. Restaurants and bars all leave their empty wine bottles out on the street, so we were whipping wine bottles at each other at 2:00 A.M. walking up the middle of Yonge Street. To this day, I can't believe none of us got run over or got arrested.

I stole a flag from the prep and put it over Jim Hayhurst. He slept with the Canadian flag on him all night. I ripped off one of those ugly bird washing ornaments out of someone's garden and stuck it in Dave Turner's bed. Dave woke up with this thing in his bed. Another time we were out until 5:00 A.M. and Greg Connor and I slept in the UCC cricket pavilion. We did stuff like that all the time.

Eric Kierans, who is a big businessman, had a daughter at BSS who had just been given a new convertible Audi Coupe. She was seeing a friend of ours, J.P., at the time. She was wasted at a party, so she said to J.P., "Keep my keys so I don't drive." J.P. had his hand out, but I grabbed the keys as she dropped them. None of them even noticed. We went out and drove around Forest Hill in her car. We parked it under a lawn sprinkler. All the car windows were open and the car roof was open. The sprinkler went into the open car all night. Was she ever pissed the next day! The car had about two feet of water in it. Nothing ever seemed to happen to us, so we just kept pushing.

We did get grounded a lot, but we'd just have panzos pizzas in the basement and watch movies and TV. There would always be somebody else to hang out with. You never got a gating alone. Then people would drop by. It would be, "It's a slow Friday night. Let's go see Lincoln." There would be twenty people in the basement. We'd pull girls in the window and hang out and watch movies.

One thing happened that should have woken us up. There were twin brothers, Eric and Steve From, in my year. Steve From was killed on a bike tour in Grade 11 over in Europe. He had the same attitude we did: nothing can happen to us. Fly by the seat of your pants. No one really knows what happened. They found his body at the bottom of a cliff. He did the same sorts of things as we did. We could have got killed doing tons of stuff we were doing. You don't even think about it.

There was lots of cocaine at the school, but none of my close friends really did it. We all tried it once and said, "Forget it." It was definitely very easy to get cocaine or any kind of drugs you wanted at Upper Canada, but none of our group were really into it. We were all too preoccupied with our drinking games.

We used to drink at Dave Turner's all the time because the Turners were never there. His parents were in Ottawa or somewhere else. We used to practically live at the Turners' apartment on Avenue Road. We could walk down there from the school easily and hang out there on Friday and Saturday and drink. Once, five of us were playing stupid drinking games at the table. Dave and I looked up and noticed his parents' apartment was full of people. Someone who wasn't playing the game kept letting people in on the apartment buzzer. People just started to come over. Dave said, "Holy shit! Linc, you're staying over tonight." I would say, "I've got to phone and sign out of Seaton's." I would get Doug Blakey on the phone at 10:00 P.M. and tell him I was staying at Dave's.

It was tough for Dave sometimes, being the son of the Liberal leader and the prime minister. I think Mike dealt with it better because he was older. All three Turner brothers went to UCC. Mike is the oldest, Dave is the middle one and Andrew is the youngest. Their sister, Liz, went to BSS. She campaigned with her father. It didn't bother her at all. But I think it got to Dave and Andrew a bit more.

Dave used to get ribbed when we would go to parties at other people's places. You could hear people saying, "There's John Turner's kid." I think it was worse for him when he went to Western. There would be stories that he was arriving in a black stretch limousine with a garbage bag full of dope. In fact, his sister Liz drove him out in a Honda Civic. He had to put up with a lot.

Dave and I would have drinks with his mom. We'd be drinking scotch with Mrs. Turner and some of her friends. She'd say, "Hey, Linc! You want a scotch?" We'd have a couple of scotches and then we'd go to our place and my dad would serve wine at these dinner parties. Everybody would get blitzed. A lot of the time, we were drinking with our parents. Drinking wasn't something where we nipped into the closet. It was wide open. If we drank too much, the attitude was like, "You idiot. Why did you drink so much?" Our parents would be there, so it was sort of a controlled thing. There was never drinking and driving because nobody cared if you stayed over. You'd phone and say, "Mom, I'm crashing here tonight because I've had way too much to drink." She'd say, "Great! Stay there."

We had a lot of parties at my grandmother's house on Kilbarry Road, just north of UCC. Everybody called her "Nan" and would hang out with her. She was a buddy of the former school nurse, Miss Barrow. We would have keg parties and barbecues over there all the time. There would be about one hundred people in her backyard, right across from the school. We'd be playing drinking games and my grandmother would have a couple of martinis.

Dave Turner and I were always organizing parties. We'd order big fancy buses up from New York with TVs and bars, which would take us to different stewards' dances. One day, I was sitting in class. Mike Adamson comes in and says, "Linc, Mr. Sadleir would like to see you right away." I don't have any socks on and I haven't shaved. I go down and Sadleir is sitting in his office. He said, "Linc, Linc. Sit down." He said, "I understand you're in charge of this bus."

I said, "No one's going to be drinking and driving, so Dave and I have ordered a big bus. Everyone's going to be on it." He said, "Okay, that's fine. Great idea. But I'm getting phone calls from mothers from different girls' schools saying that their girls have all asked to take off from school at noon." We were picking our dates up early for the dance, so they wanted to get off early to get ready. He said, "I'm getting a lot of flak from all the headmistresses that a lot of their girls are leaving early to meet you."

Headmistresses were calling Sadleir and asking, "Who is this Linc Caylor kid who's picking up all these girls in a bus at 4:00 P.M.?" He said, "Why are you picking them up so early? To start drinking?" I said, "No, we're going straight to my grandmother's house." He said, "Oh, well, Peggy. That's fine. No problem. I'll just tell them all that." My father knew Dick Sadleir well because he was a boarder in Seaton's in the 1950s when Sadleir was a housemaster.

UCC wasn't that strict in my time. I'm sure if you pushed things too far, you'd be in a lot of trouble. If you were caught with drugs, you'd be kicked out right away. Jeremy Robinson got caught smoking drugs in the cricket pavilion. There was no doubt about it. It was a clear-cut case, so Dick Sadleir came down hard on him. If I had got caught with drugs, I would expect to be kicked out. Drugs were bad, drinking was fine. Some of the masters drank a lot. That's the way it was. I guess that's just the double standard.

Dick Sadleir said to me on graduation, "Well, Linc, it's been quite an experience. When I write my memoirs, I'm going to have a chapter named after you entitled 'The Taming of Linc.'" I said, "Thank you, sir!" I think by the time I left UCC, I was starting to get my head screwed on better. I got to university and I didn't crap out or fall apart. It was probably because of Upper Canada. I don't know what would have happened if I had been at a public school with three thousand students. I probably would have dropped out and started pumping gas.

I went to King's College in Halifax as an undergrad. John Godfrey, who was the president of King's and a UCC old boy, was probably the reason I got in. My marks were so bad. John Godfrey is a childhood friend of my mother's. My grandmother knows his father, Senator Godfrey. My mother phoned John Godfrey and said, "Remember Linc from Muskoka? He needs to go to school somewhere." So it was like, "Okay. He can come out here."

We were a strong year, a really solid group. We still have "Buds Weekends." In my first year of law school, when everyone was four years out of UCC, about twelve of us had a Buds Weekend at Charles Field-Marsham's house. I came from Ottawa and guys came from places like Halifax, Montreal, and New York. We did nothing but hang out, drink, and talk amongst ourselves for almost four days.

Mrs. Field-Marsham would come in every once in a while and make sure the place hadn't been destroyed. She would bring us food. She'd leave and come back and we'd still be sitting in our boxers and T-shirts in the kitchen with beers in our hands. She would just look at us and say, "Girls would never do something like this!" We had stuff to talk about and it would go on forever. It is something that no one can crack. Jim Hayhurst and I have been best buddies since Grade 9, Greg Connor and Sam Hardy since Grade 7. I can see myself hanging around with the same guys twenty or thirty years from now.

At law school, you have tons of views coming at you from the far left and far right and everything in between. You hear views from militant lesbians and feminists. Since my Upper Canada days, I've moved over a little on the spectrum. I'm not as conservative as we all were in high school. Feminists immediately peg me as a conservative old boy. The girl I'm seeing right now likes to think of herself, not as a militant feminist, but a feminist. But if she's hanging out with me, she can't think that UCC old boys are all that bad.

Once I had a bunch of guys up to Ottawa. We had a huge disaster of a weekend because I tried to mix my friends from Ottawa with my friends from Upper Canada – Dave Turner, Chris Hickman, Paul Capombassis, and Dave Campbell. It just didn't work. Campbell made some anti-Semitic comments and remarks that degraded women. A Jewish female friend of mine was there. It was just a nightmare. The guy hasn't changed since our days at Upper Canada.

All my law-student friends are "enlightened." Whether you are conservative or otherwise, at least you have to be aware of what everyone else thinks. I just don't think that Campbell has ever been exposed to it. He went to McGill, where there are a lot of Upper Canada guys, and hung out with them. Now he's hanging around with the Bratty brothers, Mark and Chris, from Upper Canada.

When we were at UCC, there was no doubt in our minds that we would become leaders. None of us had had any big setbacks yet. It may well happen, but most of us are still flying pretty high. We still think nothing's going to stop us, and we will be leaders in the community. That's what we felt right from the beginning. I don't know how it was instilled in us. Probably by the attitude: UCC is supreme, and we will be too. Whether it's politics or business, whatever I end up choosing in a couple of years, you just have that feeling that you'll be best at it. It's a self-confidence we got coming out of UCC. Not everybody got it, obviously, but I think a lot of us in our group did.

I don't think other schools are as tight as Upper Canada in their old-boy network. When I went to an interview with Blake Cassels, who have three hundred lawyers, two of the guys interviewing me were UCC old boys. They said, "I saw your resumé. I wanted to make sure I came in and met you." Every firm I went to, an old boy, if he happened to see my resumé, would say, "Oh, yeah. I'll see this guy. Bring him by." They'd ask, "When did you graduate? What sports did you play? What house were you in?" UCC is definitely an "in."

The power structure will change, but there will still be Upper Canada guys leading in different parts of the community. It may not always be the solid "in" it always used to be. My dad used to say that when you opened the Report on Business in the *Globe and Mail,* practically every story or profile had an old boy in it. Now you rarely see it because Toronto is so much bigger. The impact of UCC on Canada is a lot less than it was, but it's still strong.

I remember I was in my room in boarding one day and a guy walked in. I was getting ready for my football game. He knocked and said, "Mind if I come in?" There were lots of old boys wandering around the school because it was the annual Association Day. He walked in, looked around and said, "This used to be my room. What's your name?" I said, "Lincoln Caylor." He looked surprised and said, "Is your dad Jim Caylor?" I said, "Yeah." He said, "Back in the 1950s, your dad slept in that bed and I slept in that bed. Nothing has changed!"

ANDREW HEINTZMAN

1975–86

Musician, publisher

ALL OF MY MEMORIES of the prep are about fighting. When we were in Grade 3 and 4, we had a gang called the "Turtles." Many guys who are still my friends were in this gang. We would collectively terrorize Grade 7 and 8 boys, especially the ones who were incapable of defending themselves. We were like a pack of hyenas.

We had great snowball wars. Literally three hundred prep kids would march like an invading army to the upper school and attack it. The first big snowfall every year, it was just understood that we would march to the upper school at lunchtime. Usually we would find a bunch of guys having a cigarette after lunch and attack them. Eventually, they would run in and get their friends. There would be twenty upper school guys standing on top of the hill and three hundred of us prepsters on the field. Usually we'd make a couple of charges and they would beat us back. As more upper school guys came out, it would become a slaughter. We'd end up running in disarray back towards the prep. Frequently a window would be broken and then the snowball fight would be called off. The prep headmaster, Dick Howard, would put a ban on it, so it wouldn't occur again until the next year.

If we got into serious trouble, my older brother would sometimes protect us. A couple of times he defended my friends and me. At other times, he and his friends would beat us up. I never knew which side he was on. I distinctly remember his friends would find me and give me a huge face wash with snow.

I started in 1975 in the prep when I was eight. There were about twenty-four guys in our Grade 3 class and about half of us survived all the way through to Grade 13. A number of them are still my very good friends, which is amazing because Upper Canada is the most competitive place in the world. In Grade 3, we would literally cry if we lost a game called Challenge. Kids would be devastated. Even at that early age, we fed off status and competition.

Challenge was a multiplication game. If you were doing the number six, you would spin a wheel and it might land on eight. The first one to say "forty-eight" would win. The desks in our class were positioned according to our rankings in Challenge. Challenge was everything. If you were ranked number twelve in the class, you could challenge number one. The two of you would sit in front of the class and play the game. If you won, he would go to number twelve and you would go to number one. I remember Challenge being the dominating feature of that year.

I was a very anxious-to-please kid. I was a little boisterous, but I really wanted to do as well as I could. I won the form prize in Grade 3, tied with Trevor Farrow. That was a big deal to me. This was the beginning of our strange rivalry. It's amazing how early we started to be rivals. I wanted to do well in school and I did do well. I wanted to be an athlete and be on all the teams.

We organized our gang, the Turtles, like an army. There were field marshals, generals, majors, right down to privates. The four of us who organized it were field marshals. Virtually the whole class was in some way a member of the Turtles. Once we got into trouble when some of the Turtles had chased a guy around the track. Mr. Deeks said, "Okay, I know about the Turtles now. I want the field marshals to come to the front." So he knew the terminology. We knew that the whole thing was going to be called in and that we were going to get in trouble. The four of us walked up. We hadn't actually been involved in the chasing of the kid around the track, so we got let off. But he banned the Turtles.

In Grade 7 and Grade 8, fights started when guys would come and steal our basketball. That was just a sign like, "We want to fight." They would go dancing off with our ball and we would go after them and get into a fight. In the younger grades, I would walk home with a couple of my friends. Almost every day, we'd get into a fight with somebody. There were literally hundreds and hundreds of these occurrences. I just remember so many little brawls. They were mostly wrestling matches and a show of strength. You would trip the person and get them in a headlock. Once there was a fight in Grade 7 or Grade 8 behind the Patrick Johnson Arena between two kids, which turned into a huge brawl. They beat each other up very badly. It was the real thing. There were a couple of those kinds of fights.

A bunch of my friends and I were in the choir, so we would get bugged for being in the choir. That was always a cause for warfare. I remember walking up to the choir practice in the upper school and being followed by the grade older than us, who would bother us. Eventually, halfway up the field, it would turn into a rumble.

We loved it. We would always pick on the guys in UR, or upper remove, who were the Grade 9s who stayed in the prep. We would run around the halls saying, "U R dead!" We'd stake out the various doors in the prep building, figuring out where they were and how we could corner them. Sometimes the odds were on their side, sometimes the odds were on our side. I remember one of my friends, John Andersen, who was a very good athlete and a strong kid, was surrounded by eight or nine guys a grade older. He had one guy in a headlock and was just pounding him and getting pounded himself, right out in front of the prep school.

I think the violence just had something to do with the nature of the environment – the all boys' school, the competitiveness, the hierarchy. All those things just made us want to fight. A lot of sadistic things went on in that school. A lot of people were being hurt. I guess it's the same as anywhere else. Kids really got picked on. We called each other by our last names. Sometimes the names would become derogatory. You knew that every time they were being talked to, it felt like they were being ridiculed. The teachers did it too. They could be quite cruel as well.

In the upper school, I started playing in a rock band. One year, I ran the Jam, which was a rock concert in the annual Arts Festival. My band was probably the thing that I was emotionally the most attached to, besides the soccer team. My band, Odyssey, was in the Jam in Grade 9, the youngest band to ever be in it. Everyone would drink and the school would close their eyes to it. We would pack Laidlaw Hall and all hell would break loose. They took out a bunch of the pews. People would be drinking, smoking, and smoking up. It was the night of craziness.

I considered the music to be a real source of self-expression and I came to loggerheads with the administration a number of times on this issue.

One of the libraries at the upper school is called the Heintzman Music Library. My family became quite involved in what Mr. Mee, the music master, had done at the school. My father is very musical and my brother played in all the bands. I played saxophone in all the school bands. Yet, there was always tension between the official school music and the rock music, which was really closer to what I wanted to be doing.

There were numerous yelling matches, not with Mr. Mee so much as other people on the staff and other music teachers. We'd always be yelling at one another over practice and rehearsals, four months before the Jam was taking place. It would always happen that someone would leave equipment out. Masters would scream furiously at me and Turner. They had no patience for the Jam. They hated it. I was always frustrated with them because I thought they were really overlooking something important. To give Mr. Mee some credit, he did make an effort to recognize that aspect of music at Upper Canada, although in retrospect, it was pretty limited. They would have loved to shut it down.

Upper Canada went through a brief period of liberalization in the 1970s, but it started to change in the late seventies and early eighties. Our year, 1986, was a very strange year. We came head-to-head with the final puritan strain of the administration. By 1986, the school had become as conservative as it had ever been. Our year was pretty crazy. We had a real social rebellion involving an overt drug and music culture. Collectively, we really went out of our way to frustrate the establishment, which led to numerous standoffs.

Our final year was really quite crazy. I'm sure the teachers would remember it as a watershed because, after we left, the school became even more conservative. I think we were the last year that systematically tried to frustrate the whole ethic and myth of Upper Canada College. I always thought of it as a political movement.

I had a real run-in with my housemaster, Neil Mens, who ended up kicking me out as head of McHugh's House. I was the head of house for half a year. By the end, we had a real dislike for one another. It was really out in the open. I thought he played a number of dirty tricks on me. I'm sure he didn't like me at all. I thought his attitude and his philosophy of the school stood for a great many of the things that were going wrong.

He basically said, "You're bumping up against a brick wall. There is no way to change the system. The system has been here for a long time. This school is designed to turn out lawyers, doctors, and businessmen. You're looking for the wrong thing in this school. You either play by the rules of the system or you leave."

He had been at UCC for only three years and I had been there for ten years. It used to infuriate the hell out of me because I thought that I knew the school much better than him. I just didn't think that that was a good response, especially to an idealistic kid. In a way he was being quite honest with me, but I still don't think that's the right answer. I am still angry about it. The line that the administration and the teachers were taking was, "That's just the way it is." That would be their answer for a question, which really isn't any answer at all.

UCC had been my whole life and my family's life. If he had been correct in his presumption about what the school was, I would have been someone else. He didn't account for the distance I'd gone, or most of my friends for that matter. I really resented people telling me the school was a conservative system. The message was, "The system will move on. Individuals will just be lost in it."

I convinced my father and some of the other Heintzmans around me that the school was basically wrong. My dad was really on my side later on. I don't think he's had much to do with the school since. My grandfather, father, and many other family members are all old boys. I know that my father thought that the school treated myself and people like me improperly. They couldn't account for people who wanted different things out of the school and who felt that they had a right to get those things.

There were a lot of people who came into the school in later stages who could recognize immediately that it wasn't where they belonged. They took off, which was fine. But I didn't have that privilege of distance. I had already so deeply involved myself in the place that I couldn't just remove myself and leave. The love-it-or-leave-it attitude was a real problem. It was because I loved it that I couldn't leave it.

Every year has its rebels, but I think there were more rebels in our year. We did things that other years could do and the teachers wouldn't be mad at them. But they knew that every time we did it, it would be with real spite. One time, everyone painted their hair blue before we went into prayers, which really pissed them off. We made it obvious that it was "in your face!" There was a tight bunch of us who would come up with these ideas.

I was on the board of stewards. A number of the guys on the board of stewards were also the people who were getting in trouble and had complaints. One of our complaints was the snobbery of the whole system. The biggest symbol of snobbery were the "stewards' breakfasts."

We got a call from someone at Havergal College, saying, "Come to a stewards' breakfast and meet all the stewards of the other private schools in Toronto." We just thought that was completely gross and ridiculous. It still makes me mad.

So we decided to have fun with it. We were supposed to wear our school uniforms, so we all climbed out of bed in our pyjamas, got big cigars and turned up at the breakfast. All the UCC stewards walked in the front door, threw a bunch of food around, and lit up a couple of cigars. We were rude. For me, there was always a point to our actions. It was really a political gesture saying, "This is fucked! This social system is wrong."

There was large-scale drug use amongst a very high percentage of our class at particular events. A lot of people were experimenting with drugs at various times and various events and this created a kind of bond. We had a real bond. When someone was going to do something illicit or to stir things up, it was always a harder decision not to do it than to do it.

We disrupted classes in the girls' private schools. It was like we'd gone berserk. We'd turn up at Branksome Hall down in Rosedale around 10:00 A.M., open the front doors and a hundred of us would just run like crazy people through the hall. One time, word got around because by the time we got to Branksome, they had locked the front door. So we climbed into a window. It was like a fortress.

We got yelled at by the vice-principal, Mr. Adamson, who was actually one of the people I still respect. When I talked to him about my frustrations with the school, he was always really understanding. The principal, Dick Sadleir, came out on the side of discipline. He probably had to. I know that he maintained respect for all the individual boys, even though he wasn't really happy with a lot of the unruly stuff that was going on.

When I see Mr. Sadleir now, he's really interested in what I'm doing. I have founded a literary magazine called *shift*. I think he understood, as well as Adamson, the kind of frustrations I felt at UCC. I'd have really frank talks with him, where he would say, "You're really hating this, aren't you?" I'd say, "Yes, I'm really hating this." He knows my parents really well, so he was in an uncomfortable position.

We pulled off some amazing things. When the first hockey team went to the United States one time, they were drinking on the bus. It became a really big deal with the administration. Everyone had been drinking, but who brought the beer on the bus? They eventually found four guys to suspend.

The next week, we went on a long bus trip down to an art gallery in Buffalo. Modernism was taught by Marshall Webb, who was one of our allies. It was the one course that had all the potential for self expansion and growth. All the fiction we were reading was really interesting. We talked a lot about psychedelia in the sixties, art, and literature, things that were really intriguing to us.

On the way back, we all got drunk. Someone was smoking a joint in the can and kicked the window out, so there was damage to the bus. The whole thing came down on Mr. Webb's head. We got a little bit out of control. He realized that it was a bad situation, so he got mad at us. Finally, he had to tell the principal, Mr. Sadleir.

So only a couple of days later, they had to deal with yet another case where there was drinking and damage on a school bus trip. They had to suspend somebody, so they picked four guys. But this was a classic example of our class solidarity. A teacher came to me and said, "Who brought the beer on the bus? You're the only person I saw bring beer on the bus. What should we do about it?" I brought the beer on the bus, but everyone had paid for it. I didn't want to get scapegoated, so we got thirty-five or forty guys to sign a petition, including people who weren't even on the bus, saying that they brought beer on the bus.

I gave it to Mr. Sadleir myself. I said, "You wanted a list of people who brought beer on the bus. Here you go." They couldn't suspend all thirty-five people, so what were they going to do? So they made up a weird chart and got us all together in the drama room. We had to check boxes to questions like, "Did you bring beer on the bus?" and "Did you pay for it?" We refused to go along with it and the end result of it was they brought the four guys who were suspended back to school two days later. It was a real moment of victory. Absolutely nothing came of it. We really stiffed them. It was a great feeling.

By the end, I thought the teachers were screwed. I thought they were far too puritan and staid. They were just getting the job done. There was nothing really great about UCC any more. They were mindlessly maintaining an outmoded tradition, sucking out all of our vital juices. I had a tough time the last couple of years. I was ecstatic when I left.

GEOFFREY WILSON

1984–86

Banker

ANDY HEINTZMAN was pretty much our leader in our year. He was a bit rebellious. The school would never accept him as head steward. I do not think that it was an issue when Trevor Farrow was made head steward. I think that as far as Andy was concerned, he knew that the positions of authority did not like the way that he questioned them. He understood that they did not really want to accept him.

A lot of people say that Heintzman was the last straw for Dick Sadleir, who stuck around as principal for only another year. People thought that he would have left after our year, that he had had enough. But he was not going to let Andy Heintzman get to him. He was going to stick around for another year so he could be a little bit more proud. The class of 1987 were more obedient, so he could leave gracefully and save face.

Andy Heintzman certainly did challenge authority. When I go back to UCC now, I see a lot of the guys are wearing ponytails. We always had to have our hair cut really short. I think, Wow. This is the way that Andy Heintzman would have had it. Maybe it is because of Andy that the UCC kids can do this now.

I'd started high school in Ottawa. After Grade 11 at Lisgar Collegiate Institute, I went down to UCC and met with the principal, Sadleir, and Michael Adamson, the vice-principal. Mr. Adamson was an excellent vice-principal. He said, "You know, we do not have a lot of spaces, but your father was an old boy." My father, Michael Wilson, and my grandfather, Harry Wilson, both went to UCC. My grandfather was chairman of the board of governors for five years in the 1960s. Adamson said, "We would like to have you if you want to come."

I was a football player and football camp started a couple of weeks before school started in September. I was entering Grade 12 in September 1984, just as the federal election was winding down. I came down to Toronto with my father, where his riding was located, to help with the election and to go to the UCC football camp.

So the first people I knew at UCC were football players, which suited me just fine. I was boarding at Seaton's House. David Hadden, who was an old boy and a former CFL football player, was my housemaster and a great guy. We called him "Deej," "Beast," "Potato Head," whatever. He is now the headmaster of Lakefield College. He made me feel at home. As a new boy, I had to break into the teams and the social circles. It was tough coming in in Grade 12 when everybody knew each other and I was an outsider.

I made the football team in Grade 12 as a back-up linebacker. I was a back-up lineman, both inside and outside, and back-up field goal kicker. It was a fabulous team. We won the championship. Nineteen eighty-six was the last of the so-called UCC football dynasty under David Hadden. We had Mark Bratty quarterbacking us. He actually did not play the whole year, which was a disappointment, because with Mark we were untouchable. Mark could throw the football in a perfect tight spiral thirty or forty yards down the field, and then some, and hit the guy right on target.

When Bratty was injured, Trevor Farrow filled in and did a great job. He was not a natural quarterback, but he worked really hard at it. He was the head steward and everybody's friend. There was a lot of pressure on him because he could never be what Mark Bratty was. Trevor would take his licks as quarterback and was happy to do that, which was great. That is what ended up getting us that championship – Trevor going that extra mile. Definitely with the football team that year, there was a lot of expectations and pressures for us to win. We had a very talented team, so anything short of winning was a major disappointment.

The Bratty brothers were all very rebellious. Mark ended up leaving UCC and going to Appleby. They were accused of a crime and they were absolved of it. They were charged with rape. Because their father is worth a lot of money, people inevitably are going to take shots at them. A woman says, "Oh, he raped me. Send him to jail." They are the kind of guys who are easily sucked into a situation like that because they have fun. They party hard and get themselves into trouble. When you are young and everybody knows you have a lot of money, you're a target, like Eric Lindros.

When my father was in politics, he said to me, "If I had any other job, then whatever I did would be pretty much irrelevant to my peers. But when I am in politics, what I do becomes of interest to the media. If it is scrutinized by the media, then it is de facto scrutinized by the country. So be aware that when you go out and do things, people are reflecting that upon you, whether you like it or not."

When I walked in for my first meal in the UCC dining room, my father had told me to look around because I would see a portrait painting of my grandfather. He was a major figure at the school. He was part of the fundraising to rebuild the clock tower and the upper school building in the late 1950s.

When my father was running for the Conservative leadership, a newspaper reporter asked me a couple of questions and mixed things up a little bit. She worked things to her advantage and said that, after my father, I was supporting Brian Mulroney. The truth of the matter was that I had no idea who my father would be supporting, after himself, between Joe Clark and Brian Mulroney. I was in Grade 10. The headline said something like, "Michael Wilson's son supports Mulroney." Therefore, look for Mr. Wilson to go to Mulroney on the second or the third ballot.

That was an eye-opening experience for me. It is all about power, digging up a story when you have to. So from there, going into the UCC dining room, I realized that anything I did was still not only reflecting on my father but also on my grandfather and the family name.

My father has never put any pressure on me to do anything, and I think that that may be as a result of the fact that his father maybe put pressure indirectly on him. My father has never really told me as much, but I know that he is quite proud of what I am doing and what I have done. But I also know that any decision that I have ever made, it is my decision and he is quite happy with it.

Coming out of university, I had three companies that I was considering working for – Coopers and Lybrand, TD Bank, and Dominion Securities. Coopers and Lybrand is an industry that I did not really know if I wanted to get into. TD Bank and DS were in the same industry so I had to chose between the two.

Before he went into politics, my father was executive vice-president of Dominion Securities. He was number two behind Tony Fell, who is still there. For some reason, I thought that maybe my father would want me to go to DS, but by my evaluation DS was the lesser place to work. So I went to my father and said, "I am looking for advice between TD Bank and DS."

TD did not buy one of the security firms, as Scotia Bank did when they bought McLeod Young Weir. TD developed in house and had been less successful than others, but I was looking to work in an area that was considered to be quite successful. I looked around at the technology they were using and whether or not they were coming up or coming down.

I felt DS was going down and the TD was going up. So I said to my father, "What do you think of TD versus DS?" He said, "I like them both." I said, "Do you have a preference? What is your opinion?" He said, "I have no particular bias." I said, "Well, I think that TD has got a lot more future in this particular field." He said, "Well then, I do not think that it is much of a choice." He made it very easy for me.

My brother works for National Trust, which was my grandfather's firm. I think my grandfather was pretty happy to see him take a job there. My grandfather started when he was twenty and worked his whole career at National Trust. He went from mail room or delivery guy and worked his way up to the top as president. I do not think you'll see that happen again.

Financial services had always interested me as a career choice. You really have to look at what you enjoy doing. I have learned a lot from my father. Lord knows how it went from him to me. It was by osmosis or I inherited it. But I have talked to people who I went to high school and even university with and I graduated with the same degree as they did. They will come to me and say, "I think I want to get into this. Tell me about it."

I will tell them all about the relationships between bonds, equities and money markets, currencies, interest rates and purchasing power, inflation, and the whole bit. They will say, "God, how did you know that?" I do not have an answer. You can read some of it in a textbook, but if you do not really have a preconceived notion of what it is all about, it maybe goes right by you. I seem to know an awful lot more than some of the people I went to school with. My father would read the business section and maybe explain the odd thing to me. Then maybe I would start reading the business section. It was weird in high school. Everybody else reached for the sports section first. I always reached for the business section first.

Some people want to be your friend because of who your father is. I encountered it all the time, not just at UCC, but now, especially when I go into the trade room. In the money market, everything focuses on the governor of the Bank of Canada. Whatever they say sends the currency this way and the interest rates that way. People ask, "What is your father going to say today?" I'd say, "I think that he likes Canada today." Like I know.

My father and his generation felt they had to prove something to their parents. My father's good friend, an old boy named Tim Chisholm, had to prove something to his father, taking over his father's business. As I understand it, he was always looking for a pat on the back, for a comment like, "You have added a lot to the company. Way to go." I do not think he ever got that pat on the back, but he has done a hell of a lot with the company.

My father is not the kind of person who would pat me on the back and say, "You are doing great. Congratulations. Keep going." When he was talking to Charlie Baillie, the vice-chairman of the TD Bank, Charlie Baillie later came over to me and said, "Your father is very proud of you. You have done very well. I thought that I would pass that on because I do not know if he would or not." I said, "No, he would not. Thank you."

My father has done a lot for the country and a lot personally. I am not trying to outdo him. I am not trying to match him. I am not trying to gain his adoration, so long as my peers respect me for who I am and what I am doing. If he respects me and is proud of me, that is enough.

Thirty-nine out of 117 guys in the leaving class of 1986, a full third of our class, went to McGill, including Andrew Heintzman. I always thought Andy's way of looking at things was actually pretty straight forward. He'd say, "What is everybody saying? What is the consensus? I will take the opposite view and let us see somebody argue with me."

I would question my parents all the time. When you get answers that you agree with, you start to respect them. I gained an awful lot of respect for my father for his business sense and his views economically. Socially, and in terms of raising children, I can disagree a little bit more. But on an economic level, my father is a very structured individual. He will not take a position without having a firm basis for that position, and I respect that. You will put forth an argument and he will say, "You may be right." Or if you refute what he is saying, he says, "You may be right." I may be and he may be. It may just be a different way of looking at it.

I think that may be where somebody like Andrew Heintzman gets into trouble. He may attack straight on, whereas really he is just trying to push it a little bit one way. I think that is why Dick Sadleir had a bit of a problem with it at UCC, because he had a more authoritarian management style. What he said, you did. If he wanted to solicit opinions, he would solicit opinions. But he would not change his mind from the present course, which bothered Andy.

Andrew Heintzman was a mouse trying to push an elephant. When you are a student in high school, your opinions do not amount to much. You are not going to sway the senior guys. The senior guys were not going to let your opinions, views, and vocal standpoints sway them, or themselves to be seen to be swayed by them. The school was not what Andrew wanted it to be and he was frustrated. He felt that the school was trying to push him in one direction and he was trying to push the school in another direction. Guess who is going to win that battle?

JOHN SCHOEFFEL

1979–88

Law student, New York University

SOME of the teachers in the prep were crazy. I remember my French teacher in Grade 5 throwing a hardcover book at a kid and hitting him in the face. I remember the same guy made little kids – ten-year-old kids – stand up at the front of the class and then put chalk in their mouths as punishment for speaking. I remember thinking, This is completely insane. Witnessing this stuff basically intimidated me into being too careful and too scared at that age. As I look back, it seems to me disgusting. I don't want to make it sound too dramatic. UCC wasn't a prison camp, but they relied on intimidation and punishment far too much.

There were crazy things going on. The gym teacher, Muzz Greatrex, an old army type, would give kids two minutes to get dressed after swimming.

He would be timing you. At the end of two minutes, he would stomp on kids' toes if they were not ready. It's horrifying to think about kids being so frightened – pulling on clothes, not even drying off – because of this crazy old guy. Doing drills in the pool, he would constantly shriek at us and his screams reverberated through the pool area. The prep made me very fearful and closed off. Education is supposed to open you up, not close you down.

A woman named Geraldine Mabin had been my teacher from kindergarten to Grade 2 at the Institute for Child Studies, which was a completely different atmosphere from UCC. You were free. I was the president of the dog club because my interest at that time was dogs. So we set up blankets in the back of the class and read and wrote stories about dogs. Instead of taking multiple-choice tests in the gymnasium, we would go to the gymnasium and run around and pretend to be animals as she played her guitar. I have distinct memories of kids crying when they had to go home from school.

Recently I went to visit the Mabin School, which Geraldine Mabin founded after I left the institute. I went with my roommate from Harvard who was home-educated in California. The schools in his neighbourhood were so terrible that his parents decided to educate their kids at home. Since then, the three kids in his family have gone on to Harvard University and done incredibly well. They've all written books. I thought that it would be fascinating to go to Geraldine Mabin's school and see if my friend and I would appreciate it differently.

The Mabin School is not unstructured, because you have to learn your math and how to read. You have to do what everyone has to do at school, but there's much more flexibility and appeal to individual pace. They get away from the crazy bias of age classifications of education, the idea that by age five or ten you should be achieving a certain standard. It's just a crazy organizational, business type of need.

We talked to about twenty Grade 6 kids about education, my roommate's home schooling, and what they thought of their school. They said they loved school and they never wanted to go home. They were so worried about graduating to junior high school because it wouldn't offer the same quality of education. They loved their school because they felt a part of it, not because the school was based on free and unstructured playtime. They were individuals doing things they wanted to do. In that type of school environment, if you have a particular interest, you can pursue it as a means to learning all of the materials.

This enlightened approach is something completely alien to UCC. At schools like UCC, the crazy counterproductive attitude towards learning, intensified by things as subtle as the uniform and being punished for wearing white socks, is closer to a factory mentality than an ideal learning environment. So my memories of the prep are not all fond.

I've been in many different educational settings since UCC and I've had a chance to reflect from a distance. The more I think about it, my experience at the Institute for Child Studies with Geraldine Mabin had a much greater influence in shaping my creativity. In the prep, I felt that I was basically closing off a lot of doors and becoming much more interior, timid and afraid. I certainly had to overcome a lot of fears that were generated in that period. Certainly I had friends and a lot of teachers liked me, but it wasn't a very friendly place. As soon as I got into the more senior high school grades, I became more comfortable and assertive.

I did well academically, scoring in the 82 per cent to 86 per cent range. But I just hated the fact that they would differentiate students by percentage points. I was always an 82 to an 86, as opposed to an 81 to an 85. Grades are so arbitrary. Virtually everything we did was enumerated and rated and ranked, which is another of the key problems with the industrialized approach. Kids become so preoccupied that they think that if one guy gets 86 per cent, he's somehow better than another guy who gets 72 per cent. I remember one kid always would just kill himself on some assignment to try to beat me. It seemed entirely the wrong approach.

I have been guilty of falling into the trap myself, right through Harvard University. It's the way the system works. If you don't get the good grades, you don't get to the good places. It's a real skill to learn what the teachers want. At Harvard, I really learned how to read the book, write a paper, and get an A. I knew the key – how to isolate the thesis statement and put things in the style and language it takes to get an A. It's a real knack. A lot of my friends who did well got it and a lot of my friends who didn't do well, didn't. They simply didn't know how to play the system as well. One of the reasons some people send their kids to UCC is that you learn how to play the system. You learn how the system works and how to achieve within it.

UCC is one of the most competitive places I can imagine. It's strange that there's often so much pressure applied by parents on their kids. Parents are paying over twelve thousand dollars so that their kid can get into a good university and into a good money-making profession, for the most part. The emphasis is certainly on commerce, law, and the professions. They want kids achieving a set of artificial standards from a young age, regardless of the kid's personal development or interests. Generally, parents want kids to achieve at the going rate and be competitive with their classmates. If both your parents and teachers are evaluating and treating you that way, then that becomes your mentality – competitive and cutthroat. Your self-image is overdetermined by grades and academic success.

I was on the "good" end of things. I bought into the system. I don't know how a kid can resist it, unless you completely rebel against the school, which some people do. Lots of bright, talented people underachieve as a response, refusing to buy into the competitiveness and conformity. I didn't want to do badly because I was afraid of masters doing things to me.

My older brother Mark had been on the rowing team, so my parents and my brother wanted me to try out for it. I did in my first year of the upper school but I was just too small. So I ended up coxing my first year, which was one of the best experiences I had at the school. I coxed a group of Grade 11s and 12s when I was in Grade 9. They accepted me and we had fun. It was a real antidote to a lot of the things that happened at the prep. You're doing stuff like getting up at 5:00 A.M. together and going away to Princeton University for two weeks. Bonds developed in rowing that didn't in the school in general. In my Grade 10 year, I grew bigger and ended up rowing through Grade 13 and through Harvard University.

Probably the single greatest problem with UCC is that you were at school with basically rich white men. The greatest disservice the school did to me was not exposing me to the opinions and perspectives of women and other races. The administration certainly never tried, formally or informally, to teach kids to be more sensitive, or even to know that roughly one in ten people in society are gay. There was one black guy at the school when I was there, which is obviously not the real world. There were two women teachers for a while.

I was at a UCC meeting for old boys in Boston in 1991. One of the delegates asked, "What's the school's position on coeducation?" A school official said, "UCC isn't under the same economic pressure as other private schools to admit women. We have a waiting list of eight candidates for every available spot and they don't. That's why they admit women."

This argument is completely one-dimensional and simplistic. In essence, they are saying that the reason to admit women is to fill places to make money. The school as industry. They want to make money, but they can't add more students, so why add women? Not only is he not considering the fact that it would help women to gain access to equality in social positions, but he is ignoring the needs of the boys of UCC. He's not worried about their education or how the school is serving them, which should be the priority.

At Harvard, I was incredibly well prepared by UCC to do all the academics, the athletics, and the extracurriculars. But socially and politically, my whole academic training was lacking the input of half of the population. The viewpoints of UCC are basically confined and isolated. I'm sure it is changing, but at a glacial pace.

The UCC representative in Boston also said that there are studies, one of them conducted at Harvard, that show that women don't function well in a coeducational environment. That's not my experience at all. There could be some evidence for that argument, but what I'm saying is that you're not even giving women the chance to believe or not believe that conclusion. I've heard that all-girl schools are good for developing leadership and self-esteem to compete with men in the capitalist world. But unless we bring the sexes together and give them the opportunity to influence each other positively, we won't see any progress.

UCC is one of the last places anywhere to be caught up in the nine-teenth-century imperialist mentality, separating schools by gender and dressing up the kids like an army. It's time to start educating kids in a more realistic, individual way. It's simply not thoughtful or imaginative to create an industrial, artificial setting and marshal kids through it.

SEAN GAMMAGE

1983–88

Courier

I INITIALLY AGREED to go to UCC because I realized I was spending far too much time in pool halls and video game parlours with my friends. I was just hanging around on Yonge Street, not doing much of any-thing. I realized that I needed a bit of structure in my life and UCC could provide it.

But when I got to UCC, I found out I didn't want that much structure. I had absolutely no idea what to expect at UCC. Just the fact that I was wear-ing an Upper Canada College uniform freaked the hell out of me. When I went to the clothing store, Beatty's, with my mother to get sized up for the uniform, I was very glad I met two other new boys there that same day who became my best friends.

Before UCC, I had gone to schools where I was nearly a token. Only one or two others weren't white. So luckily that aspect of UCC didn't faze me in the slightest, whereas it could have fazed a lot of other guys. In my year, there were probably about ten boys who were Oriental, three or four who were East Indian, and maybe two blacks in the whole school.

I found it very difficult the first year. I was very rebellious. I would start swearing in class if I found something to be really off topic. If I thought things were going too much one boy's way, I'd swear to get attention and then start making my own point. I realized that would be the best way to get my point across.

As far as I was concerned, I had more important things to do during my high school years. I spent more time forging signatures and going down to Jarvis Collegiate. I was sitting in on classes at Jarvis because all my friends from my previous school, Gabrielle-Roy, ended up at Jarvis.

Every year, my parents would say, "The choice is yours. You can always leave UCC if you want to." I would say, "No, let's stick around for another year." I figured: I've made it through another year, so obviously I can make it through another. Wouldn't it be nice to come out of this with a diploma from Upper Canada College? I'm quite sure a UCC diploma does make a difference for a lot of university review boards.

Unfortunately, I didn't quite make it through the last year. I got kicked out at the end of Christmas exams in Grade 13. A couple of friends and I were smoking dope in one of the prefect's rooms. We didn't get caught at the time, but there was enough pressure put on a number of the prefects that it had to come down to me. It was a choice of me getting kicked out by myself or me pulling a lot of other kids down with me. So I just went out by myself. They had cornered three of the prefects and said, "Either you tell us who was involved or you are going to be the ones kicked out." I finally said, "I can't see my friends go down, considering their parents have put more into them and their years here than my parents have."

Dick Sadleir, the principal, retired two days after expelling me in 1987. He left that Christmas break as well. UCC principals have traditionally changed over in the middle of the year. One of his last pieces of business was to deal with my situation. Everybody knew what had happened. They were trying to nail me to begin with because I had been suspended and I hadn't been at school half the time. I'd been spending so much time down at Jarvis.

So they said, "The rules say that anybody caught with drugs on the property will be kicked out." They would let the other two guys off if they agreed to just admit they were involved. With me, I had too many strikes against me, so I was out. That's why I decided, okay, fine, I'll say I was the guy who got everybody involved. I'm the only guy who should be thrown out. I ended up at Earl Haig Collegiate for half a year to graduate.

When I was kicked out, my dad was disappointed that I didn't manage to con my way out of being expelled. In fact, he told me to lie. Right off the bat, he said, "Don't tell them a thing and you might get through it." My mom was happy that I had made it up to that point, but she was mad that I hadn't got through the last half year. She would have liked to have her son be able to say, "I graduated from the most prestigious school in Canada."

When I look back at it, I wish I had gone to Earl Haig a long time before I did. I would have had a lot more fun. There were girls around and you didn't have to wear uniforms. Earl Haig had special programs for academics and for the best athletes in Toronto. It was one of the two performing arts schools in Toronto, along with the Etobicoke School of the Arts. I loved it.

My parents had no idea about the drug use at Upper Canada, but they knew a lot of my friends at Jarvis did them, so they were very glad that I never went to Jarvis to begin with. They knew that if I had gone to Jarvis, chances are I wouldn't have finished high school. I just would not have had enough discipline to resist all the frivolities and distractions.

When I was at UCC for the first two years, there was a lot of cocaine use among the upper school boys. At one point, a free-base kit was found up in the third-floor math wing. There's a little doorway that goes up to the far stairwell where guys would smoke up and freebase. That's when the school started to seriously look around for drugs. In my Grade 10 year, they kicked out nine of the twenty-four kids in my class for various reasons – drugs, alcohol, streetfighting, bad grades, absenteeism. It was just a phenomenal year for getting rid of people. A couple went at Christmas and then, all of a sudden, six or seven went at the end of the year. It was like – whoa! – what happened to most of the class?"

But nothing happened when they found the free-base kit up in the attic. Drugs were completely illegal and yet nobody got nailed for it. I'm sure that the school knew a couple of the Grade 12 guys were major drug dealers, both inside and outside UCC. At UCC, they were dealing to the Grade 13s, 12s, and some of the 11s. The school must have known that I was too, because I was dealing to the lower classes, the Grade 9s, 10s, and a few of the Grade 11s. I dealt drugs just so I could keep smoking whatever I wanted to myself. A couple of the older boys in the boardinghouses had figured out scams to make money off the younger kids by selling them drugs, booze, and fake IDs. At that age, you wanted to be able to get into the clubs and get your beer and not have to worry about things.

The Upper Canada prospectus says, "Any boy caught using drugs will be expelled." But there is a fine line between who is at the top and who isn't. Certain boys have an advantage because of their parents' names and money. I could not imagine Edward Rogers, Ted Rogers' son, being expelled for anything, especially since the Rogers have given the school so much money.

Alcohol was one thing, drugs another. A lot of whether you got kicked out of UCC depended on how well you had done in the past. When I was in Grade 11, my head of house, Andrew Heintzman, and a whole bunch of other guys on the hockey team were nailed for drinking. There was an entire busload and most of them were drunk. None of them were expelled, largely because most of them were prefects or stewards.

There were times in Grade 10 when literally half of us would be stoned in class. We had a first-year teacher for English class on the first floor beside the gym and swimming pool gallery. At recess or after lunch, we would go up to the pool gallery to smoke a joint and then come back to class. I think we took a record amount of time to cover *Julius Caesar*. It took us five months! It was a lot of fun doing it stoned. It's hard to believe with so many boys doing a lot of drugs that the school didn't twig, but they didn't. Only a couple of guys were kicked out for drugs that year.

I smoked a joint just before taking my creative writing exam. That's why I got a 92 per cent average. I did my best creative work when I was high. I'd just let my mind go. I'd write down words here, there, and everywhere. I learned the spiderweb technique, where you take one word and string it to the next word and to the next word. I'd end up with the weirdest web of ideas and images. A lot of good poetry came out of me that way.

The class of 1986 was a very wild year. Mark Bratty in the 1986 year and Chris Bratty in my year, 1988, were accused of a rape up at Wasaga Beach. At one point, UCC was unsure about which Bratty they wanted to kick out. Before the rape charge, one of the Bratty brothers had blinded a guy at a drinking party. All three Bratty brothers were at the party. The youngest one, Chris, got booted out because he was the only one who was under eighteen and therefore wouldn't get nailed by the cops. The Brattys were big boys physically, both quarterbacks for the first football team in their respective years.

The racism I experienced was never at Upper Canada. I experienced it more from the WASP private school girls, who used me to shock their parents. Initially, I wasn't trying to fit into the Upper Canada mould. But by the time Grade 11 came around, I was thinking I would like to avoid trouble. I'd like to make some friends with my classmates here at Upper Canada. So I started to go out with the blonde WASP girls from BSS, Branksome Hall, and St. Clement's and I really hated it. It was the first time I'd really bowed to peer pressure, where I was saying, "I want to fit in." I didn't go so far as to wear a Roots shirt and brown cabin shoes, but I wanted to fit in. It was a big mistake. I hated it.

At first, the girls' parents would learn that I was an Upper Canada College boy. Then it was like *Guess Who's Coming to Dinner* time. They'd say to their daughter, "This is your boyfriend? Oh! Um ..." The mother would suddenly clam up. The father would become very stern and try to be in control. He'd say, "So you're taking my daughter out, are you?" "Yes, sir." "You go to Upper Canada, do you?" "Yes, sir." Yes, sir, no, sir, three bags full. I'd try to keep him very happy when I knew nothing would keep him happy.

It was terrible because I was openly trying to be white bread at that point. I grew up in white neighbourhoods, but I wasn't openly trying to be something I wasn't. Then I found out that these WASP girls were going out with me to piss off their mommy and daddy. I was being used, which didn't go over well with me. Finally in Grade 12, I said, "Forget it. I'm not going out with any more blondes again in my life."

I would never have said anything when I was at UCC, but I always knew I was bisexual. Then, I didn't show it. I wouldn't have done anything with a guy at Upper Canada to begin with. With my friends from Jarvis, we'd been having an orgy every month, guys and girls. Literally, this is no joke. I went to three or four orgies when I was seventeen and eighteen years old.

By the time I was in Grade 12 at Upper Canada, I was stripping at Club Colby's, a gay place on St. Joseph Street. Nobody at Upper Canada knew about it, but my parents found out. My mom was really mad, but my dad didn't care too much. I don't think there was anybody at UCC who I would ever have termed openly gay at that point. If they were, it didn't make a difference to me. It wasn't as if I was going to go for them. I was just completely indifferent to it.

In Grade 12 or Grade 13, I was doing a social studies project on Casey House, the AIDS hospice, with a guy named Colin Robertson who most of the other guys would have considered gay. It didn't even dawn on me that because I was associated with an AIDS project, I would automatically be considered gay.

It wouldn't have bothered me. They had seen how flamboyant I could be. I wore jewellery and huge buckles. My earrings would dangle down past my shoulder. I was probably the most flamboyant boy at UCC. On Grub Day, you pay two dollars towards the United Way and you get to wear whatever you want to assembly in Laidlaw Hall – within reason, I found out that day. Everybody would come dressed up. You sometimes had a house theme where you would be in togas or just in jeans or casual wear. One time, I came as the character Alex from the film *A Clockwork Orange* with a couple of my friends. I was wearing long johns, combat boots, a bowler hat, and carrying a cane.

For one Grub Day, I showed up in the prayer hall in garters, high heels, and stockings. I had a whip in one hand, playing up the whole S-and-M drag queen thing. A good friend of mine, Angus McMurtry, went along with me. I had a dog leash, chain, and whip. He was on all fours, wearing a diaper, and I was whipping the floor right beside him. I was seeing how far I could push it. I was yelling, "Down slave, down slave!" When he saw me, Mr. Sadleir laughed at first and then pulled a stern face. Mr. Bredin, who was my detention master and my Latin master, gave me the coldest stare.

I don't think there was any one point where it suddenly flashed on me that I was bisexual. I always enjoyed being with girls because I'm attracted to them. I always enjoyed being with guys because I could understand them. To me, there was no way I was going to pick one over the other. Gays say, "Are you bisexual because you haven't figured out that you're truly gay yet?" I say, "No." From the straight side, they say, "You haven't figured out what you truly are yet. Are you just experimenting?" I say, "No."

Just as there are differences between the black and white races, there are big differences between men and women in terms of how they deal with other people. There are different highs and lows to be had from men and women. With men, I can understand where they are coming from. There is some intimacy that I find with women that I much prefer to that of men. Sometimes I feel some guilt when I'm with men.

I consider two guys and two girls to be my best friends in the world. They are people for whom I would lay my life on the line. I love them to that degree. Should there be a difference? Should there be only love towards females? No. Should there be love towards people in general? I don't think that everybody automatically gets my love. But what's wrong with loving a man? There should be nothing wrong at all.

A lot of my friends thought I'd be gone from UCC in Grade 10. Somehow I managed to hang in there, even though there were a lot of things I could have been kicked out for. Sooner or later, they would nail me for something. Mr. Agnew would say, "Give me fifty push-ups." And Mr. Payne would always come up with something vicious. His name was quite appropriate. You just didn't want to get on his bad side. He reminds me of a cop.

One time I threatened Payne with a rifle. I was in rifles for a year and I pointed one at him. It wasn't loaded, but just doing it is a serious offence. I said, "Hey, Mr. Payne, how are we doing today?" He wasn't happy. He just stared me right in the eye and said, "Put the gun down, Gammage." I did things like that. I'm amazed to this day that I lasted four and a half years at Upper Canada College.

IAN CHARLTON

1982–89

Student, University of Toronto

M Y MEMORIES of UCC come back to sports, especially hockey and football. I was quarterback of the first team in my final year in Grade 13, which was a big thing for me. I adored it. I won the Most Valuable Player Award.

Michael Eben, who had been a famous receiver in the Canadian Football League, started coaching at UCC when I was in Grade 12. I had him again in Grade 13. He had his Ph.D. and was a fascinating guy. He told us stories about combining CFL football and getting a degree. Playing for him in the last year made me a better player. One day I remember throwing a ball that was uncatchable. Doc Eben, all of a sudden, was in his element. With one hand he miraculously brought the ball down. He was just amazing. He was a soft-spoken, learned guy who never swore and who would motivate by example.

One day someone did a journalistic piece on him. They brought in the cameras and an interviewer was going through his list of accomplishments. We were in the background listening. Doc Eben was talking about getting letters inviting him to try out for the Green Bay Packers or Dallas Cowboys. These are exciting things, especially when you were in Grade 13, thinking about your own future.

Another former CFLer, Dave Hadden, had a huge loyalty when he was coach. People just adored the guy. He was a UCC old boy who had a spectacular football career at Queen's University and with the Toronto Argonauts. Hadden is now headmaster of Lakefield College. He had a push, push, drive, drive intensity.

Most of my closest friends at UCC revolved around the hockey team. There was a camaraderie about playing first hockey that wasn't matched in anything else that I did. It was a privilege. Sean Conacher and I were very close friends. We boarded together for Grades 11, 12, and 13. Sean's father, Brian, who was an old boy and an ex-NHLer, coached us on the first hockey team. The quality of professional coaching at UCC was unbelievable. Two guys who played for the first hockey team and graduated in 1988 went to Princeton together and now play in the NHL. Mike McKee plays for the Quebec Nordiques and Andre Faust for the Philadelphia Flyers.

If I could say there was a mentor in my hockey career, it would definitely be Brian Conacher. Here was a guy who played on the 1967 Toronto Maple Leafs, the last Leaf team ever to win the Stanley Cup. He was a very modest person, not a flashy guy. But he had a wealth of stories, like playing for the Rochester Americans with Don Cherry and for the Canadian Olympic team. If you pushed him, sometimes you could get just a nugget and you would want to hold on to it.

Once, after a big game, there was a big party some of the guys were going to, even though we had a playoff game the next day. Different guys were yelling, "Don't have too many beers. Don't stay out late." Mr. Conacher yelled to a guy who was apparently going to the party, "Listen, Hawk, do it for the club." There was a hush. All of a sudden, you felt like you were sitting on the Leaf bench and Punch Imlach had said, "Do it for the club." There was something about that phrase that turned it into something more than just high school hockey.

When we won the TDCAA [Toronto District Colegiate Athletic Association] championship in 1989, we beat Michael Power in a best of three final series. We had won the first game 10-4. In the second game, we were losing 4-2 going into the third period. If we win this game, we win the whole thing. But Michael Power was playing much better. I remember when Mr. Conacher came into the dressing room between the second and third period. Usually he was the model of composure. He never swore. He came in, knocked over the sticks, and started yelling at us. We had never seen this before. The other coaches were pretty much hiding out in the washroom. They were petrified. He said, "You guys are playing like shit. What are you doing?" He was screaming and yelling for the first time. It made a serious imprint on our minds.

The player who was probably most moved by the speech was Sean. He set up the goal to make the score 4-3, then scored the goal that made it 4-4. He was always a great player, but his play was inspired. It was really neat to see how Brian's speech affected his son most of all.

When I decided to start to board in Grade 11, I immediately adored it. It was a perfect year to come in because I didn't have to put up with the Grade 9 new-boy hierarchy bullshit. Dave Austin, who is now a Rhodes Scholar and is an incredible guy, was our head of house. I got to know him and played hockey with him. Over those years, I would find myself at times walking across the oval on a beautiful, sunny day and just realizing how lucky I was. Someone cooked breakfast for me every morning. I got to play on a football and hockey team. This was great! You're not soon going to forget those times.

It was great for partying because you could stay in boarding. I would say I was going home for the weekend and then stay out late and go back to the boardinghouse. There were all these ways you could play around with the rules. Starting in Grade 11, I took it upon myself to think that I didn't have to go to class. For whatever it's worth, I gained a reputation as someone who just did not go to class. It got me into trouble with attendance. A lot of times in Grade 13, I would sleep in until 11:00 A.M. I have great memories of sleeping in, getting out of bed, and going over to my class. Everything was there on campus. You were spoiled unbelievably.

For me, the best bonding times were late at night when I would go down and play pool. I would go down to the Grade 13 room and just be kicking around, probably doing nothing at all. The house would be dead quiet and I would meet up with a couple of guys. Although it was against the rules, we would go down in the showers and smoke. It was great. Those were the best of times, the bonding times.

In Grade 13, we used to go to the strip joint at Bloor and Yonge. That was fun. The nicest times were when all the Grade 13 boardinghouse people would go. It was just neat doing something together as a group. You would come back and check in with Mr. Blakey. Everybody would have had probably one too many beers and he would know it. But nothing was wrong. It was okay. It was just off to bed and then we would get in shit later because it was one of those nights usually where you would want to take the Grade 9 kids over to BSS.

When I was a senior, sometimes we'd wake up the cutest kid in Grade 9, who was about four feet tall, at 2:00 A.M. He was an adorable guy. All the seniors loved him. We made arrangements with a girl at BSS to have her window open. Then we made him go over to BSS and sing a love ballad to her under the window in his underwear. As much as we started off with good intentions, maybe there was a couple of beers around, and a little later maybe it took a little left turn. Instead of underwear, he would have no clothes on and then there were a lot of girls around.

I didn't know any girls when I was in the prep. Then, in Grade 9, we had football parties and suddenly there were girls everywhere. Beer was around and things totally took off. When I was in Grade 10, I played on the under-sixteen junior football team. Young guys who were movers and shakers, who were on their way to do good things in their later years in the upper school, were on this team.

That year, we decided on our own that we were going to have football cheerleading tryouts. We went to the girls' private schools, like Havergal, BSS, and Branksome Hall, and put up posters that said, "Come and try out to be an under-sixteen cheerleader at UCC." We thought maybe five girls would show up. We had put phone numbers down to call in advance if they had any questions. I got a call and Jim Parkinson got a call, one girl each. They asked, "When do we come and what do we wear?" We said, "Come as you are." This was exciting stuff.

So 4:30 comes and the two girls who called are just sitting there. One was Japanese and the other was East Indian. We waited about fifteen minutes. When we went to look outside, we saw about thirty-five girls walking up the school's main avenue! There were only about ten of us. With thirty-five girls coming up the drive, we were just going crazy. We had hit the jackpot!

So there were thirty-five girls, plus the two that were already there, in the room. We said, "Thanks very much for coming. This is a tryout for the cheerleading team for the under-sixteen football team." We crowded them all into a little room and said that we would chose ten girls as cheerleaders. We said, "Walk up to the front and do a pirouette and then say your name, who you are, and name some interests."

Every single one of them did it. They came up, did their pirouette, and turned around. Then we said, "Thanks very much for coming." All of them left their phone numbers. We all sat around and decided who had the nicest figure and the nicest bums. We picked the ten cutest girls. One of them was Eric Barton's daughter. We called them up and they thought it was great.

Everybody on the team put money into a kitty for sweatshirts and skirts. Our first game was on the main oval, which the under-sixteens rarely got to play on. About five minutes into the game, our cheerleaders come running around the end zone, go to the opposite side of the field, and start doing their number. "UCC Blues" is written across their sweatshirts. They are jumping up and down, cheerleading UCC. About ten minutes later, Mr. Sadleir, the principal, walks over and says, "That's it. Go away. You can't do this. Sorry. That's the end." Mr. Sadleir said flat out, "It's sexist. You can't do it."

I'm almost embarrassed to admit it now, but the two girls who came early both probably could have done amazing cartwheels or thrown an amazing baton, but we didn't give a shit. They weren't blonde. We wanted the WASP girls from Forest Hill who looked good. The two Asian girls who had come early – tough luck, see you later.

In retrospect, I felt ashamed. There was a concept of power, the idea of picking out which girls we wanted. Each guy got to pick two girls. We'd say, "I like Tina and Jennifer, so those are the two I'm taking."

Sexism is a huge issue at the school. Everybody tries to talk about "the egalitarian 1990s," but UCC tenaciously holds on to its hard-core traditional values. In boarding, we had our laundry done for us by maids. We could even get it dry-cleaned if we wanted. You got breakfast, lunch, and dinner made. Everything was sitting right there for you. The house matron was there to sew the button that came off your shirt. There are four maids, one for each floor, who came in and swept and cleaned everything.

I wasn't one of those kids who would leave their room in a shit pile and say to the maid, "Handle that for me." I was never rude to the women who were working there. But the house matron had to put up with God knows how much. Talk about a hard job, house matron for sixty boys, the majority of whom had been waited on hand and foot since birth. The respect was not there that should have been.

UCC does teach you manners and etiquette, but it also encourages a high degree of sexist attitudes. But I don't think my time at UCC would have been the same had it been coed – the relationships, the memories, the way we did come to interact with girls. When we got together with the girls, there was a real excitement and a genuine anticipation. Maybe that is a little perverse, making kids nervous around each other, but it was exciting. There was an innocence about it that had to be healthy.

The old-boy network attitude I find unbelievable. You really try to deny that it exists. A good friend of mine at my U of T frat house, James, is a bright, talkative guy who went to North Toronto. As the chairperson for the Canadian Institute of International Affairs at the University of Toronto, he would be in charge of bringing dignitaries in. Once he brought the king of Romania to U of T for a big dinner, so they had to do a lot of organizing and security. James was just going crazy. Another guy, a UCC old boy a year older than me, came to the rescue. He picked up the phone and called Ted Rogers. Within thirty seconds, he had one hundred cellular phones. He turns to James, who was the program director, and says, "Let me take care of some other stuff for you."

The UCC guy had just tapped into the old-boy network before his very eyes. There was a look of awe in James. He said, "Is it really like that? Can you just pick up the phone?" The old boy ended up organizing the security and had money coming in from different people. James was starting to wonder if he'd missed the boat. Here is a guy who is now on a scholarship to London School of Economics, and yet someone is making him feel inferior because he can't call up Ted Rogers and get cellular phones.

When I go back to UCC now as an old boy, I no longer expect anybody to remember my face or a big goal I may have scored or touchdown pass I may have thrown. At one point, I considered a professional football career, but I decided against it. I still remember the victories at UCC, but not everyone else does. When I go back, maybe I am hoping for someone to say,

"Hey, I remember when you did that." Then, of course, someone says, "So, when did you graduate?" Only a few years down the road, no one remembers you. Life just carries on. It's funny how that happens.

BEN WIENER

1983–90

Student, University of Chicago

S OME UNFORTUNATE THINGS happened at UCC at the end of the 1980s. I think they forgot what their purpose was, or maybe there was just so much confusion about making the transition from Dick Sadleir to Eric Barton as principal. The school snapped back into a very rigid 1950s mould, perceiving anything slightly foreign as incorrect. It didn't have a secure enough sense of itself to tolerate the things it used to tolerate when it knew where it was going.

The dress code, things like the length of your hair and the colour of your socks, got stricter. I really never saw the reason why I had to wear blue or grey socks. I figured it didn't hurt them too much to let me wear whatever colour socks I wanted. I used to be able to wear cowboy boots to school. Under Sadleir, you could write your own notes to excuse yourself from absences when you were in Grade 13. That system was eliminated under Barton, who was an old boy from the 1950s who wanted to bring back a rah-rah "Blue Pride" to UCC. He reminded me of George Bush. He wouldn't say the dress code was being made stricter, it was being "revised." He used a lot of euphemisms.

Under Barton, the school was trying to raise seventeen million dollars for some new facilities. It was really annoying to be a student and realize that you're being used as a prop for the promotional fundraising video. We had to be constantly smiling in our ties and short hair because some rich old-boy donor might be walking past our class. Then they made a separate video to show to prospective Hong Kong donors, showing UCC full of smiling Oriental kids.

Barton intended to create "educable, compassionate youth" as his mandate at UCC. That was his phrase. He introduced mandatory community service as part of the curriculum, not understanding that community service doesn't necessarily create compassion. You can make somebody spend one thousand hours working at the Scott Mission, but that's not going to change the feeling of revulsion they have for the people who are out on the street.

I don't think Barton understood the dynamics of the school. Talking about how the school had become more multicultural, he was inadvertantly funny. He'd say, "We have grown more tolerant of you." He really saw the world as being composed of the Upper-Canadian WASP nobility and the recently arrived Jews and Asians who had to line up and receive an infusion of moral character.

During the Barton years, they sent some boys down to Haiti to do some community service work. Prince Philip happened to be in town and Barton wanted to introduce Prince Philip to the guys. Eric Barton says, "These boys are going off as part of a school mission to Haiti." The prince turns to Barton as if to say, "Are you crazy? Haiti? Why are they going to that fucking sewer?" Barton only lasted a couple of years as principal.

By the tenth grade, I was really turned off by the place. Certain factions really wanted to get rid of me. I was iconoclastic. I didn't have the proper respect for the institution, partly because I am an American. My parents came to Toronto from the States in the 1960s. My father teaches at York University and has no respect for authority figures, so I guess it has rubbed off on me. I was inclined to say the emperors have no clothes, which the emperors of UCC found very threatening.

When you are a teenager, you still believe that you can make a difference if you just get pissed off enough. You believe that if you make really great speeches in defence of your idea, people will actually buy it. You don't realize that if you are coming up against the law, no matter how impassioned your pleas for the liberation of the status quo, you're not going to get it through. It takes a while to learn that.

In the ninth and tenth grade, I hung out with a lot of people from public school. I was in my proletarian-wannabe stage. I spent a lot of time looking as dirty as possible, which eventually disappeared somehow. UCC grows on you. I didn't feel there was much of a difference between myself and my peers in public school in ninth grade. By tenth grade, I really did start to feel that the public school people were moving in different directions. Somehow their values and interests were ceasing to be compatible with mine. It sounds so awful to say.

But for all the misbehaving I did, I was a fairly good kid. I played sports and I did well enough academically. I was just skipping too much school. My friends and I were interested in breaking the rules as much as we could. We'd see how long we could grow our hair, how much school we could miss, how little we could do, and get away with it. In some ways, the school seemed to encourage that behaviour with the sudden new emphasis on rules, which seemed stupid, pointless, and arbitrary to us.

Duncan Payne, my football coach, was a really big, scary Scottish guy who liked to yell a lot. One day, a friend of mine, thinking he was helping me out, marked me present on a sheet when I in fact hadn't been in class for a long time. Payne caught on that the sheet had been altered. He dragged me into his office and screamed and yelled at me. I didn't know that my friend was trying to help me out, so I didn't really have much of an explanation. He ripped out all the notes that I had been writing to excuse myself, inventing phoney funerals, vasectomies, the weirdest excuses you could imagine. There were thirty or forty of them. He asked me if I had forged any of the notes. I said that I had forged all of them, at which point he turned bright red, grabbed me by the collar, and dragged me down the stairs into the principal's office. He threw open the door, threw me inside, and said, "Eric, I want him expelled right now."

They called in my parents and I got a three-day suspension. The school was really mad at me because I wouldn't tell them who I had been cutting class with. That struck me as ironic at a school that tries to teach you so much about building character. They tried to develop some sense of moral and social obligation in us on one hand and then asked us to rat on our friends on the other hand. They had a classic double standard. That was what was so funny about the place.

The classes they taught were really sophisticated, the English department and the history department particularly. I didn't really appreciate it at the time. They never actually taught dates or events. It was all completely historiographic. Getting to college was what history was all about, not learning dates. In fact, they never burdened us with a textbook in high school. I was just amazed at the sophistication. Some of the things we read in Grade 11 keep coming up again in my university classrooms.

I thought Nigel Barber was a great history teacher. He was a bit of a folk hero for his eccentric behaviour. When UCC started the Renaissance XXI fundraising campaign, there was a lot of pressure to clean up the school image. Barber left right after Eric Barton came in as principal in 1988.

Barber was a wonderfully interesting character, but you could tell he had some distaste for the job. There were things he would rather have been doing than teaching ninth-grade history. He appeared degenerate in a really androgynous way. He had a hollow face with bulging eyes and hadn't bought new clothes since the late 1950s. He'd come into class in various states of disrepair, covering his eyes. He would wear dark sunglasses in the halls, walking with one hand along the wall. There were a lot of teachers who did that after lunch.

I don't think I've ever met people who drink as much as UCC boys. Have you ever heard of another school where they serve drinks to their eighteen-year-old graduates? The UCC culture is work hard, play hard. The school sponsors a ski day in February when they invite BSS, Havergal, and Branksome Hall girls and we'd all go out and destroy ourselves. Once we pretty much destroyed John Turner's ski chalet. His son, Andrew, graduated in my year. Mr. and Mrs. Turner weren't at their chalet, so Andrew threw a weekend-long crazy party. Once you are sixteen, you are able to drive up north by yourself. Hundreds of people were pouring in and out of the chalet.

When the cops came by, they were so bewildered, they didn't know what to do. What are you going to do with the son of the former prime minister and his rowdy private school friends? You can't throw them all in the paddy wagon. We were aware of that and we exploited it. I always felt really bad for Andrew. I think it must be rough to have a father in the public eye.

At one party, the police came into the Turners' place and said, "All right, everybody leave." Nobody paid much attention. They finally got really upset. They said, "We're going to have to get tough, so why don't you all leave?" It was pretty late, so I picked up my beer and I walked to the car. I was sixteen. The police stopped me and said, "How old are you?" They tried to give me a ticket for underage drinking. I said, "Then why did you tell us to leave?" They said, "Not with a beer. Leave the beer."

They wrote out a ticket. I took it and ripped it up. They looked at me really puzzled. They didn't know what to do. I don't think they had ever been shown that kind of disrespect before. Probably up in Collingwood, people know enough to behave themselves. When I ripped up the ticket, the cops shrugged and walked off. They looked so helpless and bewildered. When we told the cops that we went to UCC, they always seemed to let us off. Whenever I got in trouble, I'd work the fact that I went to UCC into conversations with authority figures. It makes you wonder what life must be like for people who can't say that.

My friends and I always used to go the Beaver Motel every year. The entire place would be rented out by people I knew. We'd kick things through the walls, very Rolling Stones. Hordes of healthy-looking kids would come down to take over the place and make people's lives miserable. During the Ski Day weekend parties, there was the inevitable car accident. Somebody was always driving their car off the road and coming into school with big bruises or new teeth.

We also went to various Forest Hill houses for various parties, including Ted Rogers' place at Frybrook and Dunvegan Road. People would vomit on Mr. Rogers' rug or blow up Conrad Black's swimming pool with fire-crackers. There used to be a tree on Ted Rogers' front lawn where we would always hang out and sneak a butt every day at lunch.

There was no formal direction at UCC to be anything except a jock. The attitude was "Take your classes and behave yourself." One sure way to fit in was to play sports. I was always torn. I had my own interests, but they didn't fit into what the school was doing, beyond playing football. Socially, the people I identified myself with most strongly were my friends on the football team, not the guys who were really neat to chat with. They were great to talk to, but I would never go to a party with them on the weekends. As for the other schools, the Catholic schools hated us and we had a lot of contempt for them. When we would all go down to De La Salle or St. Mike's for an important hockey game, there were always fistfights. UCC guys were yelling things like, "Hey, Gino, your mother cleans my house." Whenever the opposing team scored a goal on UCC, we'd chant, "That's all right, that's okay, you'll be working for us some day."

There were also serious interfaculty fights, although I don't think punches were ever thrown. I think it's great that the school has some con-flict because it keeps everybody on their toes. If all the teachers were the same, it would be a really dull place. I remember screaming matches. We'd walk into class and listen to Marshall Webb, the English teacher, yelling and swearing, using the most filthy language about some of the science teachers. He'd say to us, "Do you know what that motherfucker wants to do?"

Marshall Webb is an old boy who came back to teach at UCC, which is a little strange. But he's a wonderful teacher. I really enjoyed having classes with him, although I really didn't like him at first. It takes a while to get past his manner. I think he is really arrogant, depending on whether he likes you. He can make you feel really small or he can be a really good guy. I can certainly imagine him being an insufferably pompous student when he was at UCC.

There is a whole English department clique who all wear nice ties and fashionable haircuts and spend a lot of time in Toronto drinking cappuc-cino. But it was teachers like Marshall Webb, Colin Lowndes, and Brad Adams, to a certain degree, who made me realize that I could really get something out of being there. They were the masters at UCC who told me it was okay to like books. I do owe them a great debt, although they are such caricatures of urban, cappuccino New York wannabes.

Some of the other teachers could be pretty savage. Public schools are checked by government and political pressure, but at private schools teach-ers can still whack you around. Sometimes teachers would lose it, pick boys up and throw them through the halls. There was no formal beating, but some teachers could be incredibly cruel to kids who were simply confused. The teachers would pick on the kids you could tell felt really insecure and awkward, reducing them to tears with verbal abuse. They were just typical confused adolescents. By the time you get out of UCC, there is very little that gets under your skin.

I felt really bad for the female teachers, who usually were fairly recent college graduates. One female teacher got absolutely no respect. She always had to call in Duncan Payne to get her classes to sit down and shut up. She would ask, "Where is your homework?" We'd laugh in her face and say, "What are you going to do about it? You're just some young broad who teaches science. Come over here and fuck me."

She was an outsider in every way. Nobody paid any attention to her. She realized that you have to be twice as tough. The tough teachers didn't take shit. If guys gave you lip, you threw them out. That was the only way to survive as a woman and to teach tenth grade science. I had her over a period of two years. Every term, she got a little less pleasant, a little more hardened. When I was at UCC, there were only two women teachers, but now there are more. There were no black or Asian teachers.

There was always juicy gossip about male teachers sleeping with students. A guy I know used to give booze to another guy in exchange for sexual favours. I think people are just starting to become aware of how homophobic and homoerotic it is at UCC. Here you are, a bunch of guys bonding ad nauseam in your jock straps. In sex ed class nothing about homosexuality was ever mentioned, and yet the place is full of gay boys and teachers. In fact, the sex-education teacher said we should use condoms or birth control because, as rich UCC kids, there were a lot of women out there who wanted to be impregnated by us to secure their economic future. That was the sort of attitude that characterized the place. They had a big model vagina that they used in sex ed class. It was right out of "Monty Python."

One day, they school brought in a speaker who talked about the effects of dropping acid. We were all thinking, This sounds really cool. The next week, about twenty guys I know went out and bought acid. We all tried it because it sounded so cool in the drug lecture. One day we all got really bored in class, so we took acid. It was wild, sitting in front of our computer screens on acid, laughing uncontrollably. Football practice was even worse. The huddles were a complete mess because half the team was on acid.

I don't know what the drug problem is like now, but the drinking problem is incredible. We used to go to the bars all the time at lunch in tenth, eleventh, twelfth grade and come back to school. I used to go out for beers with the teachers when I was sixteen. The school seemed to encourage it. At that point, you've got to ask if there's a problem or whether it's just part of the general culture. Everybody seems to function just fine. Even the rebellion is done in an established way. It's okay to go up to Muskoka to get toasted and crack up a speedboat because your father and grandfather went up to Muskoka, got toasted, and cracked up a speedboat too.

In my graduating year, 1990, there was a minor scandal. The editor of the *College Times*, a Jewish guy, Motek Sherman, wrote an editorial that was very critical of the school. The editorial opened with an image of his immigrant Jewish grandfather pointing to the school and saying that to get inside the UCC gates, to be able to toss a cricket ball on the lawn and to go to the Battalion Ball, was a symbol of acceptance by the Canadian Establishment. Once you have achieved that, nobody could take it away from you. But Motek said that in his eleven years at UCC, the school hadn't really fulfilled its promise. In fact, UCC was nothing more than an old boys' athletic club full of mindless, alienated sheep, run by a faceless bureaucracy. Looking back, I thought it was very juvenile. I think he was very consciously looking for a fight.

Then things blew up. Ian Kennish was one of the school pets that year. His mom was a trustee and he was a steward and a hockey player. I couldn't stand the guy. He got all upset and without consulting anybody, pulled the editorial from the printers before the *College Times* went to press. He took it down to Eric Barton and turned the whole thing into a massive battle over freedom of speech. For several weeks, people met to decide what to do about Motek's editorial. He certainly pushed all the right buttons.

Finally, they tempered the editorial's tone a little. Then the deal was that Ian Kennish got to write a piece that had to be included as well. His line was: "If graduating from high school is supposed to be the happiest day of your life, why is it that today we feel only sorrow?" It went on to talk about how wonderful UCC was and what a tragedy it was that we were all leaving it. Personally, I was quite happy to move on.

I didn't think there was much anti-Semitism at UCC, although I know Motek Sherman felt that he was the victim of a lot of anti-Semitism. It could be that maybe I didn't want to see it, or maybe since I didn't make a big deal out of it, it could be ignored. Maybe as long as you didn't shove your differences in people's faces, they let you get away with it, as long as you knew how you were supposed to behave.

Anytime you feel misplaced, you always look for someone to blame. It was really funny when Jewish guys I knew would complain about the Asians. Not long ago, people were saying, "These damn Jewish kids coming in now are too smart. They work too hard." Now you have assimilated

Jewish kids saying, "These damn Chinese kids coming in now are too smart. They work too hard." Everybody moves up the ladder. I don't know what the next wave of immigration will be, but there will certainly be a lot of Hong Kong people at UCC.

For all my rebellion, I was also aware of a need to belong. Sometimes I would go out for lunch at places like the Rosedale Golf Club. It's very funny when you eat lunch at a club where you know you won't be a member. In some ways, you scorn it. You think: What a fucking elitist, racist piece of shit. I don't want to be a part of it. Fuck this institution and the culture that perpetuates it. Still, it's kind of a turn-on to eat there. You find yourself saying, "Bring me another drink. Heat my steak! Nice service! Great place!" When you pay, you sign somebody else's name.

I was probably accepted at UCC because I didn't work at it. It was very easy to adapt if you didn't have too much baggage to get rid of. When I had long sideburns, the school got very upset that I was violating the dress code. I told them they were the Jewish earlocks. When I wanted to skip school, I used to invent Jewish holidays. I'd say, "Please excuse Ben from period six. He was away celebrating Bagel Day." They'd believe me. I swear to God, I celebrated Bagel Day three or four times every year.

In the end, I'm not sure how I feel about UCC. I'm torn between appreciating a sense of tradition and what I think is sensible. Something about UCC gets under your skin so that you don't want the place to change after you've left, no matter how much you wanted it to change when you were there. I now think I would be happier if the boys wore shirts with collars to class. I sound like an old fascist, but it's true.

My memories of the place become kinder the further away I get. You forget how awful it felt to be yelled at, to have to deal with an eccentric Brit like Terry Bredin sputtering in your face, being sent home to get your hair cut or change your pants, or singing some stupid hymns every morning. But it wasn't so bad. It takes a couple of years to figure out what you can get away with. The students are given just enough boundaries to react against, but enough leeway so they don't react too much. Trying to shape the futures of adolescent boys is not an enviable task.

JAMES ARTHUR
1987–93
Student, University of Toronto

I WAS THE LOSER in our year. I was always being bullied and pushed around. There were only six new boys that year who entered in Grade 8, which is not a great year to enter into UCC. Grades 3, 5, 7, and 9 are better. Even though my father and grandfather were old boys, I was an outsider. I was one of six new boys, but I was by far the least athletic and most withdrawn.

Little things just added up. For instance, I didn't know how to tie a tie after gym class. Of course, no one would show me how. The kids were too homophobic and the teachers weren't around. I didn't have my act together in the first few days of school, so I didn't know how to try out for any teams. I don't know whether I would have made it anyway. I was very unprepared.

The teachers had no control of the students in the classroom. I had a particularly weak Grade 8 form master, Herbert Sommerfeld, who had no control. The jocks would sit at the back, shoot spitballs at the people in the front, and make rude, sadistic remarks. Sommerfeld was oblivious. He would just continue writing math equations on the board.

For lunch, we were left in a classroom by ourselves without any supervision. Every day, one teacher would walk a beat around the entire prep school to check each classroom, but most of the time we were unsupervised. Guys would steal my lunch bag, dump out my stuff, knock things off my desk, flick my ears. It was just awful. One day, I just got up and left. I went home in tears.

My mom phoned the school and complained, which made matters worse. Mr. Sommerfeld called a meeting of myself, himself, and the two class representatives. In the prep, we had class representatives from each class. The four of us sat down and had a talk, but nothing was resolved.

I was very withdrawn all the way from Grade 8 through to Grade 11. I was in a capsule. I immensely disliked everyone at UCC, although I had a few friends. I'm really unathletic. I never learned how to dive, ride a bicycle, skate, or ski. Sports were awful. I really didn't like them. I think the prep was the worst year of my life.

Another guy also came to UCC from the Forest Hill program. He actually said when introducing me to people, "This is James Arthur. He's going to be the head boy like his father. He's really smart." But I had really low self-esteem. I had a low estimate of my intellectual abilities for Grades 8 and 9. I just believed I was really stupid. Then on the SATs, I did better than everyone else in class. That boosted my ego a bit.

I might have subconsciously underachieved academically as a response to the kind of environment I was in. I realized just a few days ago that all the courses that my parents forced me to take are the ones that I flunked in or came close to flunking. I wanted to take Latin and they forced me to take German. All the courses that I had my arm twisted to take, I did badly in. All the ones I chose to take, I did really well in.

I used to go on about the hierarchy at UCC, but my friends never really believed me. The same guys who were my class representatives in Grade 8 went on to be stewards in Grade 13. Things don't change at UCC. I think intelligent and responsible students are chosen, for the most part, as stewards, but they are chosen from a very small list of students who are good at sports. I could name a few really stupid, complete assholes we had as stewards, but there have been some really good, intelligent ones too.

Stewards have to have a very idealistic outlook on life, which doesn't represent the student body at all. Maybe that idealism is bred by being mollycoddled all the way through UCC and being the chosen leaders in a sort of predestined way. Perhaps because they know they are destined to be the stewards, they are pretty cheerful about the whole UCC experience.

But stewards don't represent the student body, which is fairly cynical. The stewards are basically a class unto themselves. Our head steward, Tim Kennedy, thought it would be a good idea to have the whole leaving class of 1993 involved in a group community service project for the first month of the summer after graduation. What a conehead! I have better things to do. Quite frankly, I have no interest in the school's community service project anyway. I'm not going to spend my July working on community service.

Performing thirty hours of community service is a mandatory part of the curriculum. I worked for Street Kids International for twenty hours, doing things like stuffing envelopes. I campaigned for the Cancer Society for two and a half hours, worked at the Diabetes Fundraising Gala for seven hours, and worked at Brown School for two hours. I didn't feel the experience enriched me in any way. When a sense of morality is forced on somebody, it is not morality but just another school rule.

It would be better if students were encouraged to engage in community service without the promise of bonuses to their marks, without the promise of gold and silver pins to wear on their lapels. If all those things were abolished, I think community service could be a very fine thing. If only students who sincerely cared did it and if their hours were not posted, it would be a wonderful thing. As it is, it is just part of the bureaucracy. It serves a dual purpose. One, it improves the school's image. Two, it allows noblesse oblige to dispense with some of the guilt that I'm sure members of wealthy families often feel. I only did it because I had to.

It's very hard to work outside the framework of UCC. I tried to start an underground paper in Grade 12. I made photocopies and handed it out after prayers. Certain members of the school administration got really upset about it, which was understandable, because there were some things I said that I should not have said. I made nasty and slanderous remarks about some students and some members of the administration. I didn't mention names and I didn't swear, but it was not journalism. It was garbage. I was just venting my frustration.

The school was upset because they had no control over it. When a student does something without seeking permission from members of the administration, it creates a margin for a lot of things to go wrong. Someone could very well start handing out something even worse. They were pretty upset with me. But when they brought me in and talked to me, they were very lenient. I later became humour editor of the *College Times*, but I got fired by the editor, along with a lot of other guys. I was probably a little too satirical and subtle for them.

Most of the UCC students are comatose. Most of them are vaguely cynical or have some angry notions about the school, but would rather just sort of mill around like sheep. They just want to get through, skip classes they are too bored to attend, work a bit, think about their university admission, and try not to think about the future. That's the average UCC student.

I have said a lot of bad things about the school, but I don't mean to give a one-sided impression. The school has some really great teachers. I really do believe that it gives one of the best educations in Canada, if not the best. I think all the constant jostling and competition does lead students to find their own niche and their own opportunity to develop.

For all the difficulties of my experience at UCC, I think I distinctly found my own way of dealing with things. I think I've been made stronger by UCC. I think every boy who goes there, if they can survive it and deal with it, will come out stronger than when they went in.

On the other hand, there are plenty of people crushed by it. In the spring of 1993, a kid two years younger than me shot himself. Apparently he was a very upbeat, cheerful guy. A lot of students, some who didn't even know him, were really upset. I suppose a certain amount of it is projecting their own fears and anxieties, imagining themselves in his shoes. He was boarding in Seaton's House, then moved to Jackson's, a day-boy house. There were some Grade 13 guys in Seaton's who were crying. They were just sitting around sobbing.

After his death, the school had us go to individual classes to discuss our feelings. We were broken up into our separate houses. I was not too caught up in the whole thing, but I think it helped some people. The school had a book in the library where students could go and write about the incident. The book was to be given to the boy's family.

I'm sure the aggression that UCC breeds works very well in the real world. In the business world, you need that kind of mentality to survive and get ahead. That's probably why UCC produces all the leaders it does. To some degree, however, the school has been undermined by parents who threaten to sue if anything goes wrong. When I was in Grade 10, a kid was told to cut his long hair. He didn't and his parents made a federal case out of it. The school eventually just asked him to leave or he didn't come back. I think there were some words spoken about possible court measures to secure his right to have long hair if he wanted to. But what parents need to understand is that when you are at UCC, you surrender your rights.

Because UCC depends on the outlet of aggression, I don't think coeducation would work. If there were girls there, male students would be inhibited about letting out their aggression. UCC has been a male institution for over 160 years and girls would feel very out of place there. It makes much more sense to integrate girls through the use of cooperative ventures with girls' schools or public schools. It's probably true that UCC is fundamentally sexist, but there is not much you can do about it.

We had some feminist speakers come to speak at UCC for the World Affairs Conference in February 1993. I thought Robin Morgan, the editor of *Ms.* magazine, was way off base. I was personally pretty offended by her speech in Laidlaw Hall. She said there was some rude behaviour and rude remarks by UCC students, but it was actually a St. George's student who made a rude remark to her. I'm not saying there is a difference between UCC and St. George's, but I think she should have looked more carefully before she criticized the behaviour. I think coming in with battle tactics was a mistake. She pointed at the portraits of the past principals of UCC and called them "pale males" and symbols of repressive patriarchy. She had the whole assembly stand up and observe a minute's silence in memory of the fourteen female victims of Marc Lepine in the "Montreal Massacre." When an Asian kid stood up and asked her a question after her speech, she said dismissively, "I can't imagine what it must be like to be a person of colour in a school like this."

I was really appalled. She was not taking her responsibility seriously. I think she really did a very bad job, and so did the World Affairs Conference organizing committee. It would have been a good idea to have some speeches from radical male sexist speakers. Some of the remarks made by the feminists bordered on sexism. I decided I didn't need that garbage.

A member of the faculty very sanctimoniously said, "A lot of consciousness was raised during the conference. A lot of defensiveness was shown by UCC students." Of course the students will be defensive if you punch them in the face. I don't mean to undermine the importance of sexual equality at UCC, but I think Robin Morgan just ended up aggravating the situation.

I'm not a particularly sensitive guy. I'm pretty callous when it comes to issues like community service and coeducation. I believe in social Darwinism. Some of my teachers called me a fascist. On an essay I handed in, I said that World War I was in fact an effective method of population control. The master handed it back with a page and a half of comments. He said, "I refuse to mark this. You didn't answer the question."

One day, a big guy in my class, Chuck Chang, walked into the classroom, came up to me and said, "You're in my seat. Get out of my seat." I was in a bad mood. I said, "Look, my father just died." He said, "Oh, well, you should have told me." Then he went and sat by himself, quite shaken up. He said a couple of defensive things to the rest of the class. He said, "You could have said something. I'm really sorry. I didn't know."

I came up to him at the end of the class and said, "Hey, Chuck. I'm just pulling your leg." He was mad. I never liked him anyway. I'm glad I got a chance to do that because he was one of the guys in Grade 9 who would sit behind me and kick my chair. They did things like fold little diamonds out of paper and flick them at people. They really hurt when they hit you in the back of your head. Chuck would always throw these things at me in class, so I'm glad I got a chance to even the score.

I'm always probing or mentally jabbing people. Students who can't get by physically have to be aggressive verbally or intellectually. You can't be passive at UCC. You have to be an aggressor in some respect. I've been very verbally aggressive the past few years, which has kept a lot of people at a distance. Guys who probably could have been my friends have kept a few steps away. But it helped me.

I don't know if UCC made me the way I am or not. Maybe it comes from having a very conservative, reactionary father. His views are similiar, but I don't think I'm as right wing as my father. I didn't talk to him about my problems when I was at UCC. I can't communicate with him that well. I would tell him things, but it was always a few years after the fact. I could tell him what I'm talking about now, but I wouldn't tell him I skipped twenty or thirty economic classes this year.

I think my father was more serious about his schooling than I was. He would say, "I don't understand why you skip classes, why you don't apply yourself more to your work, why you don't care more." I said, "Look, I'm in the top six for university. It really doesn't matter to me how I do in economics." He said, "But the knowledge and information that you acquire will stand you in good stead the rest of your life." I said, "I don't need to know about the intricacies of supply and demand."

My graduation wasn't some great catharsis or anything. Mentally, I had already left midway through January. We all got together in Laidlaw Hall, went up to shake hands with Mr. Blakey and receive our old-boy tie, which is navy blue with a bunch of little gold UCC crests. Up until now, you've had to buy them. Now they just bill them directly to your account.

I thought Doug Blakey was a terrible principal, very gauche and socially awkward. His speeches are uninspiring. For the leaving-class lunch, he got all of Martland's House together and said, "Tell me about locker-room culture. Tell me about stealing." A lot of things are stolen from lockers. He was never subtle when he wanted information from students or when he was trying to get a point across.

In typical UCC fashion, Blakey tried to control and co-opt the traditional leaving-class prank. He said, "I'd like your prank to be on Thursday. I want to reserve Friday for my speech." What a guy! All of Wednesday night, there were cop cars patrolling UCC, watching for any students trying to perpetrate any mischief. On Thursday, we got a smoke machine and smoked out assembly. Blakey thought, Okay, that was the prank. I guess we got off easy this year. He was actually naive enough to believe that was all we would do.

On Thursday night, about ten of us went into the library and unlocked a window. After the security guard checked out the library and decided everything was okay, we opened up the window and climbed in. We carried out thousands of books and put them behind the door of the stage in Laidlaw Hall. On Friday in prayers, a student put a winch to hold down the crank. The door slowly lifted up to reveal huge piles of books stacked six feet high. I gather the school found out the books were gone. They knew where they were, but it hadn't occurred to them that we were going to lift the door up in assembly. It went over really well.

In 1992, someone hung a huge condom in the clock tower. Another prank diverted the traffic off Avenue Road into the school grounds. They just closed off all the traffic on Avenue Road and Lonsdale and made it go through the school. There was a traffic jam right in front of the front steps. Businessmen were getting out with their cellular phones, screaming and yelling.

Then one year, some guys put ads in newspapers and magazines and sent out forged letters to old boys saying that UCC was going coeducational. Anyone who wanted to enrol their daughters at UCC simply had to come by the day of the leaving-class assembly. Applications would be taken immediately on a first-come, first-served basis.

A lot of people were fooled. Parents showed up with their daughters, all dressed up, waiting for applications to be taken. People should have clued in. The letter had forged Mr. Blakey's signature. It looked official, but there were a few things that should have tipped them off. For the school motto, "Palmam qui meruit ferat" – "Let he who merits the laurels, bear the laurels" – the letter said, "Let he or she who merits the laurels, bear the laurels." That should have tipped people off.

I don't think UCC is a bastion of Toryism, as a lot of people think. It simply intensifies what people already feel. I think UCC teaches students to be fighters and to look out for themselves. Whether or not you're happy at UCC, it doesn't really matter. You will come out aggressive, one way or the other. A closed, competitive environment, with teachers breathing down your neck, forces you to have strong character. I'm grateful for that.

I decided to go to Trinity College at U of T, like my father did, but I'm not going to be a university academic like him. I want to be a novelist, screenwriter or a literary magazine editor. I don't think I'm going to stay in Canada. I think there is too much complacency in Canada. The U.S. has a lot of false hopes and dreams, but they have the same competitive, dog-eat-dog atmosphere that you need to get ahead.

DANIEL BORINS

1984–93

Student, McGill University

IN GRADE 13, I was parking my car on Frybook Road outside the school grounds. Doug Bassett's house, a big grey mansion, was on the corner of Frybrook Road and Forest Hill Road, right beside the school. A lot of guys smoke cigarettes out on Frybrook. The BSS girls come to meet the UCC guys during lunch and hang out together.

I was in a really bad mood. I was sick of the authority figures telling me what to do and pushing me around. It was my ninth year in the school and I just wanted to get out. It had been my idea to invite the American feminist, Robin Morgan, the editor of *Ms.* magazine, to speak at the school that term. We had just had a follow-up session after her speech and I was feeling lousy.

I was leaving the school around 5:30 P.M. Two of my buddies were in their car waiting for another guy who was finishing practice. When I walked onto Frybrook, I saw Doug Bassett yelling at these guys, giving them shit just for hanging out in their car.

He was yelling, "Move the car off there!" So they moved their car off the street. He said, "No, that's no good, move it back!" So they move it back. He just kept on yelling at these kids and ordering them around. These guys were so used to taking shit from authority figures that they didn't realize what was going on. They didn't have to move their car. They had every right to park on the street. I thought, I can't believe this.

Then Bassett turns to me and says, "What are you looking at?" I said, "I'm watching you yell at these guys." He flipped. He said, "What's your name?" I said, "I don't have to tell you my name. What's your name?" He said, "My name is Douglas G. Bassett." Then he started hurling insults at me. He shouted that he was tired of smart-assed pricks smoking in front of his house all day long. I said, "Are you even here during the day?"

He was chewing me out. Then he ran into his house saying, "I'm going to get your name. I'm going to get your licence plate number." Something really set me off. I said, "Fuck you, man. What are you doing this for?" By the time I was in my car, he had written down my licence number. I drove off. It was kind of a stupid thing to do.

About three weeks later, John Symons, the minister in charge of discipline and native affairs, wanted to see me in his office. He said, "You're in a lot of trouble. I heard how rude you were to Mr. Bassett." I said, "Did it happen on school grounds?" He said, "No." I said, "Do you know the whole story?" He said, "No." I said, "Why do you think I can be in trouble for this?" He said, "You were in your uniform, weren't you?" I said, "Yes." He said, "Well, you're a poor representative of the school."

I said, "I wasn't representing the school. I was representing myself." He said, "I heard you said some pretty vulgar things." I said, "Well, Mr. Bassett said them to me first. Shouldn't he be here in the office too? Isn't Mr. Bassett a UCC old boy? Isn't he a representative of the school? I don't think I should be in trouble for this just because Doug Bassett has a more important name, higher status, or a lot more money than me. Is that what matters to you?" Symons didn't know what to say. He said, "Well, all I can say to you is, don't fight fire with fire."

Symons was pretty decent. He said, "I think you've matured a lot since you first came here. I respect your opinion and I think you are a good person. But it might have not been a wise decision." I said, "Maybe not, but I had to do it." He said, "You don't have to, but I advise writing a letter of apology to Mr. Bassett." I said, "Maybe I will, if I get one from him first." That incident symbolized something about the school to me.

A lot of people couldn't believe I did what I did. There was a belief that I had committed the ultimate offence, insulting a rich old boy of exalted status who gives money to the school. These rich old boys are like demigods. They really are. We should all be so grateful. But maybe the guy is a total scumbag. Maybe we don't want his money. They could never see it that way. At UCC, there is an indoctrination process that money and power are good. Keep your mouth shut. Submit to somebody who has more power than you. Join rank.

I remember in the prep being told if you're riding to school on the Avenue Road 5 bus, you should give your seat to old ladies. Don't throw snowballs. Be a good prep boy. I remember being read letters that people had written to the school about boys who had done something wrong. By reading us these letters, collective guilt was being cast over all of us. I thought, Why am I always a representative of the school, but the school never represents me? Isn't there any back and forth? Do they care really about me? No! It's like love it or leave it. We have a huge waiting list. Oh, but if you do leave, you're going to be a plumber. If you do leave, you're screwed. You won't have the old-boy network to draw upon.

By Grade 8, I was unhappy at UCC. I started recognizing how I had been wronged on many occasions. Once in Grade 7, a kid at the bus stop was picking on a little Form 1 kid. I said to the guy, "Why are you pushing around this kid? Would you like me to push you around?" He said, "Screw off!" and kept on doing it. So I pushed him against the glass of the bus shelter and said, "Don't touch him! I know this guy. You're going to get in a lot of trouble."

There was a little scuffle, nothing big. I didn't think anything of it. The next day, the kid's father, with the kid, stormed into the prep school office. That year, 1986, a new prep headmaster, Hamish Simpson, took over from Dick Howard. I think Dick Howard understood things a lot better as headmaster. In the late eighties, there was a change of power in both the prep and upper school. The school was already screwed up in its lack of identity and direction, and under Eric Barton it continued to be screwed up, only in increasingly new and wonderful ways.

So I got pulled out of class by Bernard Lecerf, the guy in charge of discipline in the prep, who had been my form master the year before. I felt he was like a good friend because he had been my soccer coach for two years and I liked the guy. But in the prep school office, I had the father, the kid, Hamish Simpson, and Bernard Lecerf all staring me down. I was interrogated. Somehow I came out the bad guy. They were so concerned that a guy from outside the school had a problem with UCC that they turned me into a criminal in front of the father. They made me apologize and beg for forgiveness, but I hadn't done anything wrong! They were so goddamn concerned about the school's image. I began to realize that you had absolutely no power and no voice.

I went into the upper school as the meanest little son of a bitch. I was furious. I'd see kids being wronged or something bad happen, but there was nothing I could do. I was a serious athlete, but I was also an art student. My education in art history and art theory was mostly self-taught. My parents are the founders of Edwards Books & Art. I was either hanging out in the art room or on the football field. I ended up getting the first-team football lineman award and the art prize in the same year, so the teachers couldn't figure me out or slot me. They had extensive masters' meetings where they would bring up our names and classify each student.

I'd have a run-in with a teacher in one of my classes. Next day, a teacher in another class would mention it to me. He'd say, "Borins, you think you're going to act that way with me, eh?" I would be shocked. Is there no professionalism and confidentiality? Are students not protected in any way? You're completely subject to whatever they perceive you to be. You have no voice.

I once sat for a week in the office trying to get out of a gating that I thought was wrongfully given to me. I didn't want to go to it. I wrote a letter to Duncan Payne, the teacher who gave it to me. I'm pretty sure that John Symons, the vice-principal, got a copy of the letter. Every time I sat in the office, Symons would walk out his back exit and dodge me.

So finally on Friday, Payne confronted me. He pulled me out of the dining room and said, "You little shit! Who do you think you are writing this letter to me!" He was yelling at me. I've never seen such a poor understanding of diplomacy, democracy, and rights. Here I was being verbally abused by this big guy with a loud voice. You're in an academic environment and that's the way you're supposed to learn about things?

A kid in Grade 10 killed himself in the spring of 1993. I knew the kid very marginally, even though he was in my house. I'd say hi to him. As a Grade 13 guy, I had about three guys in Grade 9 who I looked after. Whoever was taking care of that kid seemed to have forgotten about him.

Recently I sat around with a bunch of UCC guys in my apartment in

Montreal. Somebody said, "It was really fucked when that kid committed suicide last year." We all sat around talking about the funeral, what a confusing experience it was. Right after eating breakfast with his family on a regular Saturday morning, a kid takes his dad's gun, writes a note, goes into the backyard, then shoots himself. Today I'm going to blow myself away because there is nothing left for me to do.

I remember getting a call from my buddy on the Sunday night who said, "I've got really bad news. D. A. has committed suicide." I felt bad because I didn't know him well enough. I felt bad that he committed suicide. I felt bad because I blamed the school. I'm sure there are lots of other unhappy kids at UCC.

But the worst thing was that the kid was a loner. He was a really good little kid, but he wasn't the "right" kind of guy. He never was going to be popular, excel in sports, or do something that would really make him proud of himself or have a teacher who was on his side. He was one of the many faceless guys who burrow through the system. I know he had bad experiences in the boardinghouse in Grade 9, so he became a day boy in Grade 10. I wouldn't be surprised if that was part of the reason for the suicide, not that the school would admit it. But I know a friend in boarding who felt pretty damn shitty after the suicide, because sick things happen to boarders. In boarding at Upper Canada, sexual identities and feelings are sometimes manifested in violent ways. Boarders are a completely different part of Upper Canada. There are not many cross-over friendships between boarders and day boys.

So imagine a kid in Grade 9 from an ethnic Catholic family, who lived way up north, being thrown into this sick environment. One of my friends summed him up as the kind of guy who wears a thin polyester shirt where you could see the undershirt underneath. I thought that was a pretty interesting observation. I know he went to a small Waldorf school before UCC. All of a sudden, he's surrounded by nasty Grade 13 guys in boarding. He must have been thinking: I'm going crazy. I don't know how to deal with this! I can't say anything to my parents because we're really religious and we don't talk about these things. I don't know anybody at this school because I'm so different. I wear this undershirt and I don't know how to dress right. I don't know who to talk to. I don't know anybody. My housemaster doesn't even know I exist.

The funeral was up north at some kind of rented church, a hire-a-priest funeral run by a Philippino priest who didn't really speak English well. It was a weird brand of Christianity I hadn't seen before. They got my buddy who was the head of Jackson's House to read "The Lord is My Shepherd." It was lame. We were just all shaking our heads, thinking, Wow! This is crazy! The eulogy was jaw-dropping. It was like, "Don't worry, God will forgive you. We all forgive you."

It was so cold. It was really sad. When we were talking about this, one of my buddies said, "It was like a shotgun funeral. Bury the guy and let's get the fuck out of here." If a kid like Galen Weston, Jr. killed himself, or when Dano Realini died in a car crash, they become the heroes of Upper Canada College. After some guys graduate, their legacy is still felt. Certain guys were the cool UCC guys. If one of those guy dies, they achieve enshrined, godlike status.

The school tried to have crappy little counselling sessions for the younger guys. They had a few stewards saying to us, "We're going to brief you on what teenage suicide is. Now go speak to the Grade 9 boys." What, all of a sudden, makes an eighteen-year-old steward an expert on how to deal with young kids in complex emotional and social issues? It was one of the most insensitively handled things I've ever seen. The whole thing is summed up in the back of the 1993 *College Times*. There was a picture of the kid with his name and dates, 1976–1993. Nothing else. He's the blank kid, the unknown soldier, the faceless loser you'll never know, the guy who wasn't important enough to have a eulogy.

I remember a big fiasco with the cricket team a few years ago. They went down to Barbados and got high all the time. One guy went to jail there. There were stewards on the trip, but Galen Weston, Jr., didn't get his stewardship taken away. One of the guys there was the head of a house. The head of your house is not necessarily a cool guy in the house, and he is often not even remotely like the guy you'd want to have representing you. Blakey said to the househead, "I'm going to take away your stewardship unless you tell me who did drugs." Of course, he ratted on everybody. His stewardship mattered more to him than loyalty to his peers.

The guys involved were called in and just said, "Oh, Mr. Blakey, I'm sorry. I got trapped into smoking marijuana by some native islanders. I really only took a puff. I didn't mean to." Mr. Blakey gave these guys a week's suspension. Mr. Symons made one of my friends look up the word *morality* in the dictionary, copy it out, then write an essay on it. He said that once that was done, he was free, so he went over to his buddy's house with all the guys who were suspended and smoked drugs all week long.

For the longest time, I'd be so frustrated when I'd tell my parents what was going on at the school. They thought I was being weird. They thought, What's the matter with you? You're too political at a young age! Finally, one of my teachers went too far. I remember being furious and yelling at my parents. I said, "Do you think I'm some kind of a stupid shit and I don't know what's going on? Don't you understand that if I come to you and say

I'm being wronged, it's because I'm being wronged. If I have a problem with a teacher, I'm not making it up to worm my way out of something. It's because it really exists."

All of a sudden, they believed me. Then my parents became hated by all the teachers. After one parent-teacher night, oh my God, a teacher said, "I'm still bleeding from all the bullet holes from last night." I said, "What are you talking about?" He said, "Your mom and dad literally attacked me." I said, "It was probably deserved. You've been cheating me the whole year." I was completely straight with him. I said, "I don't understand why you do this with my marks. Are you punishing me for something?" He denied it, but sure enough, the marks went up to what they should be.

In a way, everything at UCC was like a game. With Tony Hearn, I remember we used to have to write a rough draft and a good copy for our English compositions. Mondays were the rough draft day and Wednesdays were the good copy day. You had to go up on Wednesdays and show him both. I hated writing a rough draft for every composition, so I would always show him the same rough draft. Three-quarters of the way through the year, he looked at the rough draft and realized it was an old one from the beginning of the year. He yelled at me about it.

Parents' Night was the next night. I was shitting, I was so nervous. But Hearn thought it was a really clever thing to do. He pretended to be mad at me, but he told my parents otherwise and my parents told me. It was like I was being rewarded for thinking of ways to cut corners. The attitude from the teachers was like, "Lie, but lie well."

In the prep, I was lucky I had a teacher like Doug Brown. In Grade 8, when he was my English teacher, it was the first time I was friends with a teacher. An adult spoke to me on an even level, where nothing was inappropriate. There were no pretensions. In class he was the best teacher on an academic level. I learned important things from him. My thought processes went beyond the conventional because there was such a rich blend of things we talked about, whether it was sex, drugs, or our emotional insecurities. It was a very comfortable learning environment. It was the first time I actually wanted to do something in school academically. I didn't want to do well just for myself. I wanted to do well for the teacher too.

Doug Brown was a guy in his forties who wore Grebs, jeans, and a button-down shirt to school. He drove a beat-up old General Motors van. His apartment had lots of beer in the fridge, tons of maps on the walls, milk crates full of records, and a shitload of books. He thinks about and studies methods and theories of teaching. He's always learning more about it. He was at the prep for about fifteen years, but each year got worse for him. He had a power struggle with John Pearce and Ted Stephenson, two senior, ultra-conservative, ultra-WASP, ultra-old-order, ultra-formulaic kinds of teachers.

There was a power struggle over the way Doug Brown wanted to teach. If you ask any prep kid, "Who is your favourite teacher?" they'll say Doug Brown, not Ted Stephenson or John Pearce. For six years, Pearce and Brown didn't speak to each other. They exchanged memos. It was the old order versus the new order.

Brown and I used to talk about how you have to stand up to people. You have to remain headstrong in the face of adversity, for the sake of the kids you're teaching. The most important thing to him has always been teaching. That is what he is so incredibly good at and it was being taken away from him. I can't believe he was pushed out because he was different, pushed out because he was in a power struggle. What about learning? What about the kids? What about the school? What is UCC, a fucking factory? A school? A corporation?

I once asked that question of a teacher, Mr. Hood, in Grade 11. He said, "What are you, a fool? Of course it's a corporation." I thought: Wow! I can't believe somebody actually admitted it, just like that. I can't believe that he could actually participate as a teacher and actually believe that UCC is a corporation, not a school, and actually show me that he has accepted it.

By accident, Doug Brown and I met at Christmas 1993, six months after I graduated from UCC. We had gone our separate ways. He finally had been forced out of the prep in the middle of the previous year. I saw him driving by in his van. So I followed him and he finally pulled over. He said, "I don't believe it. This is karma. How are you?" I was damn happy to see him. I was really hurt not to see him at my graduation. I had lost contact. I said, "What the hell happened to you?"

He said, "I've been in Montana living in a commune." I said, "Are you teaching?" He said, "No, I don't have a job." I said, "Do you have an apartment here?" He said, "No, I sleep in my van." He's homeless and unemployed. I said, "I'd be happy if you stayed at my house. It's the least I could do." He was so grateful. He followed me home. I made up a bed for him on the couch. I gave him a beer. We talked the whole night.

A lot of things came out. I talked about trying to maintain my own sense of integrity without having the school fuck me up. He said that he was scared of me because I had turned into a big guy. I used to work with weights, pumping myself up and playing football. He didn't understand. He said, "I was scared of you. You wore a football jacket." He thought I had changed. I explained that the only way I could survive at UCC was to conscientiously object and be difficult, but not in a punishable way.

As we were talking in my basement, I suddenly realized he wasn't the one giving the advice any more. I was giving it. I was the one taking care of him. So I was having this revelation: I'm taking care of this middle-aged man because there is no justice at Upper Canada College. Not one parent wrote anything in protest over Brown's departure. He was such a positive influence on so many kids, yet not one other teacher stood up for him. He doesn't do the establishment thing, so he was executed. Upper Canada executes the Doug Browns.

I remember I used to hang out with Doug Brown after school. One of the things we realized was that there were fundamental things wrong with the school. I always viewed the system as a form of thought control. You could get a good education, but UCC also could turn out amoral, screwed-up guys who don't even know it, and never will. You could become Doug Bassett and not realize how wrong you are, repeating the same mistakes that had been done to you.

I think I got an excellent education at UCC. I was allowed to excel in anything that interested me. There were almost limitless possibilities. But paradoxically, at some point, you always had to give in and conform to the ideology of the school. All the time I was there, it was like, I hate this school, but I love it. I want to stay, because I want to see if it can change.